American Presidents, Religion, and Israel

American Presidents, Religion, and Israel

The Heirs of Cyrus

Paul Charles Merkley

PRAEGER

Westport, Connecticut
London

Library of Congress Cataloging-in-Publication Data

Merkley, Paul Charles, 1934–
   American presidents, religion, and Israel : the heirs of Cyrus / Paul Charles
Merkley.
      p. cm.
   Includes bibliographical references and index.
   ISBN 0–275–98340–4 (alk. paper)
   1. United States—Foreign Relations—Israel. 2. Israel—Foreign Relations—United
States. I. Title.
E183.8.I7M48 2004
327.7305694—dc22   2004048060

British Library Cataloguing in Publication Data is available.

Library of Congress Catalog Card Number: 2004048060
ISBN: 0–275–98340–4

First published in 2004

Praeger Publishers, 88 Post Road West, Westport, CT 06881
An imprint of Greenwood Publishing Group, Inc.
www.praeger.com

Printed in the United States of America

The paper used in this book complies with the
Permanent Paper Standard issued by the National
Information Standards Organization (Z39.48–1984).

10 9 8 7 6 5 4 3 2 1

Contents

Introduction

* * *

Now the LORD had said to Abram, "Get out of your own country, from your family, and from your father's house, to a land which I will show you. I will make you a great nation; I will bless you and make your name great; and you shall be a blessing. I will bless those who bless you, and I will curse him who curses you; and in you all the families of the earth shall be blessed." (Genesis 12:1–3)[1]

* * *

In November 1953, just a few months after leaving the presidency of the United States, Harry S. Truman took up an invitation to visit the Jewish Theological Seminary in New York. Accompanying him was his good friend Eddie Jacobson, a comrade from his Army days, and his partner during the brief life, over thirty years previous, of Truman and Jacobson, Men's Haberdashery, in Kansas City. Jacobson introduced his friend to the assembled theologians: "This is the man who helped create the State of Israel." To which Truman retorted: "What do you mean, 'helped to create?' I am Cyrus. I am Cyrus."[2]

Truman's fascination with Zionism, the cause of the Jews in the Twentieth century, found confirmation in his Biblical faith. He recalled with affection and gratitude the Christian upbringing he had received, and, being a man of intellectual and moral integrity, he had no wish to suppress the recollection of this nurturing. To him, it all made sense: he had been taught in Sunday school that the Restoration of the Jews to Israel was an inseparable part of the message of the same prophets who called God's people to love their neighbors and to care for the poor. The historical Cyrus II ("the Great") was the Persian king who overthrew the Babylonian Empire in 539 B.C., and thereafter encouraged and subsidized the return to Jerusalem of the Jewish population, which been held captive in Babylon for seventy years.[3] Throughout the two-and-a-half millennia of historical calamities that followed, Cyrus remained the symbol of the righteous gentile ruler who would someday make possible the ultimate and *irreversible* return of the Jewish people to *Eretz Israel*—the restoration of their nationhood, and their security against their enemies.

Truman pondered resolutely on the extraordinary circumstances that had made him president. He studied soberly his own strengths and weakness. And he came to the perfectly calm conclusion that he was Cyrus. It was not a manner of speaking, but the largest possible sort of truth, that someone, someday, would be called upon to play the role of Cyrus on behalf of the whole generation of Jews in their time of greatest need. Not only for them, but for all their descendants. It was what all Christian Zionists believed. It was what had moved Arthur Lord Balfour to propose the Balfour Declaration and Woodrow Wilson to sign it.

Many pious Jews wrote to President Truman during his lifetime to remind him of the part played by Cyrus in the past and identifying him, Harry Truman, with Cyrus. The chief rabbi of Israel, Isaac Halevi Herzog, on the occasion of a visit to the White House early in 1949, told the president, "God put you in your mother's womb so that you would be the instrument to bring about Israel's rebirth after two thousand years." We are told by a witness to this meeting that, "On hearing these words, Truman rose from his chair and, with great emotion, tears glistening in his eyes, he turned to the chief rabbi and asked him if his actions for the sake of the Jewish people were indeed to be interpreted thus and [that] the hand of the Almighty was in the matter."[4]

To resist the establishment of the modern State of Israel, Truman believed, would stain his reputation in the history books as surely as to fail to meet the evil of soviet communism when it challenged the continuance of Western civilization in Europe. Truman never forgot that the modern State of Israel had been brought into existence by solemn decision of the United Nations, as a consequence of the same historical process that had brought about the defeat of Hitler. Those nations who opposed the decision of the world community, and who appealed to the god of battles against it, should, he believed, be answering to the world community for their obstinacy. To make an issue of Israel's "right to exist" was to make issue with the whole possibility of purpose in history. Furthermore, to say that the United States had been mistaken in sponsoring the partition of November 1947, and mistaken again in her recognition of the new State of Israel on May 14, 1948, would be to make a mockery of the existence of the United States itself, which had, after all, entered into history in a moment of time, July 4, 1776, with an appeal to the powers of the world to accept the manifest endorsement of "Nature's God."

None of the next nine presidents (that is, from Eisenhower to Clinton) reasserted in public Truman's claim to the mantle of Cyrus—the claim that underwrote Truman's commitment to Israel. At first blush, this will seem curious, because most of the presidents who succeeded Truman were raised, as he was, in an Evangelical church. Each of these presidents had heard in church the lessons drawn from Genesis about the patrimony of Abraham and had learned from a Sunday school teacher that the words referred to an obligation upon Christians to *prefer* Israel in her struggles. Each had been taught as doctrine that the restoration of the Jews to Israel was an essential element in the purposes that God has for history. In contrast to Truman, each had concluded early in his career that the "literalist" teachings of his youth should not be brought into conversations about matters of high policy conducted by the learned men who were their advisors on foreign policy. Being men of no less earnestness than Truman, each understood that he had to find a way of expressing a different policy toward Israel in language of equal moral force. From Jimmy Carter to Bill Clinton, presidents have presented themselves to the world not as the heirs of Cyrus but as champions of the peace process. In ideological terms, this has meant divesting the presidency of a role originally conceived in theological terms, in a day when the vocabulary of theology lay close to the surface of public life, in order to take on a role whose meaning is entirely secular. It is a role of equal moral grandeur, but one more suited to post-Christian times than the role of champion of Israel.

Throughout the whole of the period that figures in this book the American voting public has always been much more supportive of Israel's view of things than have their elected governments or the media elites—a circumstance that one finds routinely noted and deplored in the memos and afterwards in the memoirs of American policymakers. Most Americans, it seems to me, when they think about the historical circumstances that put Israel in place, and about the circumstances that have accompanied the half-century of her existence—her never-resolved struggle with her unreconciled neighbors, her continuing jeopardy—are moved by a vaguely mystical sense about the meaning of all of this, which is best understood as the residue of Biblical Restorationism. In the presidency of George W. Bush, it has begun to appear that this popular instinct to "bless" Israel has once again taken command, as it did in the days of Harry Truman.

*   *   *   *   *

Harry Truman's declaration of his motivation in the matter of assisting the birth of Israel and befriending it in its earliest years provides, it seems to me, unambiguous proof of a connection between religious faith and public action. I have discovered, however, that there is, among historians, such a profound bias against accepting the possibility of any connection between religious expression and the public actions of individuals or groups that even straightforward declarations of this admittedly rare kind are routinely dismissed as instances of deception (willful or naïve) or of confusion. Before I proceed, therefore, I have to deal with this issue, and with a few other matters that have occurred to readers of my earlier drafts of this manuscript and that may, possibly, occur to the present reader.

I do not pretend that I can *demonstrate* that the religious and philosophical commitments of the presidents *caused* them to take the actions that they did with regard to Israel. Neither in this book nor in my previous books (where, likewise, this issue arises) have I ever pretended that I could prove anything of the sort, either for presidents or for anyone else. All serious students of this theme know that there can be no compelling proof that belief *causes* anything. This follows from the transcendent nature of belief. But if it is not true that belief *is* the root of action, then I believe history is an utterly meaningless field of study.

I have taken as axiomatic that religion is that realm of belief in which the largest claims about the meaning of life are proffered and either chosen or rejected. I have tried to display evidence for the religious beliefs of the individual presidents, and have asked the reader to keep this evidence in mind as I summarize their actions. In modern times, historians generally shy away from the theme of religious faith as motivation for policy and deeds. And this has been particularly true—and particularly inexcusable in my view—with regard to our subject of attitudes toward Israel. The historians have pretended not to notice that presidents have religious and philosophical commitments. Yet all of the presidents, at one time or another, have left more-developed or less-developed expressions of these religious beliefs in the documentary records by which they hoped to be judged by future historians. Excluding this dimension of religious faith makes the task easier than it ought to be, and has produced results that are neater than mine. Still, it has always amazed me that historians feel free to decide for their subjects that their religious beliefs and pronouncements can be ignored. They would not dare to do the same with respect to their views on political economy—which, I suggest, can be shown to have carried little weight, relative to religious faith, as a source of thought and action. I have not argued that the religious commitments of the presidents have *driven* or *controlled* their policies and actions toward Israel, but I have argued that there is plenty of evidence that most of them have been powerfully motivated by religious faith, and that this reality is abundantly clear in the record, and should be given some pride of place in discussion of their motives, policies, and deeds.

I have not given equal attention to the religious and philosophical views of all the presidents. The fact is that the presidents of our period have not given us their insights and their thoughts in equal measure. Truman has left great quantities of autobiographical materials and many long letters full of his thinking on all issues, great and small. There is never any reason for guessing at what Truman thought he was doing and why. Jimmy Carter was always, during his public life, much readier than any president before or since (until George W. Bush) to speak frankly about his religion and his philosophy; he was, furthermore, a sedulous keeper of diaries and autobiographical materials, and he has filled out the years of an exceptionally long and active post-presidency with the writing of exceptionally wide-ranging and candid books. John F. Kennedy, by contrast, left almost nothing of value reflective of his religious beliefs. Richard Nixon did leave some limited published testimony about his religious commitments, but we have no reason to believe that he has been more honest with us about these matters than about other matters that most historians regard as more important.

With regard to the policies pursued by our presidents, the reader will note that references to archival materials get thinner as we get closer to the present. Jimmy Carter's Presidential Library is, at this writing, the latest to be sufficiently stocked and available for researchers that a visit there is required. My sections on Presidents Reagan and his successors to date have taken into account memoirs of the participants and the public record as well as published books. It will be a long time before historians have in hand primary documentation of equal value for all of the presidents discussed here. In light of all of this, it would be wrong of me to try to level the playing field and pretend that we have equally well-rounded pictures of the religious and philosophical life of all our principals and equally well-rounded accounts of all of their deeds. Something else that has contributed to the uneven character of my story is the fact that the issue of Israel did not appear with equal urgency for all the presidents. I have therefore slowed the tempo of the narrative to take advantage of the greater amount of the historical record that is available for the crucial moments in the story.

I have approached the issue of religion as a factor in the story of presidential actions toward Israel at two levels. I have offered several lengthy sections of generalization, drawn from the whole story, or a large part of it, and I have done the best I can to show how the religious commitment has governed the attitudes and the deeds of each of the presidents of the period, in order. It has been a considerable challenge to keep the several different elements of the discussion within view of each other at all times. In order to do justice to the complexities of the issue of religious motivation, I have had to develop some generalizations for a while; then, when I turn back to review policies and actions, the religious factor recedes, while I turn to summary of policy and actions of the presidents. I have to expect the reader to remember these generalizations and presume that they are at work in the back ground while I set them aside.

While I have a great deal to say in these pages about the varieties of Christian belonging, I have said very little about religious identification of Jews in this book, except for a few references to the founding fathers of the state (notably, Weizmann and Ben-Gurion) and certain Israeli politicians since then. For the most part, my interest in American Jews collectively is as a voting bloc and as advocates, through many organizations (AIPAC, Presidents' Conference, etc.) of certain policies and actions toward Israel. A central theme of my book is that, although most political commentators consider the Jewish vote to be a monolithic pro-Israel vote and most politicians adopt positions on matters of concern to Israel in light of the presumed pro-Israel position of Jews, in fact, Jews are at least as divided regarding attitudes toward the policies followed by the government of Israel as are most others. With reference to all my interests in this book, whether people call themselves Jews for "religious' or for other reasons is neither here nor there—although this is a matter that interests me greatly and about which I have done much reading.

When I deal with political results, I make comparisons between Christians of pro-Israel disposition (as one bloc) and the Jewish population (as another bloc). Here I have argued that the general population of Americans is more pro-Israel than are Jews (considered as a bloc, identified by census-takers); and, further, I have argued that Christians of conservative theology are much more Zionist than any other recognizable bloc, including the whole bloc of Jews. I have tried to show how and where this knowledge has affected the judgments of the presidents. When it comes to the presidents (none of whom was, or is likely soon to be, a Jew, and all of whom declare themselves to be Christians of one category or another), I have to take into account the character of this religious belonging and I have to make assumptions about how religious belief bears upon actions. I believe I have done all that the evidence allows. Given that the party of choice for the great majority of conservative Christians is the Republican Party, the effects of these calculations have now become blatantly clear in the presidency of George W. Bush—as I illustrate in the chapter on George W. Bush.

As for what this book "contributes" to the famous long-felt-need of scholars: I do not claim privileged access to the inside story of recent U.S. policy toward Israel. This is not what I am offering. I would, however, point to several lengthy sections that document, out of presidential archives and other primary sources, hitherto neglected evidence of the presidents' reflections on the ways in which religious commitments—their own and those of the public—affect attitudes toward Israel. The original contribution of this book amounts to the effort that I have made to knit together the biographical parts and the policy sections to suggest powerful motivations that other historians have, on secular principle, simply excluded.

I conclude with the unconcluded presidency of George W. Bush. For good and sufficient reason, the primary sources for this presidency are fewer than for any of the other presidencies. There is no presidential library, no papers, no presidential memoirs, and no memoirs of principal actors, although I have made use of what there is. As long as the manuscript of my book remains this side of publication, developments will occur and the present text will be made to seem inadequate and even wrong. This is always true of a book that concludes a historical account on the threshold of the present. I have, however, continued to bring up-to-date the Bush section as major turning-points have occurred—until the manuscript was taken away to be turned into page proofs in June 2004.

There is, however, a bonus, for my purposes, in being able to conclude with the Bush presidency; and that is that it is much easier to document the religious commitments of this president than it is of any president since Carter. It is certainly much easier than it has ever been to demonstrate connections between the principal articles of his faith and his political attitudes. In fact, the connection between religious commitment and action is so clear that I have been bold enough to conclude my book with George W. Bush resuming the mantle of Cyrus, bringing the story full circle to the position occupied by Harry Truman.

Chapter 1

The Champion of Israel

HARRY S. TRUMAN (1945–1953)
"I Am Cyrus"

Just after five o'clock in the afternoon of April 12, 1945, Vice President Harry S. Truman was passing time, enjoying a drink of bourbon with House Speaker Sam Rayburn in his hideaway office deep inside the House of Representatives, when a courier arrived telling him to come at once to the White House. He guessed the truth immediately: President Roosevelt was dead.

To the embarrassment of all present, the swearing-in at the White House had to be delayed for about an hour, while the desks and bookshelves of all the president's men were searched unsuccessfully for a Bible. An inexpensive Gideon Bible was eventually found in the desk of the White House usher.[1]

HARRY S. TRUMAN

Harry S. Truman was born in rural western Missouri in 1884 and spent his early years on his father's farm. When he was six, the family moved to the town of Independence, Missouri, where Harry attended elementary school and then high school. Harry had hoped to go on to college, but his father's independent livestock business went under, and it was necessary to resume life as a farmer again, this time on his grandmother's farm. Truman served as a captain in the U.S. Army in World War I, winning recognition for leadership of his troops in heavy action at the front. On his return, he started up a men's haberdashery store in Kansas City in partnership with one of his comrades from the war, Eddie Jacobson. The business failed after a few months. Harry Truman was then approaching forty years of age.

Truman's political career began modestly with election to local office in 1922, but then it took off suddenly in 1934 when he won the Democratic primary and then the general election for U.S. senator, at the age of fifty. In the Senate, he gained a reputation among insiders for diligence and probity and was responsible for passage of important legislation in the field of public transportation. Reelected in 1940, he was appointed to a special committee investigating national defense and gained a degree of name recognition by exposing graft and waste in a number of war industries. Inevitably, these investigations and the prosecutions that followed them caused some embarrassment for FDR, but he had the good sense to see that political capital could be won by adding to his ticket a figure with a reputation for probity but without a political network of his own.

Truman's selection as vice president was effectively orchestrated by President Franklin Roosevelt during the early hours of the 1944 Democratic National Convention. Roosevelt anticipated a revolt in conservative ranks if he kept the left-leaning incumbent, Henry Wallace, in place, but he felt a definite queasiness at the prospect of putting in the direct line of succession an ambitious figure of national standing, such as James Byrnes, who stood at his side day-by-day with the title Assistant President for the Home Front—an unpleasant reminder of his mortality. During the election, Harry Truman, as a good soldier, stood by the propaganda about FDR's buoyant good health, but he knew better: He told his family that "physically he is going to pieces" and that he, Harry Truman, would be the president before the term was out.[2] It is not easy to put oneself in Truman's situation and second-guess the ethics of all this, but we can see that there were limits to how far Harry Truman was prepared to carry the burden of absolute honesty. So effectively were President Roosevelt's public appearances managed that in the fall of 1944 people imagined they were voting for a president who was certified to live forever, and they paid little attention to the vice-presidential candidate.

Truman was not included in policy deliberations during the eighty-two days of his tenure of the office of vice president. He was not on the inside of military decision making and had no access to top-drawer intelligence. He was not privy to any of the feelers that were coming from the other side regarding terms of surrender, nor did he know anything about the secret provisions made for dividing up the postwar world, which had been made at the conference at Yalta (February 1945). Consequently, practically all of his time during his first full week in office as president (beginning Friday, April 13, 1945) was spent being briefed by the heads of all the departments and agencies of the government.

HARRY TRUMAN AND THE CAUSE OF ZION

On April 20, scarcely a week into his presidency, Harry Truman met in his office with Rabbi Stephen S. Wise, the authorized spokesman for the American branch of World Zionism. Truman recalled that meeting with Rabbi Wise many years later:

> [Rabbi Wise] said, "Mr. President, I'm not sure if you're aware of the reasons underlying the wish of the Jewish people for a homeland." He was just as polite as he could possibly be, but I've told you in those days nobody seemed to think I was *aware* of anything. I said, I knew all about the history of the Jews, and I told the rabbi I'd read all of Roosevelt's statements on Palestine and I'd read the Balfour declaration and, of course, I knew the Arab point of view. . . . I'd already had a communication from some of the "striped pants" boys [that is, the State Department] warning . . . [ellipsis in original] in effect telling me to watch my step, that I didn't really understand what was going on there, and that I ought to leave it to the experts. . . . But . . . as long as I was president, I'd see to it that *I* made policy.

Harry Truman was, indeed, exceptionally well-backgrounded on the issue of Palestine and what to do with it. While serving as a senator, Truman had been a member of organizations dedicated to a timely implementation of the Balfour Declaration, the pledge made by Britain back in 1917 to create a Jewish state in Palestine. He knew that FDR, for all his declared friendship with the leading Jewish figures in American politics and the sweeping support he received from Jewish voters, was having second thoughts on the matter of Zionism, after his interview with King Ibn Saud of Saudi Arabia in Egypt (February 10, 1945), during which, apparently, he first became aware of the intensity of Arab hostility to the Jews. Truman, by contrast, believed that America's commitment to create the Jewish state was clear and unqualified and that there must be no going back. He told Merle Miller in 1974,

> I was looking forward to [this interview with Rabbi Wise] because I knew he wanted to talk about Palestine, and that is one part of the world that has always interested me, partly because of its Biblical background of course. . . . I've always done considerable reading of the Bible. I'd read it at least twice before I went to school [*sic*] . . . The stories in the Bible . . . were to me stories about real people, and I felt I knew some of them better than *actual* people I knew. [But] it wasn't just the biblical part about Palestine that interested me. The whole history of that area of the world is just about the most complicated and interesting of any area anywhere, and I have always made a careful study of it. There has always been trouble there, always been wars from the time of Darius the Great and Ramses on.[3]

Whenever he commented on the background to the Palestine question, whether privately or publicly, Truman always took the trouble to set a up a preface for his position by offering a synopsis of the uniquely long history of the Jewish people, drawing on the Biblical story and also upon the secular history of the world into which Israel had been born. Both the scriptural and the secular-historical perspectives were acquired early, partly from Sunday school and partly from the village library.

RELIGION IN THE LIFE OF HARRY TRUMAN

At the time of his birth, Harry Truman's parents were active in the Baptist church. Later, when they moved to Independence, Harry was enrolled in the Sunday school at the First Presbyterian Church, which, he says, the family attended "every Sunday regularly for as long as we lived in Independence." In 1903, when he was eighteen, the family moved to Kansas City, and Harry went to work at a bank. There in Kansas City, Harry joined the Baptist church by adult baptism. He remained a member of the local Baptist church wherever he lived for the rest of his life. In one of the autobiographical fragments preserved in his personal papers he writes, "I'm a Baptist because I think that sect gives the common man the shortest and most direct approach to God."[4] In 1959, six years after Truman's retirement from the presidency, the National Baptist Convention, the principal body of black Baptists, held its convention in his home town of Independence, Missouri, on September 8, 1959, and Truman came to speak to them:

I am a Baptist by education and by belief that John the Baptist recognized and baptized the Savior of the World, Jesus. And, my friends, he did not sprinkle him with Jordan water; he reverently lowered him bodily below the surface of the sacred Jordan and raised him as a symbol that sin could be washed away. . . . [At the time that Jesus came to be baptized by John,] the Jews had long been awaiting a prophet who would give them a revival of the teachings of Moses, Samuel, Amos and Isaiah. And when he came, they failed to recognize him. He came to rescue the poor and the indigent from the special privilege classes. He was born in a manger. He grew up as the son of a carpenter and was one himself. But remember, he carried his mission to the people who needed the mercy of God. He constantly called attention to the Law and the prophets. . . . He reminded them of the Good Samaritan who had helped his neighbor—and Samaritans were, in that day in Jerusalem, regarded as people of your color have been in some parts of the United States.[5]

It would be difficult to think of another president (excepting only Jimmy Carter and George W. Bush) and very few public figures of any rank, who would have been ready, in the broad light of day, to make a declaration of such a straightforward Christian creedal character: "that

John recognized and baptized the Savior of the World." Truman was always aware of his identity as a baptized Christian and thought a great deal about how this reality should govern his conduct of his public responsibilities. When he was sixty-six years old, he noted in his diary that it was when he was eighteen years old (that would have been in the year of his baptism, if his recollection of both these matters is exact) that he had written down a prayer, which he then carried with him in his wallet, and read once every day:

Oh! Almighty and Everlasting God, Creator of Heaven, Earth, and the Universe: Help me to be, think, to act what is right, because it is right; make me truthful, honest and honorable in all things; make me intellectually honest for the sake of right and honor and without thought of reward to me. Give me the ability to be charitable, forgiving and patient with my fellowmen—help me to understand their motives and their shortcomings—even as Thou understandest mine! Amen, Amen, Amen.

The prayer on the other side of this page has been said by me—by Harry S. Truman—from high school days: as window washer, bottle washer, floor scrubber in an Independence, Mo., drug store, as a time-keeper on a railroad contract gang, as an employee of an untruthful and character assassinating newspaper, as a bank clerk, as a farmer riding a gang plow behind four horses and mules, as a fraternity official learning to say nothing at all if good could not be said of a man, as a public official judging the weaknesses and shortcomings of constituents, and as President of the U.S.A.[6]

With precisely the same degree of confidence in the same special providence of God, Truman said of his nation:

Divine Providence has played a great part in our history. I have the feeling that God has created us and brought us to our present position of power and strength for some great purpose. It is not given to us to know fully what that purpose is, but I think we may be sure of one thing. And that is that our country is intended to do all it can, in cooperating with other nations to help create peace and preserve peace in the world. It is given to defend the spiritual values—the moral code—against the vast forces of evil that seek to destroy them. This is a hard task. It is not one that we have asked for. At times we would like to lay it down. And, as we go on with it, we see it is full of uncertainties and sacrifices. But we need not be afraid, if we have faith.[7]

TRUMAN'S PHILOSOPHY OF HISTORY

Identification with Cyrus appealed to Harry Truman's confidence in received Truth—which, for him, as for most theologically unsophisticated Christians, was inseparably bound up in allegiances to country and to family and to received standards of civility. But, if the first line of appeal of the Cyrus story was to his religious training, the second line of appeal

was to his philosophy of history. From his boyhood, he had been a vora-
cious reader—he claimed that before he finished high school he had real
all the books in the Independence library: "three thousand books—and
some of them twice!" His favorites, he said, included the works of the historians Plutarch, Edward Gibbon, and T. H. Green, and a four-volume set
of biographies, *Great Men and Famous Women* (edited by Charles Horne).
Throughout his adult life, he kept up his reading in history, having a special interest in biographies, particularly those of American politicians and
military figures. From his substantial diaries we learn that he regularly
rehearsed, privately, to himself, a long list of all the Great Men of History,
pausing from time to time to take note of the significance of the "contribution" of this one and that. His philosophy of history was not a sophisticated one: "Real history," he said, "consists of the life and actions of great
men who occupied the stage at the time." As for what made "great men"
great, "In reading the lives of great men, I found that the first victory they
won was over themselves and carnal urges. Self-discipline with all of
them came first."[8] He was absolutely convinced that the great characters
of history were instruments of the purposes of God.

HARRY TRUMAN AND CHAIM WEIZMANN

Truman's opinion of the Jewish people in general was very high. His
opinion of the men who represented the American Zionist movement,
however, was generally low. In various post-presidential publications he
recalled unpleasant interviews with these leaders. In particular, he
recalled Rabbi Abba Hillel Silver pounding on his desk one day in 1947.[9]
His dealings with David Ben-Gurion and Moshe Sharett, in the months
prior to the creation of the state, were never genial; he guessed (correctly)
that they had a low opinion of him, and were disposed to compare him
unfavorably with FDR. Of the champions of Zionism with whom Harry
Truman dealt in the crucial period 1945–1948, only one impressed Harry
Truman as a man of large qualities—the sort of man who might be
worked onto his list of the Great Men of History—and that was Chaim
Weizmann.

   In the days when the question of the disposition of Britain's Palestine
Mandate was before the United Nations (UN), Weizmann was the preeminent spokesman for World Zionism. Weizmann learned early and never
forgot that the most powerful line of appeal to the general public of the
Christian world was to its religion. Over the years, when addressing
audiences of British or American citizens, or the various commissions of
inquiry of Great Britain or of the League of Nations, or when addressing
the UN General Assembly, Weizmann would draw deliberately upon
prophetic sections of the Hebrew scriptures in defense of the creation of

the State of Israel. In the crucial speech before the General Assembly on October 16, 1947, Weizmann recalled Isaiah's prophecy of Zion restored: "The Lord shall set His hand again the second time to recover the remnants of His people. And he shall set up an ensign for the nations, and shall assemble the outcast of Israel and gather the dispersed of Judah from the four corners of the earth."[10] This approach to the issue of Palestine and its future was irresistible to Harry Truman. Equally important: Chaim Weizmann was the only Zionist figure of the first rank at the time who had a sensible appreciation of the *limitations* of Zionist assets. He knew that, although American public opinion was well-disposed, its goodwill had its limits, and these limits were being tested unduly by strident publicity campaigns and conspicuous pressure tactics—not to mention the terrorism that was going on in Palestine. This, too, commended him to President Truman.

Like Harry Truman, Chaim Weizmann was totally confident that Providence had assigned him the task he must perform. He had enlisted as a teenager in the cause of World Zionism and had been its preeminent spokesman for most of time since the beginning of World War I. There was a powerful mystical streak in his self-image. In the month of October 1914, in the first weeks of World War I, Weizmann wrote to his Zionist colleague Shmarya Levin, "With feverish anxiety I am watching events which have for me a deep hidden meaning; it is the struggle of the pagan Siegfried against the spirit of the Bible, and the Bible will win."[11] In his diary, following shortly upon his successful lobbying at the League of Nations for the creation of the Palestine mandate, he wrote, "When I look at the Jewish community . . . in all the Western countries, when I remember the destruction in the East [that is, Eastern Europe], my heart freezes, and I come to the conclusion that only the Chosen Ones who have acquired all their moral strength from the only true Jewish source—only they are prepared and fit to assume the burden of work for the sake of others, and they will succeed in reviving the dry bones [see Ezekiel 37], so let us not complain of our destiny; it may be difficult, but it is beautiful."[12] According to his biographer Norman Rose, Weizmann "was observant, conforming to the traditions he had learned as a child, but he interpreted them in an individual, common-sense way as befitted a nineteenth-century liberal, a product of the Enlightenment. He attended synagogue on the High Holidays, enjoyed the festivals, and meticulously conducted the Passover service in Hebrew . . . [but] he was resolutely opposed to the rule of the rabbis."[13]

On hearing of FDR's death, Weizmann, like most of the leading Zionists, believed that the Jews had lost their best friend. None of the Zionists was well-informed about Harry Truman, but all assumed that a man without a university degree, a man from the South, an Evangelical Christian, a man who was not well-known to the Jewish businessmen and politicians (including themselves) who had been close to FDR and had advanced "Jewish interests" at the White House in the past, could not be expected to have the broadness of vision necessary to see the task through. A large amount of elitism figured in this general verdict. But after his first, brief meeting with the new president, Weizmann changed his attitude (December 7, 1945.) The two men established a remarkable rapport. Weizmann explained his vision of the Jewish state to Truman— how "it would realize the ancient hope by being a place where the Jewish faith could be realized in practice, while still being a secular state, based on sound democratic foundations with political machinery and institutions on the pattern of those of the United States."[14] After that first meeting, and down to the last meeting between the two (March 18, 1948) prior to Israel's declaration of her existence as a state (May 14, 1945), Truman and Weizmann were constantly in touch.

In early 1945, Zionists feared that Truman would be overwhelmed by the pressures from his State Department and his War Department, solidly opposed to the folly of permitting a Jewish state to be set down in the midst of the Arab world, but Weizmann remained confident that Truman would stand fast. On April 9, Weizmann wrote to Truman: "The choice for our people, Mr. President, is between statehood and extermination. History and providence have placed this issue in your hands, and I am confident that you will yet decide it in the spirit of the moral law."[15]

Weizmann trusted Harry Truman. Chaim Weizmann, taking all in all, could show a remarkable record with respect to his judgments of the character of gentile princes. Though he was himself a product of the Russian Pale, and had little contact as a social equal with Christians until his middle years, he formed sound notions of the thinking of Christians, the extent and the limitations of their knowledge and sympathies. He was among the first, in each case, in correctly appraising the worth and reliability to Zionism of C.P. Scott, of Arthur Balfour, David Lloyd George, and Winston Churchill. Significantly, Weizmann understood earlier than did most other Zionists (and certainly earlier than the Labor Zionists) that the British Labour leaders, whose words of allegiance to Zionism were so much more fulsome than those of the conservatives, would not prove constant friends; in addition, he rightly attributed the defection from the ranks of Zion's friends of Prime Minister Attlee and Foreign Secretary Bevin to qualities of character.

THE ROLE OF THE TRUMAN GOVERNMENT IN ESTABLISHING THE STATE OF ISRAEL

In the fall of 1947, when the UN in special session was considering the case for partition of Palestine, there was in most places of the world a generally friendly disposition toward the Jews of the world. The creation of a Jewish state commended itself to many in the period from 1945 to 1948 as a solution to a problem that would otherwise have had to be solved by massive resettlement of Jews in Europe and/or massive immigration of European Jews to America, Canada, New Zealand, South Africa, or Australia. This realization rendered many closet anti-Semites temporarily susceptible to restorationist sentiments. But the story does not end there, as anti-Zionists pretend; for restoration of the Jews had a powerful appeal within the Christian community and a long history, which owed much to the substantial vein of philo-Semitism in the Church and to popular enthusiasm for causes that could be shown to be biblically authorized. This was especially true in the United States, where the Evangelical tradition was strongest.

But this friendly disposition would not have been sufficient to win the day for the cause of the Jews had the two superpowers not shown their own support and made clear how they wanted their friends to act. As for the United States, on the matter of the General Assembly vote of November 1947, Sumner Welles, who had been FDR's undersecretary of state, and later lobbied hard among his former colleagues on behalf of Zionism, recalled: "By direct order of the White House every form of pressure, direct and indirect, was brought to bear by American officials upon the countries outside of the Moslem world that were know to be either uncertain or opposed to partition."[16] Most reliable authorities tell a similar story. President Harry S. Truman insisted publicly at the time and continued to insist ever after that the United States had not lifted a finger to direct the voting at the UN. In his *Memoirs*, Truman recalls, "The persistence of a few of the extreme Zionist leaders—actuated by political motives and engaged in political threats—disturbed and annoyed me. Some were even suggesting that we pressure sovereign nations into favorable votes in the General Assembly. I have never approved of the practice of the strong imposing their will on the weak, whether among men or nations."[17] On the other hand, Truman did not contradict friends who, in the election year that followed, appealed to Jewish voters on his behalf with the claim that his interventions had won the day.[18]

In the years when the "Palestine Question" was before the UN (1945–1948), the Zionist cause was greatly assisted by the almost unwavering tendency of Western nations to follow the lead of the United States in the largest political matters. Coincidentally, the United States was under the spell of what we might call *secular-millennialism*. The UN was still under construction, and there was no limit to the utopian expectations that it aroused in the Western world. It was the moment of World Federalism and *Esperanto*. The political world seemed infinitely malleable. In Congress, majorities of both parties had supported the Wagner-Taft Resolution of 1944, which called for implementation of the Balfour pledge by means of the creation of a Jewish homeland. The national platforms of both national parties repeated these pledges in 1944.[19] Most understood, and conceded out loud, that the Arabs would be made unhappy by the decision to create the Jewish state, but none at the time saw this as a decisive obstacle. Most believed that the Arabs would see the foolishness of their fears within some reasonably short time after the deed was done; if they did not, the rightness of the action would be unaffected.

Most of the commentary that flowed from the pens of liberal intellectuals and academics at that hour saw Zionism as an opportunity to establish a bridgehead of civilization in a premodern, prescientific neighborhood. The adversary was usually defined as "feudalism" (understood to mean the social and political arrangements that made possible the domination of Arab sheiks over their people) and "obscurantism" (the Muslim religion). It is difficult to imagine the liberal intellectual and academic community today, so full of loathing for Western civilization, sitting patiently while the case is made for the Jewish state as a bastion of "civilization" against "Arab feudalism"—despite the fact that in the intervening half-century the Arab world has advanced not at all in the direction of democracy nor toward the establishment of basic freedoms.

It is an awesome thought as well that Israel could not have come into the world without the assistance of Joseph Stalin. By the newly minted rules of the UN Charter, the decision to partition the Mandate of Palestine was one that required support of two-thirds of its current membership. Already in those days there had been many instances of a two-thirds vote being put together in the UN General Assembly in support of a matter on which the Soviet Union was opposed—something that caused growing frustration in Moscow. To accomplish this, three things were required: harmony between the United States and Western European nations (which was normal); a united voice among the nations of the Western hemisphere (which normally followed the American lead); and the compliance of at least some of the member states of Asia and Africa (most of which were newly liberated parts of European Empires). The nations belonging to this latter category were normally disposed to accept opportunities for enlarging the membership and thus the voting strength of the non-European bloc. But the issue of Palestine cut across this normal arithmetic. Britain intended to abstain—out of cussedness. Arab states and other Muslim states, which normally saw their best interest in lining up with the side taken by the Americans, did not welcome the addition of a Jewish state to their ranks. In this situation, the support of the Soviet Union and its satellites was essential.

In fact, *the creation of the State of Israel was the only major issue of the early Cold War period on which the two superpowers supported each other's position.* Abba Eban, who represented Israel at the UN and was present the day that the Soviet Union announced its support of partition, said, "There was something almost messianic in this convergence of American and Soviet ideas."[20]

Stalin's motivation was purely negative, success being measured entirely in terms of the confusion that this was causing for the West. There is no doubt that the left-wing government of Israel would have welcomed a serious courtship by the USSR There was a need for arms, and there was a need for diplomatic support in many forthcoming conflicts at the UN. Stalin helped a little on the first, by permitting Czechoslovakia to sell weapons to Israel, but he was of no help at all on the second. Had Stalin followed through with generous cultivation of Israel's goodwill, there is no doubt that the opportunities for American influence in Israel would have been drastically curtailed. No sooner had the dust settled on the first round of Arab-Israeli conflict, however, than Stalin began to demonstrate his contempt for Israel's concerns. Though she had been the first to recognize Israel de jure (just a few hours after the United States won the race to be the first to recognize her de facto), thse Soviet Union thereafter placed unconscionable restrictions on the activities of the Israeli Embassy in Moscow, and simply ignored Israel's complaints about government-directed anti-Semitism and about the restrictions on religious practice and Jewish education in the USSR and the prohibition of Jewish emigration.[21]

At the same time, the decision to proceed with the creation of the state of Israel was next to being unique as a major issue on which the United States and the UK *disagreed* at the time. Since the end of the war, the United States and the UK had been working well as a team on the issues that seemed at the time to matter most: These included the actions to rescue Greece, Turkey, and Iran from Soviet intimidation (the Truman Doctrine); actions to counter Soviet intransigence with regard to the occupation of Germany (culminating in the Berlin airlift of 1948–1949); and the decisive early steps down the road to European cooperation, which would soon issue in the formation of NATO. When it came to the Palestine question, however, all comradeship evaporated. In the documentary records are to be found extremely bitter exchanges between the two foreign offices and the two heads of government. Foreign Secretary Ernest Bevin wasted much goodwill when, at a large Labour Party gathering, he publicly accused the Americans of being keen on a homeland for Jews in Israel precisely because they were not keen on the real live Jews they already knew in New York. Also contributing to Britain's bitterness of soul at this hour was the fact that all the members of the British Commonwealth except India and Pakistan voted with the United States and the UN majority on this issue, and, thus, morally speaking, *against* Britain. Historians of the British Commonwealth see this as the turning point in the story that leads to realignment of all the roads that ran through the former British Empire so that henceforth they would all lead to Washington.[22] The Suez Crisis of 1956 completed this process.

When the Korean War began in June 1950, the success of the United States in rallying the UN for collective action against North Korea drove the USSR and her Communist allies to denounce the UN as an enemy of the cause of global liberation, which Communism claimed to serve. Further down the road, however, the Communist powers gained the ear of the new majorities, which materialized in the UN General Assembly following the decolonizing frenzy of the 1960s and 1970s. The USSR made itself the champion of the anti-Zionist cause, and following the Six-Day War of 1967, the USSR and her satellites withdrew diplomatic recognition of Israel. In those days, the so-called Third World seemed readier to follow the lead of the communist superpower than that of the Free World superpower in most matters coming before the UN. The denunciation of Zionism became the surest instrument of all for organizing the majority against the U.S. Israel's day-by-day life at the UN then became nearly insufferable. Later still, the Soviet empire collapsed, and shortly after that the USSR herself, one of the two superpowers in 1948, imploded. One consequence of this latter event was the admission to the UN of several more new nation-states, none of them friendly, most of them outright hostile, to Israel. Thus the roster of the nations—the *dramatis personae*—has changed dramatically, while the issue of Israel's "legitimacy" still holds the stage at the UN.

*   *   *   *   *

UN Resolution 181, which was passed on November 29, 1947, did not create the State of Israel, as some general accounts carelessly state, but was rather in the form of a recommendation to the UK, the mandatory power, that the plan of partition with economic union be adopted and put into force by October 1, 1948—by which date, as the British government had announced, it would have left the area. It was further stated that any attempt to alter by force this decision would be regarded by the UN as "a threat to peace or act of aggression." A Commission of five members of the UN was delegated to implement the partition plan, taking over administration of Palestine by orderly steps, as the British relinquished it. Nothing like this happened, as the British refused to cooperate with the Commission, and as the Arabs refused to acquiesce in any part of the arrangement. In fact, just a few days after the General Assembly voted for partition, Britain told the UN that she did not consider herself bound by these instructions, but would leave Palestine a few months down the road. And, in May 1948, she did.

In the light of all this (Britain's impending withdrawal, Arab and Jewish violence against each other and against the mandatory power, and the announced intention of the Arab League to enter the fray when Britain should withdraw), the State Department and War Department, in March of 1948, sought to persuade Truman that a mistake had been made and that, in the best interests of the Jewish people themselves, some further delay was necessary before Israel should declare its independence. The president authorized discussion along this line at the highest level, and some drawing-up of position papers. Then, on March 19, Warren Austin, the chief of the U.S. delegation at the UN stepped to the rostrum and announced that the United States now favored a form of "trusteeship" for the whole of Palestine.[23] This was taken by the Jewish Agency to mean that the opponents of Israel would be given another indefinite lease on their ancient campaign to prevent the birth of Israel. Truman had no intention of permitting that to happen, but he had somehow missed the point that even to raise the possibility of trusteeship seemed to deactivate the November promise to the Jews. Rather than concede that Harry Truman was not fully in control of decision making in his own administration—or, worse still, that he did not comprehend his own policy—it was necessary for the president to stand before the press (March 25, 1948) and pretend that this position was compatible with the intention of the United States to see the partition decision carried through.[24] This situation encouraged the anti-Zionist majority in the State and War Departments to renew their efforts to head off the creation of Israel.

On March 18, 1948, Chaim Weizmann (recently denied reelection by the World Zionist Congress as its president, but still it most important emissary to the powers that be) was granted a secret, off-the-record interview with President Truman, during which Truman confirmed his commitment to recognition of the forthcoming Jewish state. This allowed Weizmann to steady the nerves of the Jewish Agency over the difficult days while the American delegation at the UN was floating the trusteeship proposal.[25] Credit for making the interview possible belongs to Truman's long-standing personal friend, Eddie Jacobson.

Truman's dilemma, in seeking to bless Israel is personified in his dealings with George C. Marshall, his secretary of state since January 1947. Truman's personal regard for Marshall cannot be exaggerated: "He was one of the men you could count on to be truthful in every way, and when you find somebody like that, you have to hang on to him."[26] Marshall has few critics among the historians. He was, in private, a thoroughly admirable individual and had lived a life selflessly dedicated to public service as a soldier and statesman; he had, as George F. Kennan put it, "the imperturbability of a good conscience."[27] At first blush it may seem anomalous, in view of how much Truman needed Marshall, that Marshall's nomination proceeded through the Republican-led Senate with unprecedented swiftness—in fact, in one day. But perhaps there is no anomaly here.

What better way to guarantee a quick end to the political career of a rascal like Harry Truman than to yoke him to an honest man?

And Palestine was an issue about which George Marshall did feel strongly. Though considering himself no less sympathetic than Truman to the plight of the Jews in the years from 1945 to 1948, George Marshall was completely tone-deaf to the siren of Zionism. Having worked so closely with British political leaders, generals, and diplomats, he understood the challenge of Zionism from *their* perspective—as an embarrassing remnant from World War I, an old bit of Wilsonian idealism, left out in the sun too long. He believed it was his duty to make the president understand the issues as the British did—in the cold light of reason.

Marshall's anti-Zionist efforts did not begin with his tenure as secretary of state. He was widely believed to have influenced President Roosevelt's decision to thwart the Wagner-Taft Resolution in 1944. Marshall's opposition to partition in late 1947 and his opposition to the plan to go ahead with recognition of the state in the spring of 1948 had been fortified by his confidence, as a military man, that the Jews of Israel could not survive. Urging the Jews of Palestine to go ahead with their plans for an independent state amounted, he believed, to volunteering them for the completion of their holocaust, at the hands of the Arabs.

Possibly the darkest moment of Truman's presidency came on May 12, 1948, during a meeting that he had called for the purpose of rehearsing before his senior policy advisors the arguments for and against recognition of the Jewish state.[28] Marshall had only recently held a meeting with the leaders of the Jewish Agency, in which he had brutally advised them to give up their impossible and mischievous dream. Now, at this later meeting in the White House, Marshall spoke firmly against recognition. Clark Clifford, the president's counsel, given the task of presenting the argument in favor, rehearsed the history of the Jewish diaspora since the destruction of the Second Temple, the Balfour Declaration, the recent holocaust, and the present desperate situation of the displaced persons. He even introduced restorationist texts drawn from scripture, notably Deuteronomy 1:8: "See, I have set the land before you; go in and possess the land which the LORD swore to your fathers—to Abraham, Isaac, and Jacob—to give to them and their descendants after them."

Marshall's legendary propriety failed him utterly in that moment. "This is just straight politics," he blurted, interrupting Clifford's presentation. "I don't even understand why Clifford is here. This is a political meeting. . . . If you [President Truman] were to follow Clifford's advice and if I were to vote in the next election, I would vote against you." Everyone gasped. After the meeting Truman told Clifford "I can't afford to lose General Marshall." Looking back over forty years later, Clifford was inclined to see the stakes as being even higher than anyone did at the time: "Here was the indispensable symbol of continuity, whom President

Truman revered and needed, making a threat that, if it became public, could virtually seal the dissolution of the Truman Administration and send the Western alliance, then in the process of creation, into disarray."[29]

Though badly shaken, Truman pressed on with what he believed was the right decision. Just a few hours prior to his announcement of de facto recognition of Israel, he received through Marshall's undersecretary indication that Marshall would keep his principled objections on the matter to himself—that he would support the decision publicly when it came; he would not resign. Yet, it is important to understand that on the eve of the Democratic National Convention Truman had taken the supreme risk of losing General Marshall, the anchor of his presidency, over the matter of Israel.

The State Department's advice to President Truman—to *not* permit the United States to invest its life, property, and sacred honor on behalf of Israel—was, indeed, based on realistic calculation of the facts against Israel's victory in the coming War of Independence. Among these facts were the following:

1. Within the Mandate of Palestine as it stood in 1947, Arabs outnumbered Jews two to one, whereas the total of the Arab population that surrounded Israel outnumbered her by about fifty to one (30 million to 600,000).

2. Advance elements of five Arab armies were already engaged in the war on Israel's soil.

3. The Arab side was much better armed. Governments of the seven independent Arab government states of the region (Egypt, Iraq, Syria, Lebanon, Transjordan, Saudi Arabia, Yemen), organized since March 1945 on Britain's initiative as the League of Arab States (Arab League), were openly and legally purchasing arms, as Israel was not permitted to do. The U.S. government adhered to the arms embargo to the area—which, under the circumstances, meant an embargo on the Jews.

4. Great Britain, the closest ally of the United States, was on the other side.

The new State of Israel's first correspondence with the U.S. government was all about redressing this imbalance: about the need for lifting the arms embargo, the need for loans, and the need for de jure recognition, which would allow Israel to petition for admission to the UN and to start taking care of her diplomatic needs throughout the world.

There were areas of foreign policy that President Truman left largely untouched to the care of his State Department. One of these (of great political consequence) was China. But on the issue of Palestine, Harry S. Truman was at the center of the action, keeping himself totally informed, and, especially during the election season, playing a forward role, not always keeping his principal foreign policy advisors *au courant*. His instructions to his UN delegation to declare for partition of the Mandate of Palestine in 1947 had contradicted the advice that his State Department and his War Department had given him; his decision to ratify Israel's Declaration of Independence on May 14, 1948, by means of an immediate declaration of de facto recognition was likewise taken against the virtually unanimous advice of his senior diplomatic, military, and economic advisors. Everyone knew that a great chasm divided the pro- and anti-Israeli factions within the government, and that as Harry Truman's prospects for election grew dimmer (as they did virtually every day from that day forward) it would be harder for him to maintain a friendly policy toward Israel.

PRESIDENT TRUMAN AND THE STATE OF ISRAEL: MAY 14, 1948—JANUARY 20, 1953

The Election Season, 1948

It has to be kept in mind that, on the day when Israel declared its independence and President Harry Truman declared de facto recognition, neither Israel nor Truman was expected to be around much longer. The best-informed observers were predicting that Harry Truman would cease to be president eight months later and that Israel would be crushed even sooner.

As for Harry Truman, when the year 1948 began, it was generally conceded that Truman had no chance of election to the presidency. At the first opportunity, the mid-term election of 1946, the electorate had handed control of Congress back to the Republican Party, which had been waiting sixteen years for this moment. Since then, Truman had faced one legislative humiliation after another. All through the first half of the presidential election year, 1948, there was a steady erosion of support for Harry Truman within his own party, while the number of those declaring support for the Republican and Progressive parties was growing daily. "No President in memory, not even Herbert Hoover in his darkest days, had been treated with such open contempt by his own party," a recent biographer, David McCullough, has written.[30] Many survivors from Roosevelt's administration considered Truman an embarrassing accident, and some of these became active in unsuccessful efforts to dump him well before the Democratic National Convention of July 1948. When that did not work, his refusal to step aside led to a double defection of vitally important sectors of the party: On the left, a contingent of liberals now contemplated the candidacy of the Progressive Party leader, Henry Wallace; on the right, a contingent of segregationists looked to the candidacy of States Rights leader Strom Thurmond of South Carolina.

As we work through the record of Truman's dealings with Israel over the next few months, we have to compensate imaginatively for the knowledge *we* have but that no one had at the time: that another presidential term lay ahead for Harry Truman. Everyone whom Truman dealt with in those weeks acted on the premise that he would not be around long enough to act upon any long-range consequences of his decisions. This consideration colors all of the dealings Truman had with members of his own official family, with the Congress, with the American news media and public, and with the Israeli government. As *we* know, on November 2, 1948, Harry Truman won "against the greatest odds in the annals of politics. . . . Every expert had been proven wrong, and as was said, 'a great roar of laughter arose from the land.'"[31]

There was no doubt that Israel's cause was a sentimental favorite with the American public. It is equally true that no responsible American politician advocated risking the life of a single American soldier for the defense of the new state. This was, in any case, an academic issue, as the American army had been practically dismantled by the end of 1945. To provide an American presence adequate to defend the new state against its enemies would have exhausted the whole of the available manpower, leaving absolutely nothing with which to meet challenges to American authority in regions obviously closer to American strategic concern. It was one thing to allow Israel to come into being and quite another to keep her in being. Israelis thought of Truman's decision to recognize the state de facto as a promise of things to come. However, Truman had always argued that the United States would not send its armies to fight for Israel, and through the summer and fall of 1948 he defended the UN policy of embargo of military supplies to the area, which Israelis believed to be prejudiced against them.[32]

Before the State of Israel had, by its own declaration, been in existence for a full day, the entire army of invasion of the Arab League had crossed its borders and joined the anti-Zionist guerrilla forces. In the words of Abd al-Rahman Azzam Pasha, secretary-general of the Arab League, it was to be "a war of extermination and a momentous massacre, which will be spoken of like the Mongolian massacres and the Crusades."[33] But, although there were many disappointments for the Jewish side (notably, the necessity of negotiating a surrender and evacuation of the Jewish community in the Old City of Jerusalem), the Israelis by and large held their own, and in fact took possession of several regions of Palestine that the partition plan had envisaged as belonging to the state that the UN had proffered to the Arabs, and that they had contemptuously rejected. After about four weeks of fighting, both sides were ready to accept a ceasefire (June 11.)

When hostilities resumed (July 8), it was immediately obvious that the Israelis had made better use of the respite than had the Arabs, stocking up on arms purchased from Czechoslovakia as well as other arms that were purchased illegally in the United States and in other Western countries. During ten days of renewed fighting, Israel's position was improved notably in the vital corridor between the coast and Jerusalem and in the Lower Galilee. On the Arab side, there was less unity in this second round, because of the correct perception that Abdullah, the King of Jordan, had been playing a double game, pretending to be a champion of the Arab cause, while in fact concentrating his energies on tactics serving his intention to attach the areas of Palestine immediately adjacent (the West Bank) to his kingdom—then, in effect, using the ceasefire period to draw these areas into his regime, with the clear intention of keeping them.

During those first months of the existence of the State of Israel, coinciding with the American presidential campaign, several decisions had to be made on matters vital to Israel's continued existence. It cannot be said that the Truman administration performed to the consistent satisfaction of the Israelis on these matters. The administration started off well (in Israeli eyes), in the matter of its appointment of its first official representative to Israel: James G. McDonald, a professor of government at Columbia University, former League of Nations commissioner for refugee relief, and a declared Christian Zionist.[34] At the same time, however, McDonald was not yet designated as ambassador, given that Truman was still reluctant to concede de jure recognition to the state (which, among other things, would entitle Israel to apply for admission to the UN). Here his rationalization was that he must wait until Israel had held its first elections, thus putting its regime on a more legitimate basis. But some Israelis feared that Truman had doubts about their prospects and was keeping his commitment to Israel limited. In the same weeks and on other equally crucial matters, the anti-Zionist camp won the argument: Israel's request for a loan was not approved, nor would the president lift the embargo on sale of arms.

In the meanwhile, the UN had named a mediator, Count Folke Bernadotte of Sweden. Israel was reluctant to accept UN mediation, believing that it could only lead to giving back to the Arab side some part of what they had lost as the result of rejecting partition and rejecting Israel's independence. Israelis suspected that the same cohort of career policy advisors who had tried to talk President Truman out of recognition of Israel were now manning the Bernadotte Mission. This seemed to be borne out by its report (leaked in part before the author of the report was assassinated on September 17, 1948): It called for a partnership of Israel and Jordan within a kind of reunion of the lands covered by the mandate, with Jordan having possession both of the West Bank (including East Jerusalem) and the Negev, and Israel having Western Galilee. After two years, Jewish immigration would be controlled by the UN. Bernadotte's principal recommendations would clearly have had the effect of clawing back much of what Israel had gained on the battlefield—in effect overlooking Israel's sovereignty and compelling her to enter into a new situation of constitutional tutelage. No serious person imagined that this would come about unless the United States *compelled* Israel to get in line with the report.

Bernadotte's assassination on September 17, 1948, by Israeli terrorists muddied the waters. Israel's cause suffered an incalculable loss in world opinion because of this murder. Fortunately for Israel, none of the Arab principals had the wit to capitalize on this circumstance by now declaring support for the plan. No plan that accepted the existence of Israel was acceptable to them. (It was greatly in the interest of Abdullah of Jordan that the plan should be accepted, but he dared not break ranks publicly.)

Meanwhile, it seemed to be becoming clearer every day that Harry Truman would not be a factor of any importance much longer. Commentators (inspired by leaks from within the State Department) calculated that the loyalties of Truman's official advisers were even less firm than in May. Senior policy advisers, who had no intention of letting their careers go down with Harry Truman, were already dealing with the Republican secretary-of-state-in-waiting, John Foster Dulles—which presented little practical difficulty, given that Dulles was a member of the U.S. delegation at the UN, breaking bread on a daily basis with them. This was the domestic background when, at the annual meeting of the UN General Assembly (held that year in Paris), Secretary of State Marshall announced U.S. support of the Bernadotte Plan.[35]

At this point, the Israelis had an experience of déja vu: As in the days leading to the decision for recognition, so now the most senior State Department people responsible for the issue (notably, Marshall, Dean Rusk, and Robert Lovett) were making apparent their disgust that this "foreign policy matter" was being ground up in "domestic politics." The president was committed by the party's 1948 platform, where we read:

We approve the claims of the State of Israel to the boundaries set forth in the United Nations resolution of November 29th and consider that modifications thereof should only be made if fully acceptable to the State of Israel.

We look forward to the admission of the State of Israel to the United Nations and its full participation in the international community of nations. We pledge appropriate aid to the State of Israel in developing its economy and resources.

We favor the revision of the arms embargo to accord to the State of Israel the right of self-defense.[36]

Harry Truman, aboard his campaign train, told his traveling companions that, on the matter of the Bernadotte Plan, Marshall had acted without consulting him, but he was talked out of publicly repudiating Marshall's statement.[37] In the last days of the campaign, Truman released a statement confirming his commitment to the principles in the platform. To a crowd at Madison Square Garden he said that Israel "must be large enough, free enough, and strong enough to make its people self-supporting and secure."[38]

The Last Years of the Truman Presidency (1949–1953)

Had the Arab states left well enough alone at this point, the Americans undoubtedly would have compelled Israel, as the condition of peace, to release some considerable portion of the territories that it had acquired outside the boundaries envisaged by the partition decision of November 1947. But the Arabs would not accept the verdict of the god of battles. In the round of war that resumed in October 1948 and ended in January 1949, the Israelis completed their conquest of the Galilee, held on to the Negev, and invaded the Sinai.

At the several conferences held under UN auspices early in 1949, Israel held firm about her new, more defensible boundaries. The anti-Zionists would always insist thereafter that American complicity made it possible for the Israelis to refuse concessions. The record shows quite a different story. The State Department, as always, was determined that Israel should be made to give up large parts, at least, of her territorial windfall and should be made to welcome back or fully compensate the Palestinian-Arab refugees, estimated to number up to 600,000. President Truman made clear to the government of Israel his "disgust" at its attitude toward the refugees.[39] But America's ability—and for that matter, the world's ability—to move Israel on this and other issues vanished when it became clear that the Arab states would not deal directly with Israel. Adamant about not recognizing Israel's existence, the Arab governments would not let their delegates sit at the same table with Israeli delegates, insisting that the UN participants carry messages back and forth across the room. Thus they kept their hands clean of compromise and their Arab hearts united upon the need for more war at a better time. Arab and Israeli representatives did not meet face-to-face in diplomatic conference again until December 1973, when they met at Geneva for one day!

Israel's proclamation of independence, May 14, 1948, had guaranteed equal rights to the Arabs of Israel, and professed to welcome them to stay. But the arrival of Arab armies and the flight of Palestinian Arabs from Israel changed all that. In a formal reply on this matter to Count Bernadotte, August 1, 1948, Ben-Gurion had written: "When the Arab states are ready to conclude a peace treaty with Israel this question will come up for constructive solution as part of the general settlement, and with due regard to our counterclaims in respect of the destruction of Jewish life and property, the long-term interest of the Jewish and Arab populations, the stability of the State of Israel and the durability of the basis of peace between it and its neighbors."[40] And that, essentially, is where the matter still stands today.

Principally because the refugee issue was such a thorn in the flesh, U.S.-Israel relations were more troubled through 1949 and 1950 than they had been in 1948. But gradually President Truman came to recognize that Israel would not make unilateral concessions, admitting large numbers of refugees, when the Arab states that were raising the issue were themselves refusing to accommodate refugees on their own soil. Israel's relations with the American public improved as it became clear that the Arab states were refusing to negotiate directly with Israel about anything. Thus, the remainder of Truman's term, until January of 1953, saw steady improvement in official U.S.-Israel relations. Abba Eban describes the day he presented his credentials to President Truman as ambassador (September 5, 1950). Truman told him that "most of the striped-pants boys in the State Department are against my policy of supporting Israel. . . . [They will] soon find out who's the President of the United States."[41] In May 1951, Prime Minister Ben-Gurion made a highly successful visit to the United States, during which he talked to American supporters of Israel and with congressional leaders, and had an interview with the president, from which he carried home a $150 million grant-in-aid.

The 1948 presidential election—the first election since the assumption by the United States of its role as the leader of the Free World—fixed the issue of Israel near the center of the national political agenda. In none of the subsequent presidential elections would presidential candidates be free of the obligation to indicate how they intended to bless Israel. While other issues of foreign policy would come and go, no platform of either national party, in all the election years that followed, would neglect to include a benevolent statement about Israel. By contrast, who would have foreseen in 1948 that statements of policy toward the Soviet Union would disappear entirely from party platforms in 1992? (For that matter, who foresaw this in 1988?) Who foresaw in 1960 that the Vietnam issue would bulk large in the platform of 1964, and dominate the foreign policy planks of the platforms of 1968 and 1972, only to disappear from the platforms in 1976? Who foresaw in 1948 that the issue of Israel would still be a major one in the foreign policy planks of both national parties in 1996? Who anticipates today that it will disappear from the platform of 2004, as the Soviet Union disappeared from the platform of 1992?

SUMMARY

Harry S. Truman had the unique obligation and, as he saw it, the unique privilege of setting the parameters for official American policy toward the State of Israel, created on his watch. His commitment to the religious training of his youth, fortified by his admiration of the singular political accomplishments of the Zionist leaders, caused him to be an unwavering friend of the new state. Equally, his realistic and patriotic commitment to American interests equipped him to be a stern critic of Israel's deeds, when criticism was called for. It could never have occurred to Harry Truman that there could be anything approaching parity between the cause of the Jews in his own time and the cause of those who were defying all the recent lessons of history as well as the declared will of the UN in order to prevent Israel's continuance in a state of peace.

Chapter 2

In Pursuit of "Evenhandedness"

DWIGHT D. EISENHOWER (1953–1961)
"Millstones around Our Necks"

ISRAEL LOSES THE SENTIMENTAL ADVANTAGE, BUT REMAINS IN DANGER (1949–1956)

By the time General Eisenhower succeeded Harry Truman (January 20, 1953), Israel had lost much of the political advantage that she had enjoyed over her enemies. Paradoxically, the simple fact that Israel had survived and continued to grow in strength may have lessened her public support. It was now much easier for people of goodwill to express criticism of Israel's behavior. There were no more pictures in the newspapers describing the plight of hundreds of thousands of European Jews, victims of the Nazi wars; now the words *refugee* and *homeless* were reflexively associated with the 15 million dislocated by the partition of India—and with the Arab refugees from the Holy Land. Gone too from most people's minds was the speculation about the "Biblical meaning" behind the restoration of the Jews—speculation that had been briefly seasonable during the days of the UN debates about partition and in the days of the American administration's agonizing about recognition. Perhaps that had been only a seven-day wonder—some kind of fad. Even among Jews, it was noted that it was becoming difficult to organize rallies and letter-writing campaigns in the interests of the state. The zeal that had been typical of American Jews through 1947 and 1948 became (as Will Herberg put it at the time) "diffused into a vague though by no means insincere friendliness to the State of Israel."[1]

But Israel's enemies had lost none of their determination to drive the Jews into the sea. Diplomatic isolation of Israel deepened as most of the newly created nation-states (ribs out of the side of European empires in Africa and Asia) joined the club of nonrecognizers and swelled the anti-Zionist chorus at the UN. Because Israel was barred by Arab nations from participating in the Asian Group of members states of the UN (where it belongs geographically), she remained the only member of the UN not eligible to serve on any of the UN commissions and not eligible to have a seat on the Security Council.[2]

The Arab economic boycott of Israel was supported (at least overtly) by all European and American corporations who did business with Muslim states. British and American oil companies complied with Iraq's demand to close down the pipeline that had provided Arab oil to Haifa. Egypt demanded that the Suez Canal be closed to any ships going to and from Israel; and, after a certain amount of righteous huffing and puffing, Britain and the other Western powers acquiesced. Likewise, in 1950 Egypt established a military presence on the southeastern shore of the Sinai Peninsula, closing the Strait of Tiran to Israeli commerce—another unambiguous violation of international law that garnered no sympathy for Israel at the UN. Still, so long as this sort of day-by-day provocation of Israel did not issue in war, the attention of Americans wandered off in other directions.

THE PRESIDENTIAL ELECTION OF 1952

The foreign policy section of the Republican Party platform of 1952 focused on the increasing menace of the communist empire, made possible by "the tragic blunders" at Tehran, Yalta, and Potsdam and the "futile and immoral policy of containment" pursued by the Truman administration. Noting that, "[T]he Middle East and much of Africa seethe with anti-American sentiment," the platform pledged to put a Republican administration, "to the service of peace between Israel and the Arab states and we shall cooperate to bring economic and social stability to the area." Speaking before the committee where the platform of the Republican Party was written in 1952, Jewish groups urged that the party pledge greater military and financial support—in effect, to achieve parity with the Democratic platform on these matters. But other voices, led by the American Friends of the Middle East, were strenuously opposed; as a result of their efforts, the plank merely pledged "to continue our friendly interest in this constructive and inspiring undertaking."[3]

JOHN FOSTER DULLES

The principal draftsman of the foreign policy portions of the Republican platform was the man who was to become Eisenhower's Secretary of State: John Foster Dulles. Dulles was an exceptionally serious-minded churchman. He was raised in the Presbyterian manse in Watertown, New York, where there were family devotions to begin every day, Sunday school to attend faithfully, and (as JFD recalled) about ten church services a week to attend.[4] Dulles's concern to relate the life of faith to the life of the mind was stimulated by his studies in philosophy at Princeton (under such scholars as John Grier Hibben) and at the Sorbonne (under the renowned Henri Bergson).[5] Dulles served on a number of commissions established by the Federal Council of Churches of the United States and various ecumenical bodies working to formulate "Christian opinion" on world issues. In August 1948, Dulles attended the founding meeting of the World Council of Churches in Amsterdam, where he warned against the accommodations that Western churches seemed too ready to make for the sake of keeping in their organization the state-controlled representatives of the churches behind the Iron Curtain.

From September to December of 1948, while a member of the American delegation at the United Nations, Dulles had taken a generally pro-Israeli line, in conspicuous contrast to the anti-Israeli line pursued by Secretary of State Marshall and his team. Moshe Sharett, the acting representative of Israel to the UN and Israel's first foreign minister, wrote to Dulles on December 17, 1948: "I have nothing but admiration for your personal attitude to our delegation and the cause it had to defend. We have all appreciated deeply your helpfulness and wisdom."[6] Then, shortly after these events of 1948, Dulles was suddenly embarked (or so it seemed) on a political career. He was appointed to the Senate by Governor Dewey of New York in July 1949, to complete the remaining term of Senator Robert F. Wagner. When he was narrowly defeated in the special election that November, many analysts suggested that the Jewish vote had given the victory to Herbert Lehman, the Democrat. Thereafter, as a Republican politician and as secretary of state, Dulles never lost sight of the fact that the pro-Israeli domestic vote did not belong to his party, and (as he believed) could not be won by Republican words or deeds. Indeed, in the 1952 election, 75 percent of the Jewish vote went to the Democrats—despite which, New York State went to Eisenhower by a wide margin.[7]

Still, John Foster Dulles's reservations about the influence of Jews in American politics were mild compared to those of his new boss, Dwight D. Eisenhower.

DWIGHT D. EISENHOWER

Born in Denison, Texas, on October 14, 1890, and raised in Abilene, Kansas, Dwight David ("Ike") Eisenhower graduated from the West Point Military Academy in 1915. He did not see combat duty during World War I but did win promotion and decoration for his outstanding work as commander of a tank corps training center. Throughout his entire subsequent military career, until he was appointed commander of the North African campaign in late 1942, Eisenhower's promotions and his reputation were carried forward on his accomplishments as an administrator and a planner—that is, on desk work and public relations. He greatly impressed Chief of Staff George Marshall, who brought him to Washington, where he moved through two promotions of rank in two years and became chief of the newly organized Operations Division of the General Staff early in 1942. Having prepared the plans for the European Theater of Operations, he was then given command of U.S. forces for Europe and appointed Allied commander for the North Africa campaign. As supreme commander of the Allied Expeditionary Force for the invasion of France, Eisenhower presided over perhaps the most colossal military exercise ever undertaken, involving supervision of more than 4.5 million troops, and requiring the steady exercise of the highest level of diplomatic and political skill.

Eisenhower's name figured constantly in talk about future presidents from at least the days of the Normandy invasion. When he resigned as chief of staff of the army in order to become president of Columbia University (February 1948), it was widely believed that he was deliberately stepping to the sidelines of public life in order to avoid the blandishments of politicians of both parties seeking to drag him into the presidential contest of 1948. As if to keep everyone guessing, Eisenhower then gave up the Columbia University job after a few months to respond to a call to military duty, returning to Europe as Supreme Commander for the North Atlantic Treaty Organization (NATO). Finally, in the first week of January 1952, Massachusetts Senator Henry Cabot Lodge Jr. forced his hand by entering Eisenhower's name in the New Hampshire primary to be held on March 11; there Eisenhower's solid superiority to candidates Robert Taft and Harold Stassen was demonstrated. Yet Ike's formal declaration did not come until June, accompanied by his resignation from the Army.

Ike's enormous popularity as the leader of what he called the "Crusade for Europe" abetted a widespread mood of weariness with the incumbent Democrats, compounded by suspicion over the recent pattern of Communist advance in Asia, and frustration over the Korean stalemate. All of this accounts for a sweeping Republican victory in all three rings of the election: presidency, Senate, and House of Representatives—something that never happened again.

By choosing Eisenhower (and passing over Taft, Stassen, and the others) the party had defused criticism that it lacked experience in foreign policy matters. After all, who else in American public life could possibly claim as much personal acquaintance with all the leaders of the world (on both sides of the Iron Curtain) and such a record of direct participation in recent history? But Eisenhower had no intention of "being his own secretary of state" (as John F. Kennedy would later encourage others to say of him.) To reassure lifelong Republicans that he belonged in the party, he hinted broadly during the campaign that his choice for secretary of state was the same as Tom Dewey's and Wendell Willkie's would have been, namely, John Foster Dulles.

RELIGION IN THE LIFE OF DWIGHT D. EISENHOWER

Of the presidents since Truman, it is Dwight D. Eisenhower who had the most intense sense of history as a field where great processes were at work. Ike did not doubt that God had purposes that He was accomplishing in history, and that therefore he, Dwight Eisenhower, must be appropriately respectful of these mysteries. But it is also abundantly clear that he *did not* think of Israel as in any special sense a work of God in history. At least, that was not his thinking when he began his presidency.

In his book, *The President is Calling,* Milton Eisenhower, one of the president's brothers, speaks of the "serenity" that characterized his parents' life together, and "their utter devotion to their religious beliefs. They were fundamentalists. . . . All of us boys were raised in the River Brethren Church, which was strictly fundamentalist in doctrine."[8] An annoying disingenuousness runs through this entire memoir. For example, Milton speaks of his father's ability to read the New Testament in Greek, and then of his father's knowledge of the German language: "But he never spoke German in our presence, however, for in our early days in Abilene one was looked down upon if he spoke a foreign language, and father wanted none of that for his sons"—as if the issue were one of avoiding airs, rather than of avoiding parading the family's German origins in those days when many families were actually changing their German names to deflect their neighbors' suspicion about their patriotism. Similarly, Dwight Eisenhower, reflecting on his reluctance to speak of his personal feelings in his correspondence with friends, writes, "Anglo-Saxon men usually find it difficult to exchange direct expressions of sentiment and affection."[9]

Just as Ike's off-hand remark about Anglo-Saxon behavior serves to deflect attention from the reality of the Eisenhsower brothers' *German* nationality, so Milton's remarks about the family's pious, Bible-reading, "fundamentalist . . . River Brethren" background (the River Brethren were an offshoot of Mennonites, formed in Pennsylvania in the 1770s) serves to deflect attention from a matter that so greatly embarrassed both Milton and Dwight Eisenhower that they could find no room for it in their memoirs: the conversion of both his parents from the River Brethren to the Jehovah's Witnesses.

The distinctive theology of this latter group builds almost entirely on its unique interpretations of certain passages in the book of the Revelation (or the Apocalypse of St. John) that tell of the last days of the present world, when the key role is to be played by certain converted Jews, assigned to lead the final contest against Satan. All of this action follows upon the restoration of the Jews to Israel. There is no need for us to attempt to delineate these distinctive Witness teachings.[10] Dwight Eisenhower was never tempted to follow his parents' lead to become a Jehovah's Witness. Apart from everything else, he could not have been a Witness and have a military career, as Witnesses are forbidden to give allegiance to the earthly kingdom in any form, including those that citizens regard as the most routine duties of patriotism. Thus, while Captain Eisenhower was training soldiers for the front during World War I, his mother was courting arrest for distributing literature advocating resistance to the draft.[11] The burden of remaining simultaneously loyal to his mother and to his soldier's oath was huge. There is no need to wonder that Dwight Eisenhower had such a fear of religious zealotry of all kinds. In all his years as a public figure, including his years as president, Dwight Eisenhower gave no hint of his familiarity with the themes of Christian restorationism and the lines of thought that persuaded Harry Truman to say of himself that he was Cyrus. *This was not because he was unaware of these themes, but that he was only too well aware of them and came to despise them.*

In his presidential memoirs, Eisenhower tells us that, having been an outsider to the world of religious belonging all his adult years, but now awed by the prospect of becoming the president of the United States, he decided, on the very eve of his first Inauguration, to join the Presbyterian Church by baptism. People who take this story at face value miss the point that prior to his long years of religious avoidance there were his boyhood years of exposure to religious zealotry of a sort that had always deeply embarrassed him. Even his joining the church in January 1953 is presented to the world as a rational exercise: "Religion was one of the thoughts [sic] that I had been mulling over for several weeks." Of his reference to faith in his inaugural address, he later said, "I was seeking a way to point out that we were getting too secular. . . . We had to proclaim our faith. It was our faith in the deathless dignity of man."[12]

EISENHOWER, THE JEWS, AND ISRAEL

American Jews in 1952 did not quite know what to make of Eisenhower. All of Eisenhower's biographers note that, unlike Roosevelt and Truman, he had no Jewish friends and had only the most limited contact with their political, social, or religious leadership. As a career officer, he had certainly been exposed to the anti-Semitism rampant in officer circles in the 1920s and 1930s. But his biographers assure us that his correspondence carries no evidence of any authentically anti-Semitic expression.[13] Jewish leaders remembered him as a friend of the Jews of Europe in 1945–1947. As Allied Supreme Commander, Ike had insisted on giving all possible publicity to the cruelties of the Hitler regime against the Jews and to the intolerable plight of the Jews in displaced person (DP) camps. He had welcomed the interest shown by Zionist leaders in their situation, as when David Ben-Gurion, then still Chairman of the Jewish Agency, visited the camps under Eisenhower's sponsorship.[14] Never doubting that the vast majority wished to go to Palestine, Ike cooperated with David Ben-Gurion by sending military planes to Palestine to bring in mail, educational materials, and instructors to prepare the DPs for life in Palestine.

But Eisenhower's sympathy with the plight of the Jews in 1945–1948 is not evidence of pro-Zionism. As chief of staff after the war, he stood with George Marshall in opposing all talk of an American role in establishing the Jews in their intended state in Palestine. At the time he said that "overall it would take five to seven divisions plus air power for several years to protect British and U.S. interests, and principal centers of Jewish and Christian population," and that such use of force would merely destabilize the region, creating an opportunity for Soviet infiltration, bringing about the loss, in Eisenhower's words, of "probably the one large, undeveloped reserve in a world which may come to the limits of its oil resources within this generation without having developed any substitute."[15] Eisenhower took this line consistently in advice he gave to President Truman while he was chief of staff.

Unhappy at the time with President Truman's decision to bring Israel into existence and to give recognition to her valiant effort to remain alive, Dwight Eisenhower had never ceased to believe that the special relationship with Israel was an impediment to America's freedom to pursue a policy based upon her own best interests in the area. To Philip Klutznick, president of B'nai B'rith, Eisenhower admitted that he had not favored the establishment of the state, but "we would have to live with it."[16] Eisenhower's contacts among Jews were few, and virtually all were with those who remained loyal to the anti-Zionist American Council for Judaism, whose influence in the general Jewish community had declined sharply since 1947.

On March 8, 1956, Eisenhower related in his diary his impressions of the Ben-Gurion government—their unwillingness to respond to Arab complaints, their stubborn refusal to see that there were limits to the credit that they enjoyed with the American people.

> I cannot help reminiscing just a bit. In 1946 or 1947, I was visited by a couple of young Israelites [sic. This was his usual terminology.] who were anxious to secure arms for Israel. (I was then chief of staff of the army.) I tried to talk to these young men about the future in that region. The two of them belittled the Arabs in every way. . . . They boastfully claimed that Israel needed nothing but a few defensive arms and they would take care of themselves forever and without help of any kind from the United States. I told them they were mistaken—that I had talked to many of the Arab leaders and I was certain that they were stirring up a hornet's nest and if they could solve the initial question peacefully and without doing unnecessary violence to the self-respect and interest of the Arabs, they would profit immeasurably in the long run. I would like to see those young Israelites today.[17]

The same thought is in Dwight Eisenhower's letter to his friend, Swede Hazlitt, written November 2, 1956, at the height of the Suez crisis:

> Of course, nothing in the region would be so difficult to solve except for the underlying cause of the unrest and dissension that exists there—that is, the Arab-Israeli quarrel. This quarrel seems to have no limit either in intensity or in scope. Everybody in the Moslem and Jewish worlds is affected by it. It is so intense that the second any action is taken against one Arab state, by an outsider, all the other Arab and Moslem states seem to regard it as a Jewish plot and react violently.[18]

This is Eisenhower's most consistent thought on the Middle East: It is Israel's existence that is the "underlying cause" of everything that is out of control in the Middle East. Fix that, and everything necessary for peace and order will follow, as the night follows the day!

In General Eisenhower's mind, as in General Marshall's, the issue of Israel always remained the clearest, most powerful example of how wise foreign policy making could get poisoned by "domestic politics"— or "partisan politics," "election considerations" or "certain electoral considerations," and "pressure from certain minorities"—phrases that recur in the records of cabinet discussions on Middle Eastern issues through the Eisenhower years. He was annoyed, for example, when he learned that Republican political leaders had been consulting with Jewish groups, under pressure of the forthcoming municipal elections in New York in the fall of 1953, and he wrote to Dulles: "The political pressure from the Zionists in the Arab-Israeli controversy is a minority pressure. My Jewish friends tell me that, except for the Bronx and Brooklyn the great majority of the nation's Jewish population is anti-Zion." Dulles agreed: The Israelis, he said, were "millstones around our necks."[19]

Throughout his presidency, Eisenhower oscillated between equally unreal under-estimation and over-estimation of the Jewish vote. In March of 1954, when pro-Israeli elements in the United States were mounting a noisy campaign to persuade the administration to sell arms to Israel, Eisenhower told Rabbi Abba Hillel Silver, the most prominent Republican among the American Zionist leaders, that he could not permit American foreign policy to appear to be controlled by "domestic politics." If taking this stance meant that he would not be reelected, then "that would be quite agreeable to him." Rabbi Silver (correctly) assured him, "You can be reelected without a single Jewish vote."[20] But if this was so, then where was the heroism in *defying* the Jewish vote?

Eisenhower's victory caused great concern in Israel. The Ben-Gurion government had been accustomed to easy access to a friendly president, offsetting an unfriendly State Department. Ben-Gurion noted privately, "Until now there was only one conduit to the White House—the Israeli, from now on there will be an Arab one as well."[21] President Eisenhower and Secretary Dulles agreed that the previous administration's Middle East policy was vitiated by Truman's susceptibility to advice from American Jews. Neither ever acknowledged that, among the careerists in the State Department, there had always been an even more pronounced, indeed a virtually monolithic, bias toward the Arabs. Parker T. Hart, the director of the Near East Division in the State Department, said later: "The area experts to a man were scandalized by what happened in 1948. We had made a tremendous effort to lay the groundwork for good relations with the Arabs, and all of a sudden, when we were in good position, all our hopes were dashed."[22] Under the Eisenhower/Dulles regime, the pro-Arab viewpoint came into full possession of in-house discussion of Middle East issues. Hart now reported to Colonel Henry A. Byroade, assistant secretary of state, a man who was fully committed to the Arabist point of view. Byroade brusquely condemned the Israelis for their retaliatory raids into Gaza, Syria, and Jordan, warning the Ben-Gurion government to "drop the attitude of conqueror and the conviction that force and a policy of retaliatory killing is the only policy that your neighbors will understand. You should make your deeds correspond to your frequent utterances of the desire for peace."[23] Indeed, Byroade's denunciations of the Israelis proved too uncomfortable even for this administration and he was reassigned as ambassador to Egypt, where he developed an extreme case of clientitis, and continued to direct the Eisenhower administration along an anti-Israeli path.

Another powerful constituency, partly overlapping with the career Arabists, was the American oil industry. According to the historian Isaac Alteras, during the Truman presidency "the Aramco Oil combine used the State Department to undermine the effectiveness of every act of the President of the United States with respect to the partition of Palestine.

While under Truman their pro-Arab efforts had little success, such would not be the case with the new administration, for Eisenhower trusted wealth and temporal power, and his close friends were men in industry, oil, and banking."[24]

POINTS OF FRICTION

The period 1953 to 1956 was marked by recurring squabbling between the American and Israeli governments. In exchange of correspondence at all levels, in exchange of public statements, in public exchanges at the General Assembly of the UN-U.S. spokesmen seemed always to be making a point of pride of not taking the Israeli viewpoint on issues that arose between Israel and her neighbors or between Israel and the UN.

Among a plethora of issues that were active in those months, two were most troublesome: (1) the plight of the hundreds of thousands of Palestinian-Arab refugees (Arabs who had lived in the Mandate before 1948, and who had been displaced because of the Arab-Jewish war that began in Palestine in December 1947); and (2) Israel's policy of severe reprisal by raids across borders into Lebanon, Syria, Gaza (controlled by Egypt), and Jordan (which in those days ruled both banks of the Jordan river.) The government of Israel's view was that no reprisals at all would be necessary if the other side would refrain from initiating acts of terror. Israel's government claimed that it stood ready to negotiate in good faith about these two related issues (cross-border violence and the refugees), but was prevented from doing so while Arab states would not recognize her existence and instead persisted in the rhetoric of annihilation of the Jews.

In the long catalog of complaints against Israel, there was only one about which American politicians could not pretend to be without conviction. This was the "Jerusalem issue." What made this issue inescapable for politicians was that it was the only current issue on which the major church bodies were of like mind. Few Americans understood the politics of oil, but most Americans went to church; and most of these carried back home denominational newsletters and policy declarations from which they learned that their church had strong views about Jerusalem, and that these generally put the State of Israel in an unfortunate light.

UN Resolution 181 of November 29, 1947, had stipulated that Jerusalem should be under international control, and that neither the forthcoming Jewish state nor the forthcoming Arab state would have sovereignty there. The Jews were now being told that, because they had accepted the partition, they were bound to the stipulations regarding Jerusalem that appeared in that UN resolution. But the Arabs had rejected the whole package, and had appealed to the god of battles. In the upshot, the Kingdom of Jordan held "East Jerusalem," including the Old City, and, having expelled the Jewish minority, was now embarked on the crudest extirpation of all vestiges of the Jewish presence there and throughout the Kingdom of Jordan. Furthermore, throwing to the wind an explicit commitment made at the time of the armistice, King Abdullah, and King Hussein after him, forbade access by the Jews to *haKotel* (the Western Wall), their only holy site in the Old City of Jerusalem. The Jews, meanwhile, were in possession of most of "West Jerusalem" (the new city), in which none of the major Christian holy sites were located.

On December 9, 1949, the UN formally adopted a resolution in support of a *corpus separatum*, 100 square miles in extent, which would include all of Jerusalem and its environs, including Bethlehem. Both the Vatican and the World Council of Churches (WCC) endorsed the *corpus separatum*, thus putting all the major church bodies of the West on the same side with the entire Soviet bloc, and all the Arab and Muslim states—except, of course, Jordan. The government of Israel was having none of this. On December 13, 1949, the Knesset unanimously voted to move to Jerusalem, and on January 1, 1950, the entire government operation (except for the ministries of defense, police, and foreign affairs) went up to Jerusalem. On January 23, 1958, the Knesset solemnly proclaimed that the Holy City had "always been the capital of the Jewish nation."

For a while, the Truman government went a certain distance to present a common front with the churches on the matter of Jerusalem; but eventually that government wearied of the issue. The churches, however, did not. Still, although the Eisenhower government shared the attitude of the Vatican and the WCC on this issue, President Eisenhower and Secretary Dulles were much too preoccupied (as we shall see) quarreling with Israel over matters of greater import to make a major diplomatic assault on the Jerusalem front.

THE "NEW LOOK" IN MIDDLE EAST POLICY: THE STRATEGIC OVERVIEW

Dwight Eisenhower had always put a higher appraisal upon the strategic value of the Middle East than most did. As Supreme Commander of NATO forces, he had testified before the Senate Foreign Relations Committee on July 22, 1951: "So far as the sheer value of territory is concerned, there is no more strategically important area in the world than the Middle East, the so-called bridge to Africa and Asia. . . . We should bring in the Arab world on our side." At a press conference in Denver on June 24, 1952, he proposed formation of a Middle East alliance along NATO lines. In the Middle East, he said, "you have a problem of just cold hatred to us, and there we have got to win friends before we can even talk to them." He expressed the difference between Truman's policy and the one he intended to follow as the difference between "special relationship" and "friendly impartiality."[25]

Early in his administration, Eisenhower signaled his readiness to embark on a new policy in the Middle East by sending Secretary Dulles on a "fact-finding" tour of the Middle East, which included Egypt, Israel, Jordan, Lebanon, Syria, Iraq, Saudi Arabia, India, Pakistan, Turkey, Greece, and Libya.[26] Dulles found the new Egyptian regime obsessed with the issue of Britain's continuing presence and determined to make him understand that this was part of a general imperialist operation, in which Israel was somehow implicated. Dulles assured the Egyptians that the new American government "was trying to work out a Middle East policy on the basis of the enlightened self interest of the United States as a whole. I do not mean [the] self interest of a particular group of Americans."[27]

In Israel (according to a telegraph-style memorandum prepared in the U.S. Embassy in Tel Aviv) Dulles explained to the Ben-Gurion government that, "Arabs felt [that the] Roosevelt and Truman administrations [were] so subject to Jewish influence that [the] Arab viewpoint [was] ignored. Decisions [were] often taken under pressure [from] United States Jewish groups which felt [that] they had the right [to] exercise influence because of contributions to [the] election victory. [The] [n]ew administration, [as the] [S]ecretary pointed out, was elected by [an] overwhelming vote of [the] American people as a whole and neither owes that type of political debt to any segment nor believes in building power by cultivating particular segments of [the] population. . . . [Dulles] suggested that the Prime Minister [Ben-Gurion] might be able to help [the] United States to help Israel in this regard."[28] Whatever Dulles may have expected, the Israeli leaders did not argue this point. In fact, Ambassador Abba Eban agreed that "the constant demand by individual Jewish leaders to see the President and the secretary of state leads to negative results. . . . Israeli officials in Washington must be given priority in presenting the country's case before the American policymakers."[29]

Having completed his fact-finding tour, Dulles reported his findings to the president: "The Israeli factor and the association of the United States in the minds of the people of the area with French and British colonial and imperialistic policies are millstones around our neck"[30] Then, in a television and radio address on June 1, 1953, he reported to the American people in the same terms:

Closely huddled around Israel are over 800,000 Arab refugees, who fled from Palestine as the Israelis took over. They mostly exist in makeshift camps, with few facilities either for health, work or recreation. . . . The United States should seek to allay the deep resentment against it that has resulted from the creation of Israel. In the past we had good relations with the Arab peoples. . . . Today the Arab peoples are afraid that the United States will back the new State of Israel in aggressive expansion. They are more fearful of Zionism than of communism, and they fear lest the United States become the backer of expansionist Zionism. On the other hand the Israelis fear that ultimately the Arabs may try to push them into the seas.[31]

The speech infuriated the Israelis. It seemed that the new U.S. government had now adopted the Arab recital of recent history.

While the previously special relationship with Israel deteriorated, Eisenhower was actively seeking a close relationship with Egypt and the other Arab states of the region. Various ties of commitment, including sales of arms, were developing with Turkey, Pakistan, Iran, and Iraq, all of whom joined a pro-Western regional alliance with Britain called the Baghdad Pact (1955). (The United States was not formally a member, but was universally understood to be the true patron of the pact.) Early in 1955, Nasser of Egypt approached the American government with a proposal for a major purchase of American arms. The Eisenhower administration offered to go one better: it would make a gift of $27 million in arms, provided that Egypt give a commitment to use them only in self-defense; that it accept the services of an American team to train the Egyptians in their use; and that Egypt declare itself an ally of the West against the communist bloc. Nasser rejected these terms, but continued to talk about the possibility of arms purchases, while he secretly carried on negotiations along the same lines with the Soviets.[32] These latter negotiations resulted in a deal announced in September 1955, under which Egypt was permitted to make a major portion of her payments to the USSR in the form of Egyptian cotton.[33] There was consternation in Washington: "Against the background of recently increasingly Soviet interest in the Middle East, we must regard the Egyptian arms deal as a very serious step toward the penetration of the western position in the Arab world," Dulles wrote to the president, "and we must consider all possible steps of preventing Egypt from consummating it."[34] There was even greater consternation in Israel. Adding to the offense that her enemies were now better armed than before was the suggestion, made in public at about the same time by Secretary Dulles, that "It is difficult to be critical of countries [that is, Egypt], which, feeling themselves endangered, seek the arms which they sincerely need for defense. "[35]

Ben-Gurion had already proposed to his cabinet specific proposals for a preemptive war against Egypt; and although they had voted these down as not propitious, they had given him agreement in principle to proceed when the timing seemed better. During the Israeli election campaign of July 1956, Ben-Gurion promised Israelis that he would clear the passage of the Gulf of Aqaba: This meant that if the Egyptians did not voluntarily remove the fortifications which blocked the Straits of Tiran against the Israelis, then Israel would remove them by force.[36]

Meanwhile, Israel's friends in the United States kept up a steady campaign to persuade the Eisenhower government to meet Israel's defensive needs. At the very outset of the presidential election year of 1956, a group of prominent Democrats, including Harry Truman, Eleanor Roosevelt, and union leaders Walter Reuther and George Meany, issued a public call for defensive weapons for Israel as the necessary response to the Soviet Union's incursion into the Middle East. Forty Republican House leaders spoke up publicly in the same vein.[37] Still Eisenhower would not budge. In fact, he was prepared to pay the price of letting American arms manufacturers lose out on sales to Israel, while he secretly encouraged France and Canada to sell their best jet fighters to Israel, even though this would mean diminishing the stock of NATO.[38]

BACKGROUND TO THE SUEZ CRISIS

News of the American negotiations with Nasser during 1955 and early 1956 had angered the British, who had earlier persuaded the United States to join with herself and France in a Tri-Partite Declaration (May 25, 1950), undertaking not to sell significant amounts of military hardware to any side in the area, and to take immediate concerted action, both within and outside the UN, to prevent any violation of the armistice lines of 1949. Acceding to American pressures, Prime Minister Eden had already negotiated an agreement with Egypt (October 19, 1954) that called for withdrawal by stages of all British forces from Egypt. Soon there would be no British troops in position between Egypt and Israel. During the early months of 1956, the United States and Egypt had been negotiating, apparently amicably, over a contract to build the great Aswan High Dam together.[39] This episode ended exactly as the arms-sale negotiations had—with Nasser playing off the Americans against the Soviets. On July 19, 1956, the Eisenhower administration withdrew from negotiations without forewarning;[40] Nasser was told that his dealing with the other side amounted to "blackmail."[41]

Quickly, the Soviet Union hammered out its terms—again settling for job lots of Egyptian cotton in partial payment of the costs of the giant project. The Soviet foot was now well in the door—not only the door of Egypt, but the door that led to all the other Middle East regimes that had come or were soon to come under Nasser's influence. In the years that followed, Nasser (and for a while his successor, Anwar Sadat) found themselves signing one contract after another, piling up more and more debt, drawing onto their soil more and more Soviet and Warsaw Pact military, scientific, and trade personnel.

On July 26, 1956, Nasser suddenly announced that he had nationalized and taken possession of the Suez Canal. He took the occasion to express his contempt for the British Empire and his intent to rally the Arab world for the early liquidation of Israel: "This, O citizens, is the battle in which we are now involved. It is a battle against imperialism and the methods and tactics of imperialism, and a battle against Israel, the vanguard of imperialism. . . . They strengthened Israel so that they can annihilate us and convert us into a state of refugees. We shall all of us defend our nationalism and Arabism and we shall all work so that the Arab home-land may extend from the Atlantic Ocean to the Persian Gulf."[42]

On July 27, Prime Minister Eden wrote to Eisenhower to be sure that he grasped what was really going on here:

> Dear friend:
> We should not allow ourselves to become involved in legal quibbles about the rights of the Egyptian government to nationalize what is technically an Egyptian company, or in financial arguments about their capacity to pay the compensation which they have offered. . . . My colleagues and I are convinced that we must be ready, in the last resort, to use force to bring Nasser to his senses. . . . However, the first step must be for you and us and France to exchange views, align our policies and concert together how we can best bring the maximum pressure to bear on the Egyptian government.[43]

Meanwhile, the British chiefs of staff were summoned, and (as Eden recalled) "instructed to get ready a plan and a timetable for an operation designed to occupy and secure the canal, should other methods fail." Eden hoped that the Aswan Dam episode had demonstrated to the Americans the necessity of closing ranks at the UN and in the international body that was supposed to enforce the Suez Convention. "We expected that the United States would at least be neutral. But if assistance were not forthcoming from our friends, we had to be in a position to take action alone."[44]

On July 31, Eisenhower called an urgent meeting of his principal advisers on security matters to deal with the news of Egypt's action and these first signals from Eden of his own intentions. He informed his advisers that the British had told him that they intended (in their words) to "break Nasser," and would initiate hostilities, probably in about six weeks. Eisenhower believed this to be "very unwise . . . [and] that the British were out of date in thinking of this as a mode of action in the present circumstances . . . [as Nasser] embodies the emotional demands of people of the area for independence and for 'slapping the white Man down'. . . . [In the end,] It might well arouse the world from Dakar to the Philippine Islands against us."[45] During conversations with Eden and the British foreign secretary in London a few days later, Dulles struck an entirely different note: "A way had to be found to make Nasser disgorge what he was attempting to swallow. . . . It should be possible to create a world opinion so adverse to Nasser that he would be isolated. Then if a military operation had to be undertaken it would be more apt to succeed and have less grave repercussions than if it had been undertaken precipitately." "These were forthright words," Eden recalled (sardonically) in the subsequent days of his humiliation. "They rang in my ears for months."[46]

Over the next several weeks, Dulles pursued his strategy, which was to jawbone the matter to death in a variety of international bodies. A conference of the twenty-four countries considered (by Eden and Dulles) to be the most directly affected by the Suez situation was called in London on August 16. A Declaration followed, in which international control of the Suez Canal was reaffirmed, but in which there also appeared statements of willingness to discuss with Egypt her interests, particularly with regard to operation and profits. But Nasser, predictably, obliged the British by rejecting the Declaration altogether.

All this time, Eisenhower was aware that Britain and France were meeting on an ongoing basis to plan some concerted military action. Hinting at this knowledge, he sent a warning to Eden on September 8: "The use of military force against Egypt under present circumstances might have consequences even more serious than causing the Arabs to support Nasser. It might cause a serious misunderstanding between our two countries because I must say frankly that there is as yet no public opinion in this country which is prepared to support such a move, and the most significant public opinion that there is seems to think that the United Nations was formed to prevent this very thing."[47]

For months, Israel had been planning a military initiative against Egypt that would result in clearing the Egyptian menace from her frontiers: removing the Egyptian emplacements that denied Israel exit from the Gulf of Aqaba, and ending the constant terrorist incursions from Gaza (held by Egypt since the end of the War of Independence). Although it had denied responsibility at first, Egypt, in a formal statement of August 31, 1955, publicly took responsibility for these raids, which, in fact, had always been under Egyptian command: "Egypt has decided to despatch [sic] her heroes, the disciples of Pharaoh and the sons of Islam, and they will clean the land of Palestine." Israel had no interest in taking Egyptian territory, and was interested in the matter of the Suez Canal only to the extent that it wanted what the Constantinople Convention said all nations were entitled to: freedom of passage.

France's premier, Guy Mollet, agreed entirely with Britain's Eden that Nasser was Adolf Hitler redivivus. Nasser was publicly supporting the Algerian rebels against France, delivering anti-French propaganda to them via radio, and supplying them with arms out of his arsenals recently acquired from the Communist bloc. Of these activities Mollet said, "All this [is written] in the works of Nasser, just as Hitler's policy [was] written down in *Mein Kampf*. . . . Nasser [has] the ambition to recreate the conquests of Islam."[48] It was Israel's good fortune that at this moment in

France's dizzying history of rising and falling governments, there was a premier (Guy Mollet), a foreign minister (Christian Pineau), and a defense minister (Maurice Bourgès-Maunoury) who were all pro-Zionist—not a typical state of affairs. This situation contributed to the development of a special relationship between France and Israel, both targets of Nasser's furious new version of Arab nationalism. "Of all the major arms producers in the world, France was the only one that was not hostile and did not boycott us," recalled Shimon Peres, who played a key role in French-Israeli negotiations at this time. In 1954, Israel and France had signed an agreement for the sale of latest-model French military equipment, including jet-planes, tanks, and anti-tank weapons. Furthermore, the two were secretly collaborating on nuclear research.[49]

Planning for the action (eventually code-named Operation Musketeer) that the three nations ultimately took against Egypt began with secret meetings between middle-level French and Israeli authorities on September 1, but soon involved the senior political and military figures in both regimes. It bothered Ben-Gurion on the day that he was introduced in person to the planning sessions for the conspiracy at Sèvres (October 22–24), that the British did not seem ready to treat the Israelis as peers. It was no secret that Eden had opposed the creation of a Jewish state. "If we must have preference," he said to his personal secretary in 1941, "let me murmur in your ear that I prefer Arabs to Jews."[50] The measure of Eden's cynicism can be seen in his neglect to mention in his memoirs that he had had any prior knowledge of the action that Israel was about to take—let alone that his government, and that he personally, was brought face-to-face with the movers of the project as early as October 7.

Ben-Gurion caused consternation among the French and British co-conspirators when he proposed that the operation not take place until after the American election, and that the United States should then be let in on it before it unfolded.[51] His fear was that Eisenhower might suspect that the timing of the adventure was meant to cause him embarrassment at the polls, and that this would make him dangerously unfriendly. This is exactly what happened—as we shall see.

After much turbulent and awkward clandestine negotiation, the three parties arrived at the Sèvres Protocol. The plan was that on October 29, 1956, Israeli forces would launch a large-scale attack on Egyptian forces in Gaza and Sinai and drive them westwards toward the Suez Canal. On October 30, Britain and France would make certain public demands upon Egypt and Israel: Egypt would be told that she must withdraw to a distance of ten miles west of the canal and agree to a temporary occupation of key areas along the canal by British and French forces, while Israel should cease fire and withdraw to a line ten miles *east* of the canal. If, as expected, Egypt refused, British and French forces would commence their attack in the early morning hours of October 31—that is, thirty-six hours after the start of the operation. In addition, Israel would dispatch forces to seize the western shore of the Gulf of Aqaba and the islands of Tiran and Sanapir in order to ensure freedom of navigation in the Gulf. Ben-Gurion disliked the part of the plan that called for the British and French to pretend to be surprised by Israel's initial action, and then to call for Israel to cease this action, as though she were an aggressor and they bystanders. As Moshe Dayan put the matter to the British and French at the time, "Britain and France would play the cops and we the robber, they the saints and we the sinner."[52] Still unhappy with this aspect of the plan, Ben-Gurion signed on to the Sèvres Protocol.[53]

EISENHOWER'S RESPONSE TO THE SUEZ INTERVENTION

Indications that Israel was preparing for military action had accumulated on the desks of American intelligence analysts over the summer and fall of 1956. However, the Israelis had contrived to give the impression that their intended action would be directed at Jordan. According to the American sources, this made sense to Eisenhower, who believed that Israel had designs to recover the West Bank. Thus, he was (he claimed) put off the track of the larger plan: that is, Israel's connivance with Britain and France in action against Egypt. On October 29 at 3:20 p.m. Israeli time (8:20 a.m. in Washington, D.C.), the Sinai campaign began: Low-flying aircraft severed Egyptian telephone lines and transport planes carried 395 paratroopers to Mitla Pass, while an Israeli armored force of about 4,000 crossed the Egyptian border and quickly joined the paratroopers at the Mitla Pass.

Eisenhower was obliged to return from the campaign trail to deal with the crisis. Meanwhile, Ambassador Eban had arrived to explain everything at the State Department, where he received a very cold reception.[54] As Ben-Gurion had feared, Eisenhower assumed that the Israelis had deliberately timed this action to embarrass the president during his reelection campaign. Eisenhower told his son, "Well, it looks as if we're in for trouble. If the Israelis keep going . . . I may have to use force to stop them. . . . Then I'd lose the election. There would go New York, New Jersey, Pennsylvania, and Connecticut at least."[55] What particularly infuriated Eisenhower was that he had explicitly warned Ben-Gurion, a mere two weeks earlier, *never* to try to exploit the Jewish vote. According to his diary, he told Ben-Gurion "that he should not make any grave mistakes based upon his belief that winning a domestic election is as important to us as preserving and protecting the interests of the United Nations and of the free world in that region. . . . On a long-term basis aggression on his part cannot fail to bring catastrophe—and such friends as he would have left in the world, no matter how powerful, could not do anything about it."[56]

On Tuesday, October 30, the British and French issued their ultimatum, in the form of letters delivered by the Foreign Office to the ambassadors of Israel and Egypt in London. No one on earth believed that the British-French ultimatum was inspired by the actual events. Israel (following the "Musketeers" script) accepted the British ultimatum; but Egypt (again as anticipated) did not. The rest of the script played out as, between October 31 and November 2, Britain and France bombed Egyptian airfields, destroying most of the Egyptian air force on the ground. Simultaneously, France and the UK used their veto power against an American resolution offered in the Security Council. Thereupon, the United States moved the action to the General Assembly, taking advantage of the "Uniting for Peace Provision," which allows the General Assembly to take action in the case of Security Council deadlock.

Meanwhile, Eden had written to Eisenhower: "We have never made any secret of our belief that justice entitled us to defend our vital interests against Nasser's designs. . . . My first instinct would have been to ask you to associate yourself and our country with the declaration. But I know the constitutional and other difficulties in which you are placed. . . . [W]hen the dust settles there may well be a chance for our doing a really constructive piece of work in the line against communism."[57]

On October 31, 1956, Eisenhower spoke on television to the nation about the crisis. He explained the need to provide American leadership in the search for peace by going to the General Assembly.[58] He managed to be conciliatory toward Britain, France, and Israel, referring to them as "friends" and "allies," and conceding that there had been provocations from Egypt, but still he affirmed that American policy was to support the rule of law. At a meeting of his National Security Council at the White House, 7:15 p.m., Washington time, on November 1, Eisenhower put the matter somewhat differently: "It would be a complete mistake for this country to continue with any kind of aid to Israel, which was an aggressor. . . . In this matter, he does not care in the slightest whether he is reelected or not. He feels we must make good on our word."[59]

In the UN General Assembly, the United States sponsored a Resolution calling for "an immediate cease-fire and withdrawal of all occupying forces from Egyptian territory as soon as possible" and for a return to the lines held following the armistice agreements of 1949. Sixty-four nations supported the Resolution, five opposed (Britain, France, Israel, Australia, New Zealand), and six abstained.

Meanwhile, an uprising against communist rule in Hungary had (to the momentary chagrin of the Soviet Union) almost wiped the Middle East news from the front pages. It was quickly and brutally suppressed and its leaders liquidated. On November 3, the Soviet Union used her veto power in the Security Council (for the seventy-ninth time to date) to prevent passage of a resolution condemning her invasion of Hungary. On Monday, November 5, British and French paratroopers dropped on Egyptian cities along the Suez Canal. That same day, Soviet Prime Minister Nikolai Bulganin dispatched sharply worded letters to the leaders of Britain, France, and Israel. "We are filled with determination to use force to crush the aggressors [Britain, France, Israel], and to restore peace in the East," Bulganin proclaimed. He hinted at the use of atomic weapons. At the same time, Bulganin sent to President Eisenhower a brusque dispatch stating his intention to bring Soviet force to bear in the region to secure peace if the United States did not agree at once to some collaborative action with the USSR against Israel. In reply, Eisenhower stated that if the Soviet Union tried to intervene with force in the Middle East, the United States would respond with force against it. The prospect of Armageddon now occurred to many.

Eisenhower did not hesitate to make use of the Soviet threats when leaning on Eden, even though he knew through secret U2 aerial surveillance that the Soviet Union was taking none of the steps required to follow through with these threats. Even more effective was a powerful economic weapon: Eisenhower simply refused a British request for oil shipments to make up for those lost by Nasser's blocking of the Suez Canal and withheld support for the loans that Britain urgently requested to help stop the decline of the pound sterling.[60] To the horror of his French ally, Premier Mollet, Eden caved in: In a note that arrived at the White House at noon on election day, November 6, Eden announced that the cabinet had agreed to an immediate cease-fire. Subsequently, Eden tried to arrange a meeting with Eisenhower, but Eisenhower simply refused to talk with the prime minister until Her Majesty's government had complied with the UN resolutions without condition. But before any of this could happen, Eden had resigned on grounds of ill health.

In his memoirs, Eden sums up this story with great bitterness:

If the United States government had approached this issue in the spirit of an ally, they would have done everything in their power, short of the use of force, to support the nations whose economic security depended upon the freedom of passage through the Suez Canal. They would have closely planned their policies with their allies and held stoutly to the decisions arrived at. They would have insisted on restoring international authority in order to insulate the canal from the politics of any country. It is now clear that this was never the attitude of the United States Government. Rather did they try to gain time, coast along over difficulties as they arose and improvise policies, each following on the failure of its immediate predecessor. None of these was geared to the long-range purpose of serving a just cause. . . . The old spoor of colonialism confused the trail.[61]

JEWISH POLITICAL STRENGTH TESTED IN THE SUEZ CRISIS

The Presidential Election of 1956

Particularly awkward for American Jews was that these events were happening in the last days of the 1956 election campaign. It was their worst nightmare come true: that American Jews should, in defense of an action that the American public regarded as aiding and abetting the decayed British Empire, be asked to throw their weight against a popular American president, who at that very moment was leading the world in denunciation of the Soviet Union's actions in Hungary. As Egypt's armies melted away across the Sinai, Prime Minister Ben-Gurion delivered a triumphant speech to the Knesset, in tones that reminded many people of the victory monuments of the ancient conquerors. The Sinai campaign, he declared, was "the greatest and most glorious in the annals of our people." Gaza and Sinai, he now insisted, had never properly belonged to Egypt in the first place. Now was the moment to restore King Solomon's patrimony from the slopes of Lebanon to *Yotvat* (Tiran): "Yotvat will once more become a part of the third Kingdom of Israel." Years later Ben-Gurion admitted: "I made a few mistakes in that speech. . . . I went too far . . . the victory was too quick. I was too drunk with victory."[62]

The leaders of American Jewish groups declined the Israeli Embassy's requests to defend Israel's cause before the American public.[63]

If they were to base their decision on comparison of their official platforms, American friends of Israel would have had no difficulty choosing between the two parties in November of 1956. The Republican platform offered only a generalized and platitudinous declaration of support for Israel, in the context of a miniature essay on the geostrategic importance of the region in which Israel happens to live. The theme was, "We shall support the independence of Israel against armed aggression. The best hope for peace in the Middle East lies in the United Nations."[64] According to the Democratic platform, "the current crisis over Suez is a consequence of inept and vacillating Republican policy." It took explicit note of Egypt's illegal denial of passage to Israeli traffic through the Suez Canal, and vowed that a Democratic administration would "act to redress the dangerous imbalance of arms in the area resulting from the shipment of Communist arms to Egypt, by selling or supplying defensive weapons to Israel, and will take such steps, including security guarantees, as may be required to deter aggression and war in the area."[65]

Adlai Stevenson, the Jews, and Israel

Of all the major Democratic candidates seeking the presidential nomination for 1956, Adlai Stevenson was probably the least trusted by the Jews. During the years that he had been titular leader of the party, he had failed to proclaim a rationale for commitment to Israel's security. Speaking to the American Committee for the Weizmann Institute on December 2, 1954, Stevenson had even endorsed the administration's approach: "One cannot, in good faith, take issue with the striving of our officials and other Western nations to improve relations, cooperation, and confidence in the Arab world."[66] This was a platitude, unworthy of the candidate who presented himself as a voice of conscience in politics. Predictably, Stevenson's support of the administration's Middle East policy began to melt as the electoral season advanced. When Eisenhower refused to send arms to Israel in response to the new situation created by the USSR/ Czechoslovak-Egyptian arms deal of late 1955, Stevenson reminded Democrats of their party's history as the first and best friend of the cause of Zion: After all, he noted, it was Woodrow Wilson who had sponsored the Balfour Declaration.[67] Now he discovered that Israel was in mortal danger and insisted that the United States must honor its commitment to her security. Still, he disappointed Israel's friends by his persistent habit of attaching this talk about commitment to Israel to some on-the-other-hand talk about not wishing to prefer either side in this deep-rooted, everlasting, and unfortunate conflict. "We do not want to see an arms race in the area where the principles of Woodrow Wilson's fourteen points once shone like a lighthouse after centuries of dark oppression. . . . There is no time to lose, for the issue in the Middle East today is not just the preservation of Israel but all the values of the Christian, Hebrew and Islamic cultures."[68] This was precisely the note least likely to reassure those whose concern for Israel's present and future owed anything at all to Biblical perspectives.

Stevenson always resented the presumption of American Jews who offered him education on this issue. In a private letter dated December 20, 1955, he wrote, "I quietly asserted that it should be the policy of this government not to permit any change in the status quo by force—and the more noisy Zionists have been denouncing me as a traitor ever since, and, frankly, I'm getting damn well fed up with it. . . . Moreover, I'm about the only leading Democrat left with whom Arabs will still talk in confidence."[69]

Israel's action of October 29, 1956, Stevenson said at the time, was entirely the fault of the Eisenhower administration: "Here we stand today. We have alienated our chief European allies. We have alienated Israel. We have alienated Egypt and the Arab countries. And in the UN our main associate in Middle Eastern matters now appears to be Communist Russia—in the very week when the Red Army has been shooting down the brave people of Hungary and Poland. We have lost every point in the game."[70] But even in this moment of high dudgeon there was the characteristic Stevensonian waffle: "I would not condone the use of force, even by our friends and allies. But I say that we now have an opportunity to use our great potential moral authority, our own statesmanship, the weight of our economic power, to bring about solutions to the whole range of complex problems confronting the free world in the Middle East. The time has come to wipe the slate clean and begin anew."[71]

Perhaps Stevenson was not the sturdy friend of Israel that a Democratic president ought to be, but the verdict was already in on the incumbent president. And so Eisenhower lost the Jewish vote again.[72] And again it was shown to Jews and Republicans alike that the popular Republican president did not need the Jewish vote. As for Adlai Stevenson, he remained convinced ever after that the Suez crisis helped turn Eisenhower's merely probable victory into the landslide that humiliated Stevenson and, for a good while to come, severely tried his feelings about democracy. To one correspondent he wrote bitterly, "I was doing not so badly until the Middle East came apart and then the public was, thanks to years of conditioned ignorance, rushed into endorsing the author of our disaster." And to another, "Just think, after all those bond drive rallies I've addressed they [the Israelis] couldn't have waited another week."[73]

AFTER THE ELECTION

Israel Alone

Meanwhile, on November 7, 1956, the General Assembly of the UN had passed a resolution, sponsored by the United States, calling on Israel to withdraw from Egyptian territory. The vote was 65 to 1 (Israel). The reelection of Dwight Eisenhower had made it clear that there could not be a change of direction of U.S. policy; and without that Israel could not hope to avoid the painful business of withdrawing her forces from Gaza and Sinai (including the strategic position at Sharm el-Sheikh on the Gulf of Aqaba). The best she could hope for was that through procrastination and stubborn reiteration of her determination never to withdraw she could compel the UN and the United States (the latter was more important) to make public commitments to secure Israel's future peace as conditions of her withdrawal.

On February 20, 1957, Eisenhower gave a television address in which he condemned Israel for her noncompliance with the UN resolutions and indicated his intention to resort to stiff sanctions against Israel.[74] At once it became clear that Eisenhower had underestimated the American public's esteem for Israel and had overestimated the loss of credibility that Israel had suffered when the world first saw her entangled with the British and the French in their sordid "gunboat" exercise. Jewish organizations quickly rallied support in Congress for guarantees that would allow Israel to retreat from Sinai and Gaza. Dulles wrote to Henry Luce, "I am aware how almost impossible it is in this country to carry out a foreign policy not approved by the Jews. Marshall and Forrestal learned that. I am going to try to have one. That does not mean that I am anti-Jewish, but I believe in what George Washington said in his Farewell Address that an emotional attachment to another country should not interfere." Out of public view, the president was exploring with the secretary of treasury action to withdraw tax exemptions for contributions from Americans to Israel (through United Jewish Appeal, Israel bonds, etc.). Taken aback by the sudden shift of the public relations advantage back to Israel, Secretary Dulles telephoned his friends in the National Council of Churches and suggested that the clergy use their pulpits to mobilize support for the administration's Middle East: "The non-Jewish elements of the community have got to make themselves more felt or else there will be a disaster here."[75]

The Friends of Israel Regroup

One reason for Eisenhower's underestimation of the pro-Israel forces was that there had been a slackening of American Zionist activism following the War of Independence of 1948–1949. Membership in the Zionist Organization of America declined from 250,000 in 1948 to 87,000 in 1963.[76] Many saw this as evidence of declining ardor for Israel; but in fact it was an indication of the Jewish community's sense that, with the creation of the state and the immediate securing of its right to exist, the Zionist task was completed. When it became clear that Israel was not to be left in peace, new ways had to be found to mobilize American official and public support.

In the 1956–1957 crisis, financial donations to Jewish organizations in support of Israel reached unprecedented levels. In 1954 the American Zionist Council established the American Israel Public Affairs Committee (AIPAC) as the official lobby for Israel in Washington. AIPAC developed contacts with senators and congressmen, and distributed informational materials. Reacting to the crisis of 1956–1957, AIPAC led the campaign against the administration's sanctions. The other principal conduit of Jewish influence in the official arena was the Conference of Presidents of Major Jewish Organizations, established in 1955. It brought together both Zionist and non-Zionist organizations, including B'nai B'rith, Hadassah, Jewish War Veterans, the American Zionist Federation, and the American Jewish Congress, so that they could agree upon a common approach to official U.S. policy toward Israel.

Since the election, Israel's public image had been steadily improving. Long before Eisenhower's television address of February 20, 1957, Israel's action of October was sundered (in public memory) from the actions of Britain and France; Israel was now able to focus public attention on the circumstances that made her incursion into Sinai necessary—that is, the terrorist raids and Egypt's attempt to strangle Israel's economy through denial of access through the Suez Canal and the Gulf of Aqaba. Israeli military prowess in October had won admiration (especially when contrasted with the bumbling of the British and French, and their quick retreat under the threats of Bulganin and Eisenhower).

Now it seemed more important than it had in November that the Democrats had won the congressional side of the national election. Here, the Jewish vote and the pro-Israel vote counted for much more than it had seemed to do when all eyes were on the presidential contest. Lyndon Johnson, the majority leader since 1955, was well disposed to Israel—not least because he had ambitions for the presidency himself, and was actively seeking to prove support in Northern constituencies to balance his home support in the South and Southwest. William Knowland, Republican leader in the Senate, was also prominent in the defense of Israel, and found many Republican allies (notably, Alexander Wiley, senator from Wisconsin and the ranking Republican on the Senate Foreign Relations Committee). In a vigorous attack upon the administration's policy, Knowland said that the sanctions that the administration threatened to bring against Israel were proof of "a double standard by the United Nations that would apply one law to a small country . . . while sidestepping the question of sanctions on a larger aggressor" (that is, the Soviet Union).[77]

Despite his determination not to yield to "domestic pressure," Eisenhower ultimately did just that. Not all of Israel's demands were met—the Egyptians were not kept out of Gaza—but a United Nations Emergency Force (UNEF) was posted both in Gaza and in Sharm el-Sheikh. In addition, the administration offered a letter of understanding for the Israelis to keep, in which it was stated that "the United States is prepared to exercise the right of free passage of vessels of U.S. registry and join with others to secure general recognition of this right." With these "guarantees" from the U.S. administration in hand, the government of Israel, on March 1, 1957, accepted the UN's call to withdraw. The withdrawal took place March 4 to March 7.

In the decade that followed, Israel was able take advantage of the trepidation that the Egyptian president felt but did not admit to publicly, in order to open up Israeli traffic in the Gulf of Aqaba. It was in these years that Eilat became Israel's southern gateway to the Orient, and an oil pipeline laid from Eilat to the Mediterranean coast contributed to the economic boom of the years that followed. Above all, the dramatic demonstration of Israel's military strength and skill in the Gaza and Suez action had a chastening effect in Arab ruling circles, accounting for a decade of relative tranquility on its borders.

IMPROVED U.S.-ISRAEL RELATIONS IN THE LAST MONTHS OF THE EISENHOWER PRESIDENCY

The events of 1956–1957, by reducing the influence of Britain and France in the Middle East, seemed to open up a vacuum of authority, suggesting unlimited possibilities of mischief for Nasser and other Arab dictators to exploit, hand-in-hand with their new patron, the USSR. To address this situation (but without, of course, confessing that anything he had done or left undone had contributed to it), the president brought before a joint session of the 85th Congress on January 5, 1957, a proposal (soon dubbed the "Eisenhower Doctrine") "to cooperate with and assist any nation or group of nations in the general area of the Middle East in the development of economic strength dedicated to the maintenance of national independence . . . [and] to authorize such assistance and cooperation to include the employment of the armed forces of the United States to secure and protect the territorial integrity and political independence of such nations, requesting such aid, against overt armed aggression from any nation controlled by International Communism."[78] To secure passage of the act, Eisenhower was required to accept an amendment noting the commitment of the United States to preservation of the independence and sovereignty of nations in the area. As it turned out, Israel was the only nation in the region that formally adopted the Eisenhower Doctrine.[79]

*   *   *   *   *

The key to understanding Eisenhower's attitude toward Israel is the resentment he carried since his failure, in the days when he was chief of staff and George Marshall was secretary of state, to have persuaded the Jewish people and their American Zionist allies of the irrationality of Zionism. To Maxwell Abbell, president of the United Synagogues of America, Eisenhower once wrote, "I grew up believing that the Jews were the chosen people, that they gave us the high ethical and moral principles of our civilization."[80] This did not prevent him from believing that the Zionist venture was perverse and irrational. Indeed, he seemed to have thought that Jews, precisely because they were generally so intelligent, should have been able to see the irrationality of their goal. The whole exercise called Zionism was, to him, an embarrassing example of willful zealotry, discrediting the rationalism that, he imagined, had characterized his own journey in life since boyhood.

From the example of his own parents, Eisenhower carried the conviction that strongly held theology had a deranging effect. Dwight Eisenhower wanted nothing to do with the notion that the president of the United States stood in a providentially appointed situation as the protector of

Israel. He was not Cyrus, nor was he the heir of Cyrus. The state had come into existence against his better judgment and advice and had then gone on, in defiance of his professionally based expectations, to survive its war of independence. Well then, Israel should not count on him to save her from the fruit of her willfulness.

By 1958, however, Eisenhower, in effect, had come around to the general American viewpoint on Israel. He was still not keen on exploring the theological roots of popular Christian attitudes toward Israel, but he could not question the practical effects of Zionism. He had been wrong to think of Zionism as unballasted zealotry and he had been wrong to dismiss the American Zionists, Christians and Jews, as troublemakers. He was mightily impressed by the success of Israel's friends in Congress, who compelled him, just a few weeks after his heroic reelection victory, to write some guarantees for Israel's security into the undertakings to withdraw from Sinai. While the dignified and well-educated leaders of Europe's most advanced nations, Britain and France, thrashed about and permitted tin-pot tyrants to escape their grasp, the people of Israel had supported their leaders' constant and courageous actions—and so had the American people. And now, after the dust had settled, only Israel had formally associated herself with Eisenhower's own foreign policy in the Middle East. This was a sobering revelation for Eisenhower.

In the remaining three years of Eisenhower's presidency, Arab regimes in the Middle East became more and more unstable, mainly owing to political wrecking operations conducted by President Nasser. Throughout all this, Israel proved to the United States the value of her intelligence gathering, and in countless small ways cooperated with the U.S. government as a partner in pursuing their shared purposes in the area. Some years after his retirement, Eisenhower conceded that applying pressure to Israel to vacate Sinai in 1957 had been a mistake. Eisenhower is even quoted as saying to friends some time in his last years that stronger pressure upon him from American Jews would have helped avert this colossal blunder![81] Richard Nixon agreed: "In retrospect I believe that our actions were a serious mistake."[82]

JOHN F. KENNEDY (1961–1963)
"Old $12 Bibles"

THE RENEWED THREAT TO ISRAEL'S PEACE IN THE EARLY 1960s

The thousand days of the presidency of John F. Kennedy coincided with a moment of exceptional tranquility for Israel. As we have seen, almost immediately after the debris of the Suez crisis of 1956–1957 was cleared away, Israel began working to restore the old alliance with the U.S. government by demonstrating her value as an ally in support of the Eisenhower Doctrine. Almost daily, Israel's stock grew in U.S. official circles, as President Nasser, abetted by the USSR, noisily set about de-stabilizing conservative Arab regimes (including the regimes that possessed the vital oil resources) and promoting subversive politics in many forms—all in the name of unified Arab action against Israel. After Nasserite forces overthrew the familiar regimes in Iraq and Syria, Eisenhower moved to shore up the regimes of Israel's other immediate neighbors, Lebanon and Jordan.

Thus, the battle lines of the Cold War came to the Middle East. As the USSR drew Egypt, Syria, and Iraq into its orbit, the others were, to one degree or another, drawn into the American orbit. The United States became the principal source of arms and diplomatic support to Lebanon, Jordan, Turkey, Iran, Saudi Arabia, and Kuwait—not one of them a democracy and all active in the anti-Israel chorus at the UN. Still, Eisenhower hoped that Israel's quiet cooperation in these efforts would eventually win the goodwill of the rulers of these "moderate" regimes.

KENNEDY, THE JEWS, AND ISRAEL

The relative tranquility on the Israel-Arab front since 1957 explains the relative neglect of Israel in the 1960 platforms of both parties. Both platforms spoke vaguely of finding solutions acceptable to all, both deplored boycotts, and both deplored the life of the refugees. Neither platform bid boldly for pro-Israeli voters, but, as usual, most Jews read more comfort into the Democratic Party platform.[83]

The first thought to enter many Jewish heads when John F. Kennedy's name was floated for the presidential nomination was that this was the son of that legendary anti-Semite, Joseph Kennedy. Eventually, however, the famous Kennedy charm won the day: "We all have our fathers," he quipped. Inertial loyalty to the Democratic Party disposed Jewish voters to believe that anyone in the Democratic lists was bound to be more of a friend to Israel than was the Republican nominee, Richard Nixon—a judgment that, in the light of subsequent events, would appear dubious at best.

In the fall of 1960, Kennedy spoke to a friend about his experience of dealing with the Jewish political brokers: "I had the damnedest meeting in New York last night. I went to this party. It was given by a group of people who were big money contributors and also Zionists and they said to me, 'We know that your campaign is in terrible financial shape!' . . . The deal they offered me was that they would finance the rest of this campaign if I would agree to let them run the Middle Eastern policy for the United States for the next four years."[84]

No major crisis involving Israel occurred during the Kennedy years. Even so, it is extraordinary that none of the major accounts of the Kennedy presidency gives more than a few lines to Israel. In most of these volumes, the item *Italy*, which follows *Israel* in the index, has more lines. Yet, right through the Kennedy years, the usual enemies were tirelessly at work, using terror in Israel and abroad, steady harassment at the UN, and economic sanctions and boycotts abroad to destroy Israel's will to go on.

Only two pages in Arthur Schlesinger's thousand pages on the thousand days of Kennedy's presidency (*A Thousand Days: John F. Kennedy in the White House*) deal with Israel. Here we read, "Kennedy believed strongly in America's moral commitment to Israeli security and took steps to strengthen Israel's ability to resist aggression." This alludes to the fact that Kennedy was the first president to agree to major sales of advanced weaponry to Israel, notably Hawk anti-aircraft missiles, made available on low-interest credit terms. In so doing, he discarded the advice both of the Pentagon and the State Department. (In the two previous administrations there had been understandings with NATO governments by which Israel bought weapons from these allies so that American diplomatic overtures in the Arab world would not be put at risk.) Kennedy's initiative was to be continued under President Johnson, and in fact expanded to include the most advanced aircraft.

Schlesinger continues: "But he wished to preserve an entrée to Nasser in order both to restrain Egyptian policy toward Israel and to try to work more closely with the modernizing forces in the Arab world." This latter ambition, writes Schlesinger, led to "one of Kennedy's most interesting experiments in foreign policy."[85] This refers to Kennedy's intention, discussed within his official family, to invite President Nasser of Egypt to the United States "when political conditions permitted." Theodore Sorenson, too, refers to this intended invitation, which, however, could not be extended "until improved relations could enable him to answer the political attacks such a visit would bring from voters more sympathetic with Israel." Sorenson goes further, claiming that Kennedy was able "to persuade Nasser to hold back anti-Israel fanatics in the Arab League." (No sources are cited for this extremely unlikely claim.) In fact, Kennedy's clumsy efforts to befriend Nasser led to, among other embarrassments, his support for the "revolutionary" regime that Nasser installed in Yemen—an adventurous action that greatly outraged Saudi Arabia and the other conservative regimes of the area, as well as the British.

At one point, the Kennedy administration announced an effort to find a negotiated solution to the Palestinian refugee problem. For this, the administration brought on Joseph Johnson, president of the Carnegie Foundation for Peace, who had worked for many years with the UN on this very issue.[86] Johnson was extremely impatient with Israel's viewpoint; in any case, the Israelis, after an initial expression of interest (the price of smoothing consideration of their arms requests) eventually made clear that they would not allow Palestinian returnees on the scale or at the cost (to them) that the Johnson Plan proposed. Years later, Johnson spoke of a cabinet meeting he attended in which this issue was discussed. It was, he recalled, hopelessly befogged by domestic political consider-ations—so much so that it illustrated what the State Department's Near East officers had been telling him for years, that "In any administration, the President is the desk officer for Israel."[87]

After Eisenhower's arm's-length approach, there was now a much closer and friendlier day-to-day collaboration between the two govern-ments. In a meeting with Israeli Foreign Minister Golda Meir in Decem-ber 27 1962, Kennedy said that the United States "has a special relationship with Israel in the Middle East really comparable only to that which it has with Britain over a wide range of world affairs."[88] Kennedy was, of course, well aware of the importance of the Jewish vote. In the very close election of 1960, in which he won New York State by a mere 384,000 votes, Jewish precincts gave him a total of 800,000 votes. During a courtesy call of Prime Minister David Ben-Gurion, he said, "You know, I was elected by the Jews of New York, and I would like to do something for the Jewish people." The remark shocked Ben-Gurion. "Why should he say such a thing to a foreigner?"[89] The few clear-cut private expressions we have found about the nature of Kennedy's ties to Israel (as distinct from campaign statements and formal presidential statements) reflect his understanding that his right to be called a friend of Israel had been bought and paid for legitimately, over-the-counter, in the give-and-take of partisan politics. There is no evidence that this friendly disposition was grounded on conviction firm enough to stand in a moment when (as in the situation facing Richard Nixon in October 1973) America's own eco-nomic and security interests were put on the scales.

RELIGION IN THE LIFE OF JOHN F. KENNEDY

Of all the presidents of the twentieth century (with the possible exception of Warren Harding), John F. Kennedy is the one whose deepest moral and philosophical commitments are hardest to tap. Richard Hutcheson, whose book on the religious commitments of the presidents is the best source for such a judgment, says, "No president in history has adhered more rigorously to the classic pattern of 'moderation' [in expression of religious belonging] and to the gentlemen's agreement to keep personal faith separate from public life than he."[90] But this judgment obscures the very large point that Kennedy himself raised the issue of religious belonging in the 1960 election, addressed it at length, and in so doing began the undoing of the "gentlemen's agreement" of which Hutcheson speaks. He raised the issue reluctantly but nonetheless deliberately, and with preemptive purpose. It was so brilliantly done that most political experts believe that he turned his Catholic belonging from a political liability to a political asset. This was first done in May 1960 during the primary campaign in heavily Protestant West Virginia, where he said, "Nobody asked me if I was a Catholic when I joined the United States Navy . . . and nobody asked my brother if he was a Catholic or a Protestant before he climbed into an American bomber to fly his last mission." As president, he vowed, he would not "take orders from any Pope, any Cardinal, any Bishop or priest—not that they would try to give me orders."[91]

Kennedy's decision to open up the issue of his Catholic belonging did not follow from a lifelong habit of sharing his faith. All our sources agree that he had no interest whatever in discussing his faith, at home or abroad. There is in fact not very much that we can say with confidence about Kennedy's religious conviction. Some follow Arthur Schlesinger Jr. in simply dismissing JFK's Catholicism as a source of his philosophy: "His intelligence was fundamentally secular, or so it seemed to me. . . . Kennedy's religion was humane rather than doctrinal. He was a Catholic as Franklin Roosevelt was an Episcopalian—because he was born into the faith, lived it, and expected to die in it. . . . He had little knowledge of or interest in the Catholic dogmatic tradition. . . . One can find little organic intellectual connection between his faith and his politics."[92] Another court historian, Theodore Sorensen, recalled that, "Not once in eleven years—despite all our discussions of church-state affairs, did he ever disclose his personal views on man's relationship to God."[93] The crudest verdict I have ever found is that of Nigel Hamilton: "For Jack, love of God was, like the love of a woman, a romantic conception for which he had little use."[94] In light of any of these assessments, we would not expect Kennedy's affection for Israel to have anything to do with religious conviction—or at least any more than anything else did. Certainly, there is no reason at all to imagine that he had ever heard of the tradition of restorationism and Christian Zionism, both of which are rooted in Puritanism.

As we saw, Israeli leaders were baffled by the cynicism that Kennedy showed in his remarks to them about "the deal" that the Jewish political leaders thought that they were making when handing over funds to his campaign. Israeli leaders are capable of irony and even cynicism, in appropriate contexts. But Kennedy's ironic style was not that of the *Sabra*; rather, it was the sort cultivated by people raised in privilege, accustomed to luxury, embarrassed by moral talk. Unlike Europeans and Canadians, the Israeli leaders were not seduced by the famous Camelot style.

In his book *President Kennedy*, Richard Reeves gives us many a glimpse into the intellectual and moral atmosphere that pervaded Camelot. Early in his book, he tells of President Kennedy's attempt to explain to his wife that her quick and ready acceptance of luxurious gifts from heads of foreign governments could become politically embarrassing. On one occasion, we are told, President Kennedy learned that she was to receive a gift of splendid horses from the King of Saudi Arabia. What made these scenes so awkward, he explained privately afterwards, was that, "The Arabs give her these horses and then the Israelis come along with an old Bible worth about $12."[95]

Few of us will ever face a dilemma of this kind. But which of us can say with perfect, good conscience, that, if there came an hour when such loyalties might be tested, he would not recall that one side gave out splendid horses and the other side gave out old $12 Bibles?

LYNDON B. JOHNSON (1963–1969)

"Israel will not be alone unless it decides to go alone."

COMMON THREADS IN THE RELIGIOUS UPBRINGING AND THE PHILOSOPHICAL DISPOSITION OF EISENHOWER, JOHNSON, AND NIXON

President Eisenhower, who preceded President Kennedy, and Presidents Johnson and Nixon, who immediately succeeded Kennedy, each served through a dramatic moment when he was called upon to determine an American response to a life-threatening crisis in Israel. These three presidents (Eisenhower, Johnson, and Nixon) have in common, and in contrast to John F. Kennedy, the fact that they were all Protestants. But what they share beyond that is even more interesting, and rarely noted. *All three were raised in churches distinctly on the Fundamentalist side,* further from the center of American religious life than the Southern Baptist Harry Truman. Like John F. Kennedy, they came from a religious minority—*not* the minority of Roman Catholics but the minority called Fundamentalists. When the foundations of their political careers were laid, national politics was almost exclusively a world of mainstream Protestants: Episcopalians, Presbyterians, and Congregationalists. Each of these three men (Eisenhower, Johnson, and Nixon) turned his back eventually on the (theologically speaking) right-of-center denomination of his youth and relocated himself in one of the mainstream denominations as an adult. This is in contrast to Presidents Truman and Carter, both of whom began and ended as Southern Baptists, and it is in contrast as well to Franklin Roosevelt, who began and ended an Episcopalian. All three voted with their feet against aspects of the Evangelical-to-Fundamentalist legacy in which they had all been reared.

Eisenhower, Johnson, and Nixon all speak of gratitude for their pious rearing, yet each developed profound antipathy for those aspects of that legacy (such matters as the Divine Inspiration of Scripture) that tend to get in the way of a secular understanding of politics and history. Of particular interest to our story is the evidence of each man's antipathy, even contempt, for the part of the Evangelical heritage that produced Christian Zionism.

RELIGION IN THE LIFE OF LYNDON JOHNSON

Both Eisenhower and Johnson were raised in a part of the country where most people were Evangelicals or Fundamentalists. Both Eisenhower and Johnson abandoned the denominations in which they were raised, and moved into the Protestant center during their public lives. Both spoke grandly about belief in God as a source as civility and patriotism. Both were absolutely sincere in this matter. Both had a low opinion of religious enthusiasm. Neither had the least interest in theology or church history. Neither followed a discipline of daily Bible study or a settled routine of prayer. Neither ever belonged to a Bible-study group nor participated in any of the occasions for Christian fellowship that existed in military service or in Washington. Each carried about a very short repertoire of scriptural passages that could be worked into public addresses and occasionally into conversations. Johnson's favorite all-purpose passage was "Come let us reason together" (Isaiah 1:18).

Johnson was raised in the Church of Christ (Disciples), a denomination born in the revival of the 1830s, but as an adult he attended different churches. One reliable insider, Joseph Califano, reports that Johnson would speak cynically of the pious demeanor of others (specifically, Senator Hatfield); but he also reports him speaking of the consolations of faith in God in times of adversity.[96] Toward the end of his time as president he showed an interest in Roman Catholicism, following the lead of his daughter Lucy who had converted to Catholicism at the time of her marriage.[97]

JOHNSON, THE JEWS, AND ISRAEL

The index to Lyndon Johnson's memoirs contains a decidedly greater number of entries for *Israel* than for *Italy*. This does not prove that Johnson had an exceptional interest in the issues of the Middle East, but rather that, during his presidency, circumstance (namely, the Six-Day War of June 1967) forced him to deal with Israel on an urgent basis—something that John F. Kennedy was spared.

One may assume that Johnson's upbringing in the Bible Belt made him familiar with the traditions of restorationism and sensitive to Christian

Zionism. But there is no evidence that he looked at the story of Israel's creation and its further triumphs and tribulations from a Christian Zionist perspective. In contrast to the other presidents discussed in this chapter, he had an intense attachment to Israel, but this was essentially sentimental, not theological, philosophical, or religious. He appreciated the tenacity of the Zionists; he was drawn to the romance of the Jewish experience in Palestine. During his early days as a congressman, Johnson drew notice as a man who was prepared to do the politically unpopular work of finding permanent visas for Jewish refugees in flight from Hitler.[98] Like the majority of American politicians of both parties, he supported partition and recognition of the state. He was remembered by friends of Israel for the part he played as majority leader in the Senate in forestalling the efforts of President Eisenhower and Secretary Dulles to bring sanctions against Israel in the months following the Suez crisis.[99] (Senator Kennedy had been absent from the Senate through much of this time, owing to health problems.) He appreciated the partisan advantage of a close connection with the American Jewish organizations, and in his bids for the presidency in 1960 and 1964 he pulled out all the stops before Jewish audiences. But the government of Israel was right in guessing that his devotion to Israel had limits. It is fair to assume that the team of LBJ and Rusk would not have responded with the life-saving alacrity shown by Kissinger and Nixon at the time of Israel's desperate need in October 1973.

Lyndon Johnson, again in contrast to Kennedy, had many Jewish friends. All of them were politically important people (LBJ had no life at all outside politics), but a number were *also* personal friends and trusted counselors. His principal contacts with the American Jewish community were two holders of very high office: Arthur Goldberg, the U.S. ambassador to the UN, and Abe Fortas, a justice of the Supreme Court. Fortas had been a young New Deal lawyer when Lyndon Johnson had been a young congressman, and the two had been close allies for nearly thirty years. Ignoring the tradition that insulates high court justices from politics, LBJ sought the advice of Justice Fortas constantly, and even went so far as to bring Fortas into policy planning meetings of his White House staff.[100] President Johnson fully realized that Fortas's active participation in this decision making guaranteed that the leaders of the American Jewish community would always be up-to-speed on the administration's intentions toward Israel.

DEAN RUSK, SECRETARY OF STATE (1961–1969)

A crucial factor in this story is the long-standing anti-Israeli disposition of Dean Rusk, whom LBJ confirmed as his secretary of state. Like most

America foreign policy careerists before and since, Rusk attributed Middle East troubles to the baneful effects of religion: "I hope events will prove me wrong, but the intractable nature of the divisions between Jews and Arabs and even between moderate and extremist Arabs almost defy solution. . . . When both Jews and Arabs are convinced they're speaking for God, that makes for a tough negotiation. I've been at the table when the Arabs quoted the Koran while Jews quoted the Book of Moses, and I couldn't say, 'Oh, come on now, don't give me any of that stuff!'"[101]

Almost needless to say, Dean Rusk was raised on "that stuff"—in Cherokee County, Georgia, deep in "the Bible Belt"—as the son of an ordained Presbyterian clergyman.[102] Rusk never notes any connection between his Bible-rearing and any perspective he might have on the history of Israel (or anything else, for that matter). In fact, he displays an appalling ignorance (that is, *pretended* ignorance) of basic facts of religious history as they are taught in every Sunday school in the world. Thus, speaking of the insolubility of the Jerusalem issue, he notes that "Muslims, Jews, and Christians look upon Jerusalem as a city essential to their religions and traditions; *the city of David, Christ, and Muhammed, the center of three great religions* [emphasis added]."[103] No Muslim claims that Jerusalem is *the center* of the religion of Islam. Rather, Muslims claim that, in the light of the absolute perfection of Islam, which has eclipsed and replaced the inadequate and partial revelations of Judaism and Christianity and all other faiths, Islam is obliged to assert preemptive title to all the sites associated with the other two "Abrahamic" religions. The Jews, in contrast, have never asserted any claim to possession of any site on earth *but this one*—the site of their ancient temple. They have utterly no interest in asserting a claim to Mecca or Medina, or, for that matter, to Rome or Ephesus, or Constantinople, or Kapilavastu, or any other city. One would assume that in the course of his lengthy academic career, Dean Rusk had read enough world history to know that only from a faithful Muslim perspective could anyone say such a thing as that Jerusalem is *the city of Mohammed . . . the center of Islam.*

When it came to Middle East policy, Presidents Kennedy and Johnson both received from Dean Rusk the age-old State Department recital: "Unfortunately some people in the American Jewish community and other U.S. supporters of Israel . . . look upon anything less than an all-out pro-Israeli stance by the State Department and the U.S. government as betrayal. . . . A debate over this issue would be vicious and ugly; all sorts of latent anti-Semitism—always present on the America scene—would creep out from under the rocks. For that reason, Washington has often shown great patience with Israel publicly, while behind the scenes our objections and differences are sharply expressed."[104]

PRELUDE TO WAR

By the time Johnson came to office, Nasser of Egypt commanded the entire field of Arab radical nationalism. He now bragged openly that he was in command of all the terrorists who conducted their raids through Gaza and across Israel's borders elsewhere.

On May 16, 1967, President Nasser demanded the withdrawal from the Sinai of the UN forces, which were supposed to be supervising the truce lines to which Israel had agreed to withdraw following the Suez War. The UN Secretary, U Thant, complied immediately, without securing the agreement of any government. Meanwhile, the Arab states that regarded themselves as still in a state of war with Israel entered into a joint military command under Colonel Nasser. Thereupon, Nasser began to move his troops and tanks into the Sinai Peninsula while he publicly announced his intention to go to war at once for the purpose of liberating the Palestinians and driving the Israelis into the sea. As the first step, Nasser announced further, on May 22, that he was closing the Gulf of Aqaba to shipping bound to or from Israel.

Later, it could be seen that Nasser had been enticed into his provocations against Israel by the failure of the United States to promise to meet him with force, *as he had expected it would*. Those close to him at the time remember him as near panic when he recognized how far he had gone out on this limb and how impossible it had become politically to crawl back. Consulting ex-President Eisenhower quickly, Johnson was reassured that "the Israelis' right of access to the Gulf of Aqaba was definitely part of the 'commitment' we had made to them."[105] But not until May 23 did President Johnson condemn these actions publicly, and even then he proposed no course of action.[106] France, which had been Israel's ally in 1956, now, under President Charles De Gaulle, deserted her. Harold Wilson, Britain's prime minister, a better friend of Israel, proposed that Britain and the United States send a group of civilian ships with a powerful naval escort through the Straits of Tiran, an international waterway, as a gesture that would demonstrate to Nasser that the great powers would not abandon their rights of unrestricted passage. On May 26, this proposal was taken personally to Lyndon Johnson by Israel's foreign secretary, Abba Eban.

The accounts of this meeting that appear in Johnson's memoirs and in Eban's memoirs bear almost no resemblance to each another. Johnson describes himself as commanding the scene, calming the agitated Eban, securing the latter's gratitude for assurances, which he now made, that "we will pursue vigorously any and all possible measures to keep the straits open," while noting in sorrow that Congress, infected by the weak-kneed spirit born during the Vietnam debates, might have to be shaped up a bit before they would see this challenge as clearly as the president did.[107] In *his* account, Eban recalls himself saying that Israel would be able to refrain from the use of force only if "the maritime powers would make common cause with us. If they did, Nasser would retreat, and a victory could be won for international civility without prolonged war."

Johnson (according to Eban) used his unhappy Vietnam experience as an excuse for refusing to act as Israel required: "Without the Congress," he whined, "I am just a six-foot-four Texan." "I was astonished," Eban recalls, "that he was not too proud to avoid these self-deprecatory remarks in the presence of many of his senior associates. I thought I could see Secretary Rusk and General Wheeler wilt with embarrassment every time he said how little power of action he had."[108]

A phrase that occurred early in these talks and occurred so often that it became an administration mantra was "Israel will not be alone unless it decides to go alone." Secretary of Defense McNamara and Secretary of State Rusk intended by this to convey that the United States was opposed to Israel's taking any military initiative. Thus (to follow a metaphor suggested by William Quandt), it should be interpreted as a red light. But Justice Fortas, apparently with LBJ's permission, conveyed to Israeli authorities a different message: that, although the United States would not say so out loud, it understood and expected that an Israeli military initiative was coming, and it would protect Israel from the diplomatic consequences. In other words, it was a yellow light. All sources agree that LBJ privately encouraged Israel to believe that the United States would not let Israel lose if it came to war.

According to Secretary Rusk, "The Soviets thought they had a commitment from their Arab friends not to make the first move, and after our May 26 meeting with Israeli Foreign Minister Abba Eban and Premier Levi Eshkol's May 30 assurances, we thought we had a similar commitment from Israel. At least we and the Soviets exchanged these assurances with each other."[109]

THE SIX-DAY WAR, JUNE 5–10, 1967

On May 30, King Hussein of Jordan flew to Cairo and publicly placed his troops under Nasser's command. Egyptian and Syrian troops now moved into Jordan to take up their positions under the new command. Faced with Nasser's mobilizations and the Arab nations' declarations of intent to join with him in his war of liquidation against the Jews, Israel struck first. On the very first day of action, the Egyptian air force was destroyed, most of it on the ground. Over the next three days Egyptian forces were driven out of Sinai and Gaza, while Israeli forces drove deep into Egypt, encircling the Sinai army. Meanwhile, the troops of Syria and her allies were driven out of Golan; Jordan was driven out of East Jerusalem (including the Old City) and out of all of Palestine west of Jordan.

On June 10, Soviet Premier Kosygin told President Johnson over the "hot-line" that "a very crucial moment had arrived," one pregnant with "grave catastrophe," in light of which the Soviet Union must face the need for "independent decision." Unless Israel unconditionally halted its military advances, the Soviet Union would take "necessary actions, including military." Johnson describes the "deathly" stillness, the "tense atmosphere," the mood of "utmost gravity" in the situation room as he absorbed this message and quickly issued the orders to move the Sixth Fleet from its current situation fifty miles east of the Syrian coast to twenty-five miles east of the Syrian coast. Later that day, Israel agreed to a cease-fire. Johnson implies that moving the Sixth Fleet in closer had somehow caused the cease-fire to happen, even though nothing in the record suggests that anything other than Israel's recognition that her task was completed bore on the decision. Given that the president had shrunk from the trivial risks of the proposed Gulf of Aqaba action, what confidence could Israel have had that the full force of the United States would ever have been brought into play in the event that the Soviet Union were to intervene—as no serious person believed it would anyway?

Secretary Rusk recalls that, "The problems for us were rendered easier with an Israeli victory than an Arab victory." Nonetheless, "we were shocked as well, and angry as hell, when the Israelis launched their surprise offense," because, Rusk claims, all avenues for negotiation had not been exhausted. "But in all fairness to Israel, considering the major Arab mobilization, the movement of sizable Egyptian forces into the Sinai, the formation of an Arab high command, the Jordanian-Egyptian Treaty, the movement of Iraqi and Egyptian units into Jordan, and the stepping up of the Arabs' holy war propaganda, if the Israelis had waited for the Arabs to strike first, their situation could have been very grim." *Maybe*, he concedes gracelessly, there *was* a case for "preventive action."[110]

By the time he came to write his memoirs, Lyndon Johnson had persuaded himself that he had acted heroically on behalf of Israel during the 1967 crisis.[111] However, such was not the judgment of the government of Israel, which continued to believe that an unambiguous declaration of the American government's intention to support Israel in the weeks leading up to Nasser's threats would have averted the war altogether—saving some eight hundred Israeli lives. It was true that Israel's ambassador in the United States, Ephraim Evron, said, shortly after the crisis of June 1967 had passed, that "Lyndon Johnson saved Israel!" (referring to the president's warnings over the hot line to the Soviets not to intervene). But the Israelis guessed, and the president knew full well, that the Soviets had never intended to come to the rescue of the Arab war effort, which had already collapsed by the time the USSR had spoken up.

At the same time, Johnson's inaction won no friends for him on the other side. All the Arab protagonists in the Six-Day War broke relations with the United States immediately. Although these relations were eventually restored, none of the rulers of these governments could bring himself to concede that American policy had ever been other than totally beholden to Jewish interests.

ISRAEL'S CONTINUED ISOLATION FOLLOWING THE SIX-DAY WAR

From June 1967 forward, Israel was increasingly isolated at the UN. Most of the member-states newly admitted to the UN as result of the decolonization enthusiasm of the 1960s and 1970s went immediately into the anti-Israel bloc, where the USSR played the role of whip. At the same time, most of the NATO allies of the United States were losing enthusiasm for the cause of Israel, frequently leaving the Americans alone to vote with Israel against recurring resolutions of denunciation against Zionism that took up more and more of the time of all UN bodies. The United States played the key role in working out UN Resolution 242 (November 22, 1967), the preamble of which recognizes "the inadmissibility of the acquisition of territory by war." The body of the resolution calls for recognition by all of "the sovereignty, territorial integrity and political independence of every state in the area and their right to live in peace within secure and recognized boundaries free from threats or acts of force." In the years that followed, UN Resolution 242 would be remembered as a formula under which Israel should trade back land for peace.

In August 1967, the Conference of Arab States, meeting at Khartoum, defied UN Resolution 242, declaring instead the policy of the Three Noes: *no* peace with Israel, *no* recognition, *no* negotiation. In 1974, Yassir Arafat, the chairman of the Palestine Liberation Organization (PLO), was given the unprecedented privilege of being invited to address the UN General Assembly, as though he were a head of government. He appeared with a pistol at his side. Thereafter, the PLO enjoyed a unique "observer status" at the UN. A year later, the UN General Assembly voted to condemn Zionism as a form of "racism or racial discrimination."

To Israel's annoyance, U.S. spokesmen would never bring themselves to say out loud that Israel's initiation of the Six-Day War was a justified preemptive action. Despite the abject performance of the Arab armies and governments in the crisis of June 1967, the Soviet Union resumed its massive supply of weapons, aircraft, and advisers. By 1995 Soviet Ambassador Dobrynin felt free to write that "the authority [of the USSR] had been considerably damaged by the defeat of its clients. . . . The Soviet leadership wanted to restore its role in the Middle East and prevent the United States from dominating that strategic area. But this policy left us with little flexibility because we often blindly followed our Arab allies, who in turn used us to block many initiatives that were advanced for a peaceful settlement."[112]

Meanwhile, Arab governments boldly encouraged the Palestinians to enter upon the path of terrorism as the best way of overcoming the alleged advantage of the Zionists in conventional warfare. By the early 1970s, terrorist actions against Israel had begun to reach into Europe. At the 1972 Olympic Games, PLO terrorists murdered Israeli athletes. But Jews were not the only targets: The gangster regimes of Syria, Iraq, Libya, and later (following 1979) that of the Republic of Iran carried the work of liquidating their enemies onto the streets of European cities, silencing critics who had fled abroad. It is not clear how these actions affected Israel's cause: Did the increase in sympathy for the Israelis that followed upon these evil deeds outweigh the growing spirit of annoyance that Israel's quarrels with her neighbors were now spilling out into the streets of Western cities? Israelis were disappointed by the United States' failure to get tough on the regimes that harbored these terrorists. Knowledge of these atrocities did almost nothing to dampen the interest of the U.S. government agencies in smoothing the path to Arab capitals for U.S. capitalists and arms salesmen. As all this was occurring abroad, an anti-government, anti-authority spirit sprang from the movement of opposition to the Vietnam War at home. Among its many fruits was a cult of "liberation movements"—all of this feeding a tendency to romanticize terrorists and thus contributing to the propaganda success of the PLO and its Chairman Yassir Arafat, a public relations genius *sans pareil*.

RICHARD NIXON (1969–1974)

"The time has come to quit pandering to
Israel's intransigent position."

RICHARD NIXON, THE JEWS, AND ISRAEL

"The creation of the state of Israel in 1948," says Richard Nixon, by way of introducing the Middle East theme to the pages of his memoirs, "had planted seeds of hatred that would eventually explode into three full-scale wars."[113] Thus for Nixon, as for so many Americans, not the hatred of some people for Israel, but the *existence* of Israel was the root of the matter. This, in a nutshell, had always been the attitude of the Near Eastern wing of the State Department. On the other hand—and in strong contrast to Eisenhower—Nixon was ready to admit, privately and publicly, a powerful admiration for the Jewish social and economic experiment, and, in particular, for the victories of Israel in her several wars against vastly greater numbers. Everyone who ever shared conversation with Richard Nixon on the theme of Israel noted Nixon's admiration for the Israelis, whose preeminent virtue was that they were "tough"—a major word in Nixon's vocabulary. To his cabinet he once said, *"They're* not ashamed to be patriots"—in pointed contrast to the critics of his Vietnam policy.[114] But at the same time, Nixon recalled, "I was disturbed by the fact that their swift and overwhelming victory over the Arabs had created a feeling of overconfidence. . . . Their victory had been too great. It left a residue of hatred among their neighbors that I felt could only result in another war, particularly if the Russians were to step up military aid to their defeated Arab clients."[115] This note we have already seen in Eisenhower's thinking: that the Israelis somehow would have been better off for the educational effects of *losing*—a prescription that neither Eisenhower nor Nixon nor any patriotic American had ever offered to the American people. Certainly, this attitude did not govern Nixon's thinking on Vietnam.

Anti-Semitism (as generally understood) is not something that we have to take into account with respect to any of the other presidents we consider in this book. Nixon's case is different. The *White House Tapes* and the *Haldeman Diaries* (especially the unexpurgated version that was consulted by Richard Reeves for his book *President Nixon*) document a distinct streak of anti-Semitism—not consistently explicit, but always latent and sometimes virulent. In the transcripts of private monologues taken by Haldeman and on the tapes "the fucking Jews" or "the cocksucking Jews" are everywhere. According to Nixon, they control the press, the media, the universities; they have cells located throughout the civil service; "most are disloyal."[116]

Richard Nixon, like his Republican predecessor Dwight Eisenhower, resented the Jewish vote, precisely as he sought to cultivate it. Despite his best efforts, however, Nixon was never able to win even as much of the Jewish vote as Eisenhower did. (Nixon won about 17 percent of the Jewish vote in 1968 and 35 percent in 1972, as compared to Eisenhower's 36 percent in 1952 and 40 percent in 1956.)[117] Even more than Eisenhower, therefore, he was determined to make the evident disapproval of Jewish voters into a political asset by drawing the attention of all the other voters to his determination to keep the nation's interests above "political considerations."

RELIGION IN THE LIFE OF RICHARD NIXON

Since much has been made of Richard Nixon's Quaker background, it is important to grasp that the California Quakers among whom Richard Nixon was raised were, by his time, removed at least two generations from the pacifist, Holy Spirit–led worldview of classical Quakerism. The East Whittier Friends Church taught and practiced the essentials of mainstream Evangelical Protestantism. Like the Methodists and the Southern

Baptists, they supported revivals; and, like many other youngsters, Richard Nixon had committed his life to Christ and to Christian service during a tent revival in the 1920s.

I have found only one developed statement about his religious faith by Richard Nixon himself. This is in Chapter Five ("Religion") of a short post-presidential book, *In the Arena: A Memoir of Victory, Defeat, and Renewal* (1990). *Not* mentioned in this account is the tent-meeting story that he told to Billy Graham. After a few words about his pious church upbringing, he speaks of his days at Whittier College, where "my belief in the literal accuracy of the scriptures was shaken, although my faith remained as firm as ever." Now he understood (as he put it in a student essay at the time) that, "The resurrection symbolically teaches the great lesson that men who achieve the highest values in their lives may gain immortality."[118] Needless to say, this is not what Billy Graham preaches.

Nixon decided, after he became president, "that I wanted to do something to encourage attendance at services and to emphasize this country's basic faith in a Supreme Being." And so, in defiance of the Quaker tradition and possibly also of the Constitutional principle of separation of church and state, he brought regular Sunday services into the White House. "What better example could there be than to bring the worship service, with all its solemn meaning, right in to the White House?"[119] President Nixon's most overt act of solidarity with revival Christianity was his decision to attend a Billy Graham rally in Tennessee. Pat Buchanan, a speechwriter for Richard Nixon and a Roman Catholic, later told Richard Hutcheson, "There was a lot of politics in that—no small amount." Still, Buchanan did not doubt that Nixon was, privately, a "believing Christian."[120]

Given his upbringing in the Evangelical-to-Fundamentalist setting, we have the right to assume that he was fully aware of the Restorationist teaching and the Cyrus tradition. Still, there is nothing in the record to suggest that theological reflection figured in Nixon's calculations of his duty toward Israel. There may be a clue to the philosophical basis of his attitude toward Israel in this passage from one of his post-presidential books:

President Eisenhower used to refer to two men as "Old Testament prophets": John Foster Dulles and Ben-Gurion. I found this ironic in both cases. Dulles was a devout American Protestant who carried the doctrines of the New Testament engraved in his heart and mind. Ben-Gurion was a scholar of the Scriptures, but he described himself as secular rather than religious. "Since I invoke Torah so often," he once explained, "let me state that I don't personally believe in the God it postulates . . . I am not religious, nor were the majority of the early builders of Israel believers. Yet their passion for this land stemmed from the Book of Books. . . . [The Bible is] the single most important book in my life."[121]

The last glimpse we have of Richard Nixon, as he faced the agony of his resignation, bears powerful evidence of his guilty awareness that he had not lived the confident life of faith that he thought he had committed himself to the day when he went forward at that tent-meeting. On the night that he prepared his statement of resignation, Nixon, after some considerable drinking, called Henry Kissinger to his side and poured out his fear about facing criminal trial after his resignation. He told Kissinger about his dependence upon "his strong belief in a Supreme Being," which he was confident that Kissinger shared. Then he asked Kissinger to kneel beside him in prayer.[122]

NIXON'S RELATIONS WITH THE GOVERNMENT OF ISRAEL

Nixon decided at the outset of his presidency to hand over responsibility for initiative and coordination in foreign policy *not* to his secretary of state, William Rogers, but to his national security adviser, Henry Kissinger. This, he believed, would make it possible for the president to conduct foreign policy with only minimal contributions from the professionals. Nixon's national security adviser encouraged this approach and frequently went out of his way to remark upon the resemblance of Richard Nixon to Benjamin Disraeli and (on other days) Otto Von Bismarck.

But there was to be one exception to this new order in the foreign policy arena—namely, the "Middle East" (by which Nixon, like all the presidents with whom we have to deal, meant *the Arab-Israeli confrontation*), which was handed over to Secretary Rogers. At the time, and later in his memoirs, Nixon stated that the principal reason for this arrangement was that it would be unfortunate if U.S. policy in regard to Israel were seen to be under the direction of a Jew (that is, Henry Kissinger).[123] But this was just a cover—thrown away later when the going got tough during the Middle East crisis of October 1973. The real reason for the initial decision to take Middle East policy out of the White House and give it to the secretary of state was that Nixon saw no prospect for accomplishing anything there, where statesmen had been thrashing around for solutions for decades—in a real sense, for centuries, not to say millennia. He did not want to be seen in the vicinity of diplomatic disasters. That was what Bill Rogers was for. But in the end it proved impossible to keep the Middle East off the front burner. William Rogers was not the man, and the Rogers Plan was not the answer. We have every reason to believe that Nixon grasped both of these truths.

The Rogers Plan was a clumsy restatement of UN Resolution 242, minus the part that had any appeal to Israel: that is, the obligation for the other side to *previously* recognize Israel's right to exist and to enter, in the broad light of day, into direct negotiations with her. Nixon admits this in his memoirs: "In strictly practical terms, the provision for return of occupied territories meant that the Rogers Plan had absolutely no chance of being accepted by Israel. . . . *I knew that the Rogers Plan could never be implemented*, [italics added] but I believed that it was important to let the Arab world know that the United States did not automatically dismiss its case regarding the occupied territories or rule out a compromise settlement of the conflicting claims."[124] This, of course, was not what was said at the time.

President Nixon was pestered from his earliest days in office with the Israeli government's requests for sale to Israel of a whole range of the newest military technology, to be facilitated (as always) by loans and credits—then subsequently (as always) to be sweetened by "forgiveness" of large chunks of the loans. This campaign was assisted by the American Jewish lobbies, who were able to remind Nixon that during the 1968 campaign he had said that "the balance of power in the Middle East must be tipped in Israel's favor," and that therefore, if elected, he would "support a policy that would give Israel a technological military margin to more than offset her hostile neighbors' numerical superiority."[125] A public, head-on collision with the American Jewish community took place in late January-early February 1970, when Jewish groups organized protests to disrupt the visit to the United States of French president, Georges Pompidou, who had offended the friends of Israel by selling a large number of Mirage jetfighters to Libya. In his diary that night, Chief of Staff H.R. Haldeman recorded Nixon's words: "'This is unconscionable. The fucking Jews think they can run the world' . . . [He] also said, in front of K [Kissinger], not to let any Jews see him about Middle East. Said they can go to talk to [New York City Mayor] Lindsay and [Governor] Rockefeller about whether *they* can provide arms for Israel."[126] Activities like the Pompidou boycott, Nixon suggests in his memoirs, reflect "the unyielding and short-sighted pro-Israeli attitude prevalent in large and influential segments of the American Jewish community, Congress, the media, and in cultural and intellectual circles. In the quarter-century since the end of World War II this attitude had become so deeply ingrained that many saw the corollary of not being pro-Israeli as being anti-Israeli, or even anti-Semitic. I tried unsuccessfully to convince them that this was not the case."[127]

Nixon rejected Israel's request for new arms for nearly two years, while he secretly explored possibilities for an understanding with the Soviet Union.[128] Meanwhile, he sought to assure Israeli leaders that it was in their best interests that he *not* meet their requests. The logic behind this was that, by showing the world that he was not automatically in Israel's court on all issues, he would gain credibility in the Arab world and the trust of the Arab leaders—thus gaining the moral leverage necessary to persuade the leaders of the Arab world to join him in negotiations for a new understanding with Israel. By extension of this logic, it would also help Israel if the United States sold military hardware to the Arabs (who were daily announcing their intention to liquidate Israel the moment they became strong enough to do so). His Israeli interlocutors, not surprisingly, failed to grasp this logic. Nixon told National Security Adviser Henry Kissinger to advise Prime Minister Golda Meir:

They must recognize that our interests are basically pro-freedom and not just pro-Israel because of the Jewish vote. . . . What all this adds up to is that Mrs. Meir, Rabin, et. al., must trust RN completely. [In memoranda, etc, Richard Nixon always referred to himself in the third person.] He does not want to see Israel go down the drain and makes an absolute commitment that he will see to it that Israel always has "an edge." On the other hand, he must carry with him not just the Jewish community in New York and Pennsylvania and California and possibly Illinois which voted 95 percent against him, but he must carry with him the 60 percent of the American people who are in what is called the silent majority, and who must be depended on in the event that we have to take a strong stand against Soviet expansionism in the Mideast. . . . We are going to be in power for at least the next three years and this is going to be the policy of this country. Unless they understand it and act as if they understood it beginning now, they are down the tubes.[129]

Unfortunately, the Soviets did not want the pressure to be taken off Israel—whatever the Egyptians might want. By the end of 1971, "American intelligence agencies calculated that there were 12,000 Soviet military personnel in Egypt, including thousands of officers and men." Russians were managing the whole Egyptian air defense system, training Egyptians in the use of advanced military equipment, while actually operating the thousands of missiles and advanced aircraft which flew with Egyptian markings.[130]

As all this was put in place, Secretary of State Rogers was going through the motions of working out ineffective cease-fire agreements Despite the confession just noted (*"I knew that the Rogers Plan could never be implemented"*), Nixon spins out many pages in these same memoirs describing Rogers's fruitless journeyings, as though it had all along been about something real. Predictably, it proved only too easy for Arab politicians to pretend appreciation for Secretary Rogers's initiative, while withholding as premature any commitment to recognize Israel.

THE PRESIDENTIAL ELECTION OF 1972

After standing for nearly the whole of his first term against Israeli requests for further sales of aircraft, missiles, and other major armaments, Nixon changed direction: The Israelis' latest shopping lists were restudied and approved in the spring of 1972. Richard Nixon believed that, by now responding well to Israel's requests for arms, he had earned an increase in his share of the Jewish vote (from the roughly 17 percent of 1968). But during the year of the 1972 election, his efforts to mollify American Jews were dogged by another issue: the right of Jews to emigrate from Russia. Prominent Democratic candidates, notably Henry Jackson of Washington, had been demanding that the United States insist on a public declaration by the Soviet government of the right of Jews to emigrate as a quid pro quo for the grant of MNF (most favored nation) status to the Soviet Union—a matter under active negotiation. This exercise culminated in the Jackson-Vanik Amendment, which eventually passed in the House of Representatives by a vote of 388 to 44 (December 13, 1973)—"a stunning display of the power of the Jewish lobby in American politics," says Nixon's biographer, Stephen Ambrose.[131] (Senator Jackson, the Jewish community's favorite Democrat bar none, was a Lutheran of Norwegian ancestry, representing Washington state—a state with one of the smallest cohorts of Jewish voters in America; Congressman Charles Vanik of Illinois, also a Democrat, and of Czech descent, had long championed the cause of Eastern Europeans who were captive in the Soviet Empire.) In reality, the Kremlin leadership had been responding well to quiet diplomacy with the Nixon administration on this matter, allowing some 4,500 Jews to emigrate in the month of October 1972 alone. After the Jackson-Vanik Amendment passed (as Nixon had warned the agitators for this amendment), Brezhnev, determined not to appear to be letting outsiders influence Soviet "domestic policies," swiftly closed the exit doors.

In 1972, both party platforms had exceptionally long sections on the Middle East, with much more explicit language than usual. Both platforms promised to be generous in meeting Israel's economic and military needs. Friends of Israel noted that for the first time a major party platform committed itself to the Israeli position on the vexing matter of Jerusalem: A Democratic administration would "recognize and support the established status of Jerusalem as the capital of Israel, with free access to all its holy places provided to all faiths. As a symbol of this stand, the U.S. Embassy should be moved from Tel Aviv to Jerusalem."[132] Thus, there was every reason to imagine that a Democratic president would be better-attuned to the needs of Israel than Richard Nixon. The candidate whom the Democratic Party chose to offer the people in 1968, George McGovern, was so off-center, however, that even some Jews set aside their lifetime habits in order to vote for the Republican candidate, Richard Nixon. In the upshot, Nixon doubled his voting strength among the Jews—from 17 percent in 1968, to 35 percent in 1972.[133]

NIXON'S SECOND TERM

By the beginning of Nixon's second term, the Israeli government of Golda Meir had established reasonable rapport with the American president, and was quietly appreciative of Nixon's new willingness to sell needed military equipment. Prime Minister Meir understood full well that Nixon's governing motive was not the appeasement of Israel or of American Jewish opinion but his determination to curtail the advance of Soviet influence in the region. Unfortunately for Richard Nixon, it was not possible for many years to come to make public the details of Israeli and American cooperation in these months: These included Nixon's private encouragement of Israel's retaliations against Egypt during the so-called War of Attrition (from mid-1968 to August 1970); U.S.-Israel collaboration in intelligence-gathering; and a large number of sub-rosa diplomatic and security initiatives that were drawing the Nixon and Meir governments into a closer level of day-to-day cooperation than had ever been the case before.

A small part, but by no means the whole, of this reality was guessed by commentators during the September 1970 crisis in Jordan. Yassir Arafat's PLO had taken control of large parts of that country and was openly bidding to overturn King Hussein's regime. A civil war broke out suddenly on September 15, 1970, when Hussein decided on a preemptive strike against the PLO's regime-within-a-regime. Syrian tanks, escorted to the border by Soviet advisors, entered the scene, intending to assist the insurrection. Thereupon, President Nixon conveyed to Israel the message that he would support Israeli air strikes into Syria, and even incursions by Israeli ground forces, if necessary to get the Syrians out, and that the United States would come directly to Israel's aid if the Soviet Union took direct action in support of its client Syria. The existence of this message was soon made known in Damascus and in Moscow, and the Syrian tanks retreated to Syrian soil. King Hussein's regime had been saved.[134]

But it was not in Richard Nixon to remain grateful for long about anything. In February 1973, Nixon wrote in the margins of a memo on Middle East matters written for him by Henry Kissinger: "We are now Israel's *only* major friend in the world. . . . The time has come to quit pandering to Israel's intransigent position. Our actions over the past have led them to think we will stand with them *regardless* of how unreasonable they are."[135] However, in the months remaining between that February memo and the Yom Kippur crisis of October, Nixon took no action along these lines. There was precious little time left in a day after hours and hours of working over the White House tapes and generally trying to prevent his presidency from unraveling.

THE YOM KIPPUR WAR (OCTOBER 1973)

It was slow to dawn on the Americans that President Sadat's dramatic decision to order several thousand Soviet personnel out of Egypt in July 1972, had not really severed the Egyptian-Soviet connection; neither had it increased the prospects for a peaceful settlement. The Soviet leaders, fearful of losing their foothold in the Middle East, continued to appease Sadat by selling him even more aircraft, missiles, and tanks. Meanwhile, Egypt and Syria were working out the details of their plans for the invasion of Israel, securing pledges for hundreds of millions of dollars in support from the Arab oil-producing states, including Saudi Arabia and Qatar, and recruiting infantry brigades and massive air forces from Algeria, Morocco, Sudan, Libya, Kuwait, Saudi Arabia, and Iraq. (Jordan declined to commit herself at this stage, but did in fact throw in a brigade to assist Syria when the war came.)[136]

Throughout 1971 and 1972, President Sadat had declared repeatedly that he was about to lead the Arab nations into a war of liquidation against Israel. Henry Kissinger confessed later, "Sadat . . . had been threatening to go to war every year since 1971 . . . no threat had ever come close to being implemented. New threats of war were therefore dismissed as bluff."[137] In the same spirit, the CIA and other intelligence services discounted all the evidence of preparation for invasion being made by Egyptian and Syrian forces. As late as October 5, they were telling the president that war in the Middle East was not expected. With the greatest relish, Sadat describes, in his memoirs and elsewhere, the various stratagems he used over this period to convey to Israelis again and again the impression that war was immediately imminent; and then how he finally caught the Israelis off guard, breaking the cease-fire unannounced, and in such a way and at such a time as to take maximum advantage from the Jewish people's obligations to turn all their attentions to their God on the Day of Yom Kippur, Saturday, October 6, 1973. The inspiration for the deed followed only after countless hours on his prayer mat before *his* God.[138]

In the first week of October 1973, Israeli intelligence could see these latest preparations under way, but the government, under Prime Minister Golda Meir, decided against any preemptive strike like the one that saved the day in June of 1967, but that had put Israel on the defensive with much of Western opinion. For this reason, Israel lost the initiative for the first two days at least of the war, and incurred casualties on a much higher rate than in all its previous wars.

The first twenty-four hours went well for Sadat. On the Sinai front, a great victory was gained in the first two days by the 70,000 Egyptian troops who penetrated the Bar Lev line, manned by 500 Israelis; Egyptian armies were quickly established on the east bank of the Suez Canal.

Simultaneously, Syria recovered Golan. Then, battlefield fortunes began to turn. The counterattack by Israeli tank forces in the north drove the Syrians back (at painful cost, fighting up the heights against Syrian cannon). By October 10, the cease-fire lines established after the 1967 war were reached; and, by October 13, as the Syrians and their Iraqi and Jordanian allies retreated in despair, Israeli forces entered Syria. (Included in the Syrian forces were 5,000 Palestinian Liberation Army [PLA] fighters.)[139] Now Damascus was exposed to the possibility of direct conquest. Once the front against the Syrians and Iraqis had been secured, the Israeli forces could reinforce their southern front, where they now began to drive the Egyptians out of Sinai, and back across the Suez Canal.

At this point, however, Israel faced a crisis of an unexpected kind—the imminent exhaustion of military supplies. By October 13, the Soviet Union had flown at least a thousand tons of weapons and ammunition to Egypt and Syria, and was bringing by sea even more supplies, as well as fighting men from Algeria. Further airlifts into Syria continued for several days thereafter.[140] Israel was now in the depths of its greatest crisis, facing the real prospect of extinction. Not until many years later did American policy makers feel free to hint of their knowledge that the Israeli cabinet might be preparing to put nuclear-armed missiles on alert.[141]

At this very moment, when the U.S.-Israel alliance was facing its sternest test ever, the president of the United States was totally distracted by the Watergate crisis. On the weekend of October 5–7, Nixon was in Key Biscayne, a favorite place to retreat to when overwhelmed, dealing full-time with the challenge of responding to the demands of Special Prosecutor Cox for surrender of the White House tapes. The two weeks of Israel's agony that followed contained these events: (1) the forced resignation of Vice President Spiro Agnew (October 9); (2) the selection of Gerald Ford to succeed as Vice President (October 12); (3) Nixon's firing of Special Prosecutor Archibald Cox, and of Attorney General Elliott Richardson and Assistant Attorney General Ruckelshaus—these last events remembered collectively as "The Saturday Night Massacre" (October 20, 1973). In his memoirs, Nixon does not let on that these goings-on bore at all on his handling of the Middle East crisis. The memoirs of all the other principals do, however, make clear that he was virtually incapacitated.

During the following days, diplomatic and military responses to the situation were directed by a group called Action Group of the NSA (National Security Council), chaired by Henry Kissinger. Kissinger, who had only recently (September 18, 1973) added the office of secretary of state to his title of national security adviser, now had no rival in determining policy.

HENRY KISSINGER

Henry Kissinger was born in Furth, Bavaria, in 1923, the year of the Munich beer hall *putsch*. Excluded from state schools as a Jew, he was educated at the *Israelitische Realschule*, where the Bible and Talmud were taught daily, along with secular subjects.[142] As a boy, he was subject to abuse and beatings by Hitler youth. For this knowledge, Kissinger's various biographers depend not on Kissinger himself, but on recollections of neighbors and family. Henry Kissinger himself always preferred to leave the story untold, "That part of my childhood is *not* a key to anything." But the biographers see this disclaimer as a clue to very deep matters: It is "as though Kissinger were somehow exempting himself from the psychological scars caused by Nazism in order that his diplomatic views might be accepted as pragmatic rather than personal."[143]

Dismissed from his job at the outset of the Nazi period in 1933, Henry's father, Louis Kissinger, fled with his family to America in August 1938, just ahead of *Kristalnacht*. In the United States, Henry Kissinger attended George Washington High School in New York City and City College of New York (CCNY). He was drafted into the U.S. Army in 1943, and served as a German-language interpreter in occupied Germany in the closing months of the war. By this time, he had abandoned religious practice. "For Kissinger," says Walter Isaacson, "the holocaust destroyed the connection between God's will and history."[144] He was an undergraduate at Harvard when the partition decision was taken (November 29, 1947) and when Israel was declared a state (May 14, 1948). His roommates would recall him as strongly opposed to the creation of Israel, arguing that it would alienate Arabs and jeopardize U.S. interests in the Middle East.[145]

Kissinger's determination not to be identified with the Jewish community was frequently noted by Jewish leaders during his tenures as national security adviser and as secretary of state. His first visit to a Jewish organization did not take place until April 1976, when he attended a luncheon meeting of the American Jewish Congress in Washington. This was soon followed by a visit to the Conservative Congregation Chizuk Amuno in Baltimore in May of 1976, when he received an award from the congregation.[146] The American Jewish leadership interpreted these belated visitations in the light of Kissinger's need to defend the Ford administration's policies before the Jewish community at a time when a credible challenge for the Republican presidential nomination was being made by Ronald Reagan—a man with considerable Jewish support. In the years following his service as secretary of state, Kissinger became very defensive about allegations that he had not been loyal to Israel. "I have never forgotten that 13 members of my family died in concentration camps, nor could I ever fail to remember what it was like to live in Nazi

Germany as a member of a persecuted minority," he said to the Conference of Presidents of Jewish Organizations in January of 1977.[147]

We have noted Nixon's disposition toward anti-Semitism. Henry Kissinger was a living, breathing caricature of the thick-accented, Central European Jewish immigrant intellectual whom Nixon loved to despise. "He sometimes called Kissinger 'Jew-boy' or 'my Jew-boy,' usually when his associate in foreign policy was not in the room, but occasionally when he was."[148] Nixon's domestic policy adviser John Ehrlichman recalled, "Nixon would talk about Jewish traitors, and the Eastern Jewish Establishment—Jews at Harvard. And he'd play off Kissinger. 'Isn't that right, Henry? Don't you agree?' and Henry would respond, 'Well, Mr. President, there are Jews and Jews.'"

When the two calamities of the Yom Kippur War and the Saturday Night Massacre came into conjunction in October 1973, it was Henry Kissinger who was running the foreign policy shop, virtually unimpeded. Immediately upon hearing the news of the invasion, he put himself in contact with the leaders of Israel, the USSR, Syria, the UN, Egypt and Jordan—all this without consulting the president. During the week that followed, "Nixon did not attend a single formal meeting on the war. . . . The only official he talked to was Kissinger, which left Kissinger free to do whatever he wished and claim he was speaking for the President." Most of the key decisions were not relayed to Nixon until after they were taken and acted upon.[149]

"From the outset, "Kissinger recalls, "I was determined to use the war to start a peace process," and, to this end, it was necessary to prevent Israel from humiliating Egypt again.[150] Accordingly, Kissinger resisted carrying out President Nixon's orders for *immediate* resupply of Israel's military needs, expecting that a delay in responding to Israel's needs would make Israel more willing to allow the United States to be her champion on the United States' own terms. When he did turn to dealing with Israel's request for resupply, Kissinger encountered stubborn resistance from the Defense Department, where concern was being expressed regarding an Arab backlash that would jeopardize United States access to oil. This resistance was only overcome by the direct orders of the president as commander in chief on October 13.[151] Complicating this American rescue task was the fact that the European governments of the hour feared alienating Arab countries, who might deprive them of their oil. For this reason, Britain and France denied the Americans use of their landing facilities; as a result, much time was lost working out various sub-rosa arrangements with other smaller countries.

By October 14–15, the tide of battle had turned, as Israeli tank forces and paratroopers arrived in the midst of Israel's enemies, Egypt and Syria. On October 17, a delegation of foreign ministers of Saudi Arabia, Morocco, Algeria, and Kuwait called on President Nixon demanding that

Nixon work for a cease-fire and the immediate return of Israel to the borders that had been in place before the Yom Kippur war. This was followed by a boycott of sales of oil to the United States, decreed by the Organization of Arab Petroleum Producers.

By October 19, three divisions of Israeli troops had again crossed to the eastern side of the Suez Canal. At this point, Sadat rediscovered the value of the diplomatic support of the USSR, which he had been privately bad-mouthing to the Americans for so many months. On October 19, Nixon received an urgent message from Brezhnev asking, on Sadat's behalf, for a cease-fire in place. To this end, Brezhnev urged Nixon to send Secretary Kissinger to Moscow at once for direct negotiations. Meanwhile, the Israeli bridgehead on the West Bank of the canal had broadened, and by October 22, the Egyptian Third Army, some 20,000 men and 300 tanks, was entirely cut off in the Sinai. With victory in prospect, the Israelis, on the day that Brezhnev sent his message to Nixon, were showing little interest in the cease-fire that they had been poised to accept two days earlier.

At this point, the difference in tactics between the president and the secretary of state became conspicuous. Nixon wanted to drag Israel forthwith into negotiations with the Arab states, under joint U.S.-Soviet auspices if necessary—all this before the pro-Israeli lobby in the United States could rally behind her. While Kissinger was still in Moscow, Nixon directed him to get moving on the project for some kind of conference of all the parties in the Middle East, jointly sponsored by the United States and the USSR. "The Israelis and Arabs," Nixon wrote to Kissinger, "will never be able to approach this subject by themselves in a rational manner." But the day that Nixon sent these instruction to Kissinger in Moscow was also the day of the "Saturday Night Massacre" (October 20). Recognizing that the president was wholly distracted, Kissinger made no pretense of abiding by these instructions.

Kissinger wanted the world to see that the events of the previous two weeks had really been a contest between the two systems—the American and the Soviet—and that the Americans, having out supplied the other side and having outfaced the Soviet Union, had won. There was thus no reason for dealing the Soviet Union into any future diplomacy in the area. As a Jew, Kissinger had a greater sentimental and moral allegiance to Israel than he had ever let on, but that was not the crucial point. Israel was winning because she was the client of the United States; the other side had lost because they were the losing clients of a losing regime. Soviet Ambassador Dobrynin recalled that "Sadat at that moment [by October 20] was pleading with us to hurry with a cease-fire resolution. . . . But Kissinger, it seemed, wanted to wait a bit longer. He said he needed time for consultations with Israel to persuade it to agree to a cease-fire."[152]

By October 21, Kissinger and Brezhnev had hammered out the terms for the cease-fire to be proposed at the UN. Kissinger insisted that he was bound to consult the Israelis, and so flew off to Tel Aviv. There he found that Israel wanted more time to complete the surrounding of the Egyptian Third Army by occupation of the west side of the Suez Canal. Unable to acquiesce to this publicly, Kissinger hinted that he would "understand if there was a few hours 'slippage' in the cease-fire deadline while I was flying home."[153] In these last few days, the object of the exercise had changed altogether for Israel. It was no longer a case of saving Israel's population from the army of invasion, but rather of keeping its own armies in motion until they were absolutely compelled by the powers and the UN to stop. The longer Israel could continue fighting the more compelling would be the lesson that the Arab side would take away from this adventure and the greater the hope of redressing the terrible loss of popular confidence that the Israeli government had suffered. As always, this proved a fond hope: Despite the fact that the war began with an Arab invasion and ended with an Arab rout, the world joined with the Arab military and political leaders in remembering only how much better the Arab armies had done this time around!

On October 20, 1973, President Sadat sent a telegram to President Assad of Syria in which he offered a simple explanation for this turn of affairs: "For the last ten days . . . I have been fighting the United States [sic] on the Egyptian front, armed as she is with the most sophisticated weapons in her possession. I simply cannot fight the United States or bear the historical responsibility for having our armed forces destroyed once again."[154]

Seeing himself abandoned in the moment of his own greatest peril, Assad flew into a rage.[155] Ambassador Dobrynin recalls, "I was then in Moscow attending Politburo sessions on the crisis and heard Anwar Sadat's calls to Brezhnev on a special phone, with the Egyptian president begging 'to save me and the Egyptian capital encircled by Israeli tanks.'" At the same time, the Soviet embassy in Cairo was reporting that Sadat had "completely lost his head."[156]

On October 22, the UN Security Council passed Resolution 338, calling for a cease-fire. But Israel was in no mood to sign on. Brezhnev wrote to Nixon on October 23 "Israel has grossly violated the Security Council decision on the cease-fire in the Middle East. . . . This perfidious action . . . [requires us, the USSR and the United States] to force Israel to comply immediately." Brezhnev was making essentially the same ludicrous offer that Bulganin had made to Eisenhower on November 5, 1956, and Kosygin to Johnson on June 10, 1967. The reality was that (as Dobrynin puts it) "The Soviet leadership itself hardly had at that time the means to influence developments on the ground, which angered the Kremlin."

In any case, none of this was conveyed to the president of the United States, whom Kissinger describes at this point as totally distraught, indeed, suicidal. Instead, Kissinger summoned the Action Group of the NSA and, in the absence of both the president and the vice president (Spiro Agnew having resigned, and Gerald Ford still unconfirmed), followed the examples of previous presidents by setting American forces in conspicuous motion—in this case, putting U.S. forces on combat alert (although not the highest level of alert.) "The U.S. government," says Dobrynin, "was trying to create the impression of a dangerous crisis."[157] True; but the "impression" was being created *not* for the sake of affecting Soviet behavior but for the sake of affecting Israeli behavior. The doomsday alarm sobered the Israeli Cabinet, which began complying with the cease-fire on October 24.

On October 26, after the crisis had passed, Nixon held a press conference, during which he likened the whole affair to the Cuban Missile crisis of October 1962, and awarded himself highest honors for conspicuous bravery under fire.[158] Later, he summoned Ambassador Dobrynin to Camp David and confided in him (according to Dobrynin) that he had been led to overdramatize the story "by the siege of his political opposition and personal elements who were using the pretext of Watergate to undermine his authority." "'Please inform the general secretary [Brezhnev],' he requested, 'that as long as I live and hold the office of president I will never allow a real confrontation with the Soviet Union.'"[159]

As we have seen, Sadat's line at the end of October 1973, was that the United States had entered the war and defeated Egypt—the same lie that Nasser had promulgated during the Six-Day War. Later, another lie—no less fantastic, but more palatable to the Americans—was that the Egyptians had refrained from thoroughly cleaning-up the Israel army in order to establish the conditions for a new era of diplomacy. The one consistent feature in both lies is the assertion that all had unfolded as it should: The Israelis had now been shown the true measure of Egyptian and Arab resolve and military capacity and had been made readier to talk peace. Now they knew that possession of the Sinai did not protect them, but was an obstacle to establishing the good relations with Egypt and all the other Arab neighbors. All along, Sadat now claimed, that had been his goal.

RICHARD NIXON'S LAST EFFORT ON BEHALF OF MIDDLE EAST PEACE

On January 18, 1974, a disengagement agreement (remembered as "Sinai I"), negotiated by Henry Kissinger, was signed by Israel and Egypt. Israel agreed to withdraw its forces from Egypt west of the Suez Canal and accepted the continued presence of a limited Egyptian force in a strip of land some six miles wide east of the canal. Israel lifted its siege of the Third Army, consisting of 20,000 troops and 300 tanks. A ten-kilometer buffer zone was established by the United Nations Emergency Force (UNEF) and a reduction of forces was agreed to on both sides of this buffer. Of this agreement, Sadat writes magnanimously, "I didn't bother about the Israeli pocket [sic] because I knew that they were my prisoners on the West Bank [of the Canal] and that their presence there meant their death. On the basis of defining and maintaining the real magnitude of my territorial victory, agreement was reached."[160] Needless to say, no hint of gratitude toward the Soviet Union appears in Sadat's vainglorious recollection of those moments.

Like Lyndon Johnson, Richard Nixon in *his* memoirs remembers himself facing down a Soviet threat to start up a nuclear war—which threat (again, as with the Soviet threat faced by LBJ) the historians now regard as hollow. Again, as in the case of Lyndon Johnson, we find the Israeli principals, in *their* various memoirs, properly appreciative of actions that saved Israel in her desperate hour, but not less convinced that a greater alertness to Israel's needs and a greater willingness to risk some diplomatic hassling with Israel's enemies *prior to* the outbreak of war would have prevented the crisis from happening—and would have saved some 20,000 lives, 2,600 of them Israelis.

It is intriguing to note that Nixon's very last foreign policy exercise was an adventure in personal diplomacy—a tour of most of the major capitals of the Middle East, intended to bring all the parties to agree to negotiations with each other under U.S. auspices.[161] This took place in the second week of June 1974—by which time his impeachment seemed all but inevitable, and even his own cabinet members had ceased defending him in public. Before departing on this trip abroad, Nixon told leaders of the American Jewish community that "they had to have in mind that each new war would be more and more costly because their neighbors would learn to fight, and there were more of them." In so many words, he handed the mantle of Israel's champion back to them: "As a matter of fact, whether Israel can survive over a long period of time with a hundred million Arabs around them I think is really questionable. The only long-term hope lies in reaching some kind of settlement now while they can operate from a position of strength, and while we are having such apparent success in weaning the Arabs away from the Soviets into more responsible paths."[162]

In Syria, Nixon had a long chat with the dictator Assad, and was escorted in and out of Damascus by huge crowds singing his praises. Nixon found Assad to have "a great deal of mystique, tremendous stamina, and a lot of charm . . . elements of genius."[163] Nixon took comfort from the discovery that Assad also had problems of credibility at his own bosom: "The problems that my visit presented to President Asad were summed up in the story he told me about his eight-year-old son. The boy had watched our airport arrival ceremonies on television, and when Asad returned home that night, he went up to his father and asked, 'Wasn't that Nixon the same one you have been telling us for years is an evil man who is completely in control of the Zionists and our enemies? How could you welcome him and shake his hand.'"[164] They all enjoyed a good laugh at that.

Earlier, in Egypt, Nixon was visibly exhilarated by the enormous crowds that Sadat had turned out to meet him—more than a million in the streets (although Kissinger points out that trucks appeared to be carrying people from the back to the front of the line from time to time).[165] Nixon had no doubt that this was the measure of the world's trust in his person, their hopes for his diplomatic efforts, and also of Sadat's popularity![166] In Israel, where no one had the authority to command the masses into the streets, the reception was much less buoyant. Although they were pleased to note that this was the first visit of an American president, the new Rabin government showed little enthusiasm for Nixon's peace initiatives.[167]

As his real authority was vanishing into nothingness, Nixon was advancing into more and more grandiose imagining, ringing the ancient changes on all the old bromides about living as neighbors together and seeking by peaceful means what had been sought by war. The American public was not the least interested. Whatever the virtue of Nixon's proposals, nothing he said to the leaders of the Middle East ever made the front pages at home. Only Watergate stories qualified for the front page for the next two months.

* * * * *

This part of our story has been full of paradoxes. Despite his failure to win Jewish voters, it was Richard Nixon who forged the strongest U.S.-Israel official ties seen to that date. Richard Nixon was the first president to make the case in the broad light of day that Israel was a strategic asset to the United States in the Cold War (a notion that previous presidents had only toyed with) and also the first to act on it (during the War of Attrition with Egypt and the crisis in Jordan of 1970). By doing so, he gave a new reason for many to embrace Israel's cause. Yet, paradoxically, he was also laying the seeds of the anti-Israel thinking that began to take hold in American opinion-making circles when the Cold War ended. The truth seems to be that Israel's long-term security requires a deeply rooted public commitment of a moral and spiritual sort—of a kind that Nixon could never have brought himself to articulate, even if he believed in it.

All through his career, Richard Nixon struggled against the softhearted, idealistic legacy of his Quaker mother. In private, he spoke to Billy Graham and other well-disposed Evangelicals about his tent-meeting conversion, and there is no reason to doubt that he meant every word of it. But as soon as the door closed behind these visitors he would huddle with his minions to plan what had to be done to prove to his political opponents that he was the hardest, meanest, most unscrupulous man in politics. He was obsessed with being "tough." He was always trying to prove that he was no patsy.

In his autobiographical writing, Nixon makes a considerable point of his thoughtfulness in *not* embarrassing other people by sharing his faith with them or praying in public or making statements of an overt Christian character—and he traces all of this to the Quaker virtue of living in peace with all. He is not, however, above enjoying a giggle over scripture with like-minded friends. He recalls an occasion when he and Golda Meir were exchanging thoughts about his policy of detente with the USSR. She suggested that he might be at risk of being too trusting of the Soviets.

I responded by explaining how my approach to detente differed and told her that we had no illusions about Soviet motives. I said that, with regard to international relations, our Golden Rule was somewhat different from that of the New Testament—that it was "Do unto others as they do unto you."

At this point Henry Kissinger chimed in and added, "Plus ten percent."

Mrs. Meir smiled in agreement and said, "As long as you approach things that way, we have no fears."[168]

Either Nixon had never learned or he did not recall the foundation text of the Christian Zionist: "I will bless those who bless you [Abraham and his decendants], and I will curse him who curses you" (Genesis 12:3). The notion that Israel was so situated in God's purpose as to be able to convey blessings did not resonate with him. Nixon was the sort of person who never does a good deed without getting a receipt. In this spirit, we find him insisting that so great had been recent kindnesses to Israel that they owed him recognition that should take the form of uncomplaining acquiescence as he undertook to redress all the unhappiness that had come into the world since Israel was born. His last references to Israel are quite mean-spirited, infected by the thought that the Israelis, like everyone else, had betrayed his goodwill. In the penultimate hour of his presidency, when no one was any longer taking *him* seriously, Nixon showed his determination to exchange the role of champion of Israel for a new role. Henceforward, he would bestride all the parties; he would knock heads together in an impartial way in order to achieve a rational and permanent peace. The circumstances surrounding this last diplomatic venture were so eccentric that it would not be wise to draw conclusions regarding what a future Nixon policy might have been.

Still, all things considered, Israel was well-served by Richard Nixon. During his presidency, American aid to Israel went from $300 million to

$2.2 billion per year, and the United States became for the first time the principal arms supplier to Israel.[169]

GERALD FORD (1974–1977)

"We will remain the ultimate guarantor of Israel's freedom."

GERALD FORD: THE ROAD TO PRESIDENCY

The nomination of Gerald R. Ford to the vice presidency on October 10, 1973, was the first application of the Twenty-fifth Amendment to the Constitution. It brought him out of Congress and directly into succession to the presidency at a moment when most informed persons (including, privately, Richard Nixon himself) foresaw the likelihood that Ford would become president—the first president not elected either to the presidency or the vice presidency. In his first speech as president on August 8, 1974, Gerald Ford appealed to the nation's sense of fairness and its desire for turning over a new leaf. "Our long national nightmare is over," he claimed. For a brief while, it seemed as though Ford had turned recent history into an asset for his party. President Nixon had been held accountable, and, following an orderly process of removal, was therefore no longer president. The American public seemed drawn to Ford, whom it had not known well before, but who, all were assured, was personally honest, unassuming, uncomplicated, and not given to conspiracy.

But the honeymoon was short-lived. On Sunday, September 8 (one month exactly following Nixon's resignation in disgrace), President Ford announced "a full, free, and absolute pardon [of Richard Nixon] . . . for all offences against the United States." This deed would "firmly shut and seal the book . . . [for the sake of] domestic tranquility."[170] In an interview with Richard Hutcheson in 1987, Ford explains that Sunday seemed the appropriate day for this deed, as he was acting in the spirit of "the biblical doctrine of forgiveness."[171] But what commentators observed, instead, was that presidents always consider that Sunday is the right day for news items that they want to be as little noticed as possible. Now there was ugly talk about "a deal" with former President Nixon. Ford's popularity declined precipitously, never to approach again the level of the first few days.

The key to understanding this presidency is that Gerald Ford was, by circumstance, permitted less scope for initiative than any president since Truman. Polls showed unprecedented public cynicism, owing to Watergate and to the Vietnam War. Congress, firmly under Democratic control, had taken advantage of the people's suspicion of presidential authority to enact new restraints upon the president's freedom of action in foreign policy and national security policy. In the domestic arena, the recession that had begun under Nixon got steadily worse. Unemployment rose to 9 percent in 1975; industrial production went down by 10 percent; the federal deficit rose to $60 billion, a new high. Nothing that President Ford proposed seemed to work.

As for foreign policy, Secretary of State Kissinger was able to assist President Ford in continuing the work of broadening cooperation with China and advancing detente with the USSR. The trouble was that public enthusiasm for both projects had cooled. What most Americans remember of the international news from the Ford years is a pattern of setbacks: the fall of Vietnam and Cambodia; the appearance of new communist-supported regimes in Africa (Ethiopia, Mozambique, and Angola); and the appearance of Soviet-supplied Cuban troops in support of secessionist movements against the pro-Western regime in Namibia. Ford and Kissinger warned the people sternly that the United States could not afford to let the Vietnam syndrome turn the United States into a bystander while the cause of freedom was lost.

GERALD FORD, THE JEWS, AND ISRAEL

In the last weeks of Nixon's presidency and through the Ford presidency, Kissinger worked out disengagement agreements between Syria and Israel, and between Egypt and Israel. To implement these required a certain amount of occasional contact on the ground between Israelis and Egyptians as well as an ongoing monitoring responsibility for the United States. Out of these continuing contacts there came opportunities for sub-rosa diplomacy. In this light, Kissinger, Nixon, and Ford can be said to have smoothed the path toward the diplomatic initiative that Anwar Sadat took in the first year of Jimmy Carter's presidency. In the beginning, however, Israelis were not grateful for Kissinger's disengagement diplomacy, which they felt permitted Sadat to reequip himself while simultaneously carrying off his impersonation of a military conqueror.

We have already noted a significant increase that Republican presidential candidate Richard Nixon won in the Jewish vote in his two elections—rising from the 10 percent gained by Goldwater in 1964 to 17 percent in 1968 and 35 percent in 1972. Both cause and effect in this matter was the appearance of a substantial number of Jewish leaders publicly committed to the Republican Party. President Gerald Ford's contacts with the Jewish community were largely orchestrated by Max Fisher, an oil millionaire from Chicago, with important assisting roles by Jacob Stein, chairman of the Presidents Conference, and Rabbi Arthur Hertzberg, president of the American Jewish Congress. Most Jews, like most Americans in general, admitted gratitude toward Ford for restoring respect for the office of the president following Watergate. Jewish leaders were aware that Ford had a generally consistent record of support for Israel, going back to his first years in Congress.[172] As the 1976 campaign proceeded, many who were normally loyal Democratic voters moved into his camp.[173]

American Jews did not warm to Jimmy Carter, and remained less enthusiastic about him than about any Democratic candidate in memory. David Horowitz, a syndicated columnist for World Union Press syndicate, seeking to be of help to Gerald Ford, wrote to Ron Nessen, Ford's press secretary: "Many national Jewish leaders feel as I do that Jimmy Carter's evangelical approach goes contrary to America's traditional approach to the issue of religion." He quoted from Jimmy Carter's speech before a Disciples of Christ laymen's convention at Lafayette, Indiana, on June 19: "A truer demonstration of strength would be concern, compassion, love, devotion, sensitivity, humility—exactly the things Christ spoke about, and I believe if we can demonstrate this kind of personal awareness of our own faith we can provide the core of strength and commitment and underlying character that our nation searches for." To this Horowitz offered what he believed was the correct response for Jewish Americans: "No aspirant to the Presidency of the United States, if true to the spirit of our Constitution, can tell the American people that 'the things Christ spoke about' (with respect to the Jews, he said 'You are of your father the devil, and he was the first murderer . . .'—John 8:44) can provide the core of strength and commitment underlying the character that our nation searches for."[174] Rabbi Alexander M. Schindler, president of the Union of American Hebrew Congregations and also currently the head of the Conference of Presidents of Major American Jewish Organizations, wrote in the early summer of 1976, "It is not surprising, remembering that historically much of anti-Semitism had its roots in fundamental Christian religious doctrine, that such anxieties should stir many Jews, and so feel and express a certain discomfort when a candidate describes himself as a 'born again Christian' and discusses the details of his Christian beliefs which include moments of personal revelation."[175] Carter was saying before Jewish audiences, "I have an absolute, total commitment as a human being, as an American, as a religious person to Israel. Israel is the fulfillment of biblical prophecy." But one Jewish official spoke for many when he said, "For over 2,000 years it has never been a good thing for Jews to have mystically religious Christians around—the Crusaders, the Spanish inquisitors are examples. Jews know Carter is no anti-Semite. He just makes some of us nervous."[176]

If this really was what American Jews thought, there was an opportunity for Gerald Ford—an opportunity, but also a potential trap. He must find a way to exploit the suspicions that American Jews felt about Jimmy Carter because he was a "Fundamentalist" or an "Evangelical" (the distinction is, understandably, lost on most Jews), while not appearing to repudiate his own theological allegiances—which were virtually identical to those of Jimmy Carter.

RELIGION IN THE LIFE OF GERALD FORD

Ford's reputation as a regular churchgoer had been promoted as a qualification at the time of his nomination for the vice president. During an interview with the historian Richard Hutcheson, Ford recalled, "Both my mother and father were very devout churchgoing members. . . . During our married life when we were in Washington we attended with our children Emmanuel Church on the Hill. My wife taught Sunday School there. . . . I was not a vestryman, but I participated in various men's functions, dinners, etc."[177] Although he was always a loyal Episcopalian, Ford had moved for many years in Evangelical circles. His district, after all, was in Grand Rapids, Michigan, which has one of the major concentrations of Evangelical voters in the north and is the home of Calvin College. Among his closest friends was Billy Zeoli, who was best known for his promotion of prayer groups (called "chapels") among athletes—a special enthusiasm of the former college football player Gerald Ford. For many years, Gerald Ford had participated regularly in a small prayer group of fellow congressmen, which included John Rhodes, Melvin Laird, Al Quie, and others. Several times in his memoirs and in interviews, he maintains his indebtedness to regular scripture reading, and always illustrates the point with the same text: "Trust in the Lord with all thine heart, and lean not unto thine own understanding. In all thy ways acknowledge Him, and He shall direct your paths" (Proverbs 3:5–6). In his memoirs, Ford notes, "Fifty years before [entering the presidency], I had learned that prayer as a child in Sunday School. I can remember saying it the night I discovered that my stepfather was not my real father. I had repeated it often at sea during World War II. It was something I said whenever a crisis arose.[178] In James Cannon's biography of Gerald Ford, the same passage is cited six times.

Ford's willingness to be associated in public with Evangelical organizations and his relative openness about his faith would become lost on the public during the election season of 1975–1976. A serious challenge for the Republican nomination came from Ronald Reagan, who had broad political support in the Evangelical-to-Fundamentalist world. After the nomination was decided, Ford's rival for the November election would be Jimmy Carter, who was such a high-profile Evangelical Christian that his "religiosity" would be made the keynote of much journalistic commentary. Somehow, Ford had to take advantage of the negative appraisals of Carter, without obscuring his own commitments.

A memorandum was prepared, with the help of his campaign advisers, outlining talking points for the candidate to make in the event of being asked about religious matters in a press conference:

> As a Christian, I strive to live up to the moral code as set forth in the Ten Commandments and in the teachings of Jesus. . . . I believe a candidate's personal religion is a proper concern for voters when they are choosing their President. However, I do not believe that it is proper for any political figure to deliberately exploit religion for his or her political advantage.
>
> If I am asked about my beliefs, I will respond for I am proud of the convictions I hold.[179]

In his memoirs Ford recalls, "Throughout the campaign, Carter had talked about his religious convictions in a way that I found discomfiting. I have always felt a closeness to God and have looked to a higher being for guidance and support, but I didn't think it was appropriate to advertise my religious beliefs."[180]

THE ELECTION OF 1976

At the beginning of the election year 1976, Ford's political handlers were hoping that their candidate, assisted by the concerns expressed by so many Jewish commentators about Carter's advocacy of "born-again Christianity," could break the headlock the Democratic Party had on the Jewish vote. Nothing came of this hope. Yet, right down until the end of the race, the Gerald Ford Campaign Committee kept on clipping notices about Jimmy Carter's religious statements, and commentaries that suggested he was paying a high price for them. (Ironic though it may seem, the most convenient source for the religious views that candidate Jimmy Carter offered during the election of 1976 is a thick set of files in the Gerald R. Ford Presidential Library.)[181] White House aides were now telling reporters that, against Carter, Ford might expect to exceed the 35 percent Jewish support that Richard M. Nixon had won in 1972. Meeting with the Presidents of Major Jewish Organizations in March of 1976, Ford referred to his record of a quarter-century of commitment to Israel's survival. This was at a time that Carter was receiving only 14 percent support from Jewish voters in the Democratic primaries held in major northern states.

On the eve of Israel's twenty-eighth birthday, President Ford attended the American Jewish Committee's 70th annual meeting, where he made his principal campaign statement on Jewish issues and Israel, the highlight of which was the line, "We will remain the ultimate guarantor of Israel's freedom."[182] "A highly placed Israeli embassy officer" is quoted as saying that Ford's speech was "the warmest a President has ever made about Israel."[183] A few days earlier, Secretary Kissinger spoke to the Conservative Congregation Chizuk Amuno about the United States' obligations to Israel "as the principal supporter" of its own security, and of the administration's intention to "be understanding of Israel's special circumstances in the process of negotiations. . . . Israel's survival is inseparable from the future of human dignity."[184]

In an address on May 13, 1976, to the American Jewish Committee's 70th annual meeting, Ford had explained that his own commitment to Israel stood on two premises. One was the conviction that a strong Israel served the security interests of the United States. The other was a spiritual premise: "When America's founders created this republic 200 years ago, they saw it as a promised land. They were inspired by moral and ethical values of the Old Testament as well as by the teachings of Jesus. . . . Today, the American people, regardless of religion, see justice in this Nation's traditional and special relationship to a kindred nation in the Middle East—the State of Israel. . . . America must and America will pursue friendship with all nations, but this will never be done at the expense of American's commitment to Israel."[185]

Gerald Ford's manful effort to win Jewish support brought out a degree of solicitude for Israel and Israel's security that had seemed to be wanting in the last months of Nixon's presidency. Ford exerted himself mightily to increase military sales and various forms of financial aid to Israel in these months. Israel's friends in the United States had every reason to believe that the concessions that Israel had been forced to make to secure the disengagements agreements of 1974 and 1975 would be the last that an American president would ever ask them to make. On October 12, 1976, at a yeshiva in Brooklyn, Ford said, "From the time that I first ran for Congress in 1948, I recognized that a strong Israel is essential to the cause of peace and the national security of the United States, and I am proud of that record. . . . I stand firm in my commitment to Israel. I am proud that our delegation at the United Nations has fought and will fight any measure that condemns Zionism as racism or would deny Israel her full rights of United Nations membership. . . . Prime Minister Rabin, who has been my personal friend since he was Ambassador in the United States when I served in the Congress, said recently that relations between our two countries are at a peak. The funds for Israel in my first two years of office totaled $4,300 million. Forty percent of the total American aid to Israel since 1948 was authorized during the Ford administration."[186]

There is no reason to doubt the sincerity of Ford's effort to establish his moral commitment to Israel and to represent this effort as following from his own personal religious commitment. On the face of it, there seems to be nothing wrong, either, with the calculation that such a dec-laration would turn the trick, and bring the friends of Israel into the Republican camp at last. But in the end Jewish voters suppressed their reservations about Jimmy Carter and voted overwhelmingly to return a Democrat to the office of president of the United States, on which the survival of Israel had depended so often in the past.

Chapter 3

The Camp David Process

JIMMY CARTER (1977–1981)
"Israel is the problem towards peace."

CANDIDATE JIMMY CARTER

Jimmy Carter was born October 1, 1924, at the Wise Hospital in Plains, Georgia (population 550), but was raised in a much smaller community outside of town called Archery. Jimmy's father, Earl, owned the family home and several hundred acres of land, which were worked by more than 200 black people to produce many crops. The most reliable and valuable was peanuts. Almost all of Jimmy's childhood playmates were black—the children of the tenants on his father's farm. Jimmy's school life, however, was segregated from that of his friends, as was his church life.

After graduation from Georgia Tech, Carter entered the Annapolis Naval Academy. In the summer of 1944, he had his first assignment at sea, on the battleship USS *New York*, doing patrol duty on the east coast. In 1950, he applied for and was accepted into the program for the first atomic-powered submarine. Admiral Hyman Rickover himself made the selection, impressed by Carter's gift for mastering complex and sophisticated technical and scientific knowledge and his already-legendary capacity for hard work. Thereafter, Carter's technological knowledge came to include reactor technology and nuclear physics.

Virtually all those who got to know Jimmy Carter well in later life have commented in one way or another on his obsession with self-improvement, accounting for every hour as an opportunity to learn something valuable, displaying everything thus acquired on his mental trophy shelf for everyone to see. Once, at a press conference during his presidency, he bragged to reporters: "I read two or three books a week. I'm kind of a fast reader . . . I ordinarily read most of the books on the best seller list."[1]

Beginning in the last months of 1952, Jimmy Carter was required to return frequently to Plains, to attend the bedside of his father, who was dying of cancer at the age of sixty-eight. "I came home from the Navy to see my Daddy die, and the thought struck me that here were my roots, here were my ancestors, these were my fields I had worked in, these are the people I grew up with . . . I felt that my Daddy's life meant more, in the long run, than mine had meant, so I got out of the Navy."[2] Jimmy took charge of the family business (peanut farming and marketing) and became active in local affairs, beginning with election to the Sumter County School Board in 1955. He served in the Georgia Senate from 1963 to 1967. He was defeated in his bid for the governor's chair in 1966, but he won his second contest in 1970.

The keynote of Carter's inaugural address as governor of Georgia was that "the time for racial discrimination is over." This declaration (which was soon followed by actions which brought Georgia's black population to the center of decision making in the state's public life) won him front-page notice in the *New York Times* and a cover story in *Time* magazine a few weeks later, in which he figured as one of the South's "new voices." Under Georgia's one-term system, Jimmy Carter's governorship would end in 1974.

In March 1973, Carter accepted the invitation of Robert Strauss, chairman of the Democratic National Committee, to head up the committee's campaign drive for the 1974 midterm elections. His visits to thirty-three states under these auspices gave Carter contacts with state party leaders from all over the United States. Chosen by Strauss precisely for his lack of political fame, he was not perceived as a player in the presidential stakes, let alone the front-runner, until it was too late. Jimmy Carter won recognition as a serious contender for the Democratic nomination by entering and winning the Iowa caucus contests, whose new significance under the recently rewritten Democratic Party nomination rules he perceived before the other candidates did. At the end of the primary process, Carter had shown that he had support in all regions of the country. His fiscal conservatism provided assurance to Northern Democrats who had lost faith in high-spending liberalism, and his social-conscience progressivism drew support among black Americans.

At first, Carter had a large advantage in opinion polls. There seemed, at first, to be no end to the electoral magic in his appeal as "an outsider to the process," his emphasis on restoring basic moral virtue to public life, and his compassion. Although Gerald Ford did not lack moral virtue, he was stuck, nonetheless, with the Nixon legacy and with the steadily worsening economic situation. But as the race progressed, Carter's wide advantage narrowed dramatically.

THE "RELIGIOUS ISSUE" IN THE ELECTION OF 1976

Carter's initial successes in the primaries of 1976 trashed all the premises upon which expert judgments about the political process had been reared for at least an entire generation—something for which he was never forgiven. He was a Southerner, a one-term governor of a small state, and a farmer. Conventional wisdom held that none of the above needed to apply for the presidency. But, in expert circles, the *surest* mark of Jimmy Carter's *disqualification* for the presidency was that he *volunteered* information on his religious faith and offered to demonstrate the connection between that faith and his position on public issues.

During his presidential campaign, Carter attended Sunday church services regularly, usually returning home to Plains for the purpose, but he made no special effort to work the Evangelical vote. (The keynote speaker at the 1976 session of Carter's own Southern Baptist Convention, held in Norfolk, Virginia, was not Jimmy Carter but President Gerald Ford.) When the matter of his faith was raised in New Hampshire, neither Jimmy Carter nor the reporters knew that it was coming. At the time Jerald ter Horst reported: "It was plainly an odd line of questioning for a political rally. An awkward hush fell over the room. Listeners squirmed and reporters lowered their eyes to their notepads. Everyone was embarrassed, except the candidate. Quietly, unblinkingly, he provided his answers. Then the subject changed, and everybody was relieved . . . Five days later, Carter won a clear victory in the North Carolina presidential primary, making it five out of six. So his religious views cannot be said to be a handicap thus far . . . But . . . agnostic professionals and the Democratic intellectuals who resent Carter's intrusion into their political scenario for 1976 are fidgety over his Baptist fundamentalism."[3]

While governor of Georgia, Carter had told a convention of the Christian and Missionary Alliance, meeting in Atlanta in 1974: "My family, my business customers, the people of Georgia know that the most important thing in my life is Jesus Christ. And I know that you share my conviction as those who have a strong missionary spirit, that the most important pursuit for us in this present life and for eternity is to let others know about the grace of God in our own lives and what it can mean to them."[4] Carter knew that his openness about religion made many Americans uneasy. "I've wondered whether to talk about it at all," he confessed to a reporter from *Newsweek*, "but I feel I have a duty to the country—and maybe to God—not to say 'no comment.'"[5]

It was evident early on that most of the pundits believed that Jimmy Carter had blundered. Out of a Southern Baptist's naive zeal to be a Daniel, he had filled the air with the vocabulary of primitive Christianity and brought upon himself both ridicule and belittlement. Then, just a few weeks before election day, the November issue of *Playboy* hit the stands and was discovered to contain the "Playboy Interview with JIMMY CARTER: Candid Conversation," and the accompanying article by Robert Scheer, "Jimmy, We Hardly Know Y'all."[6] Here we find candidate Carter trying hard to underline what he had been saying for months about his policies, his qualifications, and his political commitments. The brassy interviewer, showing little interest in those matters, kept baiting him about his redneck religiosity. For the most part, Carter's response was disciplined: "There are a lot of people in this country who have the same religious faith . . . But it's always been something I've discussed very frankly throughout my adult life. Harry Truman was a Baptist. Some people get very abusive about the Baptist faith. If people want to know about it, they can read the New Testament."

At that point, Scheer turned off the recorder and moved the discussion onto a man-to-man basis. Carter claimed later that he believed he was now talking off-the-record. Under this circumstance, it might be best to use the vocabulary that an interviewer for *Playboy* would recognize. (Having spent many months of his life locked up in small submarines, Jimmy was at least as familiar with this vocabulary as the interviewer.)

I'm human and I'm tempted. And Christ set some almost impossible standards for us. Christ said, "I tell you that anyone who looks on a woman with lust has in his heart already committed adultery."

I've looked on a lot of women with lust. I've committed adultery in my heart many times. This is something that God recognizes I will do—and I have done it—and God forgives me for it . . . Christ says, Don't consider yourself better than someone else because one guy screws a whole bunch of women while the other guy is loyal to his wife. [No text is given for this.] The guy who's loyal to his wife ought not to be condescending or proud because of the relative degree of sinfulness.

Polls taken immediately afterward gave the impression that the *Playboy* article had reduced Carter's ten-point advantage to a virtual tie.[7] Using the *Atlanta Constitution* of October 12 as a source, Ford's campaign team reported to the president that throughout the South, Baptist preachers were denouncing Carter for having "brought reproach on the Christian faith" by giving an interview to *Playboy* magazine, which, they said, "represents everything repugnant to the historic Christian faith." The episode, they said, cast doubt upon his credentials as a "born again" Christian.[8]

It seems that the damage was, in part, repaired in the next few days by Carter's better performance than Ford's in the presidential debates that intervened between the *Playboy* episode and Election Day. After this see-saw, the election became a cliff-hanger again. The result was one of the closest popular elections in history.[9]

CANDIDATE JIMMY CARTER, THE JEWS, AND ISRAEL

Throughout the campaign of 1975–1976, Jimmy Carter of Georgia spoke of his commitment to protect "the integrity of Israel." In a synagogue in Elizabeth, New Jersey, in June of 1976, he declared that this commitment stood squarely on his convictions as a Christian. "I worship the same God you do. We [Baptists] study the same Bible you do . . . The survival of Israel is not a political issue. It is a moral imperative."[10] Jewish listeners were by no means assured by such words. At a Beverly Hills fundraiser before the California primary, Carter said: "I'm going to tell you something you don't like. I'm a devoted Southern Baptist . . . I ask you to learn about my faith before you permit it to cause you any concern . . . There is no conflict between us [concerning the] Separation of church and state. I worship the same God you worship."[11]

Most Jewish Democrats would probably have preferred *any other* of the leading Democratic candidates of 1976—saving, of course, George Wallace. A Jewish newspaper, the *Sentinel*, was reporting in May that in the Democratic primaries so far "Carter has shown strength among practically every category of voters except Jews . . . Carter's weakness so far is attributed to the popularity of Jackson, Carter's absence of a Jewish issues record—and fear that he is something of a religious fanatic."[12] The fact was that American Jews (or at least the more articulate ones—those who spoke for the many Jewish organizations or who wrote articles and editorials for journals of opinion) were just not as well-disposed toward Southerners as toward Northerners and Westerners. They were not as trusting of Southern Baptists as they were of politicians with allegiances to other, more-familiar "mainstream" churches, or to no churches at all. Much of this was the plainest prejudice—the fruit of unfamiliarity. In their own parochial way, Jewish presidents of Jewish organizations assumed that if Jimmy Carter was not known to them he was not known to Jews. What they *did* know (or thought they knew) was that Southern Baptists had always been especially susceptible to anti-Semitism. Everyone knew about Leo Frank, a Jew who had been lynched in Georgia in 1913.

There was certainly nothing in Jimmy Carter's character or record that gave any excuse for anyone to allege anti-Semitism. In fact throughout his career, Jimmy Carter commanded the loyalty, often quite fanatical loyalty, of Jews—*not* New York, Boston, or Philadelphia Jews, but Atlanta Jews. More revealing than any of this is the fact that Jimmy Carter's most influential adult role model (some said, his father figure) was a Jew, Admiral Hyman Rickover. One does not make a father figure of someone reviled.

Jimmy Carter's efforts to counteract Jewish suspicions of his born-again Christianity led him into declarations of Christian Zionism, which had never appeared in his record before, and, as we shall see, were at odds with the views he expressed later as president and, later still, as a former president. "I have an absolute, total commitment as a human being, as an American, as a religious person to Israel," he declared. "Israel is the fulfillment of biblical prophecy," he told the *B'nai B'rith.*[13] This may have caused more trouble than not. On the one hand, most Jews did not particularly want to hear this. In the manner of the anthropologist returning from his field, the *Sentinel* explained the many anomalies in Southern Baptist behavior: "Fundamentalist Protestants tend to be some of the strongest American supporters of Israel—the Rev. Billy Graham is one—but some Jews prefer support for secular reasons, such as limiting Soviet influence in the Middle East."[14] At the same time, this Christian-Zionist talk provoked complaint from Arab spokesmen. The *Egyptian Gazette,* which expressed official views, registered its annoyance at the candidate's effort to put the case for Israel on a Biblical basis: "No other American presidential candidate has hitherto prostrated himself to the zionists with so much ebullience."[15]

In the end, Carter won 64 percent of the Jewish vote, while Ford won 34 percent—about the same as Richard Nixon had done in 1972.[16]

Notwithstanding candidate Carter's pledge to be the best champion that Israel had ever had, the Jewish community's attitude after the election remained: *We shall see.*

A YEAR OF FAILED INITIATIVES (JANUARY 1977–MID-1978)

In his campaign for the presidency, Jimmy Carter had kept the foreign policy component of his program to a minimum, thereby complying with the post-Vietnam mood of the nation. When he did turn to the matter of America's work in the world at large he stressed that his purpose was to put foreign policy on a new basis, a moral basis, one that reflected "the goodness of the American people."

Thus, while domestic policy making dominated the agenda for the first few months of his presidency, foreign policy initiatives were largely held in reserve. However, one area of foreign policy was moved at once to the front burner—and that was the Middle East. In striking contrast to the Nixon administration, this new administration intended to give *priority* to achieving a solution to the Arab-Israeli conflict. Again in contrast to Nixon, Jimmy Carter intended to involve himself, even *conspicuously* involve himself, in the planning and proclamation of the policy. In their various memoirs, several in Carter's inner circle recall their alarm at hearing him say, very early on, that he was willing to undertake every political risk, including the possibility of losing a second term, in service to the cause of achieving a Middle East peace. Jimmy Carter set his national security adviser, Zbigniew Brzezinski, to work at once putting together policy proposals that would be universally perceived as coming from the White House, not from the State Department.

Complicating President Carter's task was the circumstance that Brzezinski, who had been Carter's principal foreign policy adviser during his campaign, was mistrusted by the friends of Israel. Here again, we have to take account of some old-fashioned bigotry: If Jimmy Carter was a Southern Baptist, Zbigniew Brzezinski was a Polish Catholic. Many American Jews were sure that they sniffed something of Polish anti-Semitism in Brzezinski's stuffy academic papers on the theme of Jews and Israel. In an article in *Foreign Policy*, summer 1975, Brzezinski had criticized the "inherently rigid" attitude of the Israelis, their inability to contemplate "trading the occupied territories for Arab acceptance of partition of the old Palestinian mandate territory between Israel and what probably would be a PLO-dominated state of Palestine on the West Bank and Gaza strip."

Given Carter's determination to proceed, Zbigniew Brzezinski recalls, "I favored as rapid movement as possible. I felt the President enjoyed maximum leverage during the first year, and that his ability to deal with the problem would decline as he approached the congressional elections in late 1978, not to speak of the later 1980 Presidential elections."[17] By February 23, the president was able to announce that Secretary Vance had visited all the Middle East countries whose cooperation would be necessary to the achievement of peace in the Middle East (that is, Israel, Egypt, Jordan, Syria, Saudi Arabia, and Lebanon). He had issued invitations for each of the heads of government of these countries or their foreign ministers to visit President Carter personally, in order to discuss the issues. Meanwhile, in just three sessions, held between January 30 and February 23, Brzezinski and his staff hammered out the new policy. Abandoning the Kissinger step-by-step approach, the policy envisaged a comprehensive Middle East settlement. The plan was to get the USSR involved again, to the extent that it would see the gain of diplomatic capital by strong-arming Syria and its friends into reviving the Geneva Conference (still in recess since December, 1973). "Geneva by Christmas" was to be the administration's watchword.

In his memoirs, Secretary Vance expresses the administration's approach:

My sense was that the heart of the Middle East question was the intrinsic right of both Jews and Arabs to live side by side in peace and security. Ejected from their homes, embittered, radicalized, living in squalor and desperation, the Palestinians remained the central, unresolved, human rights issue of the Middle East. The president and I were convinced that no lasting solution in the Middle East would be possible until, consistent with Israel's right to live in peace and security, a just answer to the Palestinian question could be found, one almost certainly leading to a Palestinian homeland and some form of self-determination.[18]

Republican administrations had always tended to behave as though "the central, unresolved human rights issue in the Middle East" was the situation of the Arabs who lived under Israeli rule. They held this belief even though the Middle Eastern world was one where all the other heads of state were dictators or absolute monarchs; where parliamentary democracy was openly despised; where freedom of political expression scarcely existed; and where, for the most part, the free exercise of religion was not known. Thus, in a purely efficient way, consideration of the Arab-Israeli conflict must precede everything else. From this it further follows that a concession from Israel would be necessary to put Middle East diplomacy in motion. Because only the United States could bring Israel to make the concession that could set the process in motion, to jump-start Middle East diplomacy, the government of the United States must give a swift kick to the backside of the Israeli government.

The first of the official visits by Middle East leaders was that of the prime minister of Israel, Yitzhak Rabin (March 7–8, 1977).[19] From every point of view, it was a failure; and, to make matters worse, it came to be seen afterwards as probably counter-productive, given that Rabin was unexpectedly driven out of office only a few weeks after the visit. Years later, Carter recalled Rabin's visit as "a particularly unpleasant surprise." In his diary that night, he recorded his thoughts on the day: "I found him very timid, very stubborn, and also somewhat ill at ease. At the working supper Speaker Tip O'Neill asked him, for instance, under what circumstances he would permit the Palestinians to be represented at the Geneva talks, and he was adamantly opposed to any meeting if the PLO or other representatives of the Palestinians were there. . . . I've never met any of the Arab leaders but I am looking forward to seeing if they are any more flexible than Rabin."[20] Brzezinski recalls,

The meeting with Rabin did not go well. The Israeli Prime Minister and Carter simply did not relate to each other well as human beings and neither could repress his antipathy. Rabin was stiff, cold, and unresponsive. Carter tried to charm him, to give him some sense of his religious interest in "the land of the Bible," and to engage him as a human being by inviting Rabin, after the State Dinner, to look in on Carter's special pride and joy, his daughter Amy, who was asleep in her White House bedroom. Rabin declined the offer with a curt "No, thank you," thereby ending any chance of establishing a rapport with a proud father.[21]

From the outset, it is fair to say, Rabin was suspicious of Carter's motives. Not that they were sinister, but, paradoxically, that they might be, in a sense, too benign: "[He was] a new president who had visions of curing all the ills of the American people and restoring its faith in the presidency. He was imbued with profound religious conviction and believed that the American electorate had charged him with the mission of carrying through a great metamorphosis in substance as well as in style."[22]

The new tension in the U.S.-Israel relationship was immediately brought to public attention. Rabin recalls that he had extracted a promise from the president not to make public the differences of policy and strategy that had emerged in their meetings. But the very next day (as Rabin tells it), "at his press conference . . . under pressure from one of the journalists . . . Carter practically committed the United States and the presidency to an explicit position—in complete contradiction to all that had been said to me during our meetings. His remarks on Israel's withdrawal to the 4 June 1967 lines, with minor modifications, was the worst part of it. No president before him had ever publicly committed the United States to such a position. Even so it never occurred to me that only ten days later Carter would speak of the need for a 'Palestinian homeland,' a further dramatic change in traditional US policy."[23]

Early in his presidency, Jimmy Carter made good on a promise that he made repeatedly to Jewish groups during the 1976 election, by signing legislation making it illegal for American firms to cooperate in boycotts against Israel.[24] This accomplishment received little notice at the time, and it was quickly forgotten. Brzezinski recalls Carter bitterly complaining at this point of the lack of appreciation from American Jews; there was talk of a "showdown" with the America-Israel Political Action Committee. Another subject for complaint was "the vexing habit of the Israeli Ambassador, Simcha Dinitz, of leaking to the Israeli press self-serving or even distorted versions of his conversations with the top officials of the Administration."[25]

As he had hoped, Jimmy Carter *did* find *all* of his Arab interlocutors to be more genial than Mr. Rabin. Indeed, the first of these exceeded all expectations.[26] As Carter later recalled, "Then, on April 4, 1977, a shining light burst on the Middle East for me. I had my first meetings with President Anwar Sadat of Egypt, a man who would change history and whom I would come to admire more than any other leader."[27] Stepping from his plane, Sadat launched immediately into a fulsome display of flattery toward his host and exaltation of himself reminiscent of the victory steles left behind by the Pharaohs of three millennia before. Of

President Carter, he said: "For so long we have been told that politics is amoral and that international relations are not the domain of idealism or spirituality, but one of expediency and the pursuit of selfish interests . . . Mr. President . . . on the first day you assumed the awesome responsibility of your office, you took pride in the fact that your society was the first one to define itself in terms of both spirituality and human liberty. You pledged to spare no effort to help shape a just and peaceful world that is truly humane."

Earlier that same day, President Carter had briefly visited the exhibition of treasures from the tomb of King Tutankhamen, which had been on exhibition in Washington, and he had told the press of his admiration of the ancient civilization of Egypt. Sadat's listeners at the welcoming ceremony were thus in the mood to be carried back in thought to Pharaonic times. But no one could have been prepared for this: "I am certain that you know, Mr. President, that Egypt ever since its emergence as a state more that 7,000 years ago, has been a land of ideals and principles. From time immemorial, the Egyptian has remained faithful to higher values and ideals which render human life more rewarding and fulfilling. His belief in the divine truth, the afterlife, and the day of judgment—all this has instilled in him an extraordinary sense of justice and a genuine conviction of the universal brotherhood of man." This is not the view of Pharaonic Egypt that is conveyed in the history of civilization textbooks that most of his listeners had once studied. But Sadat of Egypt, like Pahlevi of Iran, and like Saddam Hussein (who came to power in Iraq in the summer of 1979), had determined to count the splendors of the ancient despots as part of the cultural capital of his regime.

If we are to believe their own words, the two presidents became undying "friends," indeed "brothers," on the spot. That night, Jimmy Carter announced that Anwar Sadat was "one of my close, personal friends." The explanation for this extraordinary instant bond was that "he's a man from a small village." Sadat picked up the cue at once: "I can quite understand the way you think and act. Like you, I come from a rural area that is the heart of Egypt's farmland, where life has different dimensions and a different meaning. . . . A conscious submission to the divine will provides us with tremendous strength to deal with the continuous challenge of life . . . Mr. President and dear friends, your recent statement on the right of the Palestinians to a national homeland was welcomed by every Arab." In Sadat's memoirs, published in 1978 (before the Camp David meetings), he writes: "I must put on record that President Carter is true to himself and true to others . . . I find that I am dealing with a man who understands what I want, a man impelled by the power of religious faith, and lofty values—a farmer, like me."[28]

Anwar Sadat never lost the advantage he gained that day in the contest of personalities with the rigid, dour, Yitzhak Rabin. This advantage carried into all the later rounds, when Anwar Sadat was matched with Menachem Begin—quite a different man from Yitzhak Rabin in most respects but certainly equal to Rabin in his disdain for people who put amiability too high on the scale of priorities in the context of high politics, and in his contempt for American-style public relations.

Even after leaving the presidency, Carter persisted in what Brzezinski called his "protective concern" for Sadat. Throughout the pages of Carter's memoirs, Sadat is everywhere and always "a shining light." No one else is even in the running for this distinction. Sadat's memory and the accomplishments of the Sadat-Carter team are invoked—quite often in entirely irrelevant settings—to make a point about what is truly possible, and about how hope can triumph over despair, and courage can overcome weakness and fear.[29] The section of his presidential memoir that deals with the Egyptian-Israeli peace negotiations (and that takes up about one-quarter of the whole book) *begins* with his recollections of hearing the news of Sadat's assassination and then attending Sadat's funeral in October 1981. "In Cairo," he recalls, "we found that security was extremely tight, the normally bustling streets of the huge city seemed almost deserted. . . . The crowd of people was unstructured and slightly confused, moving ahead by fits and starts."[30]

Jimmy Carter's portrait of Anwar Sadat is, to put it mildly, not well-rounded. It never occurs to him to note the discrepancy between the legend of the single-minded devotee of peace and the fact that his murder took place as he stood in splendid, bemedaled uniform, leading his people in the annual celebration of what he always insisted was his heroic victory over the Israelis in the October War of 1973. Carter expresses puzzlement at the low-key effect of the funeral, and detects something "unstructured" about the population in attendance. But this puzzle has an answer. Quite simply, Sadat was not, in his own people's reckoning, the man of peace that the Westerners remembered, but rather was the incompetent and vain ruler of their daily lives. The biographers, Hirst and Beeson, provide a sharper description of that day, filling in much of the "structure" that Carter missed: "Anwar Sadat, the peace-maker, died at a celebration of war . . . It was his habit, every year, to relive those glorious hours [October 1973] at a grandiose parade . . . [where he] took his seat on the ornate bronze dais, decorated with impressions of Osiris and other Egyptian gods."[31] This aspect of his regime—Sadat's evocation of the glorious beginnings of Egypt's history in the despotic and pagan age of the Pharaohs, his ten presidential residences, his devotion to a cult of himself[32]—infuriated not only "fundamentalists" but all serious Muslims. Similar popular feelings had played a large part in bringing down the Shah of Iran just a few months previously.

On one occasion, President Carter was asked by reporters why it was that decisions are so slow to be made in Israel, while they are made so swiftly in Egypt. He explained:

There's a difference, as you know, between the governments in Israel and Egypt. Prime Minister Begin is constrained by the parliamentary system. He has a cabinet and a parliament, the Knesset, and he has to negotiate with them and deal with them . . . Sadat, of course, being a President, being a very strong and powerful constitutional officer in the system of government Egypt has, can speak much more quickly, make decisions much more rapidly. He has to do much less consultation with other Egyptian officials than does Begin [sic]. But I think the recent attitudes among the general public in both these countries is conducive to peace. I think Sadat has the overwhelming support of his own people. I think Begin has the overwhelming support of the people of Israel.[33]

Carter's *public* ruminations on this subject bring to mind President Franklin Roosevelt's *private* comments aboard ship, en route to Yalta: "What helps a lot is that Stalin is the only man I have to convince. Joe doesn't worry about a Congress or a Parliament. He's the whole works."[34] Sadat's self-indulgence set the tone for the political and economic elite who were bound by hoops of steel to his regime. This greed and corruption inevitably aggravated the problems of the masses and of the middle class. When, in an effort to contain the bourgeoning deficit, the government slashed the subsidies on basic commodities (a legacy of the "Arab-Socialist" practice of the martyred Nasser), "the great food riots" of January 1977 broke out, during which seventy-five people were killed in Cairo alone (by official estimates.)[35] Sadat's response was to impose emergency laws, effectively closing down all opposition.

On April 25, King Hussein of Jordan came to visit President Carter.[36] Hussein made a great impression on Jimmy Carter, who was able to note that he and Hussein were in agreement on "the principles of my public proposals," and that there was now hope for a Middle East settlement, as there had not been for "20 or 30 years."[37] This exercise served as a kind of dress rehearsal for the subsequent interview with President Assad of Syria a few days later in Geneva (following Carter's attendance at the Economic Conference held in London). Carter told reporters immediately that Assad was "great," "brilliant," and one of his "favorite leaders."[38] In his diary he noted: "It was a very interesting and enjoyable experience. There was a lot of good humor between us, and I found him to be very constructive in his attitude and somewhat flexible in dealing with some of the more crucial items involving peace, the refugee problem, and borders"[39] A few years later, we find him once again retelling the story of this "delightful conversation": "[Assad] was extremely interested in my efforts to arrange peace negotiations. We began to enjoy the discussion, parrying back and forth and attempting to outdo each other in precipitating laughter in our audience of aides and advisers around the table . . . Assad stressed to me that the origin of many problems was the arbitrary subdivision of the region by the colonial powers, Great Britain and France, without regard to natural boundaries, ethnic identity, or tribal unity. Since then, Israel's actions were even worse." And as for the present world-political setting, it was true that Syria was a closely held client of the Soviet Union; but then, "Assad depended on high levels of Soviet economic and military aid . . . when threatened by the military forces of Turkey and Israel." And, as for the kinds of complaints against his regime that figured even then in the publications of Amnesty International: "Assad claimed that the Christians and Jews in Syria were treated just like any other citizens and with fairness." Above all, Carter was impressed by Assad's self-confidence. "He never deferred to the other Syrian leaders with him, nor did he seem interested in their reaction to his comments." As he reflects on the possible source of this admirable, numinous, self-confidence possessed by Assad, it occurs to Carter that, "He seemed to derive great patience from his obvious sense of history." Consistent with his admiration for the "strong and forceful leader" is the ineffably naive summary Carter offers of the story of Assad's rise to power, in "a successful bloodless coup" in 1970. Conceding Assad's "reputation among the other Arab leaders for ruthlessness and brutality toward those Syrians who resisted his authority," he provides exoneration by noting that its source is "his singleness of purpose in protecting his region from outside interference and in expanding Syria's role as a dominant force in Middle East affairs." "As a matter of conviction and principle," Assad explained to Jimmy Carter "no Arab leader could ever agree to give up any territory no matter how great his desire for peace." In this spirit, "Assad considered Lebanon an integral part of his own community and thought it only natural [sic] that Syrian forces should have been dispatched in 1976 to stop the Lebanese civil war."[40]

In that same busy month of May, 1977, Jimmy Carter had his second state visit from an Arab monarch—Crown Prince Fahd of Saudi Arabia.[41] By the time he came to write *The Blood of Abraham* (1985), he had a well-formed picture of Saudi Arabia's history.

> During the early years of the twentieth century, the father of Khalid and Fahd, Abd Al-Aziz Al Saud, was *successful in bringing together* the different regions of the peninsula under his dominion, and in 1932 he consolidated them into the Kingdom of Saudi Arabia. With a *proper blend of force and compromise*, religious revival and agricultural reform, as well as a large number of carefully planned marriages, the King was able to overcome ethnic tribal jealousies and conflicts and to emerge as the recognized leader of a wide geographical area. . . . The Saudi leaders were able to preserve an *acceptable* balance between delivering the material advantages of a modern state and at the same time preserving the *proper degree* of religious commitment. They also offset their absolute authority with a remarkable closeness to their subjects.[42]

Even by Carter's standards, this is an astonishingly prettified version of a civil war that went on for decades and caused the deaths of several hundred thousand Arabs.[43] As for the matter of Israel, "[T]here is no doubt that the Saudi leaders share the almost unanimous Arab feelings of resentment and antagonism toward the encroachment of Israel on land that was previously occupied and ruled by their Moslem brothers." On the occasion of the royal visit (May 1977), Carter said publicly that "so far as I know, between ourselves and Saudi Arabia, there are no disturbing differences at all"—something no president has ever said of Israel. About a year later, the administration announced its intention to sell advanced aircraft and other weapons to Saudi Arabia—something candidate Carter had repeatedly denounced President Ford for suggesting.[44] As we shall see, Jimmy Carter hoped by these deeds to secure from the Saudi regime some words of support for the principle of recognition of Israel, but these hopes were absolutely disappointed, despite repeated pledges (in private) along these lines.

Jimmy Carter's visits with Middle Eastern leaders that spring did not include one with the leaders of Iraq, with whom previous administrations had refused contact because of that regime's active and vocal support of terrorists . However, even as Carter was visiting with Assad and Fahd, his administration was seeking an opening to Iraq, as part of the new administration's policy of "normalizing relationships with countries who have been our adversaries and even enemies in the past" and "aggressively challeng[ing], in a peaceful way of course, the Soviet Union and others for influence in areas of the world that we feel are crucial to us now or potentially crucial 15 or 20 years from now."[45] Even as Carter spoke with Assad in Geneva, high-ranking State Department figures were in Baghdad, seeking to improve U.S.-Iraq relations by (among other things) offering to allow General Electric to sell the Iraqis engines for their four new Italian frigates. Congress later found this proposal to be "contrary to common sense," in light of Iraq's extreme hostility to Israel and its active promotion of terrorism. As late as April, 1980, however, National Security Adviser Zbigniew Brzezinski was saying that "we see no fundamental incompatibility of interests between the United States and Iraq"—noting particularly that the two administrations saw eye-to-eye with regard to "a secure Persian Gulf."[46]

Eventually, it dawned upon Jimmy Carter that, "The more I dealt with Arab leaders, the more disparity I discovered between their private assurances and their public commitments. They would privately put forward ideas for peace and encourage us in any reasonable approach. However, the peer pressure among them was tremendous. None of them—apart from Sadat—was willing to get out in front and publicly admit a willingness to deal with Israel." Still, Carter never ceased to be dazzled by the style and bearing of the Arab rulers. All were such charmers in private—

so much better company than the dour Israelis. All were so much more open to agreement at every point. In his memoirs, Carter bends over backwards to encourage us to appreciate the extraordinary difficulties they worked under: "The threat of Palestinian terrorist attacks against some of their shaky regimes was one significant reason, but the concentration of the oil wealth in the more radical countries, such as Libya and Iraq, was perhaps more important. Saudi Arabia was both rich and moderate—but again, supporting the peace process only in private."[47] The point is clear: Had the Israeli leaders understood better the burden of oil wealth and the weight of "peer pressure," they would never have asked for so much from Saudi Arabia.

Since his meeting with Rabin, President Carter had been seeking out opportunities to make clear that his administration was prepared to stir up some new thinking about the Arab-Israeli conflict. On March 16, 1977, participating in a "town meeting" in Clinton, Massachusetts, he announced: "There has to be a homeland provided for the Palestinian refugees who have suffered for many, many years."[48] As Edward Tivna puts it, the remark about a Palestinian "homeland" was "like putting a match to a stick of dynamite and throwing it into the American Jewish community."[49] But, far from being spontaneous, the remark had been carefully rehearsed in Carter's mind. This message was reinforced later when President Carter shook the hand of the PLO representative at the United Nations. In fact, as many guessed, the administration was already dealing with the PLO through a variety of secret channels.[50]

While Carter was making these first approaches to Arab leaders, Israeli politics underwent an amazing upheaval. Yitzhak Rabin's first tenure of the office of prime minister of Israel coincides almost exactly with Gerald Ford's tenure of the office of president of the United States. He had entered office on June 3, 1974 (just in time to welcome Richard Nixon during his visit to the Middle East two weeks later—one of Nixon's last public acts as president of the United States) and was to leave office in the fifth month of the presidency of Jimmy Carter. It was during his brief tenure as prime minister that most of Henry Kissinger's shuttle diplomacy had occurred, culminating in the disengagement agreements with Egypt and with Syria in 1974 and 1975. Rabin shared the conviction of his party that they would remain in government forever—or at least for as long as Menachem Begin was the alternative. In a party executive meeting late in 1974, he had joked that Begin was "an archeological exhibit in our political life."[51] A general election was called for May 17, 1977.

No sooner had the election campaign of 1977 begun, however, than Rabin was compelled to step down as leader, when newspapers carried a story that his wife had violated the law by keeping an account of U.S. funds in a U.S. bank. This was the latest, but by no means the most damning, of a long sequence of exposés of abuse of office by highly placed

Labor figures in just the preceding few months. Despite all this, Israeli and American observers were predicting a Labor victory under Shimon Peres. On what really mattered to the Carter administration, there was every reason to prefer a Labor victory. Menachem Begin and his party had denounced at every step the process that culminated in the disengagement accords of 1974 and 1975. The platform of Likud committed it to holding, forever, Judea, Samaria, Gaza, and Golan, whereas Labor's platform explicitly endorsed UN Resolutions 242 and 388 and spoke of territorial concessions to win peace.

At the end of the election day, May 17, 1977, it was not certain who would form the new government. Of the 150 seats in the Knesset, Menachem Begin's Likud had increased its number from 39 to 43, while Labor had dropped 19 seats, to 32. Ironically, many commentators, both in the United States and in Israel, believed that President Carter had contributed unwittingly to the Likud victory by his recent talk about the Palestinians' right to a homeland. At Labor Party headquarters they said: "Just about everything Carter did helped to defeat us. . . . At least he could have kept his mouth shut until after the elections."[52] The several religious parties held the balance of power, and they ended the stalemate by agreeing to share in government with Begin.

The reaction of the president and his official family was monolithic. "Israeli citizens, the American Jewish community, and I were shocked," Carter recalls in his presidential memoirs. "None of us knew what to expect."[53] Taking the three categories in reverse order, one must concede that Jimmy Carter is fully authorized to say that *he* was shocked and is *probably* correct in saying that American citizens, taking them all in all, were, if not shocked, more surprised than pleased; but it hardly seems logical to say that "Israeli citizens were shocked," given that they had just done the deed! This is not the only time that we find declarations of this kind, that ask us to believe that Jimmy Carter knows the true mind of the people of Israel better than Menachem Begin does—and even better than they know their own mind. This habit of explaining the will of Israeli people to the elected leader of the Israeli people must have been very trying, to say the least, to Menachem Begin.

After Likud's unanticipated victory in May 1977, the pundits rushed into print with pieces explaining its inevitability. The negative side of the explanation was the public's weariness with Labor—with the party, with its dated socialism, and with its discredited leaders. Those preferring sociological explanations explained that a new generation of Israelis, which did not share the worldview of the founding generation, had finally gathered up the courage to vote against its fathers' advice. Most important, perhaps, was the accumulating effect of changes in patterns of immigration since 1948. After the wartime DPs were absorbed, the preponderance of immigration was no longer from Europe (no more than a trickle had ever come from America) but from the lands of the Near East, which had driven out their Jews in reprisal for the verdict of the United Nations in 1948 and the verdict of the god of war in 1948–1949. These Oriental (or Sephardic) Jews had lived for centuries in lands where the dominant population had not been Christian (though it might have been governed by Christian empires, as in French North Africa) but Muslim, and where Jews had not had much contact with schooling, let alone with science or modern thought. Although he was an *Ashkenazi* (an Eastern European Jew), Menachem Begin appealed to the unmixed Israeli patriotism of the *Sephardim*. He was against any territorial concessions and he expressed his opposition not in military-strategic arguments, nor by appeal to UN declarations, nor to political science, but in language they understood. Speaking to the bruised self-esteem of the Sephardic immigrants, he said that his party had always "represented the poor in possessions and the rich in faith." Then, striking the same note as Jimmy Carter had struck in the campaign of 1975–1976, Begin stated: "We are entitled to say: Let us return to the values of personal and public morality . . . As leaders, let us give a personal example of modest living, of keeping promises, of sincerity and truthfulness in speech—of credibility in political and economic affairs."

But, possibly, what won the hearts of the Oriental Jews more than anything was the fact that (as his biographers put it) "Begin's moral and humanitarian outlook is anchored in the religious tradition in which he was raised." On his first *Shabbat* as prime minister, "for the first time, Israelis saw a prime minister observing the Sabbath at his home in the traditional manner."[54] He would not conduct public business on *Shabbat*. Jimmy Carter learned this early when his ambassador was turned back from the prime minister's door with a message in his hand that he said was a request for immediate action on some matter. President Carter never repeated this mistake.[55] After Begin's election, commentators seized upon the coincidence that the Israeli public, like the American public a few months earlier, had turned for leadership to a man of personal religious piety. *Time* magazine described Begin as "a fervently religious man who frequently invokes God's name" (apparently unaware that this is a contradiction in terms) and went on to claim that "it has suddenly become popular in government circles to interject a *Baruch Hashem* ('God be blessed') or a *Toda L'el* ('Thank God') into conversations."[56]

Menachem Begin himself, on his departure for the United States a few days after his formal designation as prime minister, called attention to the hopeful fact that both he and President Carter were believers. As he put it, "We both are blessed with the historic opportunity to give substance to the religious meaning of our societies." Begin had made a firm decision to appeal to the love of Israel in which, he understood, Christians of Mr. Carter's particular stamp were nurtured. This motif was established in his first public words on arrival in the United States as prime minister: "Mr. President, I have come from the Land of Zion and Jerusalem as the spokesman for an ancient people and a young nation. God's blessing on America, the hope of the human race. Peace to your great nation."[57] Afterwards, Begin told a Jewish audience that the rabbinate in Israel had appealed to the people to pray for the success of his mission and had specified a particular Psalm for each day of his visit. The ground of his own confidence was this: "Carter knows the Bible, and that will make it easier for him to know whose land this is."[58]

For his part, Jimmy Carter sought and received from his advisors at home and abroad knowledge that would help him in his oncoming confrontation (as he expected it to be) with Begin. Carter's embassy in Israel told him that, while a sizable majority of Israelis supported Begin in his refusal to consider negotiations with the PLO, and while equally sizable majorities agreed with him that "the West Bank" belongs by historical right to Israel, a majority of Israeli Jews (53 percent) are convinced that "it will be impossible to obtain a peace settlement with the Arab countries, if Israel refuses to give up any of the West Bank territory." In a candid introduction to his memo on Jewish voters, Chief of Staff Hamilton Jordan, who had been Carter's closest personal associate in his campaign for the presidency, admits that this president's team had started with a certain disadvantage on this issue: "We are aware of its [the American Jewish community's] strength and influence, but don't understand the basis for that strength nor the way that it is used politically. It is something that was not part of our Georgia and Southern political experience and consequently not well understood." Not only are Jewish voters predominantly Democratic but they vote in greater proportion to their actual numbers than any other identifiable subgroup of the electorate—close to 90 percent in most elections. Their influence in primaries is often decisive. In New York City, the Jewish population is 20 percent, but Jews cast about 55 percent of the votes in the Democratic primaries. By contrast, only about 35 percent of eligible blacks vote in presidential elections, and fewer in primaries. Thus, although Carter received 94 percent of the black vote and only 75 percent of the Jewish vote, he received, in New York State, twice as many Jewish as black votes. Then there is the matter of Jewish financial contributions. "In 1976, over 60% of the large donors to the Democratic Party were Jewish."[59]

The challenge for the president is not understated. Several pages in Jordan's memo are given to AIPAC, which acts as the collective voice for thirty-two separate Jewish organizations on all issues affecting Israel. There is, Jordan warns, no "political counterforce" to this lobby. In the U.S. Senate, "on a given issue where the interests of Israel are clear and directly involved, AIPAC can usually count on 65–75 votes [out of 100 total.] . . . For many years, the American Jewish community has simply reflected the attitudes and goals of the government of Israel." Because he has spoken aloud of "a homeland for the Palestinians," Carter is presently held in low regard in pro-Israel circles. The situation is made worse by press reports of Carter's meetings with four Arab heads of state (invariably described in "very positive" terms), which contrast sharply with press reports of the visit with Rabin (invariably described as "very cool"). But this situation could change in the longer run. "One of the potential benefits of the recent Israeli elections is that it has caused many leaders in the American Jewish community to ponder the course the Israeli people have taken and question the wisdom of that policy.... This new situation provides us with the potential for additional influence with the Israeli government through the American Jewish community."[60]

No great expertise was needed to substantiate Hamilton Jordan's point about Begin's low standing in the American Jewish community in 1977. From the beginning, American Jews had overwhelmingly favored the left side of the Israeli political spectrum, which was in power at creation of the State and had dominated political life ever since. In 1948, at the time of an earlier visit by Begin to the United States, Albert Einstein and Hannah Arendt, among many other intellectual celebrities, had publicly denounced Begin for his "Fascist" and "Nazi" tactics. In its first editorial on the Israeli election, the *New York Times* said, "*As luck and Israeli democracy would have it*, the politics of the Middle East are now dangerously out of synch . . . *Mr. Begin's Likud did not really win the election*. It gained a handful more seats than in 1973 and emerged the leading party only because Labor, which has ruled the nation since its formation in 1948, suffered a humiliating defeat." (An odd piece of logic!) "It may not last long."[61] *Time* magazine used its best schoolyard wit to advise its readers that "Begin rhymes with Fagin."[62]

After listening to Begin speak to interviewers on the news program, "Issues and Answers," Carter told his diary: "It was frightening to watch his adamant position on issues that must be resolved if a Middle Eastern peace settlement is going to be resolved."[63] There was, therefore, every reason to fear that Mr. Begin would not prove "a shining light" to Jimmy Carter, as Anwar Sadat had done. In any case, Carter did not really want any more shining light in his life at this point. The issues were already abundantly clear to him—the result of countless hours of homework. What he needed, he thought, in prospect of Prime Minister Begin's visit, was to be well-armed with factual information against devious arguments. He knew that he had the moral advantage, as he always did.

The first meeting between Jimmy Carter and Menachem Begin took place on Tuesday, July 19, 1977.[64] Jimmy Carter brought with him to his discussion with Begin a text from the prophet Isaiah, which he intended to share with the prime minister: "And the work of righteousness shall be peace, and the effects of righteousness quietness and assurance forever"

(Isaiah 32:17). Menachem Begin had no difficulty seeing his own efforts in that light. Recalling that first meeting with Prime Minister Begin, in July of 1977, Carter writes in his presidential memoirs: "Begin gave me his views about the historical nature of Israel, which was interesting this time, although I was familiar with most of what he said from my studies of the Old Testament and more recent history. I had no idea how many times in the future I would listen to this same discourse."[65] Jimmy Carter did not appreciate people explaining to him what he already knew. In this respect, biblical history or the history of the Jews was no different from atomic theory. This was the side that some around him recall as the "SAT mentality"[66] —that once you had got up the facts about anything, then you had exhausted its truth, and were armored against the arguments: "*I was familiar with most of what he had said.*"

Begin always fails in comparison with Sadat in Jimmy Carter's recollections. But then President Sadat had many advantages over prime minister Begin. Not the least of these was the fact that Jimmy Carter was not familiar with *everything* that Sadat knew (or thought he knew), just most of it. Islam, for instance, was new to Jimmy Carter. When the subject was Islam, it was not necessary for him to grit his teeth and hear all over again what he already knew. But these deepest matters apart, Sadat had lived a life utterly unlike the life that Carter had known. Their "friendship" was based in large part *not*, as they both sedulously insisted, on their common experiences as sons of the soil, but on the opposite truth: that Sadat represented a world utterly outside Carter's experience. To his credit, Carter liked to learn. And when it came to the world outside America and Europe, he was an easy candidate for "Orientalism." Anyone who paused to put on a turban could command his respectful attention forever.

By any reasonable measure, Begin made large concessions toward meeting the president's own position. He agreed to take Israel to a Geneva Conference, if the president really believed that would accomplish anything. He would consider handing back all of the Sinai except for a strategic toehold, provided that Egypt was really serious about diplomatic negotiations. He would not absolutely foreclose the possibility of concessions on the Golan provided that Syria was truly prepared to talk about peace—something Syria's president had never even hinted at. And he was ready to work toward "autonomy," but not national self-determination, for the Palestinians of Judea, Samaria, and Gaza. He listened calmly while the president urged the case for an end to "West Bank settlement." In the press conference, the prime minister was unexpectedly flexible on the sensitive matter of who would represent the Palestinian Arabs at the Geneva Conference, allowing that persons friendly to the PLO leadership might very well be admitted, provided that they did not make a parade of their allegiance to the PLO.

"Going to Geneva" meant agreeing to a meeting of all the parties to the Arab-Israeli conflict, under conditions where the Soviet Union, no less than the United States, would be formally empowered to speak up about what should be done, to twist arms, to propose sanctions in case of failure. To Arab rulers, it meant the unpleasant prospect of acknowledging that Israel did exist—a dangerous step on the slippery slope to acknowledging her *right* to exist. To Israel, it meant the possibility of having to trade away some of the securities incorporated in the 1975 Memorandum of Understanding while being confronted with a unified Arab position on issues of life and death. Part of the difficulty for men of Menachem Begin's generation was that the very name *Geneva* evoked hateful memories of the time when that city was the capital of the League of Nations—the place where the leading Western nations of the day displayed again and again their unreadiness to protect the weak from the strong. "Manchuria," "Abyssinia," "the Rhineland," "Sudetenland"—these and many other issues of the 1930s had been brought to Geneva. Still, during his July meeting with Carter, Begin had reluctantly agreed to see the Geneva process resumed, and he had even agreed to talk about ways whereby Palestinian Arabs could be officially present and heard from.

In the following months, while the Carter administration worked at persuading Arab governments to agree to come to the forthcoming conference, Begin conducted some shuttle diplomacy of his own. First, he made a secret visit to Tehran. Then followed a public visit to Romania (the only member-state of the Warsaw bloc that maintained diplomatic relations with Israel), seeking to put to use President Ceausescu's contacts with Egypt and other Arab countries. A number of other secret initiatives were taken in these weeks: These included a meeting between Foreign Minister Dayan and Prime Minister Moraji Desai of India, a meeting between Dayan and King Hussein of Jordan, a meeting between Dayan and the Shah of Iran, and then, in early September, a meeting in Morocco between Dayan and King Hassan, during which the latter was persuaded to help establish direct contact with Egypt—this in turn leading to secret meetings between Dayan and Egypt's deputy prime minister in Morocco on September 16.[67]

In late September, Dayan came to the United States and tried, in person, to persuade President Carter that Israel was being at least as forthcoming as the parties on the other side, and was entitled to some public acknowledgement of this. Instead, he received the cold treatment from the president and his aides.[68] You are more stubborn than the Arabs and you put obstacles in the way of peace," the president told him at their first meeting. On September 29, the Carter government presented to Moshe Dayan the text of the Joint Statement with the Soviet Union regarding a Geneva Conference, which it would issue two days hence at the United

Nations. Dayan now set to work to mobilize American Jewish opinion, addressing five conferences of major Jewish organizations in the five largest cities of the United States. His message was blunt: "We are being told by Carter and Vance that if we want peace, we must accept Arab terms—we must give up the Golan Heights, the Sinai, and the West Bank. Maybe there will be peace if we do all that but there will be no Israel. We are not going to accept this."[69]

As one reads the memoirs of the Americans involved in these decisions, what strikes one most is that none of them could later adequately explain to himself, let alone to us, why everyone at the time had accepted that it would be a good thing to go to Geneva. It was as if it were just something that could not be avoided—like going to the dentist. In retrospect, the arguments that were supposed to demonstrate its inevitability collapsed in the minds of these participants—somewhere between the deed and the writing of their memoirs. Carter's interpretation of the situation was that, unless the Soviets were engaged in the process, the Arab states, all, to one degree or another, subject to Soviet influence, would not agree to play. But this seems to contradict Carter's claim, so often reiterated, both privately and publicly during these same months, that his personal diplomacy with all these Arab states had revealed that their links to the USSR were as nothing compared to their desire to work more closely with the United States and their powerful (though still undeclared) willingness to turn the corner in their attitudes toward Israel. Zbigniew Brzezinski, though he of course toed the line, believed that the costs were much higher than Carter was admitting: "Inevitably, the necessity of finding language for a text which they could sign jointly had put the United States in the position of "appear[ing] to be aligning itself with the Soviet point of view."

The United States and the USSR issued their Joint Declaration (October 1, 1977).[70] In the key passage, which spoke of "ensuring the legitimate rights of the Palestinian people," the United States appeared to be adopting the vocabulary preferred all along by the Soviet side. After another tense meeting between Dayan and Carter (October 4, 1977) a joint U.S.-Israel statement was worked out regarding procedures to be followed at the conference.

Jimmy Carter's staff prepared for him a summary of reactions to the Joint Statement appearing in the press and other media at home.[71] Pro-Israeli Senators denounced the statement. Senator Robert Dole (Republican, Kansas) said: "It appears President Carter is so determined to hold a Geneva Conference in 1977 that he will risk permanently ruptured relations with Israel to achieve it." Leaving aside the interests of Jewish-Americans, there was among the general public the impression that the administration had willfully enhanced the diplomatic role of the Soviet Union, while apparently never thinking to exact a price of admission.

Had the prospects for the Geneva process been great, the political risks might some day have come to be seen as noble. But there was no real prospect that a Geneva Conference involving all the Arab parties would accomplish anything. In this light, the exercise appears almost masochistic. In fact, all things considered, Israel was likely to be less bruised by the experience than either the United States or Egypt.

An important key to all that follows is the fact that President Sadat was even less interested than was Prime Minister Begin in seeing Geneva cranked-up again—a truth that is simply ignored in Carter's recollections. In the summer and fall of 1977, Sadat's visits to the other Arab leaders reinforced his conviction that a meeting at Geneva would ruin Egypt's hopes for any concessions from Israel. Geneva could only become a shouting match. Assad of Syria was insisting that there must be a combined Arab delegation, thus no separate voice for Egypt, despite the fact that Egypt's population was half that of the entire Arab world, and despite the fact that in all the wars with Israel to date the preponderance of casualties had always been Egyptian. The other Arab states, suspecting that Sadat would give top priority to the concerns of Egypt, and lesser priority to the territorial concerns of Syria and Jordan and the whole matter of the fate of the Palestinians, sided with Assad on this matter of a combined Arab voice. Assad of Syria, Hussein of Jordan, and whoever might get the approval of the United States and Israel to stand in as the voice of Arab Palestine would simply start up a contest to see who could emerge as the most extreme champion of the maximum demands of the PLO. Israel would only need to sit still while they tore into each other. In the cockpit at Geneva, it would be out of the question for Egypt to advance any proposals that Israel could act upon. The day when the Sinai might be returned to Egypt would be postponed, probably to the Greek *kalends*.

In his memoirs, Carter speaks of the "hopeful" and "bold" responses that Sadat made during that fall, and simply pretends that these were in response to the American administration's plans for a comprehensive peace—that is, that they were contributing to the movement toward Geneva. In fact, careful attention to what Sadat was actually doing makes it perfectly clear that Sadat was maneuvering Carter into accepting bilateral Cairo-Jerusalem negotiations in lieu of any kind of broader conference. Direct Egyptian-Israeli diplomacy had always been Israel's preference, as Sadat well knew. But to wring from Israel the major concessions he had in view, he would need to have the United States present, holding their coats. The United States, however, was not free to assist at Egyptian-Israeli diplomacy so long as it was committed to "comprehensive diplomacy," that is, to Geneva.

On October 4, 1977, Sadat wrote to President Carter (as Carter himself recalled) expressing the hope that the United States would serve as an intermediary between Egypt and Israel, and "urging that nothing be done to prevent Israel and Egypt from negotiating directly," should Geneva fail to materialize.[72] With this, Sadat put a safety net around the high-wire diplomacy that he was about to undertake, and whose ostensible purpose was to urge all the other Arab leaders to come to Geneva for comprehensive talks with the enemy. Sadat's strategy was to cause Geneva to fail before it got started, under circumstances that would allow him to pretend disappointment. Preferring not to see this, Carter portrays Sadat's note of October 4 as a typically generous and imaginative instance of Sadat's diplomacy: "I found Egypt to be the most forthcoming and cooperative nation in the Middle East in working toward a peace settlement."[73] In reality, however, Sadat's note actually brought Egypt onto the same ground with Israel: professedly ready to go to Geneva, while in fact working for direct Egyptian-Israeli diplomacy.

Ever since the spring of 1979, Carter had been hovering over Begin, seeking to work him up into more enthusiastic expressions of support for the Geneva process. Carter did not hesitate to accuse Begin of undermining the prospect for Geneva, but it does not seem to have registered with Carter in these same weeks that this is exactly what Sadat was doing too! Sadat and Begin had been conducting secret negotiations at several removes since July—of which the Americans were apparently aware. These included separate secret visits to the Romanian dictator, Nicolae Ceausescu, and to the King of Morocco, as well as the secret negotiations between the foreign ministers of Egypt and Israel in mid-September. So it was not quite a bolt-from-the-blue, as people thought, when Sadat announced, on November 9, his willingness to speak directly to the Israelis from the rostrum of the Israeli Knesset. The inspiration for this speech, Sadat tells us, came to him as he was flying back from Romania: "[The] aeroplane was passing over Mount Ararat where Noah's (peace be upon him) ark came to rest and the dove of peace, released from the ark by our forefather Noah, returned with an olive branch as a sign that the flood waters were retreating and that the shore was near . . . And I felt as if all my thoughts were as doves bearing olive branches, and that I had to select one of them."[74]

Out of this reflection came Sadat's decision to announce publicly his willingness to go to Jerusalem. This he did during a speech before the Egyptian parliament on November 9: "I am willing to go to the ends of the earth for peace. Israel will be astonished to hear me say now, before you, that I am prepared to go to their own house, to the Knesset itself, to talk to them."[75] The words were not particularly emphasized or highlighted in his delivery. Although they were greeted with applause by the audience, no particular significance was attached to this, as this audience habitually punctuated all Sadat's speeches with vigorous applause at intervals of short but equal length. (In any case, the sentence about going to the Knesset was deleted from the reports of the speech that appeared in Egypt's official newspapers—on Sadat's own instructions.)[76] Sadat had delayed the proceedings an hour and a half precisely so that Yassir Arafat could attend, and had introduced him as "a dear and wonderful colleague in our struggle." It was noticed that Arafat joined in the applause. But again, no one attached any significance to that, either. Perhaps he was nodding off, awoke to hear applause, and joined in; or perhaps he missed the point. Afterwards, Arafat claimed that he had been set up and betrayed. In any case, there was no personal contact between Arafat and Sadat after that day.[77]

Menachem Begin's initial reaction was skeptical and truculent: "He can come to Geneva . . . [This is] one of Sadat's tricks." But he quickly changed his tune, telling visiting American congressmen on November 10 that if Sadat really intended to visit Jerusalem he would be received "with all the honor befitting a President." Then two days later, in an address on Israeli television, he spoke to "Citizens of Egypt!" "There is no reason whatsoever for hostility between our peoples. . . . Let us only make peace . . . It will be a pleasure to welcome and receive your President with the traditional hospitality you and we have inherited from our common father Abraham." Then he quoted from Sura 5, verse 20, section 4, of the Qur'an: "Recall when Moses said to his people: O my people, remember the goodness of Allah toward you when he appointed prophets amongst you. O my people, enter the holy land which Allah hath written down as yours." [78] On November 15, Begin conveyed to President Carter an invitation for him to convey to Sadat, to address the Knesset.

"This [Sadat's decision to go to Jerusalem], in effect, brought to an end our strategy for going to Geneva," Brzezinski recalls. "For the next several weeks, the United States was largely a spectator." This may well have been Brzezinski's thought at the time, but it was not Jimmy Carter's. Apart from everything else, the Soviet leadership made clear to the president that it would not take kindly to being shouldered out of the Middle East, so soon after the United States had admitted its right and duty to be there—something that gave the president pause.[79] It would, indeed, be a long time after Sadat's speech to the Knesset before the president of the United States could bring himself to admit to himself and the public that Geneva was off. Jimmy Carter had already taken the initiative of appealing privately to the various Arab leaders to utter some words of encouragement to Sadat, and thus to keep Geneva alive.[80] Sadat, too, wanted the Arab leaders to speak up, but to the opposite effect. The trick, for Sadat, was to sabotage Geneva while appearing to be hell-bent on saving it. To ensure that Assad of Syria did so in clear terms, he went directly to Damascus to explain his speech of November 7.[81] As he guessed, Assad was enraged. The official Syrian press described Sadat's initiative as a "painful blow to the Arab nation . . . [It would] give the Zionist enemy gains which it has been unable to obtain in the past thirty years in spite of all the wars it has waged against the Arabs." The response of the PLO's Executive Committee was in the same vein: The Arab nation "will not forgive any ruler" for "apostasy against the dearest and most sacred goals of our people and a defilement of the blood of hundreds of thousands of martyrs who died for Palestinian and Arab land."[82] In the face of these "vituperative attacks" (as Carter calls them) from the Arab leaders, Jimmy Carter then turned to the Soviets, to urge that they use their influence with Arab leaders to the same end. To Carter's disappointment, but nobody's surprise, they would not play.[83]

President Sadat arrived at Ben-Gurion airport outside Tel Aviv as Sabbath ended, 8:03, Saturday, November 19, 1977. He was evidently enchanted by the Egyptian flags that flew everywhere, by the huge signs, in Arabic, that welcomed him to Israel, and thrilled by the Egyptian national anthem flawlessly played by an Israeli army band, and, on his entrance into Jerusalem, by the masses of Israelis of all ages who lined the streets, enthusiastically waving Egyptian and Israeli flags."[84] Sadat's long-anticipated speech before the Knesset was given in Arabic, with simultaneous translation in English, and lasted about an hour.[85] Beginning with the customary Muslim invocation, "In the name of God," he used the first few paragraphs to present an appeal to the shared religious tradition of all his hearers. "I come to you today on solid ground to shape a new life and to establish peace. We all love this land, the land of God, we all, Moslems, Christians and Jews, all worship God." Religion was central to the argument of the address: "It is so fated that my trip to you, which is a journey of peace, coincided with the Islamic feast, the holy Feast of the Sacrifice [Al-Adha] when Abraham—peace be upon him— forefather of the Arabs and Jews, submitted to God, and, not out of weakness but through a giant spiritual force and by free will, sacrificed his very own son, thus personifying a firm and unshakable belief in ideals that have had for mankind a profound significance." Sadat's own *sacrifice* was this trip to Jerusalem. He expected the leaders of Israel to reciprocate in the same spirit and on the same scale. The argument was fortified with many passages from Proverbs, Psalms, and the Prophets (notably, Zechariah) and from the Qur'an. He affirmed his own belief as a Muslim in the missions of Moses and the Prophet Jesus.

The part that Israeli ears were most keen to hear came about one-third of the way through the text, where Sadat, in effect, admitted that the Arabs were partially at fault for having rejected the presence of the Jews from the beginning, and for having refused to talk with them and deal with them since. "In all sincerity I tell you we welcome you among us with full security and safety." No Arab official had dared utter this thought before now. Afterwards, many listeners thought that they had heard the admission of Israel's right to exist as a state, on an equal basis with the Arab states in the region. Others were not so sure; after all, having the right to live in peace "among us" does not amount to having the right to be a sovereign state. What he did say clearly—and perhaps it amounted to the same thing—was that Israel was a *fait accompli*, recognized by the world: "We accept all the guarantees that you want from the two superpowers or from either of them or from the Big Five or from some of them. . . . We agree to any guarantees you accept, because in return we shall receive the same guarantees."

But having said that, Sadat did not again, to Israeli ears at least, concede another thing. "We insist on complete withdrawal from these territories, including Arab Jerusalem." When these words were uttered, Defense Minister Ezer Weizman passed a note to prime minister Begin: "We have to prepare for war." Begin nodded his agreement.[86] "Even the United States of America, your first ally . . . has opted to face up to reality and admit that the Palestinian people are entitled to legitimate rights and that the Palestine problem is the cause and essence of the conflict." He demanded that Israel should withdraw from all Arab lands, including "Arab Jerusalem." By avoiding any language that suggested recognition of Israel as a state, and by evoking the memories of the Caliph Omar (who first conquered Jerusalem for the Arabs in 637) and Saladin (who reconquered it in 1187), Sadat put the Arab title to Jerusalem in terms that Arabs everywhere would applaud. There he stood, inside the tent of Israel, not asking for concessions or listening to arguments, but demanding what was right.

Despite what Sadat said about Omar and Saladin and frequent references to the Arab people, alert Israeli and American listeners extrapolated something crucial from what was *not* said: Although there were many references to "the Palestinians," there was not a single reference to the PLO. Clearly, Sadat regarded himself as free to pursue bilateral diplomacy about Palestine with the State of Israel.

Sadat concluded, as he began, on a note of prayer to God: "From the holy Koran I quote the following verses: 'We believe in God and in what has been revealed to us and what was revealed to Abraham, Ishmael, Isaac, Jacob and the 13 Jewish tribes. And in the books given to Moses and Jesus and the prophets from the Lord.' . . . So we agree, Salam Aleikum—peace be upon you."

With his characteristic narcissism, Sadat, in his memoirs, offers us not a single word of what the Israelis had to say in response—only that "I made my speech, which was followed by speeches from Premier Begin and Opposition leader Peres." Menachem Begin, not having been given an advance text, elected to respond extemporaneously, in Hebrew (again, with simultaneous translation into English). He acknowledged the courage of Sadat's action. "We, the Jews, know how to appreciate such courage." He picked up on the most positive feature of Sadat's message: his thought about "living together." Indeed, "We shall all have to live together in this area forever and ever—the great Arab nation in its various states and countries, and the Jewish nation in its country, the Land of Israel." But Sadat was wrong in stating, as he did, that the Jewish claim stands on the Balfour Declaration of 1917: "No, Mr. President, we did not take strange land, we returned to our homeland. The link between our nation and this land is eternal. Here our prophets prophesied . . . Here the kings of Judea ruled. Here we became a nation . . . And when we were thrust far from our land, we never forgot this land, even for one day. We prayed for her. We longed for her . . . I propose, in the name of the overwhelming majority of this Parliament, that everything will be negotiable."[87]

On the day that Sadat arrived in Jerusalem, President Carter attended a special early morning service at the First Baptist Church in Washington, before watching the arrival ceremonies on television. Speaking to reporters after the service, he struck precisely the same interfaith note that Sadat had struck: "My prayer was one that recognized this whole world wants peace; that Christ, our Savior, is the Prince of Peace; that the Middle East has been particularly afflicted by war, which no one there wanted . . . Prime Minister Begin is a deeply religious man—he and I have pledged privately to pray for one another—and . . . President Sadat is a deeply religious man also. He and I have pledged privately to pray for one another . . . I think the fact that the Arabs, the Moslems, the Jews, the Christians all worship the same God and freely acknowledge it is a binding force that gives an avenue of communication and common purpose."[88] However, after viewing the proceedings on television, Carter, in private, expressed anger at the adamancy of Begin's response.[89] As for Sadat's performance, there was never anything from Carter but praise, privately and publicly expressed. Throughout the Arab world, on the other hand, as Jimmy Carter himself notes, there was nothing but hostility, punctuated by calls for assassination from the highest political and theological authorities. The Arab-American community, too, poured out bitter complaint against Carter for his generous words about Sadat and his initiatives.[90]

Even yet, President Carter was not willing to be freed from the incubus of Geneva. At his news conference of November 30, 1977, he explained: "Obviously, the leaders in Syria, even Jordan, and certainly the PLO have not recognized that Egypt is speaking for them adequately. I think, though, that in his speech to the Knesset, in his follow-up speech to the People's Assembly in Egypt, President Sadat has evoked very clearly the basic Arab position that I have understood in my private conversations with President Assad of Syria and with the King of Jordan, Hussein." Jimmy Carter was probably the only administration figure who was still committed to Geneva. Yet he could think of no better reason for this commitment than the Metternichian one—that it was legitimate. He was aware, he admitted, that "In the past, I think it's accurate to say that the Soviets have not played a constructive role in many instances because they had espoused almost completely the more adamant Arab position." Still, he ruminated aloud, "I don't think they are trying to be an obstacle to peace. Their perspective is just different from ours."[91]

Early in January, Carter told reporters: "I don't think it would be violating any confidences to say that all the Arab leaders with whom I met said they support Sadat unequivocally." While conceding that "Iraq and Libya and the more radical Arabs . . . don't want peace to prevail," he felt able to assure the reporters that Assad of Syria, Hussein of Jordan, and Fahd of Saudi Arabia, "are all perfectly willing to accept Israel now as a permanent entity in the Middle East, living in peace."[92] Carter knew full well that he was clutching at straws. On December 5, 1977, the leaders of Syria, Libya, Algeria, South Yemen, and the PLO, meeting at Tripoli, Libya, declared President Sadat guilty of "high treason against the sacrifices and struggle of our Arab people" and announced their unalterable objection to "the American-Zionist designs aimed at imposing surrender settlements upon the Arab nations . . . and striking against the movement of Arab liberation as a prelude to subjugate the Arab region and to control its destiny and to chain it to international imperialism."[93] This led to immediate severance of diplomatic relations between Egypt on the one hand and the other Arab countries. It was, no doubt, true that the leaders of Jordan, Syria, and Saudi Arabia were simultaneously telling President Carter's emissaries, behind closed doors, of their secret appreciation for his diplomacy, and of their hopes for eventual peace with Israel. But none dared say anything dimly similar out loud, lest he suffer the fate that was now cried down publicly upon Anwar Sadat—and that did eventually befall him.

In light of all this, it was now perfectly safe for President Sadat to announce that, to show his enduring commitment to the Geneva principle, he was inviting all the parties who were scheduled to have been invited to Geneva, to send representatives to a conference in Cairo to help prepare the agenda for the Geneva meeting. Given that all the Arab parties, except Egypt, had already declared their refusal to consider a Geneva Conference (now that Sadat had "betrayed the Arab people"); and given that the Soviet Union now felt that its only hope of staying in the Middle East was to assist the propaganda of the refusing parties—there was no reason for surprise or disappointment when only the representatives of Egypt, Israel, and the United States showed up at the "Cairo Preparatory conference" on December 14, 1977, and closed up shop after a few days without result.[94] Thus Sadat delivered the coup de grace to Geneva.

Ironically, something resembling the Geneva process envisaged in the Soviet-U.S. Joint Statement of October 1977, did take place fourteen years later. This was the Madrid Conference, held in the wake of the Gulf War. Before that moment came, however, much had changed. The Cold War had ended, and so had the Soviet empire. The last president of the Soviet Union was struggling to keep his job and had to be browbeaten by President George Bush into helping him dust off the Geneva machine, kept in UN storage all those years.

By early December 1977, both the Israelis and the Egyptians were assessing the prospects for serious bilateral diplomacy and each now set out to engage the United States as its best friend. In talks with the president at the White House, December 16, 1977,[95] Begin explained that Israel was now ready to give the Sinai back to Egypt, provided that there were the right security guarantees, and to give the Palestinians control over their internal affairs (autonomy), provided Israel could keep a military presence. Thereupon, Jimmy Carter telephoned Anwar Sadat and persuaded him to invite Begin to come to Egypt and present his proposals there. Ezer Weizman recalls: "Menachem Begin fell into the trap and returned from America jubilant, boasting of this success. 'All who beheld it praised it,' he repeatedly declared. Of Carter, Begin said, 'I haven't met such an intellect since Jabotinsky.' What Carter had actually said was, 'It's a very interesting plan.'"[96] Already the Carter administration was sowing skepticism about that plan through the American media.

Menachem Begin had pictured his forthcoming visit to Egypt (December 25–27, 1977) as a splendid public occasion when the Egyptians would balance out Israel's welcome of the Egyptian president just five weeks previous. That is not what happened. Begin was invited not to the Egyptian capital, but to Ismailia, the site of one of Sadat's several mansions. There was no official reception, no playing of national anthems. Egyptian flags were everywhere; Israeli flags were nowhere. Welcome signs did appear along the streets of Ismailia; but they all addressed only to "Sadat, bringer of Peace!" Begin's name did not appear in public. Foreign Minister Dayan noted that Begin was pretending to be oblivious to these insults; and his consternation grew as Sadat set about softening up the prime minister with the familiar snake oil. An unembarrassed nonbeliever, Dayan fought hard to suppress his irritation as the two principals vied to see who could draw the largest number of Biblical allusions into his addresses to each other: "Both managed to draw Moses the Lawgiver into the Ismailia event. Sadat crossed the Red Sea with him, and Begin the wilderness of Sinai. At that point I stopped listening, and conjured up the giant figure of Moses . . . who had borne such heavy burdens on his wilderness trek to the Promised Land, and had reached the threshold, only to be denied entry; Moses, the greatest of our leaders, buried in an anonymous grave."[97] Sadat affected disappointment that Begin had brought him nothing. He repeated the demands he had made from the rostrum of the Knesset: total Israeli withdrawal from the occupied Arab lands, and Palestinian self-determination: Immediately.[98] As nothing else of substance could be agreed upon, there was no communiqué.

Then, within a few days of Begin's return to Jerusalem, scattered verbal explosions carried off the meager accomplishments of the Ismailia conference. Abruptly, Sadat withdrew his foreign minister from discussions with the Israeli foreign minister and the U.S. secretary of state, which had just begun in Jerusalem (January 18, 1978).[99] Explaining his action to the Egyptian People's Assembly, President Sadat said: "I broke off the negotiations because Israel did not agree to withdraw from the Golan, the West Bank and Gaza strip before Sinai." About the same time, Begin read in the controlled Egyptian press that he, Begin, was another Shylock, insisting on his pound of flesh; Sadat should not have embraced him, but should have thrashed him within an inch of his life. Such "slanderous aspersions on the integrity and the dignity of the Jewish people," Begin replied, were of the same kind as Julius Streicher used to fill the columns of *Der Stuermer* in the 1930s. "What was this 'new spirit' we had heard so much about?"[100]

On New Year's Eve 1977 and New Year's Day 1978, President Carter met with King Hussein of Jordan and the Shah of Iran in Iran for a long conversation about the Arab-Israeli situation. The outcome was the familiar one—an expression (in private) of sweetness and light: "All three of us agreed that we ought to give Sadat our support; that the basis for a Middle East peace settlement should be UN Resolutions 242 and 338; that there should be some minor modifications of the 1967 Israeli borders; that the people in the West Bank-Gaza area should have self-determination but not the right to claim independence . . . Both the Shah and King Hussein said that they want to go after I do to Saudi Arabia and to Egypt to try to express support for Sadat."[101] If these words meant anything, the Arab-Israeli conflict was over! How could Israel back away from a united Arab proposal identical to this? Then, on January 3, 1978, in Saudi Arabia, more of the same occurred. Crown Prince Fahd and the Saudi leadership "expressed their unequivocal support for Sadat, because they wanted peace and stability in the region, but [always the same *but!*] merely smiled when I urged them to make this known through their public statements; they did not want to alienate the more militant Arabs." Like all the conservative Arab leaders, the Saudis had come to fear the PLO as a radicalizing, de-stabilizing example for the discontented among their own people. Still, "because of the powerful political influence of the PLO in international councils and the threat of terrorist attacks from some of its forces, few Arabs had the temerity to depart from their original position in a public statement." And, as always, President Carter expressed his understanding. Why President Carter gave the time of day to these two-faced statesmen will always remain a mystery. At least he enjoyed their company, as he did not enjoy the company of Menachem Begin. "The Saudi leaders were knowledgeable, tough negotiators, surprisingly frank, and good-humored."[102] Now he must leave them, and return to the hard work of knocking together the heads of Anwar Sadat and Menachem Begin.

Within a few hours of leaving the Saudi leadership, President Carter was in Aswan, Egypt, where he conveyed briefly to President Sadat the fruit of his discussions with the Iranian, Jordanian, and Saudi leaders. "There were no differences between us [that is, Sadat and Carter]," Carter recalls in his memoirs. To the assembled press Carter announced that the Egyptian position and the American position were "essentially identical . . . [namely,] that Israeli settlements on occupied territory are illegal and that they contravene the Geneva Conference decisions that were made."[103]

Nearly a year had gone by since the election of Menachem Begin. Despite Begin's belief that he was being very forthcoming and creative, Jimmy Carter could see no signs of reformation in Begin at all. It was time to make another effort to mobilize American Jews against the Israeli Government. Complicating this task, however, was the circumstance that the administration was engaged, throughout the early months of 1978, in an effort to persuade Congress to approve a program of sales of the newest arms to Egypt and Saudi Arabia. The Carter administration hit upon the idea of neutralizing (or disarming) the objections that Israelis and American friends of Israel had to sales of major arms to Israel's Arab neighbors by making up what the administration itself called "a package deal": in the same moment, advanced fighter aircraft would be sold to Saudi Arabia and Egypt and to Israel. In preparing his rationale for the arms sales to Saudi Arabia, President Carter emphasized the point that it was all being done for the sake of "the peace process." In a letter to Senator James Abourezk, May 12, 1978, Carter wrote, "Saudi Arabia has become a firm friend of the United States. As its influence dramatically expands in the world, Saudi Arabia has been not only a firm supporter of the peace process but a moderating and conciliatory force on a wide range of global issues . . . If the Saudis are forced to turn elsewhere to meet their defense needs, it will unquestionably impair the peace process. . . . The long-term interests of Israel are served by the proposed sales to Egypt and Saudi Arabia."[104]

While this issue was still hanging fire, Carter seized on the thirtieth anniversary of the founding of the Jewish state to invite some two hundred rabbis to a reception for the visiting Prime Minister Begin at the White House, May 1, 1978. This was not as clearly thought through as might have been, for, as Carter recalls, "twelve hundred people showed up at the gates. We asked all of them in, moving the entire affair out onto the South Lawn." Before this company, Jimmy Carter struck a note not heard in public since November of 1976: "The establishment of the nation of Israel is a fulfillment of biblical prophecy, and the very essence of its fulfillment."[105] A glimpse into the attitudes of Jewish religious leaders of the moment is afforded by the many letters of thanks for this occasion that flowed in afterwards.[106] Many chose the opportunity to comment unfavorably on the president's plans for the sale of arms to the Arab nations. Rabbi David Indich reminded the president of the legacy of Cyrus: "What a shame that you did not live up to that potential. But fortunately for you, it is not too late. You can still be the 'American Cyrus.'" Yet, it was clear that not all American rabbis thought in such biblical terms. Rabbi David Greenberg warned the president about the dangers of religious zeal: "Mr. Begin's emphasis on biblical borders is not only bad theology but an unfortunate impediment to peace." In Jimmy Carter's own summation: "It turned out to be a very positive and heartwarming experience, but had very little effect either in the Middle East or within our country. I still had serious political problems among American Jews, and a few days later we had to postpone two major Democratic fund-raising banquets in New York and Los Angeles because so many party members had cancelled their reservations to attend."[107] This was precisely the nightmare that Brzezinski and Carter had planned to prevent when they put the Middle East at the head of their agenda in the first weeks of the administration.

A few days after the multiplication of the rabbis, the Senate voted down a resolution to stop the sale of arms to Egypt and Saudi Arabia (May 15, 1978); and a few days after that, the president signed the authorizations. About this time, Israeli radio reported rumors that "White House aides Hamilton Jordan and Jody Powell gloated to selected newsmen they had broken the back of the Israeli lobby and are now free to make Mideast policy without outside interference. The men denied those remarks which many in Washington labeled as clearly anti-Semitic. But several authoritative sources in Washington heard them say it."[108] Whatever the truth behind the allegations, it did not sit well within the Carter administration that the Israeli news media had stooped to character assassination of this kind, especially when it might have the effect of further damaging the resources with which the president would have to fight the mid-term battles of the fall.

As Carter's second year in the presidency began, there was every reason to think that, for all the president's interventions during his first year, the prospects for peace in the Middle East were worse, not better. Almost everyone in the inner circle of the Carter administration was inclined to call an end to these efforts at mediation, before American credibility got any further reduced. But Jimmy Carter was not yet ready to let go. In fact, he was inwardly persuaded that these were precisely the conditions out of which diplomatic miracles are made.

A YEAR OF ACCOMPLISHMENT:
CAMP DAVID AND THE ISRAEL-EGYPT PEACE TREATY
(SEPTEMBER 1978 TO FEBRUARY 1979)

In one of his post-presidential books, Jimmy Carter recalls that the idea occurred first to Rosalynn: "I was disappointed at this lack of progress. One day, Rosalynn and I were walking down a woodland path at Camp David, the secluded presidential retreat in Maryland, talking about how beautiful and peaceful it was. Rosalynn said, 'Jimmy, if we could only get Prime Minister Begin and President Sadat up here on this mountain for a few days, I believe they might consider how they could prevent another war between their countries.' That gave me the idea, and a few days later I invited both men to join me for a series of private talks."[109]

Early in August, the decision was made to invite the president of Egypt and the prime minister of Israel to join with the president of the United States in concerted negotiations at the presidential retreat at Camp David, Maryland. Secretary Vance personally carried the letters of invitation to Sadat and Begin, and the three principals made simultaneous public announcements of the plan on August 8, 1978.[110] In their immediate responses to the invitation, the two principals behaved according to form. Sadat was dramatic: This was "the last chance for peace." Begin rejected this thought: "In life," he said, "there are never last chances. There are always new chances." Carter's circle noted these responses, and mentally assigned the first points to the Egyptian side. But in an interview just before departing, Begin was a little more upbeat. He recalled that just a few months ago "a very warm personal relationship" had developed between himself and Sadat, but that this had suffered as result of "some bitter name-calling in Egypt." He would ask President Sadat again, "Let us be friends!"[111] All three principals agreed to refrain from pessimistic predictions. They also agreed that during the conference there would be no contact with the press, other than briefings to be handled exclusively by the White House press officer, Jody Powell.[112]

As a political realist, Jimmy Carter stood head and shoulders above everyone in his circle—Brzezinski, Vance, Jordan, all of them—and therefore did not minimize the risks. If he involved himself again directly, it would mean giving his undivided attention to the issue. It would be like Woodrow Wilson going to Paris and Franklin Roosevelt going to Yalta— with the large difference that the hopes and dreams of the American people themselves did not seem to most people to be directly bound up in this present issue. He would have to convince the American public that it was right for him to take leave of absence, so to speak, from his obligations to run the country at a time when the economy was in shambles, and when the United States was being challenged around the world by the triumphalist foreign policy of Leonid Brezhnev. And if he should take this leave-of-absence and there should be no dramatic advance toward peace (as seemed probable), he would be exposed as a failure on the very eve of mid-term elections.

Foreign policy historian Gaddis Smith writes: "[T]he fact that he devoted thirty percent of his memoirs to the Middle East, and eighty-five pages to Camp David alone, is an accurate measure of his involvement."[113] Even by Carter's heroic standards, the amount of homework he did for this occasion is awe-inspiring. Carter ordered Brzezinski and Vance to produce separate (and massive) briefing books, without consulting each other, so that he would be assured of the widest range of understanding of the issues. He was not much impressed with either of them.[114] In addition to mastering the history behind the issues and the current political, geographical, sociological and other realities, "I studied thick books on the personalities of the two leaders, prepared for me by specialists in the United States intelligence services and the State Department. These books told me about each man's family relationships, religious beliefs, early experiences, health and most important friends; also about how he had won office, how he responded to pressure, and what his hobbies and personal habits were."[115] In addition, he claims, "Before it was all over, I would also have mastered major portions of a good dictionary and thesaurus, and would have become an amateur semanticist as well."[116] Throughout the conference, Carter took notes of everything that was said, and after each session dictated it all to secretaries.[117]

But much more important to the success of the conference than this intellectual preparation was Carter's effort to frame a theological context for the deliberations—one which would inspire the principals to think of themselves as standing under a possibility of not merely human but divine reward or judgment. Accordingly, on the first day of their meeting, the three leaders agreed to the text of a request to the people of the world for prayer for the success of their deliberations. This joint appeal to the world for prayer amounted to the only statement from the principals until the conference ended.[118] (Typically, Carter contrasts Sadat's speedy acquiescence with Begin's insistence on seeing the text of the prayer. "This characteristic response," he notes, "was a prelude to our relationship at Camp David.")[119] As well, the president provided for each contingent to hold religious services at their customary times: Muslims on Friday, Jews on Saturday, and Christians on Sunday, all to be held in the same small room.

The basic difference in approach of the two delegations was manifested immediately on arrival (September 5, 1978)—for those with eyes to see. Begin, on arriving, introduced all members of his party individually to President Carter, describing their offices and responsibilities. Sadat, on the other hand, "walked off at once with the Carters, without so much as a look back at his staff, as if he had been totally unaware of their presence aboard his plane."[120] Carter recalls: "While at Camp David, Sadat wanted to make Egypt's decisions himself; he did not like to have aides present when he was with me, and seemed somewhat uncomfortable when they were around him. His closest advisers, the Vice President and Prime Minister, were in Cairo managing the affairs of Egypt. Throughout our stay at Camp David, Sadat spent little time with his staff. In contrast, Begin relied heavily on his aides and advisers . . . [I]n Sadat's case, the leader was much more forthcoming than his chief advisers, and in Begin's case, the advisers were more inclined to work out difficult problems than was their leader."[121]

To some degree, no doubt, the difference in behavior recorded here reflects difference in personalities; and it is merely in these terms that Carter presents the picture. But to a much greater degree it reflects the differences in constitutional realities—the difference between a parliamentary democracy and a single-party authoritarian state. In a setting like the present one, there are advantages enjoyed by the man who is "the whole works." This fundamental contrast in the constitutional character of Arab regimes on the one hand and that of Israel on the other has always been a feature of the drama of American's dealings with the players in the Middle East. But crammed into this "wooden O," the tiny stage of Camp David, its effects were dramatically obvious.

On arrival, Sadat was, as always, effusively friendly. Carter saw at once that he was "eager to conclude a total settlement of the issues, not merely to establish general procedures for the future. He was convinced that Begin did not want an agreement and would try to delay progress as much as possible." He told Carter: "I will try to protect you by putting forward good proposals and make it unnecessary for any United States proposals to be offered." Begin, by contrast, though courteous, was restrained in making his greetings, and clearly determined to resist the "atmosphere of informality," which, Carter recalls, "I had wanted to generate." Begin immediately wanted to talk about formalities: procedures to be followed, the time and place of meetings, keeping of records, and so forth.

Begin expressed disappointment that Sadat had announced he was too tired to begin immediately. So Jimmy Carter spent the first evening being talked to by Menachem Begin—always a downer for the president. Carter's recollection of the moment has a petty quality: "Begin . . . seemed to look on himself as a man of destiny, cast in a biblical role as one charged with the future of God's chosen people." Begin launched into a tedious résumé of the 3,000 years of Jewish history. Carter noticed that Begin "always referred to the West Bank by the two biblical names [Judea and Samaria]—I presume to engender the notion that this was the promised land which God Himself had given to the Jews." As for the present business, it was "the old Israeli negotiating positions."[122]

Jimmy Carter admits that he did not have a clear idea, in advance, of how long they would all being staying at Camp David: perhaps "three days, or a little longer if necessary. We never imagined it would take thirteen long, hard days and nights before an agreement would be finally reached."[123] All in all, it is to Carter's credit that he did not intend to force a result by setting up a time-clock. In the end, as we shall see, it probably helped a great deal that he was able to build up in the hearts of the two principals some sense of obligation to him and to the United States by rescheduling his commitments from day to day until a result was achieved.

At the first session of the principals, Begin dwelt upon how difficult it was all going to be, given the many, many matters at issue. But he concluded his opening remarks with the thought that Egypt and Israel needed to turn the page of history, and make a new beginning. At first, Sadat responded in like spirit, and there were several somewhat unfocused exchanges. Then Sadat asked leave to make a prepared statement—which proved to be a recital of all the grievances of the Arab people since the dawn of time and all the demands that Sadat had made back in November at the Knesset's rostrum. They had not been improved an iota by the months of coming and going of Israeli and Egyptian negotiators and American messengers. Carter had been given a preview by Sadat in their late morning meeting, and had been disappointed by its adamancy. Sadat had explained, however, that (in Carter's words) he "wanted a strong initial proposal on the record, to appease his fellow Egyptians and the Arab world, but during the negotiations he would be willing to make major concessions (within carefully prescribed limits), so that his final proposal would prove to everyone the reasonableness of his approach." To avert the explosion that he expected on the other side of the table, President Carter made a little joke "that if he [Begin] would sign the document as written, it would save us all a lot of time." Then he thanked President Sadat for all the work that had gone into his presentation.

Begin, however, was not unhappy in the least: He was convinced that Sadat's performance had tipped the scales of moral advantage to the Israeli side. Jimmy Carter, who had never dealt with Middle Eastern rug merchants, was at first puzzled by Begin's complacent response; but, later it struck him: "Begin had been relieved because it was so ridiculously harsh."[124] Thereafter, Begin carried around a copy of Sadat's statement, and would shake it under Carter's nose from time to time. When Carter tried to assure him that these were not to be taken with full seriousness—that Sadat, in conversations with him, had indicated his intention to retreat from them—Begin retorted: "I do not see how honorable men can put forward one thing publicly and say a different thing privately."[125]

At the second meeting of the three principals, Carter, Begin, and Sadat, there was a heated exchange. Among other unpromising subjects, they got onto the matter of who had conquered whom. They actually got to pointing fingers and pounding tables.[126] At one point, Begin noted that Israel had given a warm welcome to Sadat, who had so recently "feigned routine autumn maneuvers and then deliberately attacked us at the precise moment he knew that we would be in our synagogues." This was a "strategic deception," Sadat explained. "Deception is deception," was Begin's reply.[127] At another point, Sadat shouted, "Premier Begin, you want land!" He spoke of "the Israeli settlements on my land!" "All restraint was now gone," Carter recalls. "Their faces were flushed, and the niceties of diplomatic language and protocol were stripped away." Carter found it hard to fathom this behavior—especially as, occasionally, there were inappropriate and irrelevant outbursts of laughter; for example, after each had accused the other of being behind the hashish trade through the Sinai! After much talking over each other's heads, Sadat announced angrily that it was all over, and stood up to leave. Soon, both principals were headed for the door, and it became necessary for President Carter literally to dash to the door ahead of them to bar the way. Without looking at each other again, each reluctantly pledged to stay at Camp David a little longer and then left the room.

Before they left, Carter volunteered to draw up a list of all the things about which they disagreed. It was a long list. It was, in short, everything. Carter now decided that there must be no more direct meetings of the principals. Despite his hopes, despite all the parade of "informality," and despite the effort at first-naming, the two were "personally incompatible."[128] Apart from Sunday afternoon, when they all took time out to have a tour of the Battlefield at Gettysburg, Sadat and Begin were never again in the same place at the same. So the president shaped up a new "negotiating technique," which, he says, "eventually opened up the road to an agreement . . . I would draft a proposal I considered reasonable, take it to Sadat for quick approval or slight modification, and then spend hours or days working on the same point with the Israeli delegation . . . I was never far from a good dictionary and thesaurus. . . . Would the Israelis withdraw 'out of' certain areas or 'into' military encampments? What was meant by 'autonomy,' 'self-rule,' 'devolution,' 'Palestinian people,' 'authority,' 'minor modifications,' 'refugees,' 'insure, ensure, or guarantee,' and so forth. The Egyptians were never involved in these kinds of discussions with me. On any controversial issue, I never consulted Sadat's aides, but always went directly to their leader."[129]

Apart from one lengthy meeting with the whole Egyptian delegation at the end of the third day (September 8, during which Sadat appears to have done almost all the talking), Carter's dealings with the Egyptians were, in fact, dealings with Sadat (that is, one-on-one), as, in effect, they had been since February of 1977. Carter's dealings with the Israelis were quite different. On the evening of the first session, the U.S. delegation decided that in the days ahead they would divide their resources and recombine in a variety of dialogues with several members of the Israeli delegation, as opportunity afforded. Thus, in the days that followed, Vance, Brzezinski, and Brown met with Weizman, Dayan, and Attorney General Aharon Barak in various combinations and permutations. It should be noted that Begin did not merely permit but actually encouraged these dealings between the members of the U.S. team and individual members of his own. Likewise, he encouraged members of his delegation to deal alone with Sadat. Thus, Sadat met privately with Defense Minister Weizman and also with Dayan.[130] After a few more days of this, Carter was doing everything possible not to deal with Begin, dealing only with Dayan, Weizman, and Barak. (At one point, Jimmy Carter revealed to Rosalynn his conviction that "Begin is a psycho.")[131]

For Begin personally, although not for Weizman or Dayan, the toughest issue of all was the settlements—both those in the Gaza Strip and West Bank, which Israel intended to go on governing, and those in Sinai, which Egypt would soon be governing if there was to be an agreement. Begin had told Brzezinski: "My right eye will fall out, my right hand will fall off, before I ever agree to the dismantling of a single Jewish settlement."[132] He literally begged Carter not to ask him, before the Egyptians, to consider this matter, as he was bound by a religious oath and no longer had the freedom even to talk about it. Both Weizman and Dayan, however, although differing between them on the specifics, believed there were ways to minimize, if not to eliminate altogether, the offensive aspect of the settlements. Both agreed that the tiny Sinai settlements could be traded away in return for effective demilitarizing of the Sinai, supported by ironclad American guarantees and American financial compensation for the purpose of building new airbases in the Negev and to compensate for loss of the economic benefits from the Sinai (oil, tourism, etc.). As for the settlements in the West Bank and Gaza, perhaps the civilian settlements could be plucked out, leaving only a few, which would essentially be living quarters for small military units, thereby retaining (in fact, improving) the security value with a smaller Israeli presence. Ariel Sharon, the minister of agriculture, phoned from Israel at one point to tell Begin that he would approve the dismantling of the Sinai settlements if this stood in the way of a peace agreement.[133] Sharon's response was surprising because he was responsible for decisions about settlement-building and because he had long been regarded as the most absolute believer in the right of Israelis to build as they wished.

On the evening of Tuesday, September 12, Carter reluctantly agreed to Begin's request for a serious talk—in fact, "the most serious talk I have ever had in my life, except once when I discussed the future of Israel with Jabotinsky." It was very heavy going. They disagreed fundamentally about the interpretation of UN Resolution 242—now an important point, because under Carter's proposals there was to be, in the statement of agreement at the end of the conference, some reference to this Resolution and how it governed their present and future decisions. There was still disagreement over details of "autonomy." At the mention of Jerusalem, Begin explained that his position was exactly that of King David: "*If I forget thee, O Jerusalem, let my right hand forget her cunning.*" And they disagreed more than ever, it seemed, about the Sinai settlements. When Begin told Carter that he was constrained on all these matters by his responsibility to represent the will of the Israeli people, Carter hit him over the head (figuratively) with polls that, he alleged, showed that the majority of Israelis wanted a peace treaty and were prepared to trade away the Sinai and the Sinai settlements to have it. "I was distressed by his attitude, and, perhaps ill-advisedly, said that my position represented the Israeli people better than his."

On Friday, the eleventh day, "I informed everyone that I would have to return to the White House on Sunday, the thirteenth day, and this ultimatum fixed a final deadline for our talks." But on that same day, both Sadat and Begin took back from their subordinates much of the compromising language, and sent the documents back to Carter so mutilated that Carter momentarily considered announcing defeat. A draft statement admitting the failure was drawn up by Carter, and accepted by Sadat and Begin.

At this moment (Friday morning), news was brought to Carter that Sadat was leaving. The helicopter had been ordered and he was packing.

It was a terrible moment. Now, even my hopes for a harmonious departure were gone. I sat quietly and assessed the significance of this development—a rupture between Sadat and me, and its consequences for my country and for the Middle East power balance. I envisioned the ultimate alliance of most of the Arab nations to the Soviet Union, perhaps joined by Egypt after a few months had passed. I told Vance that the best thing for us to do now, to salvage what we could, would be to refuse to sign any document with either country—just to terminate the talks and announce that we had all done our best and failed.

Then I asked Brown and Vance to leave me. When they were gone, I remained alone in the little study where most of the negotiations had taken place. I moved over to the window and looked out to the Catoctin Mountains and prayed fervently for a few minutes that somehow we could find peace.

Then he marched over to Sadat's cabin and talked him out of leaving.

That night Sadat and Carter watched the prizefights on television. Mohammed Ali defeated Leon Spinks, and received a phone call of congratulations from the two presidents at 1:30 a.m.[134]

On the morning of Saturday, September 16, Carter had separate interviews with the two principals—first with Sadat, then with Begin.[135] Carter brought with him two documents that had been worked out without Begin's involvement since Tuesday: one was a document about Sinai; the other was "A Framework for Peace."[136] As for the Sinai settlements, about which Begin was insisting that he was bound in a personal, religiously binding oath, a solution was put forth: when Begin presented this part of the agreement to the Knesset he would declare that he was free to vote against it. Dayan, Weizman, and the other Israelis had already assured Carter and the Americans that the majority in the Knesset would vote for it, because it was a move known to be popular with the Israeli public.

The "Framework" included an undertaking to work toward autonomy for the Palestinians, which, it was stated, would require the cooperation of Jordan and of the Palestinians and which provided for the involvement of other countries neighboring Israel in the peace process. In order not to make solution of these matters any harder, Israel undertook to make no further Jewish settlements in the West Bank while the negotiations leading to an Israeli-Egyptian Peace Treaty were incomplete: This undertaking was contained in a letter between Carter and Begin, to be made public later. (This would present great problems in the weeks following Camp David, as we shall see.)

Included in the draft of the "Framework" was a paragraph about Jerusalem. It is called a city of peace, holy to Judaism, Christianity, and Islam. All persons shall have free access to it, free exercise of worship, and the right to visit and travel to the holy places without distinction or discrimination. It was agreed that Jerusalem would never again be a divided city and that the holy places of each faith should be under the administration and full authority of their representatives, that a municipal council drawn from the inhabitants should supervise the affairs of the city. But here a complication arose. The principal obstacle in the way of getting agreement on anything more specific than these platitudes was the American position! For thirty years now, the United States had supported the official United Nations view that Jerusalem should be internationalized, and therefore that Israel's incorporation of East Jerusalem into the larger city was illegal. Sadat wanted language pledging "return" of the Holy City to a sovereign Palestine. Israel wanted recognition of its sovereignty over Jerusalem. The solution that the Americans were proposing was that President Carter and President Sadat should write official letters to each other, each stating his government's view—which exchange would appear among the official documents of the conference. Israel would not be expected to agree to this language, or even to respond. But the letters would be part of the record. When Carter proposed this device, Begin rejected it.

President Sadat understood the risk of angering other Arabs and Muslims by failing to get Israel to agree in principle to end its occupation of East Jerusalem (including the Old City). Still, given that this was an issue on which there were no substantial differences within the Israel delegation, nor within the Israeli public, there was no possibility of getting

Begin to sign a statement regarding Jerusalem that could satisfy Muslims. The other participants noted that Sadat's pursuit of this issue was by no means as wholehearted as his pursuit of the matter of Palestinian self-rule, let alone the matter of Sinai. But Jimmy Carter would not let the matter go! Somehow, the Jerusalem issue was more important to President Carter than to President Sadat.

The key to this anomaly is that Jimmy Carter *alone of the three principals* still needed to pretend that the Camp David meetings was a prelude to a larger "comprehensive" settlement. Believing that the Arab and the Muslim world was as serious as it claimed to be about its "rights" to East Jerusalem, Carter had all along believed that it was an absolute requirement for the *United States,* whatever Egypt or Israel felt, to have in the package something reflecting the fidelity of the United States to its position, stated again and again in the UN, that Israeli occupation of East Jerusalem was illegal, and that this issue was thus a fit matter for present and future diplomacy. This, Carter must have thought, was the minimum proof he must have of his prowess as a champion of Muslim rights, without which he could not return to the work of bringing Saudi Arabia and other "moderate" Arab states into "the peace process."

Thus, we must note carefully that when Jimmy Carter made that famous walk over to the cabin that housed Prime Minister Begin, it was to get his approval *of this matter only*—that is, to the inclusion (on the side) of an exchange of letters between Egypt and the United States about Jerusalem. The other issues were now behind them. This story is told at length in *Keeping Faith*,[137] and at even greater length on a recording, in his own voice, over and over again, hundreds of times every day, at the Camp David exhibit at the Jimmy Carter Museum in Atlanta. The version in *Talking Peace* (1993) reads,

> In the end, something unexpected almost miraculously helped to break the deadlock. We had made some photos of the three of us, and Begin had asked me to sign one for each of his eight grandchildren. Sadat had already signed them. My secretary suggested that I personalize them, and on each photograph I wrote in the name of one grandchild above my signature. Although Begin had become quite unfriendly toward me because of the pressure I was putting on him and Sadat, I decided to take the photographs over to his cabin personally. As he looked at the pictures and read the names aloud, he became very emotional. He was thinking, I am sure, about his responsibility to his people and about what happens to children in war. Both of us had tears in our eyes. He promised to review the language of my latest revision.[138]

Moments later, Begin called Carter at his cabin to state that he had changed his mind: He would now agree to accept the letters on Jerusalem into the record. This removed the last obstacle to signing the accords.

Speaking at the televised signing ceremony in the White House, on Sunday, September 17, 1977,[139] President Carter recalled that, "When we first arrived at Camp David, the first thing upon which we agreed was to the people of the world to pray that our negotiations would be successful. These prayers have been answered far beyond our expectations." President Sadat, responding, did not refer at all to Menachem Begin or to the State of Israel, contenting himself with thanking "Dear President Carter." In contrast, Prime Minister Begin addressed his remarks not only to President Carter but also to "Mr. President of the Arab Republic of Egypt." "We had some difficult moments," he revealed. "But ultimately, ladies and gentlemen, the President of the United States won the day." As for "my friend, President Sadat . . . we met for the first time in our lives, last November, in Jerusalem. He came to us as a guest, a former enemy, and during our first meeting we became friends. In the Jewish teachings, there is a tradition that the greatest achievement of a human being is to turn his enemy in to a friend, and this we do in reciprocity."

The next day, Sadat and Begin attended a joint session of Congress where President Carter presented his report.[140]

Finally, let me say that for many years the Middle East has been a textbook for pessimism, a demonstration that diplomatic ingenuity was no match for intractable human conflicts. Today we are privileged to see the chance for one of the sometimes rare, bright moments in human history—a chance that may offer the way to peace . . . The prayers at Camp David were the same as those of the shepherd King David, who prayed in the 85th Psalm, "Wilt thou not revive us again: that thy people may rejoice in thee? . . . I will hear what God the Lord will speak: for he will speak peace unto his people, and unto his saints; but let them not return again to folly."

And I would like to say, as a Christian, to these two friends of mine, the words of Jesus, "Blessed are the peacemakers, for they shall be the children of God."

A mountain of congratulatory telegrams grew up in the next few days.[141] No doubt, the accolades were deserved. After a decent interval, however, commentators began to note that the Camp David settlement was going to prove enormously costly to the American taxpayer. In fact, "Carter, despite repeatedly insisting that he was not going to 'buy' Middle East peace, ended up spending more than $5 billion to cement the Camp David accords."[142] This figure includes $3 billion to build new Israeli airbases to replace those surrendered in the Sinai. During the remainder of Jimmy Carter's term, military and economic aid to Israel was greatly increased, and Egypt now became the second greatest recipient of U.S. aid.

Despite what the world may have thought it heard on September 17 and September 18, the spirit of Camp David had done nothing to alleviate Jimmy Carter's suspicious attitude toward Menachem Begin. Reverting to his old ways, Carter immediately set about trying to gain more leverage against the Israeli government by calling "key Jewish leaders" to a meeting with himself (September 19).[143] The hubris virtually oozes from his diary entry on the meeting: It had been "delightful, full of fun and good cheer . . . I pointed out in a nice way that the controversies that I had put on the table that caused the strain had been the source of ultimate success, and hoped that they would not only work to repair the political damage, but to restrain Begin, who is acting in a completely irresponsible way."[144]

On Sunday, September 24, the Israeli Cabinet accepted the Camp David Accords, eleven to two, with three abstentions. On Monday, September 25, Prime Minister Begin presented the Accords to the Knesset, where, after some seventeen hours of debate, they were approved eighty-four to nineteen, with seventeen abstentions (September 28, 1978).[145] Some further six weeks of haggling were required before Egyptian and Israeli foreign ministers, meeting in Washington, could come up with the text of a draft for a peace treaty. At the last minute, the government of Egypt rejected it, calling for clarifications and modifications.[146] It was now clear that Menachem Begin was far more eager to have the peace treaty signed than Anwar Sadat was. Sadat knew that the deed would amount to burning the last symbolic bridge of Egyptian solidarity with the rest of the Arab world, which was still dedicated to the Three Noes announced at the Arab summit in Khartoum.

Any fair-minded reader of the record between September of 1978 and March of 1979 will discover that President Sadat was at least a match for Prime Minister Begin in raising ever new difficulties about ratifying the accords and proceeding toward signature of the treaty. Carter's previously demonstrated tendency to side with Sadat's interpretation of things would get steadily more pronounced and the patience of American friends of Israel would eventually wear very thin—to the point (as we shall see) of causing grave harm to Carter in the domestic political arena. At a press conference (December 7, 1978), when reporters asked, "Would you consider the establishment of four new settlements on the West Bank to be a violation of the Camp David agreements?" Carter answered promptly:

Yes, I would. My interpretation of the Camp David agreements—and, as you know, Prime Minister Menachem Begin disagrees with this interpretation—is that there was a moratorium on the establishment of new settlements until the agreements had been reached on how to establish the autonomous government in the West Bank and the Gaza Strip . . . I might say I don't want that to be an obstacle to the Egyptian and Israeli peace progress. But that's my own personal opinion, and that's my recollection of what occurred at Camp David. It's the only extant difference, and it's already been explored in the press.[147]

We know from Carter's memoirs and from documents in the Jimmy Carter Library that he felt even more strongly about this matter: that Begin was "continu[ing] to disavow the basic principles of the accord."[148] Pro-Israeli elements in the United States now denounced Carter for abandoning Israel and embracing Sadat.[149] Speaking before the Conference of Presidents of Major Jewish Organizations, on December 18, 1978, the retiring Israeli ambassador to the United States, Simcha Dinitz, criticized President Carter for issuing "an ultimatum."[150]

By the end of the year, it looked as though the Camp David process had ground to a halt. Perhaps the situation was worse than *before* Camp David! Perhaps it was even worse than it had been a whole year ago, when the euphoria following Sadat's visit to Jerusalem was already succumbing to the effects of the debacle of the personal diplomacy between Sadat and Begin. And the worst part of all was that this moment of apparent failure of the Camp David process, the one shining moment in the Carter presidency to date, now coincided with the first moments of a foreign policy problem that would soon turn into a nightmare and would ultimately defeat Carter's bid for reelection two years later. In Iran, the regime of Shah Reza Pahlevi had begun to totter. In January 1979 the Shah was forced out, and a few weeks thereafter, the Islamist regime of the Ayatollah Khomeini took over. Within months, Iraq and Iran would be in an all-out war.

On December 27, 1979, Soviet troops invaded Afghanistan, making it (so it appeared) the first Middle Eastern state to be actually clawed into the empire of Communism. Would Iran be next? All these happenings seemed to expose the incompleteness of American understanding of the forces that governed political life in the Middle East. Why on earth should anyone imagine that Jimmy Carter understood these forces better than anyone else—given that he had uttered so much anodyne nonsense in recent months about the forces of stability represented by his "friend," the Shah of Iran? Coincidentally, serious cracks suddenly appeared in the facade of detente with the Soviet Union. As the world seemed to be getting more and more out of American control, it became more and more important for Jimmy Carter to rescue the one authentic ornament of his foreign policy: the Camp David Process.

The target date envisaged at Camp David for signature of the Treaty of Mutual Recognition between Israel and Egypt (mid-December 1978) was missed. Friends of Israel in the media and in politics believed that this was because of the President's pro-Egyptian bias. On December 21, Congressman Jonathan B. Bingham, from the Twenty-second District of New York, wrote to the president: "There seems to have been a clear shift in the United States' role from that of a mediator to that of a special pleader for the Egyptian position. . . . You, yourself, have called the Egyptian position 'very generous.' Statements by yourself, Secretary Vance, Jody Powell and others make it clear that your Administration blames Israel for the current deadlock."[151] Many other congressmen and senators spoke out in the same vein about the issue.

Only another exercise in personal diplomacy could save the situation. On March 5, 1979, therefore, President Carter announced that he had decided to go directly to the scene.[152] Carter's first stop was in Egypt (March 8–10, 1979), where he was met by wildly cheering crowds in Cairo and in Alexandria. (We have already made note of this occasion.) The American president made the following statement to the People's Assembly, March 10, 1979:

> We who are engaged in this great work, the work of peace, are of varied faiths. Some of us are Moslems; some are Jews; some are Christians. The forms of our faith are different. We worship the same God . . . I would like to quote the words of the Holy Koran: "If thine adversary incline towards peace, do thou also incline towards peace and trust in God, for he is the one that heareth and knoweth all things." . . . Now I would like to quote from the words of the Old Testament: "Depart from evil and do good; seek peace, and pursue it." And now I would like to quote from the words of Jesus in the Sermon on the Mount: "Blessed are the peacemakers, for they shall be called the children of God."

Carter recalls that Sadat proved to be most cooperative. "In my private visits with Sadat he emphasized again and again that his main concern was about me, and that he wanted my trip to be a 'smashing success.' But he directed me to negotiate fairly, in the best interests of Egypt and Israel. It was imperative to him that the United States and Egypt stand together, no matter what might be the outcome of the negotiations." Sadat did, however, caution Carter, before he headed off to see Menachem Begin, that "Begin may wish to back out if he gets a chance, or wait until after 1980 when there is a President in the White House who may not be so equally balanced between the Israeli and Arab interests."[153] Then he signed on to the memorandum that Carter said represented Begin's terms for proceeding with a Peace Treaty, as outlined to him in talks in Washington talks just a few days previous.

In Jerusalem (March 10–13, 1979), the American president found a much more subdued reception. To Carter's great astonishment and even greater annoyance, Prime Minister Begin, in the privacy of the latter's study in his home in Jerusalem, now told him that the document he had shown to Sadat and that Sadat had approved needed to be discussed and approved by the cabinet and the Knesset, before he, as prime minister, could sign on. This made no sense to Carter, other than as a tactic to escape from a commitment. Zbigniew Brzezinski recorded in his journal that day "the enormous contrast between a dialogue involving Begin and Carter and one between Carter and Sadat[:] . . . Carter's discussions with Sadat were punctuated by comments such as 'I will represent your interests as if they were my own. You are my brother.' Or Sadat saying to the President, 'My people admire you. I shall always be proud of your friendship, of our brotherhood.' Carter to Sadat: 'I hope I will never let you down. You are probably the most admired statesman in the United States.' Sadat to Carter: 'My people and I are grateful to you.' In contrast, exchanges between Carter and Begin were icy, and even mutual praise was formalistic and devoid of personal feeling."[154]

The next morning, Carter took aside the president of Israel and secured his assurance that Begin had misstated his constitutional obligations. Nonetheless, Carter agreed to pay the price of attending the Israeli cabinet meeting. "Begin asked me to preside over the cabinet meeting," Carter recalled, "and in spite of many interruptions, I finally completed my remarks." Then followed "hours talking about the difference between 'derogate,' 'is not consistent with,' and 'contravene.' The only thing we accomplished during the entire afternoon was to agree on 'contravene'!" Then on Monday, there was a second cabinet meeting, followed by an appearance before the Knesset. Carter was appalled by the noisy carrying-on of the members. In addition to many meetings of Americans and Israelis in various subgroups, there was a meeting of the president with the Foreign Relations Committee, which was no more decorous. Carter thought that all the noise meant that he had failed. He was preparing to draft a statement explaining his defeat, when word came that Begin had now accepted the document signed by Sadat, with a few qualifications.

Carter flew back to Cairo at once (March 13) to present Sadat with the results of his personal diplomacy. Carter recalls: "I told him, 'You will be pleased.' He responded, 'My people in Egypt are furious at how the Israelis have treated our friend Jimmy Carter.' I answered, 'It wasn't bad.'"[155] Sadat gave his agreement without further fuss.

On March 26, 1979, the formal signing of the treaty took place on the South Lawn of the White House.[156]

CARTER'S EFFORTS TO BRING ARAB REGIMES ON-SIDE

Jimmy Carter never gave up on his mission to win the goodwill of the Arab dictators. During the last months of 1978, as he had done in the early months of 1977, he met personally with as many of them as he could and set his secretary of state upon the others. Carter's determination to bring Jordan on board nearly wrecked the process. His attempts to explain to King Hussein how the mechanism for Palestinian autonomy would actually work led to denunciations by the Israelis (because he seemed to minimize Israel's continuing security role in the area) and by the PLO (because it countenanced a security role for Israel at all.) These two parties, the Kingdom of Jordan and the PLO, now publicly buried the hatchet (which they had been brandishing since Black September 1970) and agreed that it was the PLO that rightfully spoke for the Palestinian nation.[157] Carter's effort at seduction of the Jordanians had backfired, the PLO was violently denouncing the agreements, and no Palestinian notable would dare get out of line with Arafat. In light of these events, Israel could now argue that no practical steps were possible along the road to autonomy, while continuing to enjoy the luxury of declaring her commitment in principle to that goal.

As he had always done, President Carter went on giving credence to "private messages to us [which] made it clear that the Saudis were supportive of the peace process," that Assad of Syria was "cautious but leaving the door open, not wishing to be cast alone to the Soviets;" and that "King Hussein seemed to be interested and constructive."[158] In October, the Crown Prince of Saudi Arabia told him (in the utmost confidence of course) "that your speech at the opening of the peace talks had been the final convincing argument that the Palestinians should accept the Camp David formula." Fahd gave his personal assurances that "the Saudis would try to hold the Arab nations together in a positive attitude toward us and Egypt during a forthcoming meeting of Arab leaders in Iraq early in November."[159] Sure enough, when the Arab nations held their summit in Baghdad (November 1–5, 1978), the Saudis gave no hint of the things they had been saying to Jimmy Carter, but joined in, without dissent, in condemnation of the Camp David Agreements. The oil-rich states raised their subsidies to the front-line anti-Zionist states (Syria, Jordan, and the PLO), while a parallel effort was apparently made in secret to bribe Sadat of Egypt away from his Camp David commitments.[160] Carter, always ready to forgive the gracious Saudis, puts the best light on this performance: "They maintained to us, perhaps accurately, that the conference would have been much more drastic without their moderating influence."[161] This thinking ignores the fact that Saudi money kept the PLO alive and massively contributed to the budgets of Syria and several other Arab countries, not to mention Arab and Muslim causes of all kinds. Contrary to what Jimmy Carter pretended to believe, in this company the vote of Saudi Arabia was the vote of all. Meanwhile, Soviet president, Leonid Brezhnev, still resentful at the collapse of the Geneva initiative a year earlier, wrote to President Carter "to urge me" (Carter recalls) "to abandon the Camp David process and return to the Geneva Conference format."[162]

Still Carter imagined that the actual signing of the treaty between Israel and Egypt (March 1979) would succeed, where the Camp David Accords had failed, in enticing the Arab states to come out of the closet. Instead, yet another Arab summit was held, following which fifteen Arab states withdrew their diplomatic relations with Egypt (April 19, 1979). Saudi Arabia showed not the least loyalty to Jimmy Carter, joining the Arab condemnations and the diplomatic quarantine and afterwards leading the way in OPEC's production decisions, which resulted in the tripling of world oil prices during 1979.[163] Still, speaking to a reporter from Israeli television a few days later, the president said he anticipated that Syria, Jordan, and Saudi Arabia would soon want to cooperate in the peace process, "when it becomes evident that the advantages of peace directly improve the quality of life of the Israelis and the Egyptians."[164]

President Carter never gave up hope that President Assad of Syria could be recruited, eventually, for the peace process. In the meanwhile, nothing must be done to cause Assad unnecessary offense. While Assad went on drawing down financial support and military support from the Soviet Union; while he continued to expand the training camps for terrorists on his soil and to subsidize their work abroad; while he went on expanding his empire within Lebanon—Carter, for his part, continued to keep a light in the window. During October 1978, in the immediate wake of the Camp David negotiations, Chairman Clarence Long of the Foreign Operations Subcommittee of the House Committee on Appropriations expressed his disapproval of the government's intention to provide some $90 million in "economic support funds" for Syria. Carter wrote to him to try to help him see how this must look to the people of Syria: "During the negotiations to implement the Camp David accords, it is very important to have an awareness in Syria and other Arab countries that we are fair, and they have confidence in us."[165]

JIMMY CARTER AND THE PLO

In the summer of 1979, Egypt and Israel began their negotiations to work out the conditions for the Palestinian autonomy to which they had committed in the Camp David Accords. In August 1979, Carter appointed Robert Strauss, a wealthy Texas oil magnate and a Jew, as his "Ambassador at Large for the Middle East Negotiations."[166] As the Israelis had suspected all along, Sadat now showed, in private, little interest in this matter, about which he had been making so much righteous fuss over the preceding two years. American officials now began to note "the contempt with which he [Sadat] spoke of his fellow Arabs. He kept referring to them as nomads or Bedouin who count for little."[167] Quite apart from this, Egypt had no authority to speak for the Palestinians, as the PLO, Jordan, and the rest of the Arab world was now in formal assembly committed against the Camp David process and united on the principle that only the PLO spoke for the Palestinians. During negotiations with Israel, Egypt adopted a maximalist approach, demanding more from "autonomy" than Israel had ever contemplated. Israel's strategy was to appear to take the discussions more seriously than it really did, in the hope that world opinion would give it points for goodwill—confident, at the same time, that the Palestinian/Arab side would not get its act together soon enough to pick up on any opportunities that Israeli concessions appeared to afford.

Publicly, Carter had always spoken harshly of the PLO and its leader, Yassir Arafat. Arafat's response to Camp David was that it was "a dirty deal and Carter will pay for it"[168]—which, in Arafat's normal usage, was a call for his assassination. At about the same time, Carter compared the PLO to the Ku Klux Klan.[169] But then, in August 1979, Carter was quoted as saying that the Palestinian cause was like "the civil rights movement in the United States."[170] What was going on? In response to the predictable outrage of Israelis and pro-Israeli Americans, Carter now sought an early opportunity to say: "I am against any creation of a separate Palestinian state."[171] Then, almost immediately, the president was at work on an amendment to UN Resolution 242, which would, in effect, commit the world body (and thus Israel) to finding an answer to "Palestinian rights," and thus (the logic ran) make it possible for the PLO to accept 242 and 338, and thus bring the PLO into the peace process. The Israelis soon made it clear that they would stop talking to Ambassador Strauss if the Carter administration continued down this path.[172]

From time to time, official and unofficial emissaries of the Carter administration would bring the president news that Arafat secretly admired him and would choose an opportune moment to say an encouraging word about the peace process. But Arafat's *public* reaction to Sadat's initiative in November 1977 and then to the Camp David Accords was so violent that Carter seemed to have put that hope out of his mind for the time being. Israelis and American friends of Israel were never entirely confident, however, that Carter was clean on the PLO issue. Many guessed (correctly) that, like other presidents before him, Carter had ways of getting messages to and from the PLO leadership without actually letting his own people *meet* with them.[173] They also guessed that there were people in his official family who wanted to come out of the closet on this issue. The more straightforward of these advisers used the argument that it would serve the cause of peace for the United States to talk with the less-than-lovely but politically relevant PLO, and that the administration would score points with the American public for being frank about it. There were even some around Carter who liked to think in Progressive–Third World terms, and saw something romantic in the PLO's ongoing guerrilla war. (These advisers had soul mates in other corners of the foreign policy mansion who were seeking, for instance, to direct the administration's Central American policy into paths of friendship toward so-called liberation movements in Nicaragua, Chile, El Salvador, and Honduras). As this line of thinking was particularly attractive to African-American intellectuals, it was not to be wondered at that the administration's principal African-American spokesman on foreign policy matters, Andrew Young, the U.S. Ambassador to the UN (a Georgian, and a long-time political intimate of Carter's) would occasionally advance the argument within the administration for direct dealings with the PLO.

On August 13, 1979, Young met secretly with the PLO's official observer at the UN. This action violated the Memorandum of Understanding, signed by Kissinger in 1975 and given to the Israelis to hold. Jimmy Carter had repeatedly affirmed his commitment to the Memorandum and had angrily denied repeated rumors that his administration was privately violating it.[174] Ambassador Young resigned; but thereafter he caused the administration further grief by saying out loud that the government's refusal to talk to the PLO was "kind of foolish," and that Israel's positions were "stubborn and intransigent."[175] Carter himself has said of the incident that "a mountain was made of a mole-hill."[176]

Thus Carter got the worst of both worlds, politically speaking. Jews were angry that he did not state explicitly that Young's removal was for the crime of meeting with the PLO—which left many to believe that his heart had been with Young on the matter. And blacks were even angrier, because the most visible African American in the government had been made a scapegoat. Meanwhile, in November 1979, Bob Strauss stepped down as special ambassador, in order to take over the president's reelection campaign. Predictably, many black people saw in this yet another piece of evidence of the capture of the Democratic Party by its wealthy Jews. These developments undoubtedly contributed to the developing estrangement between African American and Jewish voters. Black Democrats were becoming more outspoken on foreign policy issues, and many of these were attracted to "Third World" rhetoric, in which anti-Zionism was and is a dominant strain.

Until the end of his presidency, Carter remained obsessed by the illusion that "moderate Arab" support for the peace process could be won by demonstrations of generous concern for the Palestinians. An opportunity afforded itself in February 1980, when Morocco and Jordan introduced a resolution to the Security Council calling upon Israel "to dismantle the existing settlements and in particular to cease, on an urgent basis, the establishment, construction and planning of settlements in the Arab territories occupied since 1967, including Jerusalem." A few hours before the vote, the United States' new Ambassador at the UN, Donald McHenry, who had supported the resolution, promised the president not to vote for the resolution until the phrase "including Jerusalem" was removed. But the offending language was still clinging to the resolution when the U.S. delegation voted for it. Carter's attempt to explain all this as due to lack of alertness somewhere down the line of responsibility in the American delegation,[177] made the matter worse. The Israelis and pro-Israeli Americans were asked to believe that the United States had simply *stumbled* into the company of the enemies of Israel. The Arabs persisted in believing that the United States could not pursue the policy it believed in, because of the president's fear of the political weight of the American Jews. Secretary Vance, who had supported the original language wholeheartedly, went on to defend the spirit of the resolution before the Senate Foreign Relations Committee, even after the president found it necessary to renounce it. According to some sources, Vance simply refused to obey the president when instructed to renounce the resolution publicly.[178]

Vance had always chafed at being prevented from expressing publicly, with the bark off, the opinion of Begin and his government that he knew he shared with the president and which he knew that President Carter would have to disguise as the 1980 election progressed. He was angry when Jimmy Carter handed over custody of Israeli-Arab issues to Robert Strauss and he became angrier still when the latter got so badly out of his depth in the conduct of the diplomacy that the administration lost the confidence of both principals: Israel and Egypt.[179] Testifying before a Congressional Committee on March 20, 1980, Vance denounced Israel for expanding settlements in the West Bank and Gaza. A few days later, he resigned, the immediate occasion being his opposition to the president's aborted effort to rescue the American hostages in Tehran by helicopter, but the deeper cause being the growing gap between the president and himself over many matters of policy—not least, the policy toward Israel.

THE ELECTION OF 1980

Perversely, it seemed at the beginning that President Carter was going to benefit from the Tehran crisis, as the public instinctively rallied to the president. Senator Ted Kennedy's early bid to capture the nomination suffered from this circumstance. But later, as the situation of the hostages got worse, Kennedy returned to the contest, joined by Governor Jerry Brown of California. This domestic political action coincided with Carter's attempt to rescue the hostages (April 1980)—which not only failed as a military operation, but served as the occasion for the resignation of Cyrus Vance. A few days later, Kennedy won the New York Democratic primary, evidently by taking the bulk of the Jewish vote. By now, Carter seemed to have won enough votes from previous primaries to have virtually secured the nomination; and thus it could be argued that Jewish voters of New York knew they could send a message to the president about the November election without in reality jeopardizing his prospects for being in it.

Carter had a terrible time answering to American Jews and American friends of Israel for his stewardship in this last year of his presidency. Leonid Brezhnev and the Ayatollah Khomeini were delivering daily humiliations to the United States while friends of Israel said that the

Carter administration's overtures to the PLO and disparagement of Israel only served the causes of these two global bullies. At a Democratic National Committee fundraising dinner held in Florida in July, Carter bragged, "In the last 32 years our Nation has provided Israel with 22 billions of dollars of aid. I'm glad to say that since I've been President, a very short time, about half that amount has been requested from Congress, about $11 billion. This is not a handout from us to a people, no matter how worthy or how much they are in need of a strong defense credibility; it's a real paying investment in our own future, in our democratic principles, and in our own strength and security."[180] This was still his message on the eve of voting: "[Consider] what we have done for Israel. . . . Half the total aid that Israel has received in 32 years has come in the last 3 1/2 years as an investment in our nation's own security, a typical commitment of the Democrats, begun by Harry Truman."[181] But in the upshot, Carter became the only Democrat in our period to fail to receive less than 50 percent of the Jewish vote. He got about 45 percent, Republican candidate Ronald Reagan got 39 percent, and a third candidate, the Independent John Anderson, got 15 percent.[182] At the same time, Carter got only 41.0 percent of the vote of the whole electorate, whereas Reagan got 50.7 percent. The Electoral College arithmetic was even more humiliating: 49 to 489.

Carter's defeat was no matter for regret in Israel, but it certainly was to President Sadat, who remembered his friend telling him that after his election he would be released from the tyranny of the American Jewish voters and would thereupon become able to work more wholeheartedly with him in a common front against the truculent Israelis. Still, believing, like most people everywhere, that it was the hostage crisis that had ruined Carter's political career, he could not help but feel that Jimmy Carter had himself to blame: "What sort of superpower is it," he said, "that allows itself to be humiliated in such a way without reacting with real force?"[183]

RETROSPECT ON JIMMY CARTER: THE EVANGELICAL ANTI-CYRUS

We recall that, on the eve of his first meeting with President Jimmy Carter, the newly elected Prime Minister of Israel, Menachem Begin, vouchsafed to an audience of American Jews: "Jimmy Carter knows the Bible, and that will make it easier for him to know whose land this is." Projecting from his basically sound but incomplete reading of the divisions among Christians, he concluded that Jimmy Carter, because he was observant, an Evangelical (often characterized as a Fundamentalist), a reader of the Bible, a Baptist, a Sunday school teacher—must therefore be *theologically committed* to prefer Israel's claims to *Eretz Israel*. In short, he assumed that Jimmy Carter was a Christian Zionist. But despite what audiences of American Jews may have thought they heard during the primary contests of 1976, Jimmy Carter was not a Christian Zionist.

In his presidential memoirs, Carter speaks of his lifelong "interest in the area" acquired "through our weekly Bible study." Still, when he visited Israel as governor of Georgia in May 1973, Carter, by his own account, could spare little time to visit any places of Christian pilgrimage. "I was torn between the pleasure of visiting the Christian holy places I had longed to see since I was a child and the knowledge that I should be preparing for a future career"—that is, the business of his meeting Israeli politicians, in advance of his declaration of candidacy as president 18 months later.[184] Jimmy Carter, the Christian layman, was visiting "the area," "the Holy Land"; Jimmy Carter, the ambitious political leader, was visiting Israeli politicians.

Israelis (especially those who deal with tourists) learn early in life that, when it comes to American and European Christians, enthusiasm for "the Holy Land" does not normally translate into enthusiasm for Israel. The mind and heart of the Christian Holy Land–enthusiast is often closed to arguments based upon the Zionist understanding that *Eretz Israel* is the land that God has set aside for the Jews—the land in which He reared them, which He gave to them to be a possession forever, and to which He returned them. Looking back in 1977 upon the creation of the State of Israel in 1948, Carter wrote that "the Jews who had survived the Holocaust deserved their own nation and that they had a right to live in peace among their neighbors. I considered this homeland for the Jews to be *compatible with* the teachings of the Bible hence ordained by God."[185] This is far from the position that Begin expected him to hold—that is, the position of the Christian Zionist, to whom it is a requirement of faith to *prefer* the preservation ("the blessing") of Israel. It is, instead, the thinking of a Christian liberal-moralist.

In Carter's book, *The Blood of Abraham*, published in 1985, we find the views he was now ready to express in writing for the world to see, having had some time to digest the experiences of his presidency, and to do more reading, listening, and talking. By 1985, Jimmy Carter was no longer pretending to hold the Christian Zionist views which he had professed before Jewish audiences in 1976. *Now he came forth as a champion of Christian anti-Zionism.* Rereading the history of the Holy Land, Carter was now struck by the *parity* between the Israeli and Palestinian historical claims: "*For Jews*, Israel has been the fulfillment of biblical prophecy and the culmination of a dream to establish and live under a government of their own choice. The Palestinians, like the Jews, claim to be driven by religious conviction based on the promises of God, and they consider themselves to have comprised the admixture of all peoples including the ancient Hebrews who dwelt in Palestine, their homeland, since earliest biblical times."[186] If the Jews claim that they descend from the people of Israel whom the Bible and other ancient sources describe as being in possession of the land in ancient times, then the non-Jews of Palestine today must be the descendants of all those others who were there, both *before* the Israelis and *since*: *"all peoples including the ancient Hebrews who dwelt in Palestine, their homeland, since earliest biblical times"*—that is, the Canaanites, the Amorites, the Hittites, the Perizzites, the Hivites, the Jebusites, as well as the Philistines and *the ancient Hebrews*! And they must have continued to be present ever since! Thus, the Arabs of Palestine become the "Palestinians," one of that worldwide company of *aboriginal peoples* whose history is marked by victimization at the hands of a succession of imperialists.

This counter-history, which features the story of how the Canaanites became the Palestinians, has broad appeal today and is virtually entrenched among anti-Zionist Christian theologians and in the church establishment in the Middle East, represented by the Middle East Council of Churches (MECC). To enter into argument with it is a hopeless task, as it stands entirely on reiterated invention. That this thesis ever got off the ground in the first place is a telling illustration of the low estate of historical thinking in church circles. Something like it is *necessary*, however, if there is to be parity between the Zionist and the Palestinian title to the Holy Land. And it is this consideration that commended it to Jimmy Carter, a man whose historical learning is as shallow as his scientific and technological knowledge is broad.

From the beginning to the end of his labors on behalf of peace in the Middle East, Jimmy Carter never lost his awe for the eternal meanings that people of faith attach to issues of title in the Holy Land. Even if he had wished to set all these religious issues aside, his reputation as an Evangelical Christian guaranteed that they would be raised in his presence. At a question-and-answer session at a town meeting with New Hampshire high school students on February 18, 1978, he was asked: "What do you think about the bible prophecy in Isaiah 19, verses 23 and 24[187] being fulfilled in our times, when Egypt and Syria will be aligning themselves with Israel in the last days? and in what way has being a born-again Christian affected your role as President?" Carter answered,

Very fine. I believe that one of the great, positive factors in eventually finding a resolution of the differences in the Middle East is the deep religious conviction of both Prime Minister Begin and President Sadat. They and we, as Christians, worship the same God. Our religious beliefs differ in some degrees [sic] but there's a special interrelationship between the Arabs in Egypt and the Jews in Israel. They recognize Abraham as a common father of them all. I think they understand, as you say, the prophecies in Isaiah as applying to both peoples, that peace between Egypt and Israel is foreordained by God, and that they can play a role in carrying out God's purposes.[188]

Jimmy Carter, as we have noted already, had boundless confidence in his ability to master the texts that contained the facts that he needed to solve problems of all kinds. In *The Blood of Abraham*, he tells us that, "In preparing for the Middle East peace discussions, I had made a brief study of the Koran, which made my discussions with Sadat much more meaningful."[189] (How does one make a *brief* study of the Qur'an?) In February 1978, he told the audience at the National Prayer Breakfast: "A few weeks ago, I was in India. As part of my preparation for meeting with Indian leaders, I read the Bhagavad Gita." (Briefly?) The theme of his address that day was his broadening appreciation of the effects of religious faith in the lives of so many of the statesmen with whom he had been dealing in recent months. While in India, Carter "visited the site where Mahatma Gandhi's body was cremated and thought about his simple, deeply committed life, his knowledge of Christianity and Judaism, his worship of God . . . [In my conversation with Prime Minister Desai,] this was a common thread that ran through the conversations between us—how we shared something." He further recalled a conversation with Crown Prince Fahd of Saudi Arabia, in which the latter had spoken of "how a common religious faith and their responsibilities to hold together the interest in the holy places of Islam gave him confidence in the future and guidance on how his own life should be expended in the service of others." He spoke of Menachem Begin: "Throughout his conversations with me in the quiet, lonely, private times together, and even when he talks with others in a larger group, there's a fervor of a deeply committed, religious man who again worships the same God I do and you do." And as for Sadat, "He never fails to point out that the Egyptians and the Jews are sons of Abraham, worship the same God, share a common heritage and a common faith, and that this is a transcendent thing, quite often forgotten, but still there, that it doesn't change."[190]

During the election seasons of 1976 and 1980, Carter declared a hearty pro-Israel position; but in between, he pursued a policy much less friendly to Israel's own views of its needs and interests than that pursued by any president up to that date. Like Harry Truman, Carter was a Baptist, and well-versed in the Bible from Sunday school years and beyond. Unlike Truman, Carter had dabbled in contemporary Protestant theology and in philosophy of religion. Like Truman, he addressed the Cyrus tradition; but unlike Truman, he became convinced that that tradition had become harmful to the cause of achieving "a just and equitable solution to the Arab-Israeli conflict." And so he sought to disengage the office of the presidency and the foreign policy of the United States from the tradition, in order to be free to pursue policies that were certainly no less consistent, in philosophical and theological terms, than those required of a Christian Zionist but that were self-consciously and explicitly anti-Zionist.

In *The Blood of Abraham*, Carter reviews the "promises of God" made to the "seed of Abraham." Paraphrasing Genesis 17:20–21, Carter says, that "he [God] would establish a covenant with Isaac and that Ishmael would beget twelve princes and also a great nation."[191] A significant misreading of the text occurs here. The words are "*my* covenant I will establish in Isaac" (not yet born). By turning "my covenant" into "a covenant," and elsewhere by substituting the vague terms "promise" and "promises," Carter obscures the technical meaning of the expression, "my covenant." Everything that is said in the Old Testament about the future of the Arabs (descendants of Ishmael) as well as everything that is said about the future of the Israelis (descendants of Isaac and Jacob) Carter equalizes as *promises*—promises to the seed of Isaac, promises to the seed of Ishmael, promises to the Jews, promises to the Palestinians, promises to the Christians. It is significant that Carter attributes his reformed perspective on these matters to Anwar Sadat: "In my discussions of these religious conflicts with President Anwar Sadat of Egypt, he mentioned frequently, and almost casually, the brotherhood of Arab and Jew and how they were both the sons of Abraham. His references to the patriarch caused me to reexamine the ancient biblical story of Abraham and his early descendants, looking at their adventures for the first time *from a Jewish, a Christian, and an Arab point of view simultaneously.*"[192] In light of this, we should give some thought to Sadat's standard of biblical exegesis, which can be illustrated by the following: "The assassination of Arab brethren like Goliath, by Jewish sheep-herders like David, is the sort of shameful ignominy that we must yet set aright in the domain of the occupied Palestinian homeland."[193]

A matter of special interest to Christians is the covenant that God later makes with King David and his "house." Conservative theologians understand this to be an eternal promise, in the light of which Christians should understand that the God of Israel has always reigned in Zion, and that the Jews, after their centuries of scattering will be reunited in Zion, and governed eventually by David's heir, or David *redivivus*—that is, Messiah. Jimmy Carter affirms his belief that "God promised David that because of his faithfulness, his kingdom would be established forever." But Carter has nothing to say about the promise to restore the Jews to Zion. Instead, he draws from the subsequent history of Jewish disobedience and of their scattering the anti-Zionist conclusion, which is technically called *supersessionism* or *replacement* (that the church has inherited all the promises that God made to the Jews), while amplifying the doctrine to write the Muslims into the inheritance:

Jews consider the covenants made by God with Abraham, Isaac, Jacob, and Moses to apply exclusively to them. Moslems also consider some of this history profoundly significant and derive from it the justification for their assured place in the eyes of God, as later revealed to Mohammed. It is also of crucial importance to Christians in all lands, who know Jesus, the descendant of King David as the fulfillment of God's early promises of a permanent blessing and an unending kingdom among all the nations of the earth. For Christians and Moslems, therefore, the promises of God are not just for the people of Moses. Christians believe that Abraham was blessed by God because of his faith, not because of his race, and that he is the father of all who share his faith in God.[194]

Readers who do not count themselves as adherents to any of the three communities of faith that figure in this recital may resent being dragged into questions of biblical exegesis. They may find themselves echoing the words of Dean Rusk (noted earlier), "Oh, come on now, don't give me any of that stuff!" But as a historian of these events the reader has to consider that Jimmy Carter, a serious Christian, *knew* that he must have answers to these questions. And the bottom line, Carter knows, has to do with the truth claims of all three faiths: Judaism, Christianity, and Islam.

JIMMY CARTER'S POST-PRESIDENTIAL CAMPAIGN AGAINST ISRAEL

Jimmy Carter's version of the recent history of the Middle East conflict became more blatantly anti-Israeli as every year went by. In *The Blood of Abraham*, Sadat's version of the story seems to control everything. The outcome of the Six-Day War of 1967, we are told, created a situation intolerable to the Arab world: "With their swift victory in the 1967 war, the Israelis tripled the amount of land they controlled at the expense of Egypt, Jordan, the Palestinians, and Syria, who for several years lived with almost absolute confidence in Israel's military invincibility."[195] As for the next major episode, a telling clue to the bias in Carter's account is to be found in the index, where, under "Y," one finds: "Yom Kippur War, see 1973 war." Carter achieves evenhandedness by simply leaving out reference to Sadat's unilateral breaking of the cease-fire which began the war. There is no hint of judgment on Egypt, Syria, and their coconspirators for the decision to attack during the Jewish High Holidays. Note *is* taken of the fact that one side did attack the other; but this is done only in order to make a point about the wisdom shown by the attacker, and the culpable laxity of the attacked: "Then, in October of 1973, came the surprise attack by Syria and Egypt. Israel's defenses eventually proved adequate, but the Arab forces did well enough to restore their psychological sense of equity. They regained sufficient pride and self-confidence to permit the Egyptian and Syrian leaders to accept limited withdrawal agreements with Israel, even though the Israelis continued to occupy substantial portions of their territory."[196]

Needless to say, Israel sees this war in another light—*not* as a providentially given occasion for redressing the uneven outcomes of previous wars, so that somebody's self-esteem could be raised, but, rather, as a dishonorable assault during the holiest time of the Jewish year, an action conceived in dishonor, *and intended to result in Israel's destruction*. When the intended conquest had this quite different result, the aggressors announced, as we have seen, that this was indeed the very result they had intended. Jimmy Carter never asks: Why would the governments of Egypt and Syria—enjoying a population advantage of about twelve to one against Israel;[197] having the assistance on the field of combat and in the air of the armed forces contributed by ten other countries (Algeria, Jordan, Iraq, Libya, Morocco, Saudi Arabia, Sudan, Tunisia, and Yemen— and North Korea); having the moral support of all the wealthy, oil-producing nations, the Communist nations, and most of the Third World; choosing a moment when, as Sadat states bluntly, "European opinion in 1973 was anti-Israel and pro-Arab, contrary to what it had been in 1967";[198] having an enormous advantage in military hardware and manpower on both major fronts[199]—plan, and then launch, a war *not intending to win* but intending rather (if we are to believe Anwar Sadat and Jimmy Carter) to have it end with the other side's troops on their soil, their capitals (Cairo and Damascus) in threat of siege, and thousands of their troops surrounded?

Now and then, Sadat *would* get a little too far-fetched as he explained all of this to the Americans. In the notes he took during that first visit that President Sadat made to the White House, Zbigniew Brzezinski wrote: "[Sadat was] warm, gracious, even ingratiating . . . However, he also had a tendency to let himself be carried away by his own words. My worry is that Sadat does not seem to differentiate clearly between fact and fiction . . . [as, e.g.,] describing to us with considerable emotion how [in October 1973] he had the Israeli armed forces encircled on the West Bank of the Nile, with 400 Israeli tanks ringed by 800 Egyptian tanks which were about to annihilate the Israelis when the cease-fire finally came."[200] But the American officials never actually argued with Sadat about such trifles. That would be rude.

In Carter's accounts of the October War, there is not a word of admiration for Israel's endurance in the face of the assault upon her life, for her overcoming of her despair, a spiritual triumph that allowed her to turn away catastrophe and to defeat the combined Arab armies. During the Yom Kippur War, Israel suffered the deaths of over 2,800 of her soldiers—a proportion of her population that would be approximately equivalent to 200,000 American casualties, which is (proportionately) roughly three and a half times the loss in war dead that the United States incurred in the entire Vietnam War. None of this figures in Jimmy Carter's account of the War—neither in *Keeping Faith* nor in *The Blood of Abraham*. Instead, leaving the dead to bury their dead, his account focuses almost entirely on the providentially improved opportunities for diplomacy. Carter commends the European nations for achieving, during the days of October 1973, "an attitude that was more balanced toward the Arab-Israeli conflict . . . a show of unanimity by the Europeans on behalf of the Arab nations . . . a clear break with the United States and Israel."[201] If these words mean what they clearly say, Israelis should be very grateful that it was Richard Nixon (for whom 35 percent of Jews voted in 1972) and not Jimmy Carter (for whom 64 percent of Jews voted in 1976), who was president in October 1973.

Carter's recollections of his dealings with Israeli politicians became more negative, while his recollections of his dealings with Egypt grew more positive with each passing year. In *The Blood of Abraham* (1985), he goes back to that day in 1979 when he was invited into the very cockpit of Israeli politics:

> When I addressed the Knesset, it was a shock to observe the degree of freedom permitted the members of the parliament in their relatively undisciplined exchanges. Although I concluded my remarks with few interruptions, it was almost impossible for either the Prime Minister or the opposition leader to speak. Instead of being embarrassed by the constant interruptions and by the physical removal of one of the members from the chamber, Prime Minister Begin seemed to relish the verbal combat and expressed pride in how unrestrained the shouted argument was. During an especially vituperative exchange, he leaned over to me and said proudly, "This is democracy in action."[202]

Many good friends of Israel have, from to time, suggested that much could be gained by improving the decorum of the proceedings in the Knesset. Carter's comments, however, are not offered in that friendly spirit, but rather reveal a culpable insensitivity to the peculiar political style of a democracy as authentic as that of the nation that elected him president. *All of Carter's references to the Israeli political process betray this same judgmental spirit.*

Visiting Cairo a few hours after the disagreeable encounter with Israeli politics, Carter observed a much more presentable political scene. Enormous, happy crowds appeared everywhere; not an unkind word appeared on any of the signs that people waved. To Jimmy Carter, this proved that President Sadat was universally beloved. At the formal banquet, he said:

> I have never seen so many people as were along our route today from Cairo to Alexandria, and it was the most impressive political event that I have ever witnessed—hundreds of thousands of Egyptian citizens, millions of Egyptian citizens. The number itself was impressive, but the most impressive aspect of this tremendous outpouring of emotion was their love and respect for their President and their obvious appreciation for our common search for peace . . . I said today, as we watched the adoring crowds shouting out their slogan of a pledge of their heart and soul for President Sadat, that I would certainly hate to run against him for a public office in Egypt. But I would add very quickly that I would also hate to run

against him for a public office in the United States of America. (*Laughter* [in original]) I think it's accurate to say that he's, perhaps, the most popular person in our own country.[203]

Carter's appreciation of the role of religion in the public life of the Jews seems also to have declined in these same years. Despite efforts by journalists to portray Jimmy Carter as a man under the spell of a childlike faith, the fact is that, as a sensitive and well-read Christian, with much practical experience of the realities of everyday life in the Church, Jimmy Carter had always had a realistic appreciation for the negative and destructive possibilities inherent in religious belief. He became much more candid about this reality in his later books than in his earlier writing and speaking. In the years following his return to Plains, he saw his own local Southern Baptist congregation divide over the challenge of racial fraternity, and was compelled in conscience to leave it and help in forming another church. He completely lost sympathy for the new conservative direction in the Southern Baptist Church. With respect to our present theme, Carter reluctantly came to the conclusion that, "To a remarkable degree, 'the will of God' is the basis for both esoteric debates and the most vicious terrorist attacks among the Jews, Moslems, and Christians . . . Tragically for 'the People of the Book' who profess to worship the same God, the scriptures are a source of more difference than agreement, inspiring more hatred than love, more war than peace."[204]

All of this raises questions about Jimmy Carter's understanding of the religion of the Jews. During the visit to Israel in May 1973, which we have already noted, he had mentioned to Prime Minister Golda Meir, "that during biblical times, the Israelites triumphed when they were close to God and were defeated when unfaithful. She laughed aloud and agreed with me, but added that this was not a matter of concern to her because there were certainly enough 'orthodox' Jews around."[205] It seems that, over time, Carter came to see more virtue in Golda Meir's secularist perspective. More and more he noted the *de*stabilizing effects of the small religious parties, and came to believe that their behavior was an object lesson about the dangers of religion in public life. He came to see the religious parties as "a few elected representatives whose interests are narrowly focused on precise interpretations of scriptures," and who thus keep Israeli politics in constant turmoil. They thought of themselves as guardians of the will of God, with respect, for example, to maintaining Jewish sovereignty over biblical Israel—something that was constantly complicating the American government's necessary work of persuading Israel to trade land for peace.

Somewhere between the end of Jimmy Carter's presidency and the writing of *The Blood of Abraham*, Judaism lost something of the advantage that it normally enjoys in the esteem of a Southern Baptist, and Islam gained greatly—in a way that would not cheer most Southern Baptists. There is now something more like parity in his appreciation of the moral validity of these two other "Abrahamic" faiths. Thus, while Sadat is increasingly remembered as a genial conversationalist, with a gift for widening Carter's religious horizons, Begin is increasingly remembered as a pious bore who used religious talk for political purpose. It does not occur to Carter that there might be a political purpose in Sadat's determination (following Muslim tradition) to attach Arab history to Abraham, and thus to the Holy Land and to Jerusalem. By 1985, when Carter thinks of Begin, what comes to mind is his "deep fundamentalist convictions, based on a rigid interpretation of scriptures." Now it seems ominous to Carter that Begin's campaign crowds were wont to greet him, "Begin, King of Israel."[206] It now occurs to him that Menachem Begin's attitude on the interfaith matter was far from satisfactory. "A dedicated student of the Bible, on occasion he quoted scriptural passages, such as, 'If I forget thee, O Jerusalem, let my right hand forget her cunning,' in order to emphasize why he would not share authority in Jerusalem. I do not recall any occasion, however, when he initiated a discussion about Christianity or Islam or participated in any comparative analysis of religious beliefs. In fact, Sadat's comments on our sharing the blood of Abraham seemed to cause Begin some slight embarrassment."[207]

In the years following the publication of *the Blood of Abraham*, Carter's hostility toward Menachem Begin grew deeper and deeper. At the time of Carter's second postpresidential visit to the Middle East, in March 1987, ex-President Carter publicly renewed his complaint that Begin had never seriously intended to abide by the Camp David Accords.[208] As the 1980s went on, it became clear to Carter that Yitzhak Shamir, the Likud, and indeed the entire right wing were a united phalanx against peace. He advised Secretary of State Shultz: "In the long run, they [the Israeli government] will have to be run over, with maximum support from the Jews and others around the world who are interested in a stable, secure and peaceful region."[209] At the outset of the 1990s, he thought he saw signs of hope in the return to power of the Israeli left, led by Yitzhak Rabin and Shimon Peres. But by the mid-1990s, he had given up on the left as well. "Israel is the problem towards peace," he said in an address before the Council on Foreign Relations in 1983. This remained his theme song throughout the eighties and the nineties.[210]

By the later 1980s, Carter was telling friends that he regretted not inviting the PLO to Camp David in 1978. In the mid-1980s, Carter conveyed that thought to Yassir Arafat himself. Regular correspondence followed,[211] and in Paris on April 4, 1990, the two met for the first time. "Now in an atmosphere of cordiality, Arafat had accepted the [Camp David] accords and forgiven Carter for excluding him in 1978. Carter felt that a burden he had been carrying for years had been lifted. . . . Then they dried their tears, embraced, and said farewell."[212]

Chapter 4

Living with the Legacy of Camp David

RONALD REAGAN (1981–1989)
"For a while, our policy seemed to be working."

The American presidential election of 1980 severely tested American Jews. Even though Jimmy Carter was perceived to be the least sensitive of all recent presidents to the security needs of Israel, a slight majority of Jews voted for him against Ronald Reagan, whose sweeping victory was made possible by the defection from the Democratic Party of every other component of the old New Deal coalition except blacks.

THE ELECTION OF 1980: THE RELIGIOUS RIGHT DISCOVERED

Here I must introduce an autobiographical note. My introduction to the themes of this research began on January 1, 1981, when I arrived with my family in Jerusalem to take up an appointment for a term as a visiting scholar in the departments of American Studies and Comparative Religion at the Hebrew University. Postelection analysis was the liveliest field of conversation within these departments, and the Israeli scholars were very keen to have the views of the visitors. No one seemed eager to defend Jimmy Carter, but few would admit to having voted for Reagan. Most of the Americans were Democrats, and almost all of the Israelis were in the anti-Begin camp domestically (supporting either Labor or one of the smaller left-of-center parties). Related to this was much discussion of a new phenomenon on the American political scene: the neo-conservatives (neocons), defined as thinkers or politicians reared in left-wing assumptions but now taking up the defense of American patriotic values against the tide of anti-Americanism which followed the Vietnam and Watergate period, and at the same time trying to resist or slow down the steady empowering of government that accompanied the Great Society. The best-known of these neocons (including Norman Podhoretz, Irving Kristol, and Gertrude Himmelfarb) were associated with *Commentary* magazine, the influential journal of opinion funded by the American Jewish Committee, others with William Kristol's *Weekly Standard*, but a few were associated with the *New Republic*. Many of these neocons had declared their support for the Republican Ronald Reagan, and had a lot of explaining to do.

The thorniest nettle that the Jewish Reaganites had to pluck was the widespread impression that the resurgence of the Republican Party was caused, somehow, by the rush into politics of precisely the sort of people whom Jews have feared in the past. Contributing to Reagan's victory, although by no means deciding it, was the defection of Evangelicals from Jimmy Carter, who had presented himself as one of their own in 1976, but had since pursued policies out of line with the Evangelical consensus (for example, on the homosexual challenge, on abortion, on school prayer, and many other issues of domestic concern). The "Religious Right was a theme of great interest. I was invited to present a paper and lead a discussion on the increasing presence of Christians in the politics of the United States. Most of the enquiries had to do with the appearance of the Moral Majority movement led by Jerry Falwell, and, in particular, the mysterious matter of Christian pro-Zionism.

Coinciding with the emergence of the Christian Right in the United States was the appearance in Israel of bodies of Evangelicals who were promoting Christian support for the State of Israel. These included *Bridges for Peace, Christians for Israel, International Christian Embassy Jerusalem*, and others.[1] During the American election year of 1980, Prime Minister Begin had made gestures of friendship toward these organizations, for example, conferring the Jabotinsky Medal upon Jerry Falwell for his constant friendship toward Israel. A longtime American Zionist leader, Alexander M. Schindler (president of the Union of American Hebrew [Reform] Congregations, and past chairman of the Conference of Presidents of Major American Jewish Organizations), writing in the *Jerusalem Post*, asked: "Is Jerry Falwell good for the Jews?"

At first blush the answer . . . is a clear *yes*. After all, Falwell ranks among Israel's staunchest supporters. Israel has too few friends as it is. Moreover, the Moral Majority is an emerging political force of some consequence. Why not cooperate with them? . . . [However,] a more careful consideration of the ends and means of America's new right prompts an entirely different response. . . . This new political force—which gained considerable strength in the campaign just past [1980]—

seeks nothing less than to Christianize America, to make it a republic ruled by Christ. . . . Such a climate, in my judgment, is bad for civil liberties, human rights, social justice, interfaith understanding, and mutual respect among Americans. Therefore, it is bad for Jews.

More significant to Schindler than the presidential election victory was the defeat of several Senate liberals (Bayh, Nelson, McGovern, and Church) who had been among Israel's most stalwart friends. Schindler's intemperate letter to the *Jerusalem Post* received a response from Shmuel Katz, a longtime ally of Begin in the *Herut* party: "The Moral Majority movement in the U.S. has shown its support for Israel, and this sympathy deserves to be reciprocal."[2]

By 1980, it was no longer clear that the Democratic Party was better disposed to Israel than was the Republican Party. Ronald Reagan went even further than Gerald Ford had gone in expressions of partiality to the cause of Israel. But to most Jews it seemed that his effort was not designed so much to garner Jewish votes as to secure the support of Christian Zionists, who were now mainly located in the Republican Party. The anomaly was that few congressional Republicans had significant cohorts of Jewish voters in their districts. It was all extremely puzzling.

RELIGION IN THE LIFE OF RONALD REAGAN

Ronald Reagan was born in Tampico, Illinois, in 1911 and spent his boyhood years in several small towns in that state. Like most of the presidents of our period, Ronald Reagan took church membership of his own volition as a youngster, joining the Disciples of Christ, the church of his mother, by baptism at the age of twelve.[3] Later he graduated from the denomination's college at Eureka, Illinois.[4] After he left home, Ronald Reagan was never again a regular and consistent churchgoer. As president, he coolly insisted that it was only his concern not to put the Secret Service to a lot of trouble and not to put bystanders at risk that he declined to go to church.[5] As an adult he showed no interest in theology or any branch of religious study. He was never active in Bible study groups or regular fellowships either within the denomination of his youth or in any other denomination, nor, indeed, within any interdenominational setting nor, for that matter, in the nondenominational world of para-Church where Evangelical and charismatic fellowships flourish.

Still, it is abundantly clear that Ronald Reagan always retained the basic trust in God that informed his childhood.[6] In speeches and in his several books, he makes a considerable point of his belief in the power of prayer. In a diary entry that he recalls in his memoirs, we find these words: "I have always prayed a lot; in those days [at college], I prayed things would go better for our country, for our family, and for Dixon. I even prayed before football games. . . . I had never faced a kickoff without a prayer. "[7] One biographer, Dinesh D'Souza, was told by many persons interviewed by him of occasions when Reagan would ask a visitor to get down with him on his knees to pray together about the issue under discussion.[8] In Reagan's diary are passages in which he rehearses the challenge of expressing his faith to others. As his father-in-law lies near death, Reagan realizes that "I want so much to speak to him about faith. He's always been an agnostic; now I think he knows fear for probably the first time in his life. . . . I believed strongly in a supreme being and wanted to convince him he was wrong and should see a minister before he died and acknowledge a belief and a faith in God, so I could not resist writing and urging him to do so."[9] When he accepted the nomination of the Republican Party for the presidency at the Republican National Convention in 1980, he concluded his acceptance speech with a moment for everyone present to offer prayer.

By anyone's definition, Ronald Reagan was helplessly superstitious: He did all the Irish things—knocking on wood, carrying a good-luck penny—and occasionally dipped into further fields. Reagan's religiosity was exceptionally pervasive and resistant to focus. In his diary on March 30, 1982, he notes a moment of great interest that day: "Bunch of Congressmen came in for photos, one from Tampico area brought mementoes from my birthplace and a picture that is eerie. The day before Election day, Nov. 3, 1980, a photo was taken of a rainbow. The end came down exactly on the building where I was born."[10] He encouraged his wife's reliance on her astrologer—a matter that got the administration in trouble when it developed that the First Lady's astrologer overruled the most senior advisers in determination of the official schedule.[11] But Reagan lacked the application to make astrology a part of his life, as it was of Nancy's.

His determination to speak of his faith before friendly audiences and his equal determination to locate his largest views about the world in the context of that faith often caused alarmed reactions in the press. A notable occasion was the speech remembered by most as the "Evil Empire" speech, given to the National Association of Evangelicals, March 8, 1983. At the time, he was under much pressure from a "nuclear freeze" movement at home and abroad demanding that the United States undertake unilateral reduction and even total elimination of its nuclear weaponry. Clergymen, Reagan recalls, were in the front ranks in all of their demonstrations: "I wanted to reach them, as well as other Americans who—like my daughter Patti—were being told the path to peace was via a freeze on the development and deployment of nuclear weapons that, if implemented, would leave the Soviets in a position of nuclear superiority over us." And thus, in his speech to the Evangelicals, Ronald Reagan asked his listeners to recall that as good Marxist-Leninists, the Soviet leaders have openly and publicly declared that the only morality they recognize is that which will further their cause, which is world revolution. . . . I think the refusal of many influential people to accept this elementary fact of Soviet doctrine illustrates a historical reluctance to see totalitarian powers for what they are. . . . We will never give away our freedom. We will never abandon our belief in God. . . . Let us pray for the salvation of all those who live in totalitarian darkness—pray that they will discover the joy of knowing God. But until they do, let us be aware that while they preach the supremacy of the state, declare its omnipotence over individual man, and predict an eventual domination of all peoples on earth, they are the focus of evil in the modern world.

The worst enemy of the cause of freedom, Reagan went on to say, is relativism—the temptation to escape a serious attitude toward the world situation by pretending that there is no difference between good and evil—which opens up the corollary temptation to pretend moral superiority by "blithely declaring yourselves above it all."[12] In his autobiography, Reagan explains that his real intended target was not the domestic critics but the Soviet leader Yuri Andropov: The speech provided a means of reaching him to make sure that he understood the issues. Given this conviction, he decided to ignore the advice of Nancy Reagan, that he "lower the temperature of my rhetoric."[13]

Reagan's confidence in the Lord's appointment over his life is boldly stated in his memoirs. For example, as he recalls the assassination attempt of March 30, 1981, he thinks of the attempted assassin, "a mixed-up young man from a fine family. That day, I asked the Lord to heal him, and to this day, I still do. After I left the hospital and was back in the White House, I wrote a few words about the shooting in my diary that concluded: 'Whatever happens now I owe my life to God and will try to serve him in every way I can.'"[14] During his years as governor of California, Ronald Reagan was sought out by certain preachers and authors who commanded large audiences in the Evangelical community of that state and across the country and who were convinced that he bore the marks of divine appointment to the highest office in the land for their generation. A delegation approached Reagan and told him in the firmest terms to accept this appointment and to act in its light. Their spokesman, George Otis, had "a Word of the Lord" for him: "If you walk uprightly before Me, you will reside at 1600 Pennsylvania Avenue."[15] (There is no reference to this well-documented occasion in Reagan's own autobiography.)

In his book *Reagan's America* Garry Wills compares and contrasts the religious life of Jimmy Carter and Ronald Reagan. Wills notes that Carter's actual practice of his religion was immeasurably more conscientious and self-conscious than was Reagan's, yet it became a political burden to him. In contrast, Reagan drew political advantage from the public's perception of his "normal" religious life. Wills astutely notes that "had a story like that of George Otis's prophecy been told about Jimmy Carter, it might well have prevented his election to the presidency. There was an initial suspicion of Carter's religion as 'kooky.' But Reagan is so manifestly a normal American that any signs of his good luck were welcomed like a good horoscope." Wills recalls the essay, *Varieties of Religious Experience*, in which William James drew his famous distinction between the religion of the once-born and the twice-born.

Carter's religion is what William James called that of the "sick soul"—a religion of man's fall, of the need for repentance, of humility. In its Calvinist form, that "classical" religion was important in the early history of America. But America has increasingly preferred the religion that James called "healthy-mindedness," which replaces sin with sadness, the real enemy of human nature. . . . It is actually a pledge of one's religious acceptability, in such, circles, to feel one has a lucky star; that the individual, like the nation (or the football team), is favored by heaven. Humility, never a national virtue to strenuous patriots (or football players), is not even a personal virtue now, except in the Reagan sense of affability.[16]

How ironic it is that it was Carter who, in 1976, brought into the mainstream of politics the very people who would desert him for Reagan!

In 1980, even Southern evangelical voters deserted a President who, in most ways, reflected their background better than Reagan did. Jimmy Carter was more devout by ordinary standards (like church attendance), better acquainted with the Bible, far more active in church affairs (like doing missionary work), more willing to talk about his born-again experience. Despite all these discrete points of contact between his experience and theirs, religious voters found that Carter lacked the higher confidence in man, man's products, and America. . . . He believed in original sin.[17]

A ROCKY BEGINNING TO RELATIONS BETWEEN THE REAGAN ADMINISTRATION AND ISRAEL: THE AWACS ISSUE

Relations between the new Reagan administration and the incumbent government of Israel got off to a rocky start. As Reagan's presidency began, the two governments were engaged in a donnybrook around the decision of the United States government to sell a range of top-grade military equipment to Saudi Arabia—one of the many Arab states still in a formal state of war with Israel. Most important was a fleet of AWACS (Airborne Warning and Control System)—flying radar stations that could spot incoming aircraft and missiles and alert defensive systems on the ground but that could also serve as an aerial spy system.[18] The new government was simply signing on to a program approaching completion in the last days of the Carter administration. In justifying the sales, Carter had made a great point of the Saudi government's alleged readiness to become an active partner for peace, despite all their public denunciations of Israel, of Camp David, and of Egypt. The political problem was that candidate Reagan had opposed the sale of AWACS to the Saudis. Now President Reagan restudied the issue and "decided to go ahead with it because I was told the planes would not materially change the balance of power in the Arab-Israeli conflict. I thought that the Arab world would regard it as a gesture showing that we desired to be evenhanded in the Middle East."[19]

As debate over AWACS was just getting heated there came news that the Israeli air force had destroyed without warning the nuclear reactor at Osiraq, about ten miles outside Baghdad, Iraq (June 7, 1981). It was quickly noted that in this action the Israelis had used American-made aircraft and technology supposed to be used only for defensive purposes. The president of the United States truthfully declared that his government had not been advised in advance and he joined formally in the universal deploration of the deed.[20] Those who guessed that Reagan was privately satisfied to see this Israeli action were right. In his diary for June 1981, he wrote: "[Begin] should have told us and the French. We could have done something to remove the threat. . . . Under the law I have no choice but to ask Congress to investigate and see if there has been a violation of the law regarding use of American-produced planes for offensive purposes. Frankly, if Congress should decide that, I'll grant a Presidential waiver. Iraq is technically still at war with Israel and I believe they were preparing to build an atom bomb."[21] It occurred to Secretary of State Alexander Haig that "Begin's action . . . might well be judged less severely by history than by the opinion of the day."[22] Official U.S. retribution took mild forms: For several months, shipment of certain military equipment already committed to Israel was delayed and other programs of cooperation were suspended for the time being.

Ironically, Israel's action against Osiraq strengthened the administration's case for AWACS when it was disclosed that Israeli planes had traveled to their target over Saudi Arabia's airspace. Even as opinion in Congress was tipping in favor of the AWACS deal, assisted by the energetic personal lobbying of the president, Prime Minister Begin contacted Jerry Falwell by phone and recruited him to assist in defending Israel's decision before the American public. Falwell agreed, making many references to the issue in speeches and interviews in these weeks.[23] (At the same time, Ronald Reagan had persuaded his friend Billy Graham to use *his* influence to persuade certain senators to vote with the administration on the issue.)[24]

Begin, meanwhile, won reelection as prime minister on the last day of June 1981—something thought improbable at the beginning of his campaign a few weeks earlier and now attributed by many commentators,

Israeli and American, to Begin's sturdy defiance of the administration on the AWACS matter. This caused further ill will within the Reagan administration.[25] On September 9, 1981, the newly reelected Prime Minister Begin met with President Reagan in an effort to persuade him to drop the AWACS plan.[26] At their meeting, Reagan, knowing that Begin was scheduled to appear before congressional committees, secured (or so he believed) assurance from Begin that he would refrain from actively lobbying while in the United States. Although most commentators feel that Begin did not technically violate this pledge, Reagan took a very dim view of Begin's testimony before the congressional committees, and Begin lost merit points with Reagan.[27] Within the administration, there was now a considerable cohort, including Reagan's Chief of Staff James Baker and Vice President George Bush, who were determined to curtail Israel's advantage with the administration by speaking out firmly against their lobbying methods. The choice, they told the congressmen, was "Reagan or Begin."[28]

Reagan won the battle for AWACS by a narrow vote on October 29, 1981. As solace for this defeat, Israel received a promise from the administration of $200 million in military assistance funds (above those already committed in the budget). About the same time, talks were going on between the two governments on the idea of a strategic cooperation agreement—a form of partnership between Israel and United States in the regional defense of the Middle East. As defined by Robert C. McFarland (at that time counsel to the State Department and assigned to work out the agreement) it was a way for "the Reagan administration [to] put down its marker on the survival and security of Israel," a way of "elevating Israel to the status of ally . . . on a level equal to the United Kingdom, France, Germany and other states."[29] An obstacle, McFarland found, was "opposition from the Pentagon to enhancing U.S. relations with Israel. Since the early 1970s, the Pentagon, both uniformed and civilian personnel, had tended to view U.S. relations with Israel and the Arab states as a zero sum game, prohibiting us from working with both at the same time. Because they saw our strategic interests as centered in access to the region's oil, which is all located in Arab states, the military believed our interests were best served by strong relationships with those states. Now, with the pro-Arab Caspar Weinberger at the helm of Defense, that position had solidified." The agreement was, however, drawn up: It included provisions for the United States to locate military equipment and supplies in Israel to be available in case of trouble in the region and for American use of Israeli naval facilities and cooperation on security issues and other matters. A memorandum to proceed with the agreement was signed by President Reagan in November of 1982. But almost immediately, the administration announced that it would not proceed after all—the reason being the administration's disapproval of the announcement in December by the government of Israel that henceforth Israeli law would apply to Golan—a portion of Syrian territory acquired during the 1973 war.[30]

LEBANON

Lebanon was one of the Arab states that had participated in the war to prevent the birth of Israel in 1948. Lebanon had participated in every war since and was still in a formal state of war with Israel. Most people in the West assumed that because Lebanon had a high proportion of Christian citizens and was uniquely oriented toward the West as a place of commerce and culture, there would be found there moderate voices ready to accept the creation of a Jewish state and ready to contemplate some degree of cooperation between such a state and Lebanon as allies against the powerful religious and social forces in the Arab world that had always impeded social change and reconciliation with Europe and its values. Since its inception, Lebanon had lived under a constitution that sought to provide a context for security for all the minorities of the land. But ever since 1948, the voice of Arab nationalism had grown louder and louder. The fragile political contract had nearly been swept away in the Eisenhower years under battering from pro-Nasserite nationalists. A decade of peace and prosperity ensued. Then, in 1971, there began a steady descent into chaos, initiated by the arrival in the country of the forces of Yassir Arafat, in flight from Jordan. During 1975 and 1976 alone, 60,000 Lebanese were killed in the civil war that engulfed the nation.[31] The political and military situation became further complicated when the leaders of the Arab nations meeting in Cairo, alarmed at the prospect that Lebanon would pass into the hands of the PLO and that they would be faced with this bitter enemy of their domestic peace drawing them into another losing war against Israel, agreed to sanction Syria's decision to bring an army of its own, characterized as an Arab Deterrent Force, directly onto the scene—ostensibly to prevent the warring elements from destroying each other. Incidentally, and paradoxically, Syria's sterner presence was seen as a positive step by many in the West who were concerned about the imminent liquidation of the Christians in the land. This situation raised the stakes for Israel: If she should now seek to intervene militarily, Israel would automatically be at war with Syria, a closely held client of the Soviet Union.

All the usual patrons of the terrorist organizations—Syria, Iraq, Iran, Saudi Arabia, Libya, and the Soviet Union—kept alive in Lebanon favored groups, which spent much of their time in bloody territorial disputes with each other. Israel's response to this situation was to ally herself with a Christian nationalist military force, under the leadership of a certain General Haddad, located in southern Lebanon, while also maintaining less-visible contacts with other Christian nationalist forces throughout the country. The Palestinian fighters themselves were located mainly in the south, but pockets of "Palestinian refugees" were located throughout the country, and especially in the vicinities of the most heavily populated cities, where they were kept alive physically by UN relief aid and spiritually by a constant diet of anti-Israel rhetoric. Arafat's Palestine Liberation Army, funded by Syria and other Arab regimes, asserted its credentials as the liberator of Palestine by conducting cross-border terrorist raids and occasional guerrilla landings along the seacoast and supporting agents within Israel who carried out terrorist actions against civilians in its name.

President Reagan and the other principal figures on the U.S. side at this time all felt confident (on no evidence whatsoever) that Arafat was sincerely seeking to bring terrorist activities against Israel to a halt, and that he would welcome an honorable occasion to join the peace process. The notion was that, although Arafat could not be expected at this point to declare this vital truth, he would step forth in due course and make a statement accepting Israel's right to exist, and then negotiations between Israel and all the Arab parties, with Palestine a full partner, would become possible. Dangling this hope before the Americans' eyes, Arafat was able to draw out the American envoy Philip Habib, who after many months announced a cease-fire (July 24, 1981). But then, after a lull, terrorist actions resumed, and Israel became convinced that the only way out of her Lebanese quandary was to physically remove the PLO.

Speaking with Secretary of State Haig on September 1981, Prime Minister Begin drew his attention to a notable buildup of Syrian armor, heavy artillery, and ground-to-ground rockets going on in Lebanon and let him know in no uncertain terms that he (Begin) might have to intervene in Lebanon "as a matter of conscience." Haig recalls that on this occasion he warned Begin against any such action unless taken in the context of an "internationally recognized provocation." But other reliable sources quote him as saying something quite different: that the United States would not substitute its judgment for Israel's own in this matter.[32] This scenario will remind us of the clumsy diplomatic dialogue that went on between Britain and the United States (that is, between Eden, on one side, and Eisenhower and Dulles on the other) during the weeks when the Suez intervention was being prepared. The same question arises: Did the Israelis have the right to believe that the Americans had really given a green light, or was it a yellow light or a red light?

In any case, on June 6, 1982, Israel invaded Lebanon, beginning a campaign called "Peace in Galilee." Within hours, Israel destroyed 82 Syrian aircraft, virtually the whole Syrian air force, without a single loss, rendering Syria incapable (or so it would seem) of continuing its regime in southern Lebanon. Within a few days, Israeli troops had reached Beirut, and a stern pacification of the Palestinian forces embedded in the refugee camps had begun. Within hours, President Reagan received a message on the hot line from President Brezhnev of the Soviet Union: "The facts indicate that the Israeli invasion is a previously planned operation, whose preparation the U.S. must have known about." President Reagan rejected the allegation as "totally without foundation."[33]

This Israeli invasion of Lebanon coincided with a transition in responsibility in the Reagan administration's foreign policy, occasioned by the firing of Alexander Haig (disguised as a resignation). Although the fundamental reason for Haig's removal was his inability to get along with colleagues and to follow the instructions of the president, the Israelis knew that Haig had been the most pro-Israeli of the president's top advisors and that he favored letting Israel finish the work it had begun in Lebanon, seeing this as an opportunity to close down the Soviet Union's patronage of Arab regimes in the area.[34] The new secretary of state, George Shultz, did not share Haig's view of the strategic value of Israel. Shultz had been president of Bechtel Corporation, a powerful partner of Saudi Arabia. Under Shultz, there would be no winking at the undeclared parts of Operation Peace in Galilee. As Shultz now expressed it, U.S. policy in Lebanon would be to "attain a cease-fire between the Israeli and Syrian forces; use the Israeli presence and threat as a means to negotiate the evacuation of the PLO from Beirut, and in turn use that prospect to keep Israeli forces out of that Arab capital; lay the groundwork for putting in place an international peacekeeping force . . . work for a diplomatic arrangement that would get all foreign forces out of Lebanon; and use the opportunity to help Lebanon get back on its feet, assert its national identity, and, if possible, establish some sort of stable relationship with Israel."[35]

On June 21, 1982, Prime Minister Begin met with Reagan in the White House and was scolded for Israel's brutal attack on Beirut.[36] After the meeting, Begin and Reagan issued a joint statement calling for all foreign forces to leave Lebanon.[37] A few days later, U.S. Special Envoy Philip Habib met with certain PLO figures (not including Arafat) and received assurance that Arafat agreed in principle to accept U.S. proposals for evacuation. At the same time, the PLO representatives insisted that the United States must negotiate with other governments to find a place for them to go. In addition, there must be a Multi-National Force (MNF) to supervise their safe withdrawal. It was a long time before the Americans could find an Arab government willing to let Arafat on his soil. It seemed, "Arab governments did not trust the PLO and, for all their pro-Palestinian rhetoric, worried more about a potential PLO threat to them than about the fate of the besieged PLO."[38]

So long as Israel remained militarily active in Lebanon there would be no way for her to win the heart of Ronald Reagan. Meeting the press before a meeting with Israeli Foreign Minister Yitzhak Shamir, Reagan admitted out loud: "I lost patience a long time ago" with Israel.[39] He berated the Israelis for what he had seen on television—the terrible effects on the civilian population of Israeli raids. At this point, the administration began the practice of dealing with the Israeli opposition, almost on a par with the government of Israel. On August 19, 1982, there was a meeting in the White House with Shimon Peres, whom Reagan found to be "less combative and much more reasonable than Begin."[40] We have noted the complaints of Reagan and other American principals about Israeli lobbying in the arena of American politics, but we should likewise keep in mind that this administration and all those that followed worked energetically inside Israeli politics to try to assist the elements that they believed were better fit to serve as interlocutors with themselves and the Arab side, seeking their advice in private, taking their part (invisibly) in internal Israeli cabinet politics, and even (as we shall see in the Clinton years) actively assisting their political campaigns. Until the presidency of George W. Bush, the partner of choice was always the Labor Party's principal figure, either inside or outside government.

On August 5, UN Security Council Resolution 517 censured Israel for its intervention in Lebanon. The United States abstained from the resolution but only because the council would not agree to include language supporting the necessity of the PLO departing from Lebanon. On August 10, Israel suddenly renewed its bombardment of Beirut, insisting that the PLO was not abiding by the cease-fire supposed to be in place to assist negotiations for exit of the PLO. Robert McFarland makes clear what principally drove Ronald Reagan's responses to these events: "The pictures [on television] were spectacularly vivid and, absent any historical context of the Middle East conflict, thoroughly devastating. You could see the F-4s diving down, raining bombs on the buildings, flames shooting into the air, napalm all over the place, and women carrying babies and dragging little children running and screaming and falling in the streets. It was horrific."[41] Reagan recalls: "King Faud [of Saudi Arabia] called begging me to do something. I told him I was calling P.M. Begin immediately. And I did. I was angry. I told [Begin] it had to stop or our entire future relationship was endangered. I used the word 'Holocaust' deliberately and said the symbol of his country was becoming 'a picture of a seven month child with its arms blown off.' He told me he had ordered the bombing stopped."[42] Robert McFarland, present with other national security advisers as Reagan spoke to Begin on the phone, recalls, "I was beginning, in fact, to feel on somewhat shaky ground, and personally vulnerable, since I had been the person espousing the notion of elevating Israel to the level of ally and promoting the program of strategic partnership. My assertions had been based on the belief that Israel would engage in such a relationship in good faith, take our interests into account, and share with us their larger vision. Instead, we were being exploited by a prime minister and minister of defense [Ariel Sharon] who seemed to believe that Israel's vital interest had to be secured without taking the President of the United States into account, and that whatever they needed from the United States could be secured through the exercise of their influence on the U.S. Congress."[43]

Under the impact of Reagan's call, Begin immediately ordered a ceasefire (August 19, 1982). Again Special Envoy Philip Habib came to the scene. It was agreed that U.S. Marines and smaller forces from two other European nations, France and Italy, would secure the route along which the PLO would evacuate the city. There was bitter debate within the Reagan administration regarding the instructions for the mission of the Marines.[44] Secretary Shultz led those who wanted an active role and a mandate to continue until the mission was completed; but the debate was won by Secretary of Defense Caspar Weinberger, who wanted a restricted disposition and only for the period of time needed to supervise safe evacuation, then withdrawal—something, Shultz said, that would be read "throughout [the] Middle East . . . [as a] message of weakness."[45]

Under protection from this MNF, Arafat left Beirut, August 30/September 1. Altogether, some 5,000 PLO personnel plus 3,600 Syrians went by sea or by land over mountains to Syria.[46] At once, a mood of optimism took hold: Now the United States could turn its attention to what seemed the straightforward task of securing the withdrawal of the toothless Syrians as part of an agreement for the withdrawal of the victorious Israeli forces. What could be simpler? Now Lebanon could be restored to the Lebanese. The Marines were withdrawn (September 10–16).

Meanwhile, Lebanon held its presidential elections. The president-elect, Bashir Gemayel, leader of the major Christian faction, called Phalange, was summoned peremptorily to Jerusalem and told that he must sign on to an immediate peace treaty with Israel (September 2, 1982).[47] Then everything came apart again, when Bashir Gemayel was assassinated on September 14, 1982, a few days before his inauguration could take place. Lebanese Christians blamed the Palestinians and bloody massacres resumed in the Palestinian areas. Hereupon, Israel broke its pledge to the United States and entered the center of Beirut. From this point, "a mist of bitterness hung over every American-Israeli official encounter," Shultz recalls.[48] On September 17, there took place a murderous assault upon the Sabra and Shatila Palestinian refugee camps by Christian militia, facilitated by the withdrawal of the U.S. Marines. It was clear that Israeli commanders had cleared the path into the camps for the Christian armies; it was possible that cooperation went even further. Immediately, the United States demanded withdrawal of Israeli forces from Beirut and offered to bring the Marines back as an earnest of its intention to keep the warring parties subdued. The other two members of the MNF did likewise.[49]

Thus, on September 21 Israeli forces moved out of Beirut and the vicinity altogether, having failed to gain any benefit from their entire adventure in Lebanon. Perhaps, however, Lebanon had benefited. Perhaps the American presence could secure the degree of stability necessary to resume the political work interrupted by the murder of Bashir Gemayel.

Meanwhile, the government of Israel announced an inquiry into possible Israeli responsibility for the massacres in the Palestinian camps. The Kahan commission concluded (February 7, 1983) that the Israeli military, although innocent of actual participation in the deeds, should have anticipated that permitting the Phalangist armies into the camps carried potential for massacre. The resignation of Minister of Defense Sharon followed at once.[50]

PEACEMAKING

A landmark little-noted at the time was passed on April 25, 1982, the day that Israel completed its transfer of the Sinai to Egypt, as required by the Camp David Accords and the Egypt-Israel Treaty of 1979. Those who did take note of this event could conclude that the last piece of unfinished business between Egypt and Israel was now accomplished. Egypt, which had never shown true enthusiasm for the task of pretending to act on the behalf of the Palestinians, now lost all interest in the issue. The Reagan administration, on the other hand, recognized that it had inherited a commitment to work toward a solution for the Palestinian situation. Reagan's policy seems straightforward enough: "I had hoped to build on the peace process in the Middle East that had been started by Jimmy Carter at Camp David."

Reagan, we should note, read the history of the region precisely as Carter did: "With the creation of the new homeland for the Jews [in 1948], the Arabs who had been occupying Palestine for centuries became a stateless people. . . . Even though Israel claimed its ancestors' occupancy of the land gave it a right to the land in modern times, the Palestinians exerted an ancestral claim of their own on the West Bank: their ancestors too had lived there for centuries."[51] This is not the understanding of a Christian Zionist.

Secretary of State Alexander Haig had begun preparations for his role as peacemaker by visiting the Middle East in April 1981. He was determined to see the issue in a larger context. The tendency to focus on the Palestinian issue distracted the West from consideration of the fact that many Middle East conflicts, and especially those around the Persian Gulf, had little to do with Israel and could not be solved by Israeli concessions. Still, an effort should be made, and at the middle level of the State Department a group was set to work studying the documents and preparing a presidential initiative. But then the Lebanese crisis put all talk of negotiations for peace to the back of the agenda.

In the immediate wake of the evacuation of the PLO from Beirut, in September 1982 Haig's successor, George Shultz, stepped forward to propose a "fresh start." "Self-determination" of the Palestinians was to be the key. But this administration, unlike the Carter administration, ruled out as impracticable the option of statehood; instead, association with Jordan would be the goal.[52] In practical terms, this would mean finding a Palestinian leadership distinct from the PLO—something that should be easy now that the PLO was discredited at last before the whole world. On September 1, 1982, coinciding with PLO evacuation, President Reagan announced a new United States plan incorporating the elements of Shultz's "fresh start" and henceforth referred to as the Reagan Plan. It called for "self-government by the Palestinians of the West Bank and Gaza in association with Jordan." On the road to "full autonomy," there must be "free elections for a self-governing Palestinian authority . . . to prove to the Palestinians that they can run their own affairs and that such autonomy poses no threat to Israel's security." In exchange for having American support for this least painful of all conceivable options, Israel must accept a wholehearted freeze upon settlements. This seemed the right moment, following several painful weeks of conflict with the government of Israel over its Lebanese adventure, to remind everyone that "American's commitment to the security of Israel is ironclad, and, I might add, so is mine."[53]

Former President Carter stepped up to offer praise for the plan, and agreed that it was consistent with Camp David, but Prime Minister Begin stepped up just as quickly to reject it outright. "The Israeli government was going all out to strangle the infant initiative in its cradle," Shultz recalls.[54] However, it was soon discovered that American Jews generally supported the plan, and so the mind of the Israelis could be changed. What was most needed (and entirely lacking) was an Arab party to join the plan. An Arab summit conference held in September 1982 demanded a separate state for the Palestinians and denounced this most recent American-Israeli ploy to deny them one.

Despite the government of Israel's rejection of the Reagan Plan, Israel's standing remained high enough throughout the nation and in Congress that, despite the administration's objection, Congress passed a supplement in U.S. aid to Israel in December 1982. "I was astonished and disheartened," Shultz recalled. "This brought home to me vividly Israel's leverage in our Congress."[55]

LEBANON AGAIN

U.S.-Israel relations had not been improved by these several weeks of close contact. McFarland is blunt: "Throughout the ensuing three weeks of hostilities, the Israeli government repeatedly lied to Washington about its intentions. . . . We would have understood their strategic purpose in pushing the PLO out of southern Lebanon to free their northern territories from attack, had they shared it with us; this was a legitimate security interest and deserved our support. But we could not have agreed to their broader desire to annihilate the PLO. As bad as we thought that PLO leader Yasser Arafat was, the alternative would have been an even more radical Palestinian group led by fanatics such as Abu Moussa or Abu Nidal."[56] But now the withdrawal of the PLO from Beirut and the subsequent withdrawal of the MNF left a vacuum, into which immediately rushed all the forces that had defied the Lebanese government and army in the past, soon to be joined by a range of new disturbers—Iranian-backed Shiites and various terrorist organizations funded and manned by many Arab governments, including Saudi Arabia, Syria, Iran, and Libya. Then, in horror, the Americans discovered that PLO fighters had infiltrated the scene once more. Arafat, mysteriously back in Lebanon, started up another war among all the destabilizing parties. By this time, Syria had shifted its investments from Arafat's Fatah to several rival groups who defied Arafat's assertion of supremacy over the Palestinian cause. Arafat had to be rescued and escorted out of Lebanon again (this time under a deal negotiated by Saudi Arabia). This time, he and his forces were distributed among several training camps in Tunisia, Iraq, Algeria, and Sudan.

In April 1983, Secretary Shultz met Prime Minister Begin in Jerusalem to work out a draft treaty between Lebanon and Israel. But now the Lebanese were backing away from their earlier tentative agreement, insisting that Israel must withdraw from all of Lebanon, even the south. As it was generally understood that the national government in Beirut would be much more secure and its armies much less taxed if the south remained within the Israeli orbit, it seemed obvious that President Amin Gemayel, living in constant fear of assassination, was not speaking his own thoughts but those of Syria.

Lacking knowledge of the history of the region, Ronald Reagan had no other way of appreciating the uniqueness of this moment. Syria had begun to encroach upon Lebanon the day after she came into the world as an independent state (1946) and had been forestalled again and again, but only when confronted by European powers who knew her intention to wipe out Lebanon and had reasons of their own for wishing to keep Lebanon alive. Hence, there had been for Syria two steps forward, one step backward for nearly forty years. Now this same Syria, whose population despised the Lebanese as citified and pro-Western and only partially Muslim, disarmed in a moment, humiliated before her peers, an object of acute embarrassment to her sponsor, the Soviet Union (who, incidentally, let it be known as loudly as possible that the liquidation of the Syrian air force had nothing whatever to do with the quality of the goods and everything to do with the incompetence of the Syrian pilots)[57]—this Syria had nowhere to go, and nothing she could do but bluff. And so she bluffed.

What Ronald Reagan could see was violence, which Israel had somehow started up out of nowhere. He could also see clearly that Israel was desperate to leave, having lost, apparently, the precious unity of national purpose that had previously seen her through crisis after crisis. And so Reagan retreated into criminal naivety. He would compel the Israelis to agree to a withdrawal of her own armies and those of Syria—not simultaneously of course, but Israel going first. The presence of U.S. Marines on Lebanese soil was to be a pledge of American intention to see it all through.

On May 17, 1983, at Qiryat Shemoni in Israel, the governments of Israel and Lebanon signed a draft treaty between their two countries.[58] The single term of the treaty that could be implemented at once was Israel's withdrawal of its troops from Lebanon (except for a defensive region in southern Lebanon). But even before the Israelis could begin the actual withdrawal, Syria's President Assad, supported by the Soviets, denounced the treaty and declared his refusal to talk about withdrawal of Syrian forces—one of the conditions embodied in the Lebanon-Israel treaty. Syria's presence in Lebanon, Syria insisted, was "sanctioned" by the Arab League.

Now there was a price for the United States to pay for its shortsightedness. The Reagan administration was now in the awkward position of having to urge Israel, in private and in public, to stay in Lebanon, in the face of Syrian refusal to leave.[59] Syria was about to escape the consequences of its defeat, and U.S. policy was to blame. As an earnest of his new seriousness of purpose, President Reagan gave notice on August 25, 1983, that the Marines would stay in Lebanon, along with the MNF. Nobody believed that 500 Marines would take on all the forces of disorder, plus the Syrian army. And so it was reasonable to assume that this small American force was to be the precursor of a full-sized American commitment on the ground, dedicated to enforcing the integrity and self-government of Lebanon. Such a force could cooperate with Israel in measures of defense that were proportionate to Israel's need. Such a force would cause the Soviet Union at least to see the futility of trying to gain advantage over the United States in a region that was of no real value to her (the Soviet Union). Such a force could have been the harbinger of real peace in the region.

So desperate were the Israelis to leave Lebanon behind that the government of Israel now proceeded (beginning September 3, 1983), as noiselessly as possible, to withdraw its own forces, using the treaty with Lebanon as dignified cover. But the president of Syria was not ready to call it a day. Instead, he now raised the stakes by championing the Druze, who had their own ancient scores to settle against both the Christians and the Sunni Muslims in the vicinity of Beirut. The Druze militia, with Syria's support, now closed out the military and civilian authority of the government of Lebanon at the heart of the nation. As more and more armies sprang out of the soil and more and more blood was shed in the name of causes that the State Department had never heard of before, Syria began to seem something solid, a rock in the chaos of swirling forces. As the American public's attention moved to other matters, President Assad of Syria would summon President Amin Gemayel to Damascus and order him to repudiate the draft treaty with Israel—which he did (May 1984).

Support for American military presence in the area was declining by the day in Congress, where the decision was made to invoke the War Powers Act—an issue not raised before, as U.S. troops had not been designated as combatants. On September 28, 1983, the administration agreed to cooperate, signing on to the eighteen-month renewal of its mandate provided for in the act.[60] There was never any prospect that Syrian and U.S. forces would directly confront each other in Lebanon, given the enormous advantage of the U.S. army if it came in full force. But it never came to that. It was the terrorist organizations, funded by Arab governments and Muslim philanthropists throughout the world, that accomplished for Syria what it could never have accomplished of itself. On April 18, 1983, terrorists attacked the U.S. Embassy in Beirut, killing sixteen Americans.[61] Then, on October 23, 1983, suicide bombers drove a truck into the U.S. Marine headquarters at the Beirut airport, killing 251 men, while a simultaneous attack on the French barracks killed 58 more.

At first, Reagan reiterated in the firmest possible language his commitment to the mission of the Marines.[62] But inside the administration everything was now under review. Shultz recalls, "I continued to argue, especially to the president, that the US must persevere in Lebanon." Donald Rumsfeld, who had been President Ford's secretary of defense and who was now special envoy to the Middle East, reported to Shultz his conviction that Assad of Syria would yield to reality and make terms to withdraw provided that the United States maintained its steady presence on the ground and in the air (through constant aerial surveillance against Syrian forces).[63] This prospect did not suit the Defense Department. The key voices in the administration against a continuing role in the region, along the lines recommended by Rumsfeld, were Secretary Weinberger and Vice President Bush. They encouraged "a virtual stampede to get out," Shultz notes. At one of these meetings, Shultz noted that "the vice-President said that there is nothing more important than getting those marines out. [But, said Shultz,] we need some thinking about our interests worldwide and what the stakes are, what it means to have staying power in difficult and ambiguous situations."[64] Syria, exploiting the clear division in ranks of the American policy makers, simply walked away from the negotiations for its withdrawal, confident that the United States, like Israel now, was too divided to carry out any punishment for Syria's refusal to comply. At this point, there were some 57,000 Syrian military in Lebanon.[65]

In his autobiography, Ronald Reagan recalls speaking to the foreign minister of Lebanon on a day in February 1983 and telling him that "I was more determined than ever that the withdrawal of all foreign troops from Lebanon would resume soon, and until that day happened, our marines would remain in Lebanon. He said that it had been his experience with American presidents that they at first seemed willing to tackle the problem of Lebanon, but that they 'advanced so far and then retreated.' I told him I didn't have a reverse gear." As late as December 10, 1983, Reagan could still assert that only when "internal security is established and withdrawal of foreign forces is assured, the marines will leave."[66] As late as February 3, 1984, he said publicly that "If we get out, that means the end of Lebanon."[67]

But suddenly, on February 7, 1984, Reagan found the reverse gear. It was announced that the U.S. Marines had now been ordered to leave Beirut and "redeploy offshore," in order "to enhance the safety of American and other MNF personnel in Lebanon."[68] Thus ended the American role as a peacekeeper in Lebanon. "Our troops," Shultz recalled, "left in a rush amid ridicule from the French and utter disappointment and despair from the Lebanese. The Italians left as they saw us departing. . . . I knew then that our staying power under pressure would come into question time and again—and not just in the Middle East."[69]

REAGAN ABANDONS HIS COMMITMENT
TO THE INTEGRITY OF LEBANON AND THE
SECURITY OF ISRAEL (FEBRUARY 1984)

In his autobiography, Reagan reviews and defends his decision to walk away from his commitment to secure the peace of Lebanon and of Israel:

For a while, our policy seemed to be working. There was genuine peace on the streets of Beirut. . . . Still, as we were learning, the situation in Beirut was much more difficult and complex than we initially believed. . . . I believed the last thing we should do was turn tail and leave. If we did that, it would say to the terrorists of the world that all it took to change American foreign policy was to murder some Americans.

If we walked away, we'd also be giving up on the moral commitments to Israel that had originally sent our marines to Lebanon. We'd be abandoning all the progress made during almost two years of trying to mediate a settlement in the Middle East. We'd be saying that the sacrifice of those marines had been for nothing. We'd be inviting the Russians to supplant the United States as the most influential superpower in the Middle East.

Then, having sedulously listed all that was about to be thrown away, Reagan simply throws away the list. "Yet, the irrationality of Middle Eastern politics forced us to rethink our policy there. . . . We had to pull out. By then, there was no question about it: Our policy wasn't working. We couldn't stay there and run the risk of another suicide attack on our marines."[70] The moral descent described here is breathtaking.

In a moment in time, February 1984, President Ronald Reagan simply walked away from what he always said was his "iron clad commitment to the security of Israel," and did so, furthermore, under circumstances bound to call in question before the world that other precious consideration that he himself noted: America's reputation as a nation that would never "turn tail and leave." Reagan's abandonment of the Lebanese mission, and with it his abandonment of Israel, came at the very moment when a show of constant purpose would surely have cleared the field of Israel's most substantial enemies—the Syrians and the PLO—and would have strengthened her to face her enemies of the future.

How can we explain this? Candidate Ronald Reagan had made all the usual noises on the issue of Israel. He had talked of the "unlimited commitment" to a homeland for the Jews which had made it possible for Israel to come into existence and about "the sacred character" of his own commitment. Now, however, when Israel faced the humiliation of retreat from Lebanon, while Syria stood by mocking her and poised to return and while Lebanon (having at last achieved an elected government) was preparing to go back under the yoke of Syria, Reagan simply walked away.

What was the root of Reagan's commitment to Israel? Here we must return to the thoughts about Reagan's theological commitments that we left behind a few paragraphs ago.

Long before the events we have been describing, many commentators were telling the American people that Reagan's attitude toward the Middle East was governed by his fascination with biblical teaching about End Times. Reagan's biographer Lou Cannon describes Reagan as "hooked on Armageddon. . . . He was especially fascinated by the founding of the State of Israel in 1948, an event crucial to those who accept the intricate story of Armageddon as a literal forecast of the end of the world. . . . [He told someone in 1971] that 'For the first time ever, everything is in place for the battle of Armageddon and the second coming of Christ.'"[71] In the course of one of the televised presidential debates in October 1984, a reporter told him, "You've been quoted as saying that you do believe that we are heading for some kind of biblical Armageddon," and wanted to know whether this view affected the plans of his Defense Department "to fight and prevail in a nuclear war." Reagan's answer was that "no one knows whether Armageddon . . . is a thousand years away or day after tomorrow. So, I have never seriously warned and said we must plan according to Armageddon."[72] The issue did not seem to interest many voters, and the Democratic candidate, Walter Mondale, let it go.

There is an appalling amount of sheer misinformation about scriptural texts and about Jewish and Christian theology to be gleaned from these solemn secularist excursions into biblical eschatology (the correct technical-theological term, rarely used by secular commentators). For example, there is the notion of a chain of potent references to "Armageddon" ("the intricate story of Armageddon," Daniel Schorr calls it, or "the theology of Armageddon," as Cannon calls it) running through scripture, whereas, in fact, the word appears only once in Christian scripture (Revelation 16:16) and only once (cryptically, in Zechariah 12:11) in Hebrew scripture. These secular researchers into "Armageddon thinking" insist that there is a monolithic understanding among "literalists" about the details of the scenario that is to accompany the last days, whereas there are so many scenarios and so many subplots within the many scenarios that huge reference books have to be consulted to sort them out. The bottom line is that there is little point in attempting to critique the critique of Ronald Reagan's alleged Armageddon fixation—for the simple and sufficient reason that there is nothing to suggest that Ronald Reagan was any more familiar with biblical eschatology than with any other department of Christian theology.

Reagan's theology was essentially a freelance affair. Reagan's references to "Bible prophecies" are never accompanied by chapter and verse, and suggest no familiarity with any of the particular prophets, with their historical settings, or with their sequence. From a repertoire of anecdotes dimly recalled (anecdotes about movies or about the G.I.s at the front or about the Holocaust or about the welfare recipients living in luxury) he would suddenly draw out a line or a phrase—perhaps a reference that had been brought to recent attention by a popular television evangelist with a large national audience. For instance, at the time of the Chernobyl nuclear disaster in Ukraine, someone brought to public attention that *Chernobyl* appears as the Ukrainian equivalent of *Wormwood* (see Revelation 8:11), and Ronald Reagan was among those who thought this might be a striking echo of an event that is supposed to belong to the last days.[73] But there is no evidence that he did anything about it!

When Ronald Reagan walked away from Lebanon, leaving Israel to face (as it turned out) another two decades of deadly assault upon her northern population from the reestablished PLO and an ever-growing constellation of terrorist organizations like Hezbollah and Islamic Jihad—it did not occur to him, as it would have occurred to a biblically literate Christian Zionist, that this amounted to failure to "bless" Israel or to "prefer" Israel in her everlasting conflict with her ancient enemies. Such understanding as Reagan may have had of the Christian Zionist perspective came and went; it was of a piece with his interest in astrology and his alertness to avoid bad luck. Ronald Reagan had never been securely in the camp of the Evangelical Christian Zionists. He visited this company from time to time, and when he was among them it all made sense. When he left it, he forgot about it. The same can be said of most Americans, for whom there is a vaguely spiritual or mystical awareness of the cause of Zion that draws from the reservoir of revivalism—a reservoir long buried and receding further below the surface every day because of the advance of secular culture.

PEACEMAKING RESUMED

The Reagan Plan for Peace between Israel and the Arabs, announced in September 1982, looked toward "some form of shared, overlapping, or interwoven sovereignties across Israel, the West Bank, and Jordan"—a "mixed sovereignty." This goal was to be reached via an international conference. Jordan was the key to this solution. President Carter had failed to get from Hussein a public declaration of support for the Camp David accords; it was perhaps the greatest disappointment to befall his peacekeeping efforts during his last year in office. Under Reagan, efforts continued along secret channels to recruit Hussein's public support for the Reagan Plan. It is a tortuous story, only for the strong of heart. At times, there were several parallel channels of negotiations, and in the years to follow there would be many more. It all led nowhere.[74] There were negotiations between Shimon Peres and King Hussein, between Shultz and King Hussein, Mubarek and King Hussein, Mubarek and Arafat, Mubarek and Peres, and so on—many permutations and combinations. The State Department was aware of these negotiations, at least in general terms, and, although he had to bite his tongue while the negotiations went ahead, knowledge of them emboldened the secretary of state to believe that progress was near. At one point, Peres reported to Shultz that he had an agreement in hand with Hussein, but that first the Americans must impose this upon Yitzhak Shamir (who had become prime minister when Begin resigned in August 1983). Prime Minister Shamir was, understandably, resentful at having been kept outside of this loop, and raised difficulties immediately—superfluously, as it turned out, because Hussein afterwards disowned the whole process and denied everything.[75] Subsequent secret talks between Shamir and Hussein ended the same way in 1988.[76] These various negotiations were, of course, kept secret from Arafat, the PLO, and other Arab governments. On July 31, 1988, however, Hussein bowed to the reality that the dedicated deniers of Israel's existence would never permit him to achieve peace with Israel; he announced that "in deference to the will of the PLO" Jordan was renouncing all claims to jurisdiction in the West Bank. The Jordanian option was now finished; the PLO was now the only game in town.[77]

Even while urging Hussein to participate in the peace process, the United States was simultaneously negotiating with Hussein with a view to making Jordan a partner in securing the area in the event of future Persian Gulf trouble. Donald Rumsfeld, the special envoy to the Middle East, was assigned to this task. But Hussein soon withered under the menace of Soviet-backed Syria and withdrew from these negotiations as well (March 1984). Rumsfeld was compelled to carry back to Washington Hussein's judgment that by its withdrawal from Lebanon a few weeks earlier the United States had demonstrated to Jordan that it lacked commitment to the security of the region.[78]

The end of Israel's invasion of Lebanon also marks the beginning of a particularly confusing and bitter period in the domestic-political life of Israel. On September 15, 1983, without prior notice, Menachem Begin had stepped down as prime minister, utterly dispirited and ready to sink into a reclusive life that lasted until his death in 1992. In the Israeli election of July 1984, both major parties, Likud and Alignment (Labor), lost small numbers of seats. All in all, there was a shift to the right, benefiting the many smaller parties. Out of this came a National Unity government (September 1984), whose principals were committed to a most unusual contract by which the leaders of the two major parties (Peres and Shamir) would assume the prime minister's chair in rotation for a two-year period. Peres went first (1984–1986), with Shamir as foreign minister; then the roles were reversed (1986–1988). Throughout the four years of this first Unity government, and in fact until March 1990, Yitzhak Rabin was the minister of defense. The Reagan administration exercised a clear preference for Peres, seeking opportunities to deal with him rather than with Shamir even during the period when he was nominally reporting to Shamir, and not being too fussy about keeping Shamir informed. The true dimension of this double-dealing did not become clear until memoir-writing time arrived.

The Israeli election of November 1, 1988 (nearly coinciding with the election of George H. W. Bush), resulted in a virtual tie between the two major parties, but it was Shamir who, again, succeeded in talking the most important of the smaller parties onto his team. And so another National Unity government began (with Shamir as prime minister, Peres as minister of finance, Rabin as minister of defense and Moshe Arens as foreign minister) and continued until March 1990.

CONTACTS BETWEEN THE U.S. GOVERNMENT
AND THE PLO IN THE LAST DAYS OF THE REAGAN
ADMINISTRATION (DECEMBER 1988)

During its last year, the Reagan administration again took up the effort to get the warring parties back on the path toward a negotiated peace. Now that Hussein had ruled himself and the Jordanian option out, there was nothing left but to deal somehow with the PLO, which had the full support (at least nominally) of all the Arab governments. In the last months of the Reagan presidency, the strategy turned on the possibility of bringing Arafat under pressure to make some kind of declaration of acceptance of Israel's right to exist that would permit the United States to engage with the PLO. Shultz recalled, "I would hear again and again from credible people that the PLO and Arafat were 'about to change.' Again and again, the predicted developments proved elusive."[79] A dogged effort to get Arafat to declare his support of these conditions constituted the "Shultz initiative."[80]

Paradoxically, some ground for hope was seen in the Intifada, an evidently spontaneous popular uprising against the Israelis that began in December 1987. This development seemed to prove that the PLO did not have a monopoly on the politics of the area, that there might be an emerging indigenous leadership in Arab Palestine.[81] Some elements in the government of Israel, undergoing daily rebuke by world opinion for the severity of her reaction to this popular uprising, were attracted to the hope of dealing with indigenous leadership that would be governed by real concern for the daily life of the people and not infatuated by rhetoric about the eternal and sacred struggle to drive the Jews into the sea. In the same way, Shultz believed that the leaders of most of the Arab regimes were being sobered up by the Intifada.

Early in 1988, Secretary of State Shultz went to the Middle East to explore possibilities of starting up a dialogue between Israel and the Palestinians. On February 25, 1988, Shultz hosted a meeting in Jerusalem to which he invited Israeli leaders and a number of Arab Palestinian personalities believed to have some independent standing in the community. On the eve of the meeting, Arafat announced that by order of the PLO no Palestinian was permitted to meet with Shultz, under threat of death. Shultz's meeting in Jerusalem went ahead without any Palestinians present.[82] This dilemma stalked all future efforts to bring in Palestinian personalities of political importance.

In the last weeks of the Reagan administration, Secretary Shultz made one final, and partly successful, effort to wring some cooperation out of Arafat. On November 26, 1988, the American government denied Arafat the visa necessary to attend the UN meeting on account of "convincing evidence" of PLO terrorism.[83] Although the General Assembly indulged

Arafat by moving its meeting to Geneva for this occasion, the Americans' point registered—namely, that the United States had an unlimited number of ways of reducing Arafat's access to world opinion and his freedom of action generally. Arafat seemed to get the message because on December 14, 1988, he held a press conference during which he came close enough to meeting Shultz's terms that the government of the United States could announce that "The Palestine Liberation Organization (PLO) today issued a statement in which it accepted UN Security Council Resolutions 242 and 338, recognized Israel's right to exist in peace and security, and renounced terrorism. As a result the United States is prepared for a substantive dialogue with PLO representatives."[84]

It seemed that Arafat had at last waived the Three Noes that had governed Arab attitudes toward Israel since the Khartoum conference of 1967. In response, on December 14, 1988, the government of the United States formally revoked its long-standing commitment *not* to enter into discussion with the PLO.[85] Shultz recalls, "I was skeptical of the PLO's ability to maintain a consistent and constructive position, but I was glad that a self-imposed prohibition to American diplomacy was now a matter of history. I was also glad to have forced some important words out of Arafat's mouth. Words are important. Once issued, they can never be taken back."[86] In retrospect, the moment would lose its millennial quality. Indeed, by May 1990 the administration of George H. W. Bush was driven by the PLO's blatant involvement in a number of new terrorist atrocities to reinstate the ban on official contact with the PLO.[87]

THE STATE OF THE U.S.-ISRAEL ALLIANCE AT THE END OF THE REAGAN YEARS

Israel's standing in world opinion had undoubtedly suffered during the Reagan years, and it seemed at first that this trend might continue through the Bush years. The impression abroad was that Israel was determined to go its own way and to ignore UN opinion if necessary. The air raid against the Iraqi nuclear facility, the Lebanese adventure, and the Intifada were the principal stories with an Israeli angle during that time— the latter two events yielding, day after day, graphic pictures of brutal behavior toward civilians. Little attention was given in the media to the sacrifice that Israel had made in hewing to her pledge to withdraw from Sinai; and, of course, there was no public awareness at all of the exhausting hours of secret diplomacy for the sake of peaceful resolution of problems that went on with Hussein of Jordan and through other secret channels in the Arab world during these years. The general impression was one of truculence—unwillingness to follow world opinion on the issues that affected her. By reaction, pro-Israeli Americans became more vocal during these same years, as the impression grew that Israel was unfairly treated by the press and by the politicians and that it was the duty of the friends of Israel to organize more effectively and speak louder.

As for our principal theme, the peace process, these years display the features to which we must become accustomed now for the remainder of our period. The secretary of state steps forward with a plan, which then gets upgraded to become the president's plan. There is a round of "visits to the region" by the secretary of state—and then another round, and then another one. Hints are dropped of imminent declarations on behalf of peace with Israel from Syria, Lebanon, Jordan, Iraq, and Saudi Arabia. The news weeklies carry cover stories featuring the secretary of state's promising efforts on behalf of Middle East peace. Then, the bubble bursts. Everybody denies everything.

Despite their disappointment at Reagan's failure to respond to the opportunity opened up by Israel's intervention in Lebanon, many American Jews and other friends of Israel believed that Reagan had a sounder view of the realities of world affairs than did the Democratic presidential candidates of the period. Notable in this company were the neocon intellectuals, many of whom were hired on to the Reagan administration in mid-level positions and would continue there through the next presidency, and would return (in some cases) during the presidency of George W. Bush. Many more were associated with the increasingly influential think tanks which worked to educate public opinion along the new foreign policy lines. In these neocon ranks, Jews were particularly prominent, both inside and outside the government. Thus even though Reagan did not appoint any Jews to his cabinet (the first time this had been the case since the Truman administration), Jews were more than able to defend their perspective on foreign policy matters within the State Department and before the public. Of great importance for the future was that Republican Zionism now had an updated intellectual defense. Increasingly drawn to neocon thinking about world affairs, certain leaders of AIPAC and the American Jewish figures who were its principal funders and spokesmen developed close relationships with the Reagan administration. "Through the 1980s," J. J. Goldberg notes, "AIPAC lobbyists regularly helped the Reagan administration line up Democratic congressional support on unlikely issues from Central America to Sub-Saharan Africa. . . . In return, the Reagan administration set about making itself into the most pro-Israel administration in history. . . . Israel's annual U.S. aid package, already higher than any other country's, was edged even higher. Loans were made into grants. Supplemental grants were added."[88]

The principal flaw in this situation, however, from the point of view of Republican Party loyalists, was that on *domestic* issues it was the liberal adversaries of the neocons who were still winning the hearts of most Jewish organizations and, apparently, most Jewish voters. From the first days of the Reagan administration, the major Jewish organizations opposed and fought it vigorously on virtually every domestic issue of the day—from abortion to school prayer. Hence, in the end, the gratitude that many Jews felt and expressed for Reagan's friendship to Israel and the affinity that most felt for the general world-political view of the administration did not translate into support at the polls. Reagan actually lost Jewish votes in his 1984 reelection bid, dropping from 40 percent to 33 percent. The Democrat Walter Mondale, who lost every state except his own Minnesota, won two-thirds of the Jewish vote.[89] To this day, the Jewish shift to the right that neocons were predicting in 1980 has not materialized.

GEORGE H. W. BUSH (1989–1993)
"When you're serious about peace, call us!"

GEORGE BUSH BEFORE THE PRESIDENCY

Unlike the other Presidents with whom we have dealt here so far, with the one exception of Kennedy, George Herbert Walker Bush was born to wealth and privilege. His grandfathers on both sides were wealthy businessmen, one the owner of a major investment bank, the other a manufacturer of steel products. Born in 1924, he was raised in lavish homes in Massachusetts, Connecticut, and Maine, educated at an elite school (Phillips Academy) and at Yale University. His father, Prescott Bush, served as U.S. Senator from Connecticut (1952–1962). George Bush enlisted for the war the moment he turned eighteen, becoming possibly the youngest fighter pilot to participate in the war. It was an action-filled career, in which the highlight was being shot down in the Pacific and rescued by a submarine.

After the war, Bush set out to find a career apart from the family interests on the East Coast, but this required the bankrolling of his father and his father's associates. Because the object of the exercise was to display before the world his entrepreneurial talent, he moved as far away as possible from familiar eastern U.S. terrain, entering the ranks of the entrepreneurs in the oil business in Texas. Bush's career in the oil-rigging business was marked by ups and downs, but he was able to build a network of loyal friends who assisted his political ambitions. Texas in those days was still overwhelmingly Democratic, but the most recent presidential elections (beginning, modestly, with that of Eisenhower in 1952) were disclosing a long-range trend toward the Republican Party. Bush gave up the seat he held in Congress (1966–1970) in order to run for the Senate. As expected, this effort failed; but, as had also been expected, it marked him as a good soldier in President Nixon's campaign to make the Republican Party the party of the majority in the South. Thus he was drawn close to the Nixon administration, serving under a series of appointments in which he proved his capacity for hard work and loyalty. He became, in swift succession, ambassador to the UN (1971–1973), chairman of the Republican National Committee during the Watergate months (1973–1974), head of the American delegation to China (1974–1975), and director of the CIA (under Ford, 1976–1977). When he ran for the Republican nomination for president in 1980 this long résumé constituted his principal qualification for the office. He cheerfully accepted nomination for the vice presidency, and served President Reagan with conspicuous loyalty through his two terms. In 1988 he won election by a comfortable margin over the Democrat, Michael Dukakis.

RELIGION IN THE LIFE OF GEORGE BUSH

George Herbert Walker Bush was born into a family whose members had been usually Episcopalian as far back as anyone knew. The family was accustomed to attending church regularly and was also subject to Christian instruction in the home. Prescott Bush read a Bible lesson at the breakfast table each day.[90] Here and there in his campaign autobiography we find reference to Bush's faith in the personal reality of God. The most developed reference is in connection with the story of the loss of his daughter to leukemia at the age of three in 1953.

> Prayer had always been an important part of our lives, but never more so than during those six months. Barbara and I sustained each other; but in the end it was our faith that truly sustained us, as gradually but surely, Robin slipped away. She was three years and ten months old when she died. To this day, like every parent who has ever lost a child, we wonder why; yet we know that, whatever the reason, she is in God's loving arms.[91]

But in Bush's mind, God is not merely concerned with our personal and daily lives. He presides as well over the great matters that figure in history, and so everything that happens in that realm is no less to be seen in the light of divine purposes. Speaking to the National Religious Broadcasters in the early days of the Gulf War, Bush said "Saddam tried to cast this conflict as a religious war, but it has nothing to do with religion per se. It has, on the other hand, everything to do with what religion embodies: good versus evil, right versus wrong. . . . America has always been a religious nation, perhaps never more than now. Just look at the last several weeks—churches, synagogues, mosques, reporting record attendance at services."[92] In the months following the Gulf War, several commentators noticed a tendency for President Bush to present that victory as proof of America's existing under the special providence of God.

With reference to our interests in this book, we should note that there is nothing on record to suggest that George Bush was familiar with the themes of Christian restorationism and Christian Zionism, which, as we have argued, figured in the religious nurture of most of the presidents of this period and which have left in the political culture at least a vague residue. These themes have never figured in mainline Episcopal thinking any more than in Roman Catholic teaching. Bush did, however, have many friends in the Evangelical world, notably Billy Graham, and is known to have spent many hours of conversation with him when Graham was his houseguest on many occasions in his summer place in Maine. We do know that the cause of Israel was very close to the heart of Billy Graham and was promoted in many ways by his organization.[93] But whether he ever shared his perspectives on this matter with George Bush is purely a matter of conjecture. Certainly nothing in Bush's words or actions suggests that he saw the issue of the support of Israel in a theological context.

FOREIGN POLICY OF GEORGE BUSH

In strong contrast to Ronald Reagan, George Bush gave foreign policy the highest priority at the beginning of his administration. This was signaled immediately by his appointment of his closest long-time political ally, his campaign manager in 1980 (as he would be again in 1992), a wealthy Texan, James A. Baker, III. Given the fast bond between Bush and Baker, there was never any doubt during this presidency that foreign policy belonged to Baker.

No one should offer his first word of criticism about the record of President George Herbert Walker Bush until he has reflected carefully upon the fact that his presidency began in "the most eventful year in history . . . the most startling, promising and consequential year, ever . . . the most momentous months in mankind's history."[94] What made this year so "momentous" was, of course the fall of European communism, which took place swiftly during the summer and fall of 1989, leaving only the Soviet Union itself to succumb by the end of 1990. The Cold War was suddenly over, and everything that for over forty years had been taken as wisdom about the global realities that must govern U.S. policies was suddenly irrelevant. In the first hours of Bush's watch as president, the USSR withdrew her interest in being a world power. A few months into this presidency, the USSR succumbed altogether. No longer would the Soviet Union sponsor anti-U.S. governments in Africa. Cuba's subsidies vanished forever, as did those of the many revolutionary movements in Central America. In the Middle East, the former client states (notably Syria and Iraq) and the many terrorist movements were cut off from support of the Russian taxpayer. No one who had the attention of policymakers any-where in the world saw this coming.

There is therefore good reason why George Bush misread the signs of the times, first resisting the evidences of the beginning of the end of the Cold War, then, in recoil, overrating the strengths of the successors to the communist leaders, and finally overstating the possibilities for radical new beginning in a world in which there was only one superpower—"the New World Order." Our theme, no less than all the other foreign policy themes, has to be seen in light of the dizzying pace of change in world-political realities that marked the Bush years.

EARLIEST DEALINGS WITH THE GOVERNMENT OF ISRAEL

Secretary Baker was eager to avoid the "pitfall" (as he called it) that was Israel-Arab relations. "This rather bleak and somewhat selfish assess-ment," he recalls, "was anchored in my conclusion that there was no real evidence to believe the climate was ripe for generating any momentum in a conflict that had defied resolution for nearly half a century. But it was buttressed by my own experience as White House Chief of Staff in the first Reagan term, where aggressive and well-intentioned diplomacy had produced little more than stalemate, and a disastrous intervention in Beirut, which took 241 American lives. I remember remarking several times to my transition staff that all secretaries of state are inevitably sucked into the Middle East, where they expend an inordinate amount of time and effort in an enterprise with few prospects of success." Richard Nixon's advice to the new secretary of state was, "It's time for some even-handedness out there. But basically, the Middle East is insoluble. Stay away from it."[95]

During debates about policy toward Israel in the innermost circle of the Reagan White House, George Bush (then vice president, specially charged with "crisis management") and James Baker (the chief of staff) were the leaders of the group most dedicated to restraining Israel's free-dom of action.[96] Apart from this general bias, Baker had little trust in the current Israeli leader, Yitzhak Shamir, and would eventually find it diffi-cult to speak calmly with him or about him. The other side of this coin was that the Israelis remembered Baker as the man who, as Reagan's chief of staff, had led the administration's successful effort to carry through the AWACS sale in 1981. He was tagged thereafter, with some good reason, as one who sought to diminish the influence that Jews and friends of Israel had in public opinion and in the Congress.[97]

In spite of himself, however, Baker signed on to an effort, begun in the State Department in the last months of Shultz's tenure, to persuade the government of Israel to accept a plan for empowering a reliable Palestinian delegation so that an international conference could be held.[98] Baker's readiness to lean on Israeli politicians and citizens was revealed in many acts and words, not least in a speech to an AIPAC gathering in May 22, 1989, when he warned, "now is the time to lay aside, once and for all, the unrealistic vision of a Greater Israel. . . . Foreswear annexation. Stop settlement activity. . . . Reach out to the Palestinians as neighbors who deserve political rights"[99]—thus seeming to subscribe to the common judgment on the American left that Shamir and his party were continuing to add impediments to peace, intending to wear down the other side and ultimately achieve the boundaries of a Greater Israel, as envisioned by Jabotinsky. During the first year of the Bush administration, Baker facilitated a series of surreptitious meetings involving, at one time or another, Peres, Rabin, President Mubarek and his Foreign Minister, and certain emissaries of Arafat, preparing the ground for announcement of guidelines for a forthcoming international conference to settle the "Arab-Israeli dispute"—a prospect which Prime Minister Shamir was known to loathe. Baker calculated that the announcement by himself of a proposal along the lines foreseen in these negotiations would win support among most Israelis and would improve the political fortunes of the Labor leaders, Peres and Rabin; this in turn would compel Shamir either to step aside or get behind the plan. In this confidence, Baker had simply withheld knowledge of these negotiations from Prime Minister Shamir and his Foreign Minister, Moshe Arens.[100] Rabin's biographer, Dan Kurzman, notes, "Rabin realized it was unusual [sic] for a government official to conspire with a foreign power to shape the policy of his superior [Yitzhak Shamir]. But the Intifada was raging, and a solution, Rabin felt, had to be found before Israel sank deeper into quicksand."[101] The very complicated Baker proposals involved elections in the area, a scheme for screening out a number of reliable Palestinian Arabs who would not be controlled by the PLO, and other specifics about accrediting a "Palestinian delegation" to an international conference. When every "i" was dotted, Baker presented the plan to Shamir and Arens. Shamir must have known that it would all come to nothing, as the PLO declared that anyone signing on without PLO clearance would simply be killed. Nonetheless, Shamir stalled, and then negotiated some more.

In March 1990 Shimon Peres, the Labor leader, decided to withdraw from the Unity Government and to try to form a government under his own leadership. Bush and Baker, noting that, as always, the Labor Party leader was showing greater readiness than the Likud Party leader to cooperate with American peace initiatives, looked on with undisguised partisan interest while parliamentary negotiations proceeded. Peres's efforts to form a government failed, however—one vote short! And so—

to the horror of James Baker—Yitzhak Shamir came back with another government, which lasted from June 11, 1990, until the election of June 1992.

On June 13, 1990, while appearing before the House Foreign Affairs Committee, Baker publicly scolded Shamir for having no serious intention about negotiating. "What is needed is some really good-faith affirmative efforts on the part of our good friends in Israel." Should he be wrong about this, Baker suggested, he would welcome a telephone call *right now*—and then he read out to the world the telephone number of the White House switchboard. "When you're serious about peace, call us!" It is not normal diplomatic practice to hold up to ridicule before the world the leader of the other side in a negotiation among friends. Baker's blatant partisanship simply hardened Shamir's refusal to sign on.[102]

PERSIAN GULF CRISIS

Shortly before George Bush became president, the Iran-Iraq War ended. This event had dominated the thinking of American Middle East policy advisors for the previous decade. During 1984, the Reagan administration had reviewed the issue of American relations with Iraq, which had been severed at the time of the Six-Day War, and these were formally renewed in November 1984. This initiative was encouraged by Israel, says Shultz, as "a U.S. dialogue with Iraq constituted at least a means of communication with a state that rejected Israel."[103] Still, the U.S. remained quietly concerned about renewal by Iraq of its secret nuclear weapons programs and its research into chemical weapons. Since Iran had made itself America's sworn enemy during the hostage crisis that ended Carter's presidency, the government of the United States, following that ancient piece of illogic that "the enemy of my enemy is my friend," tilted secretly to the side of Iraq. A deliberate decision was made to suppress knowledge that the administration had regarding Saddam's possession and early use of chemical weapons,[104] of many abuses of the Iraqi dictator against his citizens, and of such matters as Saddam's resale of American grain sold to him to feed his citizens to gain cash to be applied to more war making.

Still, Iran did not crumble quickly as the Americans had expected, but rather the Ayatollah Khomeini whipped up the population to a frenzy of martyrdom, turning the great advantage of his larger population against the better-equipped Iraqis. And so the war went on for a decade. During these same years the Israelis, working a Faustian bargain of their own, were secretly assisting the Iranian side through secret sales and other kinds of help—all this, despite the Ayatollah's denunciation of Israel as Satan! (It was Israel's covert contacts in Iran who served as the sirens leading members of the Reagan's National Security team into what would be become the Iran-Contra affair.)

In its first days, the Bush administration sought quietly to reassure Saddam Hussein that it had some sympathy for the case that he was making about an historical tie between Iraq (Babylon) and the area around the Straits, on which Kuwait now stood. While it was engaged in these discussions, the Bush administration had to pretend not to be offended by Saddam's public denunciation of the United States as the enemy of Islam, the partner of Satan Israel. This was as nothing, however, compared to what happened to Kuwait and Saudi Arabia. As soon as the war ended, Saddam demanded that these profligate sponsors of his war now forgive the billions of dollars in aid, on the ground that Iraq had fought on behalf of all Arabs. It had been, he said, a war of the poor against the rich— always a winning hand in the mass politics of the Middle East, the same card played with such dramatic results by Nasser thirty years earlier. This talk made Saddam extremely popular in Gaza and on the West Bank and in Jordan.

It would be said afterward that American diplomats had been so ready to talk with Saddam and to entertain his interpretation of local history that Saddam could not have helped but think that the Americans were prepared to acquiesce in whatever action he might see fit to take. Yet the most responsible students of the story say that Saddam should have understood that the United States would not permit the unilateral solution that Saddam had in mind and that he suddenly carried out on August 2, 1990—the invasion of Kuwait. The Kuwaiti princes and the elite fled the kingdom at once, retreating for the most part to European resorts. The large body of Palestinian expatriates who provided so much of the low-paid labor in the kingdom went on a rampage. In Jordan and in the Palestinian Arab world, Hussein was acclaimed. Arafat rushed to Baghdad to embrace Saddam (January 6, 1991): "I say, welcome to war. . . . Iraq and Palestine represent a common will. We will be side by side, and after the battle, God willing, we will pray together in Jerusalem. The Iraqi fighters and the Palestinian stone-throwers have an appointment with victory."[105]

As early as August 3, 1990, Baker had secured a joint statement with the Soviet Foreign Minister, Eduard Shevardnadze, denouncing "this blatant transgression of basic norms of civilized conduct." Baker's suggestion that this moment should be considered the true end of the Cold War is a good one.[106] Once the UN had formally denounced Iraq's invasion of Kuwait, the United States took the lead in proposing action. Negotiations with Saudi Arabia led to an agreement whereby 400,000 troops were brought into Saudi Arabia. Much delicate negotiation went into appeasing the powerful anti-Western feelings of the population that for at least two generations had been indoctrinated with Wahhabism, the most fanatical of all the extant forms of Islam, which teaches the duty of Muslims to eradicate Judaism and Christianity as opportunity affords. The Americans conceded every point at issue—for example, that there should be no Christian symbols, no Bibles, and no worship services, and that there should be no alcoholic beverages at all.[107]

On November 29, 1990, the UN agreed to sponsor an international force, to be led by the United States and supported by other nations. It was like the Korean intervention in June 1950, with the important difference that this action was mandated by the Security Council with the Soviet Union voting in favor and China cooperating by withholding her veto. After painful debate, the Congress passed legislation approving U.S. participation in this war, under the terms agreed at the UN. (The vote in the House was 250-183, and in the Senate 52-47.)

FORMER PRESIDENT CARTER OFFERS AN
ALTERNATIVE SOLUTION TO THE GULF PROBLEM

In the months that followed Saddam Hussein's conquest of Kuwait, former President Jimmy Carter worked ceaselessly to prevent the international action against Iraq that eventually reversed that conquest.[108] He publicly accused the Bush administration of refusing to follow up all the many possibilities for peaceful negotiation of the issue that were being offered around the world. There was also a range of secret initiatives. He wrote personally to the leaders of the major powers and urged them not to cooperate with the Bush-Baker initiatives: Instead, Carter advised, they should hand over the matter to "an Arab League effort," which would bring about peace *in the whole region* by linking the solution of the Kuwait matter to the issue that is the source of all unhappiness among the Arabs—Israel's occupation of Palestine. The goal of the policy that Carter would be pursuing were he still president would not be to punish Iraq but to use the present crisis to establish a Palestinian state.

During the 1990s, Carter became, in the most literal sense, a ghostwriter for Arafat, whom he liked to address as "my brother." As he worked on what became the draft of the speech that Arafat gave to the Security Council of the United Nations on May 20, 1990, he told Arafat:

> The objective of the speech should be to secure maximum sympathy and support of other world leaders, especially including Americans and Israelis. The Likud leaders are now on the defensive, and must not be given any excuse for continuing their present abusive policies. . . . [You should refer to various reports of Israeli cruelty in the West Bank and Gaza.] Then ask: "What would you do, if these were your children and grandchildren? As the Palestinian leader, I share the responsibility for them. Our response has been to urge peace talks, but the Israeli leaders have refused, and our children continue to suffer. Our people, who face

Israeli bullets, have no weapons: only a few stones remaining when our homes are destroyed by Israeli bulldozers. . . ." The thrust of the speech should be to bring, not only the world's political leaders, but every parent and grandparent, into a realization of the excessively patient suffering of the Palestinians.[109]

Tirelessly, Carter sought out opportunities to denounce Israel's rule over the Palestinians. At the same time, he romanticized the way of the Palestinians. He conveyed privately to Yassir Arafat his "congratulations" on the accomplishments of the Intifada (ignoring the fact that all informed observers knew that the PLO had had nothing at all to do with starting it). By a strange logical and moral inversion, the rock-throwing boys of the Intifada became for Carter embodiments of *Gandhi's preaching of nonviolence*: They were "instant heroes" exhibiting "an unprecedented commitment to their cause and a surprising threshold for absorbing pain." In so doing, he told the world through the op-ed page of the *New York Times*, "they are appealing directly to the conscience of the world. . . . They have preemptively attacked Israel's most cherished characteristic: its moral fiber."[110]

By now, Carter no longer pretended goodwill toward Israel. Yet, he would not let go of the notion that he was universally recognized as the creator of the Camp David Spirit, and therefore the embodiment of impartiality. Believing, and stating aloud again and again, that the Republican leaders in the White House and the State Department were unfit to negotiate impartial settlement of the Arab-Israeli dispute, given the enormous political weight of the Jewish vote, Carter sought to use his Carter Center to finish the unfinished work of the Camp David Accords. His conviction of the impartiality of his organization was unaffected by the circumstance that several millions of dollars of financial support for his center came from Palestinian Arab businessmen, and millions more from Pakistani and other Muslim financiers who ran the Bank of Credit and Commerce International, which would eventually come to ruin in one of the biggest banking scandals of the century.[111]

A few days before Operation Desert Storm was to begin, Carter wrote secretly to Assad of Syria, Mubarek of Egypt and Faud of Saudi Arabia, and urged them to withdraw their support of the allied initiative: "The advances you have made in guiding your nation's progress might well be lost. This war might also postpone indefinitely any efforts to resolve the Palestine issue." The story of Carter's secret initiatives did not emerge for many years. When it did, some Bush administration figures concluded that Carter's actions had verged on treason. Secretary of Defense Dick Cheney (later to be vice president under George W. Bush) said: "For him to go behind our backs and ask world leaders to denounce our war policy was reprehensible, totally inappropriate, for a former President."[112]

Only a minority of Americans agreed with Jimmy Carter on the Gulf War issue. Yet most, it seems, gave him the benefit of the doubt, believing that he was wrong for the right reason—because he abhorred violence and believed that anything was better than to pour down death and destruction upon the people of Iraq. Yet his own Carter Doctrine of January 23, 1980 ("Any attempt by an outside force to gain control of the Persian Gulf region will be regarded as an assault on the vital interests of the United States of America, and such force will be repelled by any means necessary, including military force") was the explicit foundation of the Bush administration's action.

There was no reason to believe that Carter had a monopoly on moral anguish at that hour. The larger truth was that his animosity toward Israel had become so intense that, just like the Arab leaders, he now saw everything that went wrong in the region as being *caused by* Israel. In this light, the Gulf War presented a marvelous opportunity to put the peace process back on the track that he had opened up at Camp David some twelve years previous, but that had then been closed down again because Israel had unilaterally sabotaged it. Conferring closely and continuously with his "brother" Yassir Arafat, Carter took up the PLO leader's mandate to champion *his* own "solution" of the problem, which was to establish in the world's mind the linkage between the problems caused by Iraq's invasion of Kuwait and the issue of Israel's occupation of Palestine. The immediate withdrawal of Israel from Palestine would not only (somehow) cause Hussein to withdraw from Kuwait, but would reunite the Arabs as brothers again, give them the self-respect they had always been denied, and thus cause all unhappiness to cease. This linkage was publicly announced by Jimmy Carter from the outset, but little noticed. In a speech in Arizona on September 29, 1990, he said, "No matter how you look at what's happening in Kuwait, no matter how you look at what's happening in Lebanon, the core issue is now, and will continue to be, Israel-Palestine."[113] In an op-ed piece in the *New York Times* on January 2, 1991, Jimmy Carter disclosed the key to the whole situation: "Now is a propitious time for Israel to come forward with a genuine peace initiative, shifting the onus of the consequences of Saddam Hussein's invasion to Israel."[114]

THE PROSPECT OF A NEW WORLD ORDER

Desert Storm, the American-led, UN-sanctioned military action to liberate Kuwait, began on January 15, 1991. The first phase was an aerial bombardment of Iraq that went on for six weeks and involved, to some degree or another, the forces of twenty-eight nations. Then the invasion on the ground began on February 24. One hundred hours later, the Iraqi forces requested and received a cease-fire, which ended the war.[115] Even the most optimistic had not guessed how brief it would be and how low the cost would be on the Allied side.

It was a remarkable military triumph, prepared by a unique triumph of diplomacy. All the Arab states, except Iraq, Jordan, and Libya, supported the action—at least with words. Egypt, the largest Arab, nation, participated (modestly) in the military action. Among the Americans, there was a sense that Bush, by this war, had accomplished what Jimmy Carter had failed to do—that is, to establish in the minds and hearts of the Arab nations the reality that all had a common cause in crushing rogue forces in the Middle East. Surely these same governments could be persuaded to see the many terrorist organizations in this same light. And, above all, surely they would now see the wisdom agreeing to talk with Israel for the sake of the peace of the entire region.

Early in the aerial war, Saddam Hussein had sought to deflect Arab rage away from himself and toward Israel, thus forcing Arab states to abandon the alliance and join in what would have been a hugely popular jihad against Israel. In pursuit of this hope, Saddam launched missile attacks against Israel. For over a month (January 18–February 24), missiles landed in and around Tel Aviv. As this prospect was looming, Bush had sent messengers to Israel to persuade the government of Yitzhak Shamir that it must not give assistance to Saddam's plot to undo the alliance by responding in any way that would put the Arab people of Iraq under attack from Israel. To gain compliance with this request, Bush sent a detachment with Patriot missiles supposed to be capable of shooting down the rather low-grade and antiquated Soviet-made missiles that Baghdad was using, although it is not clear that any ever did.[116] It was a great encouragement for Israelis to know that American military were actually on their soil, sharing directly in Israel's direct defense. The Shamir government held up its side of the bargain scrupulously, despite having to face much domestic criticism for giving up Israel's freedom of action in its own defense.

By their acquiescence to American leadership and direction in the Gulf War, most of the Arab governments gained esteem in American eyes. At the same time, the kingdom of Jordan and the PLO, the two parties with whom Israel was supposed to be contemplating direct negotiation for peace, had both *lost* considerable esteem. Jordan now paid the price for declaring support of Saddam and permitting passage of goods into Iraq—the abrupt withdrawal of U.S. aid. Simultaneously, the PLO was cut off by its most generous financial supporters, Saudi Arabia, Kuwait, and the Gulf states. This last fact surely meant that Arafat now had nowhere to go and must look realistically at last at a negotiated solution to his homelessness. This seemed to present an opportunity to Israel.

In the days that followed the victory over Iraq and in many subsequent speeches President Bush spoke of a New World Order made possible by the outcome of this war. Given that Russia, the ex-superpower, seemed so willing to follow the American lead in so many major world problems (if only to the extent of not using her veto power at the UN while occasionally protesting about lack of consultation); and given that there was now a Security Council that could, under the right circumstances, think and act as one, as the founders of that body had intended; and given that Arab governments had shown their willingness to cooperate in statesmanlike ways—then there ought not to be any limit to how the world could be redesigned.

PRESIDENT BUSH RENEWS THE PEACE PROCESS

Whatever Israelis may have expected, the Bush administration had no intention of affording good conduct credits to Israel in the renewed round of peacemaking that began at once. In his speech to Congress, March 6, 1991, declaring victory over Iraq, Bush immediately brought the Israel-Palestinian conflict back to front and center: "The time has come to put an end to the Arab-Israeli dispute."[117] Shortly afterward, Secretary Baker set off on what would prove to be the first of eight tours of the region before the end of the year. On October 18, 1991, the United States and the Soviet Union announced jointly that they intended to sponsor a conference in Madrid to include all parties to the Arab-Israeli dispute.[118] There were many ways for the United States to coax the parties to participate, and Secretary Baker had apparently been using all of them, for notices of acceptance had already been received from Israel, Syria, Lebanon, and from a joint Palestinian-Jordanian delegation whose members had been approved by Israel and the United States.

The international conference at Madrid which began on October 30, 1991, was, in effect, the Geneva Conference that Jimmy Carter had so assiduously pursued. The major difference was that the USSR was now literally in its last hours and the various successor governments of the Warsaw bloc had no interest whatever in playing big power games in this region. To secure the participation of Mikhail Gorbachev it was necessary for the United States to pick up Russia's share of the tab.[119] President Gorbachev attended the first meeting briefly and then went back to face the crisis that ended in the dissolution of the USSR and of his own public career.

Israel had agreed to attend on the condition that there be a joint–Jordanian-Palestinian delegation. Although forced to pretend not to know that the delegates were answerable for everything to the PLO, Israel required that the PLO not be considered a party to the negotiations and that any overt declaration by a delegate of his subservience to the PLO would disqualify him. As it developed, Arafat was to some degree eclipsed in world opinion by the appearance of a Palestinian delegation that included some persons of standing in the Arab community of Palestine and who certainly presented a more intelligent and endearing presence than the veteran terrorist. Still, the Palestinian delegation made clear to the Americans and the Israelis that they would make no decisions that were not cleared in advance with Arafat in Algeria.

The opening sessions were rocky. Insults were exchanged, delegates stood up to leave and recesses were called to calm the scene. But eventually a business-like atmosphere was achieved.

THE U.S.-ISRAEL RELATIONSHIP IN THE LAST MONTHS OF THE BUSH PRESIDENCY

In May 25, 1990, Congress approved a request for $400 million in guarantees by the U.S. government of loans to be undertaken by Israel for the purpose of building housing to accommodate the several hundred thousand immigrants from the Soviet Union and the former Soviet empire admitted in recent years. Because of the staunch public position of Bush and Baker—that the United States would not countenance any of its own money going to extend settlements in the disputed territories—the government of Yitzhak Shamir gave assurances in private, but was soon violating them in reality.[120] Then in January 1991 the government of Israel came back to the government of the United States seeking $13 billion in additional aid from the United States. In its itemized request list there appeared $3 billion as compensation for damages done during Scud attacks—"an audacious gambit" said Secretary Baker. This request was renewed (after some adjustments resulting from the administration's first response) after the summer recess of Congress, in September 1991. As Congress was considering the issue, Israel's housing minister, Ariel Sharon, was engaging in aggressive settlement-building, in defiance of the American government's well-documented determination not to let American money be used to abet Israeli encroachment on the disputed lands. In September 1991, President Bush spoke out at a press conference about the unseemly contest over this issue in Congress: "A debate [on this request] now could well destroy our ability to bring one or more of the parties to the peace table. . . . I am up against some powerful political forces . . . very strong and effective groups that go up to the Hill . . . something like a thousand lobbyists. . . . We've only got one lonely little guy down here [the President]. . . . But I'm going to fight for what I believe. . . . The question [is not] . . . whether it's good 1992 politics. What's important here is that we give this process a chance. . . . And I don't care if I get one vote. . . . I believe the American people will be with me."[121] Bush won the immediate contest, as, faced by threat of veto, the Congress removed the loan guarantee provision from the financial aid bill and passed it (April 1992). But this only postponed the loan guarantee matter, bringing it into sharper focus in time for the election contest of 1992.

Meanwhile, Shimon Peres had lost the leadership of the Labor Party in its internal primary elections, and, following the election of June 23, 1992, Yitzhak Rabin had become prime minister again after fifteen years. Commentators in the United States and in Israel had generally concluded that Shamir's constant yanking and pulling against the U.S. government in so many matters had finally diminished him in Israel—or, to put it another way, that Bush's steadfast policy regarding the guarantees had cost Shamir his job. Rabin's new government had a broader base of support in the Knesset than any of recent years and had the additional virtue, from the point of view of the administration, that it did not include right-wing elements that had exercised so much control over Shamir while including left-wing elements committed to the pursuit of negotiated peace. In August 1992, after a quick visit to Israel, Baker reported to Bush, "I have just finished visiting a different Israel. The mood is different and the atmosphere is one of hope." Rabin met President Bush in the White House and assured him that, under his new government, there would be a virtual freeze in new settlement activities other than "those in strategic areas"; some of these latter might, however, be "thickened," he avowed.[122] Satisfied by this explanation, President Bush withdrew his objection to the loan guarantee bill when it passed on October, 5, 1992.

THE ELECTION OF 1992

During the first two years or so of the Bush presidency, Israel was still suffering to some extent in public opinion from the reputation for truculence, which it gained during the Reagan years. But the Gulf War caused a shift in public attitudes regarding the entire region of the Middle East, in light of which Israel's attitudes could be better justified. On the other side of the ledger, Israel's world-political situation was greatly improved during these same years by a broadening of normal diplomatic and commercial contact. Several years earlier (1979), Egypt had been the first Arab state to normalize diplomatic relations. Although further recognition by Arab nations would not come for a few more years (Jordan in 1994, and Mauritania in October 1999) much quiet cooperation on practical matters (commerce and management of resources) was worked out at the multilateral conferences that Madrid had spawned. Whatever they were saying to their own populations, leaders of several Arab states were beginning already to calculate the advantages of improving their relations with Israel. During 1991 and 1992, Israel enjoyed a virtual rush of decisions for recognition from nations that had previously refused it. Eastern European nations, which had been compelled to toe the anti-Zionist line of the Soviet Union, overthrew their communist governments in 1989 and 1990, and thereafter demonstrated their appreciation of the economic and other advantages that would follow from dealing with Israel as an equal. The USSR itself resumed diplomatic relations with Israel in October 1991. India and China, the two largest nations on earth, extended formal recognition in the same month, January 1992. On December 30, 1993, Israel and the Vatican signed the *Fundamental Agreement between the Holy See and the State of Israel*, which committed the two parties to mutual recognition.

And it was during these years and through George Bush's efforts that the UN rescinded the "Zionism is racism" declaration of November 10, 1975. Although of no practical effect, this action cost the Bush administration considerable time and effort in international lobbying and should certainly weigh more than it does in the recollection of the friends of Israel. Still, the general verdict among friends of Israel was that the Republican administration had proved too slow to perceive Israel's needs. This insight served to confirm the loyalty that most Jews had to Democratic Party, slowing down for the time being the drift toward the Republican Party.

In his last year, President Bush was faced with explaining to the electorate both the actions and the words that he had directed toward Israel since the end of the Gulf War. The issue of Israel in Republican counsels was further complicated by the entry into the 1992 Republican primaries of the former Nixon-speechwriter and right-wing commentator, Patrick Buchanan. His statements on immigration and his statements on the Middle East both caused alarm in the ranks of American Jews. As for the latter, he said, "There are only two groups beating the drums for war in the Middle East—the Israeli defense ministry and the amen corner in the United States."[123] Such sentiments caused confusion among liberal commentators, who, for the most part, assumed that a pro-Israel attitude was one face of the monolithic "Religious Right." Buchanan had made himself the champion of Judaeo-Christian values under assault in the media and from government, yet here he was, deliberately cutting himself adrift from a major part of the Republican congregation—"the amen corner," those Evangelicals committed to seeing that the U.S. government should pursue a consistently pro-Israel policy.

There was no doubt that Buchanan represented a substantial section of Republicans, what might be called "classical isolationists," of the school that had gone to the margins of the party after Eisenhower defeated Taft in 1952. Seeking to keep America's national interest defined in material terms and preferring a world in which there are no obstacles to free trade, classical isolationists had been well aware that the empire of the Soviet Union was the principal contemporary obstacle to globalism on U.S. terms; thus, the most ideological of the anti-Soviet Republicans had always come from this camp. But the collapse of the Soviet empire changed all this forever. During the 1992 campaign, *Commentary* magazine debated the question, "Is Pat Buchanan an Anti-Semite?" This was unjust, and in any case missed the point, since Buchanan's resentment of Israel was not because it is the land of the Jews but because it had made its defense an obligation of honor upon the United States, and hence a continuing obstacle to freedom of action in the part of the world where the oil comes from.

But the contest for the Republican nomination did not turn on foreign policy debates—let alone upon the question of Israel. And neither did the election. All the grandiose talk about a New World Order was quickly forgotten as President Bush belatedly confronted the issue that the public really cared about: the economy. A pathetic sign of President Bush's failure to keep world affairs on the agenda was the fact that he had to appeal to his old friend Jim Baker to resign as secretary of state, something Baker did with painfully visible reluctance on August 13, 1992, in order to become Bush's chief of staff—effectively his reelection campaign manager.[124] Whatever plans Bush might have for his second term, at this point the motto seemed to be "A pox on foreign policy." By the act of reassigning his most loyal friend to the campaign room while handing the State Department over to an acting secretary (Lawrence Eagleburger), President Bush diminished the prestige of American foreign policy making in the eyes of most of the world.

BILL CLINTON (1993–2001)
"I'm a colossal failure, and you made me one."

EARLY LIFE OF BILL CLINTON

It is difficult to think of anything very substantial that is common to the early life of Bill Clinton and either of the two men named George Bush who are the bookends to his presidency. There is, however, a great deal that is common to the early life of Bill Clinton and Jimmy Carter. Neither *inherited* anything that would prove of material value in advancing a political career—not money, not family connection, not acquaintance with the great world of power. Like Jimmy Carter, William Jefferson Clinton was born in a small southern town—*not* the Old South, but the Border South, in Arkansas, the site of bitter battles during the Civil War, and the site as well of one of the most memorable battles of the civil rights struggle of the 1950s and 1960s: Little Rock.

Bill Clinton (born 1946) was raised in a family of even more modest means than the Carter family. Whereas Jimmy Carter's family was close-knit, with ramifications throughout the state of Georgia, Bill Clinton's family was virtually isolated from the local family history of Hope, Arkansas. In fact, *Clinton* was not his original family name, but was taken by him legally at the age of sixteen in an effort to add a little regularity to his relationship with his mother's second husband, a philandering alcoholic named Roger Clinton. His single mother left Bill for a lengthy portion of his childhood in the care of his grandparents while she secured an education in Shreveport, Louisiana, and then for much of the time while she followed a local career as an anesthetist's nurse. When an opportunity came to leave Hope, Bill Clinton's mother took it. From the time he was six, Bill Clinton lived in Hot Springs, a city with a reputation for fast living and rather dark politics owing to its famous resorts, racetracks, and illegal but wide-open gambling casino. No place less like Plains, Georgia, could be imagined.

When Carter entered politics it was at the local level, and it was in order to advance the concerns that grow out of local community that he moved into state politics. Bill Clinton used his excellent academic record at Georgetown University School of Foreign Service in Washington and several political connections cultivated early to achieve a privileged access to the company of politicians, first in Washington, where he was an aide to Senator Fulbright of Arkansas, and then, via a Rhodes Scholarship at Oxford, to a well-situated generation of young men and women already headed for careers in national government. Clinton never completed the program that he had undertaken at Oxford while under his scholarship; Jimmy Carter, by contrast, always completed everything he began. After Oxford, Clinton did acquire a degree at Yale Law School (1973), then moved back to Arkansas. Back home, he dedicated himself to pursuit of a political career for which his base would be Arkansas but whose goal, from the beginning, was national office. Both Clinton and Carter were regarded as moderate Southern governors (Jimmy Carter, 1970–1974, and Clinton 1979–1981, 1983–1992).

RELIGION IN THE LIFE OF BILL CLINTON

Both Jimmy Carter and Bill Clinton were Southern Baptists. In Carter's case, Baptist belonging followed easily from the family's long history of membership in their local church. Bill Clinton was born into a family where the thought of going to church on Sunday or any other day did not usually occur. We are told that Bill Clinton sought out the Baptist Church himself when he was eight and began going regularly to church and Sunday school alone, with his Bible in his hand (as is the Southern Baptist way). Later, he sang regularly in the choir, and the fact that the service at his church was televised meant that Bill Clinton's presence in the choir was a matter of record, Sunday after Sunday, throughout the state. Apart from the choir, however, he never was active in church affairs; unlike Carter, he never developed any intellectual interest in doctrine or other matters that might have occurred to an intellectual who owed some part of his energies to the service of his church.

Even by the standards of most politicians, let alone the case of Jimmy Carter, we find a remarkable evasiveness in Clinton's public commentary on the role of religion in his life or in the lives of others, other than that it is very important and very real. To a White House Interfaith Breakfast gathering on August 30, 1993, he said,

> I am often troubled as I try hard here to create a new sense of common purpose. . . . I am convinced that we are in a period of historic significance, profound change here in this country and throughout the world, and that no one is wise enough to see the end of all of it, that we have to be guided by a few basic principles and an absolute conviction that we can create a common good in America. But it's hard for me to take a totally secular approach to the fact that there are cities in this country where the average murderer is now under the age of sixteen. . . . Now, *there may not be a religious answer* to the policy question of whether it's a good thing that all these kids can get their hands on semiautomatic weapons. But *there certainly is something that is far more than secular* about what is happening to a country where we are losing millions of our young people and where they shoot each other with abandon.[125]

In other settings, President Clinton struck a more recognizably Baptist note: He told a group of religious news editors on October 3, 1994, that "he read the Bible and other religious books for guidance and to cope with the isolation of the Presidency. . . . 'The Bible is the authoritative Word of God and contains all truth.'"[126]

Bill and Hillary Clinton both attended church regularly during the eighties and early nineties, the years of his governorship, but they attended different churches—she the United Methodist, he the Southern Baptist. There is a notable difference in the way in which Bill Clinton and his wife Hillary have presented their different appreciations of religious faith—a difference that reflects to some degree the different histories of the two denominations, but probably has more to do with differences in intellectual style. Bill Clinton stresses the matter of consolation for the individual in the knowledge of God's love and providence, whereas Hillary stresses the effect of religion as an impulse to play a public role. Both have promoted the teachings of a number of non-Christian specialists in spiritual living. An influential confidant of the Clintons was Jean Houston (co-director of the Foundation for Mind Research), a mind-reader and spiritualist, whose personal spiritual contact is Athena, the Greek goddess of wisdom, with whom she communicates by computer; the process is called, "docking with one's angel."[127]

Bill Clinton was constantly under assault during his presidency from preachers who had access to national audiences through television broadcast of their religious services and their programs of commentary. Pat Robertson's Christian Broadcasting Network was always on his case.

Jerry Falwell, who presided over the Old Time Gospel Hour, blatantly challenged Bill Clinton's fitness for office, extending his on-air attack through sale of videos (*Circle of Power*, and *The Clinton Chronicles*); these exposed a history of vicious criminal behavior by the president that included not only sexual misdemeanors but complicity in cover-up of evidence in extant criminal and congressional inquiries and even complicity in the murder of political opponents.[128] Given the viciousness and the recklessness of much of this attack, Bill Clinton's public response will seem restrained: "I think the truth is that there are people who don't believe [my Christian faith] . . . is genuine because they disagree with me politically. . . . I think everybody knows that they [specifically, the Christian Coalition] are basically an arm of the Republican Party."[129]

CLINTON'S EARLY DEALINGS WITH ISRAEL

Both George Shultz and James Baker, secretaries of state to the two previous presidents, had postponed as long as seemed possible their activity on behalf of the peace process in the Middle East, but each had eventually gritted his teeth and started up efforts at diplomacy with Israel and her enemies. The experience in both cases proved extremely unpleasant, and it was still unclear at the end of the presidency of George Bush whether anything good was ever likely to follow. President Clinton's experience with the same process was strikingly different. In fact, he was drawn into the peace process at a moment when the long-awaited breakthrough seemed to have occurred—and to have done so without any American involvement whatever! When it came, the opportunity to join in was (in the words of Elizabeth Drew) like "a gift seemingly sent from the heavens."[130]

The gift in question took the form of a communication to President Clinton from the government of Israel on September 9, 1993, to the effect that, out of view of the entire world, Israel and the PLO had negotiated and initialed an agreement of mutual recognition and a plan for advancing quickly to resolution of all the issues between the Israelis and the Palestinians.[131] This accomplishment would make it possible for President to Clinton to appear *literally as the presiding genius* over the beginning of the end of the Arab-Israeli conflict!

Prime Minister Rabin and President Clinton had met on March 15 in the White House.[132] Rabin told the President, "I have a mandate to take calculated risks for peace. I have been a warrior, a general for too long." Clinton responded, "If you are going to do that, my role, the role of the United States, is not to tell you how to do it, or when to do it—my role is to minimize those risks." Rabin's biographer, states that Rabin had hoped for the reelection of Bush in 1992—and this not because Bush had been particularly sympathetic but because the two men were roughly of an age and both had military experience and, in general, a sense of history's larger possibilities. "Rabin was not a general who sought the company of draft-dodgers" (that is, the likes of Bill Clinton), says Rabin's biographer. Rabin eventually became persuaded that Clinton was at least as well-disposed to Israel as Bush, but it took a while for this to happen.[133]

Israel's initial experience of the diplomacy practised by Secretary of State Warren Christopher was unfortunate. During the early months of 1993, Christopher had some lengthy discussions with Assad of Syria, intended to clear a path for direct Israeli-Syrian diplomacy. Rabin was given to understand that Assad was all but ready to come on board the peace process and was only waiting for the arrival of a sufficiently generous offer from the Israelis with regard to the future of Golan. Either the Americans had not understood what Assad was saying or they had understood his adamancy full well but believed that Rabin could be maneuvered into a prior commitment to give back all of the Golan in order to prime the pump; in any case, these negotiations went nowhere. This episode left Syrian-Israeli relations more volatile than ever, while leaving the Rabin government skeptical about both the diplomatic skills and the good will of the Clinton administration.[134]

For about a year, the Madrid conference had ground on without progress on any significant issue. Early in the proceedings the principal business (the bilateral talks) was moved to Washington. A veritable constellation of other multilateral conferences met at other locales, including Moscow, Rome, London, and Switzerland, to deal with a great range of issues affecting the entire region; at some of these multilateral conferences Arab states (Egypt, Jordan, Saudi Arabia, Oman, Morocco, and Tunisia) and even states outside the region participated. In the bilateral setting, it became clear that the Jordanians and the Palestinians were really two distinct groups, with distinct issues to pursue. It was likewise clear that the members of the official Palestinian delegations were strictly controlled by Arafat—a fact that puzzled many Americans and Europeans who could not help but prefer the style of these delegates. How much their expressed loyalty to Arafat was owing to deference and how much to simple animal fear, the Israelis and Americans could not tell.

In February 1993, Foreign Minister Peres presented Prime Minister Rabin with the news that an entirely separate and secret channel of contact had been opened with the PLO some weeks earlier in Oslo, under the good offices of the deputy foreign minister of Norway and certain civilian academics. Because Israeli law forbade direct dealings with the PLO, the Israeli individuals involved would have to present a plan soon and receive the blessing of the government of Israel or close down their contacts, lest a scandal follow. Arafat, like Rabin, needed to keep the Madrid process in place as a distraction for the press while the real negotiations were going on elsewhere, and to this end he gave incomplete and misleading information to the official delegation about certain "secret channels."[135]

On August 17, 1993, Peres flew to Oslo, where he initialed the Oslo Accords. Few details were confirmed at this stage, and so there would have to be further negotiations toward implementing the Declaration of Principles and a formal ratification to be concluded by the end of 1993. For now, the principal terms of the declaration were: (1) that Israeli troops would withdraw from Gaza and from Jericho by April 1994 and the PLO would begin immediately to administer a Palestinian Interim Self-Government Authority whose eventual boundaries would be determined in subsequent negotiations; (2) Israel and the Palestinians would enter into an agreement for economic cooperation and regional development; (3) elections would be held in the Palestinian areas for an executive council in July 1994, with the Arabs of East Jerusalem being allowed to join in the election. Thereafter, the Palestine Council would have responsibility for all government functions except defense and foreign affairs, although Israeli settlements would remain under Israeli control; negotiations on the final status of the territories and on all the related issues (the question of Jerusalem, settlements, water, final borders, etc.) would begin by the end of 1995 and continue for five years.

The Rabin government had made a Machiavellian decision: to turn to Arafat, and, in effect, to impose upon the Palestinians his band of freedom fighters who, for the most part, had lived abroad through recent decades. This unelected organization was now to be saluted as the legitimate leadership of the Palestinian people. This would happen *precisely because* all sides knew that the PLO had less command than ever before on the affections of Arab governments and, with every passing day, less command of public opinion in the territories, as Hamas and Islamic Jihad broadened their hold on the popular imagination.

The U.S. government had not been a party to the Oslo negotiations. The Israelis were concerned about the possibility of leaks if the pool of participants was broadened, and wished to enjoy the option of deniability to the end, if necessary. When Rabin approached Secretary Christopher with news of the agreement (September 8), it was not clear how the Americans would respond.[136] There was reason to fear that they might feel that they had been duped into investing their continuing energies and solemn talk (not to mention their money) on the Madrid-Washington process, which would now appear to have been a Potemkin village. However, if there *was* any of that in the State Department, there was none of it in the White House—rather there was unbounded joy.

"A GIFT FROM THE HEAVENS": THE SIGNING OF
THE OSLO PEACE ACCORDS SEPTEMBER 13, 1993

The news about Oslo came at a low moment for the White House. The first nine months of the Clinton presidency had been marked by pratfalls. During the first two weeks of the presidency the approval rating fell 20 points, as the public reacted to Clinton's very first policy initiative, which was his attempt to remove by presidential initiative and in a moment of time the objection of the military to open acceptance of homosexual behavior in its ranks. Colin Powell, the chairman of the joint chiefs of staff, widely admired and already being talked of as a Republican candidate for the presidency in 1996, openly opposed the president's initiative, and it was necessary for Clinton to crawl down. The result was the "don't ask, don't tell" policy, which almost everyone agreed made things worse.[137] Then there was the fiasco of Hillary Clinton's commission of inquiry into the health insurance issue, followed by a succession of reversals of other presidential initiatives by Congress.

Through these same months, the administration dithered about every major foreign policy matter of the day. It had no answer to Serbia's effort to crush the independence of Bosnia. The contingent of U.S. forces left by President Bush in Somalia to support the peacekeeping effort of the UN was abruptly withdrawn when public opinion turned hostile following the failure of a helicopter mission to capture the evil genius who was keeping the civil conflict alive. Within weeks there was a similar moment in Haiti when a contingent of U.S. military sent to assist the restoration of the legitimate president of Haiti turned around and went home because of the unfriendly response they met at the pier in Port au Prince. In both cases, it seemed that public opinion had been moved by pictures of violence done to American forces and that President Clinton had been moved to follow it, for lack of some better notion of what the United States had armed forces for. In the pages of the foremost journal of foreign policy, Clinton would soon be belittled for going at foreign policy issues with the mindset of a social worker.[138] In light of this recent history, the invitation to join the Oslo process did indeed seem "a gift from the heavens."

On September 11 1992, Rabin received a phone call from President Clinton, congratulating him on the news of the Oslo Agreement, and proposing a signing ceremony on the White House lawn. It was clear then, and would continue to be clear until virtually the last weeks of Clinton's presidency, that he had little notion of how painful it was for the principals in this conflict to sign on to this agreement. Some among the Israeli negotiators at Madrid and Washington noted that much more had been given away than had ever been contemplated in Israeli deliberations at Madrid, while among the Palestinian delegates at Oslo there was also outrage because (as they believed) Israel had demanded a higher price for their concessions to Arafat than they were entitled to. The Palestinian delegate Hanan Ashrawi said to Abu Mazen (who as foreign minister of the PLO, would sign the accords): "It's clear that the ones who initialed this agreement have not lived under occupation."[139] But Arafat did not apologize: "There are not two leaderships, here," he had told them forcefully,[140] and they all got in line.[141] The Israelis, too, were unprepared, and would need much time to absorb the idea of the inveterate enemy as the certified partner for peace.

In short, it was not a good idea (as would eventually become clear) to raise the expectations of the whole world. Afterwards, when the awful gap between promise and reality emerged, there would be powerful reactions against this moment, with great damage done to public life in Israel and in the Arab world. Yitzhak Rabin was extremely reluctant to agree to a role in the intended ceremony, given the distaste he had acquired for Arafat and the PLO after thirty years of living with the victims of their terrorism. He anticipated trouble as photos would circulate forever of him and Arafat shaking hands; and, indeed, the troubling effect of those images would lead to his assassination. Bill Clinton, however, was simply dazzled by the promise of the moment, and was not prepared to let Yitzhak Rabin hold himself in reserve for the sake of the hard bargaining and political wrangling that lay ahead. In effect, Clinton gave him a choice between appearing with Arafat or permitting Arafat to dominate the proceedings, appearing before the world as the victor in the contest to be the champion of peace.[142]

The Israelis and the Americans spent many hours on the phone trying to work out the staging of the event. The Clinton people wanted there to be a handshake, but also wanted to forestall Arafat's kissing Rabin, after the Arab fashion. Bill Clinton and Anthony Lake, the national security advisor, personally rehearsed and then shared with Rabin the exact maneuver for accomplishing a handshake while blocking the approach for the unwanted kiss.[143]

The Oslo Agreement was signed on September 13, 1993 (on the very desk that Menachem Begin and Anwar Sadat used to sign the Camp David Peace Accords of September 1978), on the White House Lawn, before an immediate audience comprising the entire Congress of the United States plus the entire diplomatic corps, several foreign dignitaries (including Russian Foreign Minister Andrei Kozyrev), plus the Supreme Court and many others to a total of 3,000 guests.[144] There was as well a worldwide audience of perhaps as many as 1 billion[145] (including no doubt the present reader) watching it all in real-time. It is safe to say that no one in the history of the world ever committed himself to anything before a greater audience or with greater ceremony. Clinton's speech was filled with biblical references, as well as references to the Qur'an. Shimon

Peres and Mahmoud Abbas (Abu Mazen) signed as the respective foreign ministers, while Rabin and Arafat looked on. When Rabin followed through with the agreed handshake, the audience roared and stood up. Moments later, the entire Congress of the United States was seen and heard to utter "Amen" before the whole world, on the prompting of Prime Minister of Israel Yitzhak Rabin—a thing so improbable that many wept.

At that moment, every person of goodwill in the whole world seemed ready to believe that the lion had lain down with the lamb and that Bill Clinton had made this possible.

It did not work out that way, however, and in the end, Bill Clinton would pay a heavy price for his part in advancing this illusion.

BILL CLINTON AND ISRAEL

All this raises the question of Bill Clinton's attitude toward Israel. On many public occasions Bill Clinton spoke of his devotion to Israel in biblical terms—indeed, in what sounded like Christian Zionist terms. "This whole thing is immensely interesting for Christians," he said. "Well, I mean, it's our Holy Land too. I never will forget, the only time I went to Israel was with my pastor, who told me after I got back that he thought one day I would be President, and since at that time I was the youngest ex-governor in America—I was 34—I didn't think he knew what he was talking about. And he said, 'Just remember, God will never forgive you if you turn your back on Israel.' It was an amazing thing."[146] The night before the ceremonial signing of the Oslo Accords, Clinton, unable to sleep for excitement, read through the Book of Joshua.[147] What led him to this book, he said, was his recollection (presumably from Sunday school) of the story of fall of Jericho.

But surely the book of Joshua is the book of the Bible *least* appropriate for the business in hand—the division of the Land of Israel! Clinton had never looked closely at the dreadful and bloody story of the modern conflict in Israel. Equally, one may doubt that he truly realized in his imagination the bloody facts described in the book of Joshua: He could not have chosen it as the text of the day if he had. When opportunities afforded in the months ahead to talk about the issues of the conflict in public, Clinton never rehearsed before the world the history of the situation but rather trotted out the shallow thinking of the protagonists of Conflict Resolution or resorted to banalities about living together as neighbors. Although not necessarily intending to discount Clinton's sincerity, many commentators (and notably Israeli ones) have pointed out that there is much that is vague, confused, and sometimes downright erroneous about the biblical exegesis that gets into Clinton's remarks.

When Clinton went to Israel in order to witness the signing of the Israeli-Jordanian peace treaty, an Israeli journalist described the experience as "more like visiting Disney World than witnessing the ceremonial signing of a historic peace treaty." At the signing ceremony, Clinton substantially misquoted Jesus' Sermon on the Mount: "Here in this region, which is the home of not only both your faiths, but mine, I say: 'Blessed are the peacemakers, for they shall inherit the earth.'"[148] What Jesus said was, "Blessed are the peacemakers, for they will be called sons of God" (Matthew 5:9).

PARTIAL IMPLEMENTATION OF THE OSLO ACCORDS, TO THE ASSASSINATION OF YITZHAK RABIN, NOVEMBER 5, 1995

Over the weekend leading to the White House ceremony on September 13, 1993, and in the days that followed, the president himself and several other administration figures (who had only learned about the possible agreement that Wednesday, September 8) gave interviews describing what was about to happen as a foreign policy achievement that followed from the commitment of the previous administration and the present one to the Madrid Process.[149] President Clinton told the Arab news media that he intended to be "extremely involved," in future[150]—and it must be said that he fulfilled that pledge abundantly.

The nearly universal judgment in September, 1993, was that it was the beginning of peace in the Middle East. In reality, however, peace had not come and would never come during the remaining years of Clinton's presidency. As Israelis stepped out onto the road to Utopia, they were immediately met by terrorism on a scale never seen before. At first it was delivered by the elements excluded from participation in Arafat's agreement with the Israelis—notably, Hamas and Islamic Jihad, radical Islamist movements. During the Intifada, the popularity of Hamas had grown, along with disdain for the PLO, particularly among the young. In addition to the arms that it received from sponsors among Arab governments (notably, Saudi Arabia), Hamas also received large quantities of money, which it put to use in distributing medical services and so on to the populace.

Soon, a powerful anti-Oslo movement formed in Israel. Among religiously observant Israelis the slogans had to do with reclaiming the biblical boundaries of *Eretz Israel*, whereas among the secularists they had to do with recovering full command of the requirements of national security. Some opponents of the "Oslo surrender" conspired to derail diplomacy forever through violence.

On May 4, 1994, Rabin and Arafat formally signed the Declaration of Principles in Cairo, in the presence of Secretary Christopher and President Mubarek of Egypt. Later that month Israeli civil and military authorities withdrew from Jericho and Gaza. This was followed a few days later by the triumphant arrival of Arafat to Jericho and to Gaza, and his installation as the acknowledged head of the Interim Palestine Authority. The boundaries of the PA would thereafter be widened in the course of many more negotiations. The PA was to form a police force of 10,000 (later raised by agreement to 30,000), to be armed by the Israelis. Rabin attempted to calm Israelis who could not understand why Israel was now arming the enemy. "Stop being afraid," he said, "there is no danger that these guns will be used against us. The purpose of this ammunition for the Palestinian police is to be used in their vigilant fight against the HAMAS. They won't dream of using it against us, since they know very well that if they use these guns against us once, at that moment the Oslo Accords will be annulled and the IDF will return to all the places that have been given to them. The Oslo Accords, despite what the opposition claims, is not irrevocable."[151]

Although he made entirely different noises publicly, Arafat's standing instruction to his commanders was to "kill a settler every day."[152] The government of Israel chose not to notice that the PA's defensive force had become a much larger army, nor that much of the ammunition presented to the Palestinian Army by the IDF was making its way into the stockrooms of the terrorist organizations. Only a few days after signing the accord in Cairo, Arafat visited a mosque in Johannesburg, South Africa, where he proclaimed (May, 1994): "The jihad will continue. . . . Jerusalem is not only of the Palestinian people but of the entire Islamic nation. . . . You must come to fight, to begin the jihad to liberate Jerusalem, your first shrine [sic]." As for the Oslo Accords, Arafat stated, "I regard this agreement as no more than the agreement signed between our prophet Muhammad and the Quraysh in Mecca"[153]—which is to say, a commitment to be repudiated once our side has gained the upper hand again. When confronted with transcripts of these words, Arafat's spokesmen would explain that jihad really means "a sacred campaign," a peaceful struggle for the minds and the hearts. To Rabin, Arafat explained that this rhetoric was necessary in order to neutralize Hamas and the others, and Rabin pretended to believe this. Still, Arafat went on making fiery speeches about the sacred duty of continuing as martyrs until all the entire Holy Land of Palestine is liberated. On January 30, 1996, in a speech to forty Arab diplomats in Stockholm, on the theme "the Impending Collapse of Israel," he proclaimed, "We will take over everything, including all of Jerusalem . . . Within five years we will have six to seven million Arabs living on the West Bank and Jerusalem. All Palestinian Arabs will be welcomed back by us. You understand that we plan to eliminate the State of Israel and establish a purely Palestinian State. We will make life unbearable for Jews by psychological warfare and population explosion; Jews will not want to live among Arabs. . . . I have no use for Jews. They are and remain Jews. We now need all the help we can get from you in our battle for a united Palestine under total

Arab-Muslim domination."[154] Rabin was always reluctant to admit his knowledge of Arafat's inflammatory statements, which were categorically forbidden under the Oslo terms.[155]

By mid-year 1995, it was noted that only 37 percent of the Israeli public wished to continue with the peace talks. Rabin did not deny this reality but said that he was determined to proceed with the remaining stages however unpopular. On September 23, 1995, at Taba on the Egyptian border, the details for implementing the remaining portions of the Agreement were signed. Then on September 28, 1995, in the White House, there was yet another signing ceremony: Arafat and Rabin and Peres all signed the document that contained the results of all the negotiations to date, which is usually called Oslo II. President Mubarek and King Hussein were present as witnesses, and President Clinton brought as guests representatives of Syria and Lebanon; this was meant to underline his conviction that this moment would prove a harbinger of a general peace in the Arab neighborhood.[156] Oslo II provided for the gradual addition to the Gaza-Jericho base of almost all the remaining disputed areas by stages, with Israeli military withdrawing as the PA assumed responsibility for security.

Meanwhile, at another White House ceremony, Prime Minister Rabin and King Hussein had signed a declaration of the end of the state of war between them.[157] This led in October 1994 to the signing of a formal treaty of peace, this time on the border between Israel and Jordan, but with President Clinton again presiding.[158] In line with this agreement, Rabin conceded to the king of Jordan the responsibility for Muslim and Christian Holy Places in Jerusalem—something not cleared with Arafat, who denounced these terms and appointed his own parallel dignitaries, whom the Palestinians were generally disposed to obey.[159]

As 1995 advanced, Israeli protests against the Oslo process became increasingly unrestrained. At a huge anti-Oslo rally in Jerusalem's Zion Square on October 5, 1995, posters displayed Rabin in Nazi uniform. Some rabbis were quoted as justifying assassination of one who has betrayed Israel. (The usual proof text was Numbers 25, the story of Zimri.)[160] A month later came the assassination of Yitzhak Rabin, immediately following his address to a large rally of supporters of the peace process (November 4, 1995), in Tel Aviv.

PRESIDENT CLINTON TAKES UP AN ACTIVE ROLE AS PEACEMAKER

After Rabin was gone, Clinton saw him as a surrogate father figure and himself as his political legatee. In his office there was a bust of Rabin, and elsewhere throughout the living quarters of the White House there were "private shrines to Rabin"—a plate of soil from the grave and the yarmulke he had worn at Rabin's funeral, as well as other mementos.[161] Faithful to this legacy, Clinton wholeheartedly joined in the task assumed by Shimon Peres who became prime minister once again (November 22, 1995) and was soon facing an election campaign. Clinton provided political expertise and encouraged major contributors to his own Democratic Party to contribute to Peres's campaign.[162] President Clinton's visit to Israel (March 14, 1996) in the very midst of the political campaign, in order to negotiate directly with Prime Minister Peres on a counter-terrorism treaty,[163] followed by his invitation to Peres to come to Washington for another signing ceremony (April 30, 1996)[164] were inevitably perceived in Israel and in the United States as intended to assist Peres's election.

As was always the case when Peres ran as incumbent prime minister, the campaign opened with public opinion apparently favorable, and closed with it hostile. Thus in June 1996, Binyamin Netanyahu of Likud became prime minister. Clinton took the defeat of his candidate Peres very badly. At once he took note of the narrow parliamentary base that Netanyahu had to work with and began to undermine him. Netanyahu had originally opposed the Oslo Accords, and although during his campaign he declared that honoring the agreement was obligatory upon the next Israeli government he also insisted that he would proceed no further along that path until the other side put an end to all violence. He made this view clear during his first visit to the White House (July 9, 1996).[165] The Clinton administration, however, took the view that Arafat was as much an opponent of violence as was Netanyahu and that the Israelis must make generous concessions to him in order to sustain his leadership among his people and thus begin the inevitable reversal of the appeal of the true champions of violence on both sides. During the next few months, Clinton held frequent separate meetings with Arafat and with Netanyahu in the White House. (Because more than one individual would hold the position of prime minister of Israel during Clinton's eight years, Arafat would sign the guest book many more times than any of them, and would, in fact, do so more frequently than any head of government or head of state in the same period.) At the end of September 1996, Clinton managed to get Netanyahu and Arafat together in Washington for their first extensive meeting, but little was accomplished.[166]

On December 5, 1996, President Clinton appointed his new secretary of state, Madeleine Albright. Unlike Warren Christopher, who had the reputation of a foreign policy technician rather than a global thinker, and who was always prepared to travel to wherever he felt he was needed (he made two dozen trips to the Middle East alone in his four years as secretary), Albright was dedicated to a foreign policy based less on travel and more on ideas.[167] Now that the United States was freed from the distraction of the Cold War, it was time for the nation to use its long domestic experience in accommodating cultural and racial differences to recommend and to begin to implement just solutions to unresolved antagonisms around the world that were based on hereditary hatreds and historical fixations. To this end, the United States must drop the note of embarrassment about the use of force that characterized Clinton's earlier actions. The new aggressive tone that came into Balkan policy was a first-fruit of this approach—and by most reckonings, one that did credit to the United States.

Albright's attitude toward the problem of Israel was shaped by her general strategic thinking but was also affected by the matter of her own racial identity. Shortly after her appointment, an article in the *Washington Post* in the spring of 1997 spoke of her recent "discovery" of her partly Jewish background, a factor in the flight from Europe of her father, a Czechoslovak diplomat, in the 1930s. In fact, both of her parents were Jewish; three of her four grandparents and a dozen other close relatives in Czechoslovakia had died as victims of the Holocaust. Jews found her declaration of previous ignorance about this background difficult to take at face value.[168] Whether this matter affected her actual behavior toward the Israelis during her tenure as secretary of state, and if so in what direction, there was a widespread perception that she had to try harder to prove herself on this issue than on others. Secretary Albright took a consistently hard-boiled approach to Netanyahu, frequently spilling out into shouting matches—and it was assumed that in this she was reflecting the private attitude of the president.[169] She exploited every opportunity to bring American Jewish opinion (much more friendly to the Labor side) to bear upon the Israeli prime minister.

The pattern of frequent but separate visits of Arafat and Netanyahu to the White House continued through 1997, but nothing was accomplished. From Clinton's point of view, *nothing* was actually *less than nothing*, for as he said at a Democratic National Committee dinner in New York, January 8, 1998, "The real problem with the Middle East Process is it's like a living organism that gets sick if it doesn't move, you know. It's got to move. You've got to just keep something happening."[170] With this thought, and despite their being no objective grounds for believing that either side was in a mood to make the concession that the other side demanded, President Clinton announced another "Summit Meeting" to take place in Washington in January 1998.

A few days before the conference was to begin, Prime Minister Netanyahu attended a mass meeting organized by Evangelical Protestant leaders who sought to gird up his loins for the meeting with the Clinton administration. Organized as the "National Unity Coalition for Israel" mainly through the efforts of Voices United for Israel and featuring speakers from the Christian Coalition and the National Religious

Broadcasters, the meeting was attended by about 1,000. The theme was that American Christians are opposed to any further concessions of territory to the Palestinians.[171] The Israeli prime minister was publicly scolded by many American Jewish leaders for his association with these disreputable Fundamentalists and in particular with Jerry Falwell, who was known to be one of the public figures whom the president detested most. However, the media suddenly lost all interest in Israel the moment that the first news of the Monica Lewinsky affair broke on January 21.[172]

Though greatly burdened (to say the least) by this embarrassing and possibly lethal issue, Bill Clinton was not about to de distracted. As he put it in one press conference, "getting up and going to your job every day," was always the best medicine for dealing with troubles. And so President Clinton managed to give many hours, in his usual unstinting way, to personal diplomacy with the two principals.[173] Still, the feeling was abroad that the two principals could more easily resist the president's pressures upon them by dint of the fact that the public was not much interested in this issue at the moment. Because Prime Minister Netanyahu had been targeted by the president to make the initial concessions, he gained the most from the measure of relief that Monica Lewinsky afforded. (One particularly zealous and imaginative religious teacher in Israel called on Israelis to think of Miss Lewinsky in the light of Esther 4:14, and to bless her name.) During the press conferences before and after the summit, few reporters dared disappoint their editors by actually pursuing questions about the Middle East. This remained true, more or less, until the end of the impeachment trial before the Senate in February 1999.

When Netanyahu visited the president again in April 1998, another even larger rally was got together by the same organizations, where speakers included several of the televangelists and leaders of Christian Zionist organizations, as well as such heavyweight political leaders as Dick Armey (majority leader in the House), Dick Gephardt (minority leader in the House), and Tom Delay, Republican whip in the House.[174]

Toward the end of September 1998, President Clinton announced another summit conference to deal with a situation that was, if anything, worse than it had been when the January summit took place. This one would be held at the Aspen Institute Wye River Conference Center in Maryland, beginning October 15.[175] The major change since the earlier "summit" was that Netanyahu's domestic political situation had became very shaky: His Knesset majority was in jeopardy from day to day, and a new, apparently popular Labor leader, Ehud Barak, was in the wings. Witnesses to the Wye meetings say that Netanyahu "openly disparaged Arafat . . . [that] Foreign Minister Ariel Sharon refused to address him in anything but the third person" and that for this behavior Clinton angrily rebuked both.[176] At the end, the Wye River Memorandum was signed at a ceremony in the White House.[177] "The peace process [which] for 18 months . . . has been paralyzed" said the president (contradicting the more sanguine line that he had been giving to reporters until now) had now come back to life. Additional territories were to be handed over at once to the PA, and a detailed plan was announced for moving most of what remained of the disputed territories to the PA by stages; the PLO agreed to cooperate with the CIA in turning over terrorists to Israel and to join in a "continuous security cooperation with Israel and a comprehensive plan against terrorism and its support infrastructure." Upon ratification of the agreement, permanent status talks would begin. The major concession from Arafat's side was a vague commitment to rewrite the Palestinian National Charter so as to remove the commitment to the liquidation of Israel. President Clinton promised to come to the land and preside while Arafat's Palestine National Council made this adjustment to the PLO charter in public.

Later that same day, despite having pursued these negotiations without any sleep for the previous "36 hours and 30 minutes," Clinton kept a commitment to appear at the celebration of the 160th anniversary of the Metropolitan African Methodist Episcopal Church in Washington. Of the work just done, he said, "I felt so blessed to have had the opportunity to engage in these labors, to do this for our country, for the cause of peace, for the land of our faiths, the home of Christianity, Judaism and Islam. I felt that it was part of my job as President, my mission as a Christian, and my personal journey of atonement. And I am grateful that God gave me the chance to do this for the last 9 days."[178]

On December 14, 1998, Clinton presided over what the official U.S. record describes as a meeting of "the Palestine National Council, the Palestinian Executive committee, leaders of business and religion," during which Arafat called for a show of hands in favor of revising the Palestinian Covenant.[179] Afterwards this was discovered to be a worthless gesture: The meeting of assorted Palestinian dignitaries had no constitutional standing at all, and so the document would stand as before.[180] Pretending ignorance of the constitutional niceties, Clinton had assured the government and the people of Israel that when this deed was done the Palestinian Covenant would no longer call for the destruction of Israel and that the ultimate gesture of Palestinian reconciliation to Israel's existence had been made.[181] A day later (December 15), Clinton, Netanyahu and Arafat stood together to announce the formation of a "steering committee" to take responsibility for moving forward the matters left unresolved by the Wye Declaration.[182]

The reporters who followed the president on this Middle East trip had little interest in its announced purpose and an overwhelming need to know how the president felt about the impending impeachment. (December 12, the day Clinton left for Israel, was also the day that the

House Judiciary Committee voted for the Articles of Impeachment.) None of the reporters was informed enough to raise the matter of the blatant constitutional irregularity of the conduct of the meeting in Gaza. At one point in the press conference of December 13, Prime Minister Netanyahu literally begged the reporters to ask at least one question that was about the present business.[183]

As early as the summer of 1998, the Clinton administration was eagerly anticipating a change for the better in Israeli leadership. Ehud Barak, the new leader of the Labor Party and of the opposition in the Knesset was welcomed in Washington and given a reception by the State Department on a par with that of a visiting head of government.[184] During his visit to Jerusalem in December of 1998, Clinton met privately with Barak and urged him not to accede to Netanyahu's call for a national unity government, pledging, in effect, to do everything possible to help him win the upcoming election.[185] Shortly after that, the Knesset was disbanded and a general election was called. Several of Bill Clinton's own campaign consultants, including James Carville, Robert Shrum, and Stanley Greenberg, were hired on by the Barak campaign. During these weeks Carville, by his own admission at the time, "regularly [briefed] the President on the progress of the Labor leader's campaign." Again, Clinton directed major supporters of the Democratic Party to give generously to the Barak campaign. Stories reflecting the Clinton government's unhappiness with Netanyahu's pursuit of the path of peace were leaked to the media.[186]

The election, May 17, 1999, made Ehud Barak prime minister, but left the distribution of parties in the Knesset very much as before. Barak was confident, however, that the public wanted its government to be much more forthcoming than Netanyahu had been in negotiations with the other side. He resolved to act boldly, confident that he would draw more of the parties and the leading political personalities to him as he won back the trust of Arafat.

Before making his concentrated approach to the negotiations with Arafat, however, Barak tried a round of negotiations with Syria. While preliminary discussions with the Syrians were under way, Barak resolved to withdraw unilaterally and unconditionally from Lebanon, expecting Syria to see this as opening up the way for Syria's own eventual withdrawal and creating a new context for serious diplomacy. The actual withdrawal took place swiftly on May 24, 2000. Throughout the PA this was proclaimed a victory of Palestinian resistance to Israel, further inspiring the hope that Israel could be worn down by unremitting terrorism. Arafat proclaimed that Hezbollah (the Iranian-funded and Iranian-trained terrorist organization located in southern Lebanon that had made daily life in Northern Israel so insecure since the mid-eighties) was henceforth to be the model for the next phase of the Palestinian struggle.[187]

The Clinton administration, like the Bush administration, was determined to force the pace of Israeli-Syrian diplomacy in order to achieve momentum that could be applied on all the other diplomatic fronts. President Clinton met twice personally with President Assad of Syria, the first time in January of 1994 in Geneva[188] and the second in Damascus, October 1994.[189] Syria's Assad was, as always, playing the Sphinx; and, as always, the Americans imagined they heard the sound of words suggesting important concessions. Private and public pressure was put on Barak to commit to Israel's complete retreat from Golan. To move things along, Secretary Albright said publicly, "Middle East stability is endangered by Israel's remaining in the Golan Heights."[190] In the following months, the secretary of state and other senior officials presided over countless diplomatic sessions involving the Israelis and the Syrians, notably a well-publicized conference at Shepherdstown, West Virginia (January 2000). All of these encounters, including the latter, ended in total failure. Assad ended where he began, demanding Israel's complete capitulation to Syria's terms while conceding nothing.[191] (Hafez al-Assad died on June 10, 2000.)

Direct contacts between Prime Minister Barak and President Clinton began with a meeting in the White House on July 15, 1999—the first of many such meetings. There was roughly the same number of visits of Arafat to the White House in the same period. Through late 1999 and early 2000 there were as well many meetings between Barak and Arafat. There was a Trilateral Summit in Oslo in November of 1999 and meetings in Egypt as well as in the United States and in Europe. By June of 2000, Barak had made so many unreciprocated concessions to the other side (the Palestinians, the Syrians, and the Lebanese) that public opinion virtually panicked, and the Knesset took this as a signal to start the process leading to new elections for the Knesset.

The Israeli public could find no way of reconciling the reassuring talk of their prime minister with the increasingly inflammatory sermons that emanated from the many mosques through the land. In Jerusalem, the imam of the al-Aqsa Mosque denounced all commitments that the PLO was making to Israel and decreed that this was all contrary to Islam. According to the imam, the government of Arafat did not deserve the obedience of the people: "The corruption starts from the top . . . [This is a regime that] permits alcohol . . . [and] the establishment of casinos . . . [and] portrays sincere active Muslims as terrorists and fundamentalists. The rulers are responsible for subjugating the Muslim Ummah to the imperialist infidels." But worst of all, he said, "They want to efface the Islam concepts that talk about the Jews in order for the next generation of Muslims to accept the existence of Israel as a fact and as an advantage. . . . Islam says about Jews that they are enemies. Islam says about the Jews: 'Fight them,' 'Kill them,' Drive them out.' Islam says about Jews that they are infidels. But these corrupt rulers [the PA] want us to say that the Jews are brothers in belief, that they are cousins, that they are our neighbors, that they are our partners in the peace process." Most devastating of all, in the ears of anyone sincerely devoted to the peace process, was the imam's pronouncement that a Palestinian state was not and could not be the desire of the hearts of the Palestinian people. A Palestinian state, the imam declared, is not a worthy goal. In fact, it detracts from pursuit of the only goal that Palestinians should seek: the one worldwide Muslim state, the Ummah, guided by one universal Muslim authority, the Caliph, as in the days of Islam's beginnings. Allah will not be thwarted, the imam declared: "It will be established over the thrones of these corrupt agents to the imperialist infidels. It will liberate this Masjid [the al-Aqsa Mosque], it will kill Jews, and it will open Rome [that is, overthrow Christianity]. This means that the coming Islamic state will become a superpower!" As the speaker intended, sermons in this vein would always be punctuated by the roars of the worshippers; shouting "Slaughter the Jews!" the crowds would then pour out onto the Temple Mount, pouring stones down upon the heads of Jewish worshipers below, compelling the Israeli police to rush up to the area and start up the crowd-control measures that always brought at least colorful injuries and usually the deaths of boys and young men, and that always resulted in pictures illustrating Israeli violence against civilians. Arafat, though committed under the Oslo Accords to prevent incitement against Israel from whatever quarter, instead permitted these sermons to be broadcast and rebroadcast over the Palestinian television authority and thence throughout the Muslim world.[192]

At the time of the Wye Accord (October 1998), the pundits were speaking of many hopeful signs pointing to an improvement in Israeli-Palestinian relations, among which most included President Clinton's willingness to be directly involved. Now, halfway through the last year of Clinton's presidency, virtually everything agreed upon at the Wye conference had unraveled. There was now a school of thought that said that Clinton's willingness to be directly involved had been what caused it all to go wrong! Clinton's response to these voices was to step out boldly and take command of the peace process. He knew, and the other principals knew, that his successor would likely want to avoid being ground up in this time-consuming and spiritually draining effort (as proved to be the case). He knew also that Prime Minister Barak might soon have to quit the field, as parliamentary support for his government had just sunk to thirty-two members out of 120. Barak, like Rabin in similar circumstances, vowed to continue, "even if I have the support of only . . . a quarter of the Knesset." And so it was time for another summit—this one to be held at Camp David, beginning July 6, 2000, and continuing, if necessary, for ten days.

THE SECOND INTIFADA

Barak arrived at Camp David carrying a list of concessions ready to be announced. The most important was that there would be a Palestinian state with its capital located in a neighborhood within Jerusalem and having sovereign jurisdiction over a part of Jerusalem—previously an unthinkable concession. Israel would accept the return of a limited number of Arab refugees, while others would be allowed to settle in the forthcoming Palestinian state; $30 billion would be set aside for compensation of Arab refugees from the 1948 war who could not return to homes in what had become the State of Israel. Insiders who have since published recollections of the Camp David meeting describe Clinton's utter astonishment as Arafat rejected every one of Barak's concessions. Gritting his teeth, Clinton lectured Arafat: "A summit's purpose is to have discussions that are based on sincere intentions and you, the Palestinians, did not come to this summit with sincere intentions"[193] Now Arafat asserted an unqualified claim to all of Jerusalem—something that he had never dared to suggest in previous negotiations, knowing that such a claim would have shut everything down. It was not enough to have the Palestinian capital in a corner of the city, nor was it sufficient that the Palestinian state should have (as Barak offered) custody of all the Christian as well as the Muslim sites: "Jerusalem," Arafat said, "is not only a Palestinian city; it is an Arabic, Islamic and Christian city." It must all be included in the Palestinian capital. Then he threw into the face of Barak the claim that Muslim spokesmen had been making for years, but that the Jews had assumed was fantasy: The Jews have no claim to the so-called Temple Mount because there had never been a Temple there—nothing, in fact, until the Muslims built their Mosques.[194]

Other members of the Palestinian delegation made clear that they wished to have the deal accepted, but Arafat rejected it all (July 25). His further insistence on the "right of return" of all the descendants of all the Palestinians who had ever been refugees over half a century was, of course, an invitation to Israel to commit suicide. Barak knew that he would have to defend all this after the conference, as he had promised a plebiscite, and so Clinton promised to lend unstinting time and energy to support such a campaign. At the same time, he promised to Arafat he would personally travel around the world in order to raise the tens of billions of dollars for economic development of Palestine. It was clear that Clinton was determined to build a legacy for himself by securing peace in the Middle East.

But even to have permitted these things to be discussed was denounced by the Muslim authorities in Jerusalem: "The great treason that we face today occurred only when Palestine was separated from the Islamic Creed: It happened when the Arab nationalists took their part in solving what they called then 'the Palestinian problem' and handed it over to the secular PLO. . . . It should be clear that Palestine is not owned by the Palestinians. It . . . belongs to all the Muslims. . . . Any permanent agreement with the disbelievers is void automatically. The permanent agreement means the canceling of jihad, which can never happen."[195]

Returning to the Palestinian Authority, Arafat huddled with his own party and with the leaders of the several terrorist associations and coordinated plans for what was now to be the definitive phase of the struggle: the overthrow of Israel by destruction of the nerve of its population through unremitting terrorism. Shortly, Arafat issued a declaration ordering the entire teenage population of West Bank and Gaza to attend military-style summer camps for training in terrorism.[196]

Sensing that the Israeli public would not approve Barak's offer to concede unilaterally Israel's sovereignty over any part of Jerusalem, Ariel Sharon, leader of the Likud, announced that it was time to cease acquiescing in the Muslim authority's assertion of its undivided possession of the Temple Mount that had taken place over the previous two years. He would remind all and sundry that Israel's sovereignty had never been conceded, and he would assert the right of a non-Muslim to walk on this part of the land of Israel by walking on to the Temple Mount (September 28, 2000). Generally overlooked afterwards was the fact that Prime Minister Barak had given formal notice of Sharon's intention to the Palestinian leadership several days in advance and had received the assurance of Arafat himself that the visit would be allowed to happen without trouble. Sharon's visit offered an opportunity for Barak to prove his point that it was to everybody's best interest to give to a Palestinian state custody of all the holy sites in Jerusalem. But even as Barak and Arafat were negotiating, Arafat's organization was stockpiling the stones, bottles, and other kinds of projectiles and drilling the boys and young men in their parts for the spontaneous demonstrations to follow upon Sharon's "provocative" walk.[197] Immediately mobs streamed through Jerusalem and throughout the land there was a wave of violence against lives and property, which has become known as the Second Intifada.[198]

There was virtually universal condemnation of Sharon's action, from which Washington did not dissent. In joining the chorus of denunciation of Sharon, Clinton had to overlook the evidence that Israeli intelligence had shown him of the negotiations between Barak and Arafat which were supposed to have made it possible for Sharon's visit to proceed as a nonevent.[199] On October 9, in the Security Council of the UN, the United States abstained from voting on a resolution that condemned Israel's "excessive use of force" in handling the Al-Aqsa riots.

"A COLOSSAL FAILURE"

We have seen how Presidents Nixon and Carter became aroused to almost manic levels of activity in their last months in the presidency as they sought to accomplish, in a brilliant diplomatic stroke, what had always eluded every statesman before them: a definitive peace in the Middle East. An even more extreme example of this syndrome is Bill Clinton. Obsessed by the task of putting the memory of his presidency on the highest plateau, dogged by the embarrassment of sex scandals and other stains to his reputation, he was determined that he would not leave the presidency before compelling the erstwhile peace partners to deliver the goods.

To make sense of this, we must reflect on what might be called the "mystical" attraction of this issue for Americans. Dimly recalled Sunday school lessons or Old Testament readings preceding the Homily have fixed in people's minds the sense that ancient Israel had been the site of the oldest human conflicts and that the prophets had anticipated from the beginning that, somehow, the ultimate political work of causing enemies to live together, each under his own vine and fig tree, had to be done here where ancient Israel struggled against enemies. To achieve the peace that the prophets spoke about would have such a stunning effect on the whole of mankind that everything else about a president would forever be seen in the glow of that millennial accomplishment.

Bill Clinton's case is an almost pathological instance of how blind the most pragmatic of politicians can become when presented with the opportunity to become immortal. Even following the Camp David II debacle, Clinton would not give up. He met with Arafat and Barak in New York during the Millennium Summit at the UN, but without result. There were subsequent meetings with the same outcome between Albright and Arafat in Paris.[200] Clinton's last effort on behalf of the peace process started in mid-December 2000, when Palestinian and Israeli teams of negotiators met at Bolling Airforce Base (December 19–23), and it carried through the dying days. Although Barak had resigned because of lack of support in the Knesset and was now acting prime minister pending elections to be held in February, he now offered to the Palestinians terms even more generous than those he had put on the table at Camp David: The Palestinians would gain control of 95 percent of the West Bank and all of an enlarged Gaza, and a secured land-link in between; the Arab sections of Jerusalem would become the capital of a Palestinian state; Palestinians would have full authority over Muslim and Christian holy places; Israel would withdraw from sixty-three settlements in the West Bank; and there would be a limited return of refugees, with compensation from a $30 million reparation fund. Again, only Arafat stood out against acceptance; and again Arafat's was the only vote that counted on the Palestinian side. As late as January 1, 2001, Clinton met with Arafat in the White House and offered to get on the phone to wring further concessions from Barak on such matters as the timing for Israel's complete evacuation of the Jordan Valley, and the several other difficulties that Arafat had discovered in recent days. A few days after Clinton's terms as president ended, Arafat and Barak met at Taba (January 21–27) to talk it all over again. This conference, like all the others, accomplished nothing.[201]

In fact, Arafat had never envisaged a future without him and without conflict. He had no plans for peace and reconstruction. His sacred objective throughout had been the destruction of Israel. Barak had presented him with the dilemma he thought he would never face—surrendering virtually everything that the other side had ever *publicly* asked for except the requirement for Israel to commit suicide. To accept the Camp David package would be to accept the end of conflict. And so it made perfect sense to him to start up a new wave of violence.

As the last sands were running out, it dawned on Bill Clinton that Arafat had never cared at all for Clinton's reputation or his peace of mind. On January 17, Arafat placed a personal telephone call to Clinton, praising him fulsomely, as "a great man." Clinton replied: "The hell I am . . . I'm a colossal failure, and you made me one."[202]

Chapter 5

The Worldwide War on Terrorism: Its Impact on Presidential Attitudes Toward Israel

GEORGE W. BUSH (2001–)

"They hate Christianity. They hate Judaism.
They hate everything that is not them."

RELIGION IN THE LIFE OF GEORGE W. BUSH

The first of the insider memoirs to come out of the George W. Bush White House begins with these words: "'Missed you at Bible study.' These were, quite literally, the very first words I heard spoken inside the Bush White House."[1] George W. Bush is the most overtly pious man to have held the presidency, at least since Jimmy Carter. Christian piety takes many forms, of course. In the case of George W. Bush it is that distinct form that has evolved from American Revivalism, what is nowadays generally called Evangelicalism. Bush views himself as a man converted from a careless and culpable life by decision in a moment of time to accept Jesus Christ as the Lord of his life. When at an all-candidates meeting previous to the Iowa Republican caucus of 2000, candidates were asked, "What political philosopher do you most identify with?" George Bush's answer was, "Christ, because he changed my heart." Asked then to follow up, he explained, "When you turn your heart and your life over to Christ, when you accept Christ as the Savior, it changes your heart. It changes your life. And that's what happened to me."[2] To a group of religious leaders, meeting with him in the Oval Office, Bush confessed: "You know, I had a drinking problem . . . There is only one reason that I am in the Oval Office and not in a bar. I found faith. I found God. I am here because of the power of prayer."[3] His self-conscious commitment to Christ is expressed in such observable matters as regular attendance at church on Sunday morning, offering grace before a meal when he is the host, and taking the time to bow his head before beginning a meal when he is not, regardless of the company he is in.[4]

As a boy, George W. Bush attended First Presbyterian Church in Midland, Texas, until the family moved to Houston in 1959 and began attending the Episcopal Church there. When the family was in Kennebunkport, Maine, they attended his father's Episcopal Church. During the early 1980s, he became alarmed that a tendency to anger and a weakness for alcohol were threatening his ability to retain the respect of his wife, his parents, and his friends. During the summer of 1985, Billy Graham, who made frequent visits to the Bush family and was always available for advice on the phone, convinced him that he needed to make the solemn decision to put his life under the control of Jesus Christ. This marked the beginning of what he speaks of as his "renewal."[5] He signaled his intention to begin anew by undertaking total abstinence from alcohol—a resolve that he has kept ever since.

To the graduating class at commencement at Yale University in May 2001, Bush said, "When I left here, I didn't have much in the way of a life plan. I knew some people who thought they did. But it turned out that we were all in for ups and downs, most of them unexpected. Life takes its own turns, makes its own demands, writes its own story. And along the way, we start to realize that we are not the author."[6] Bush believes that "there is a value system that cannot be compromised—God-given values . . . There are values of freedom and the human condition and mothers loving their children. What's very important as we articulate foreign policy through our diplomacy and military action is that it never look like we are the author of these values. . . . We are all God's children."[7] He believes firmly that "I am in God's hands." He believes that "the war against terror will be a monumental struggle between good and evil. But good will prevail."[8]

Bush has a plain man's understanding about the connection between personal faith and personal behavior. For example, according to some sources, a compelling factor in his decision to seek the presidency in 2000 was his alarm at how Bill Clinton had demeaned the office of the presidency, inspiring contempt and cynicism, ultimately lowering the national moral climate by his sexual misbehavior in the very office in which he was conducting his responsibilities as president.[9] An important key to the pattern of Bush's dealings with other politicians and world leaders is that he takes into account what he knows of the faith commitments of others.[10] Commentators who imagine that they have a more detached or perhaps a more "nuanced" philosophy find George Bush to be "moralistic."

David Frum speaks of the "modern evangelical culture," which permeates the Bush White House. Cabinet meetings begin with prayer. Profanity and coarse talk generally are not indulged.[11] A single individual cannot impose "a culture," unless, of course he is a dictator; thus we need to understand that, while by no means all of those who serve him in the highest offices share his Evangelical commitment, enough of them do that he has been able to sustain without discomfort around his daily working life a style that reflects his personal piety.[12] Among those of greatest influence in the inner circle are several who have spoken in interviews of their personal faith in Christ and whose own lifestyle has this same conservative Christian stamp, notably Vice President Dick Cheney, Commerce Secretary Don Evans, and National Security Advisor Condoleezza Rice (the daughter of a Presbyterian clergyman and educator and herself an active Presbyterian layperson).[13] Bush's principal speechwriter, with an influential voice on policy, is Michael Gerson, who majored in Theology at Wheaton College and was a colleague of the Christian activist and commentator Charles Colson.[14] Secretary of State Colin Powell is at least in tune with this prevailing spirit: A serious and devoted Episcopalian, he expresses repeatedly in his autobiography his distress at the "modernism" that has overtaken his denomination.[15]

GEORGE W. BUSH, THE JEWS, AND ISRAEL

David Frum, himself a Jew, and a member of the Bush official family during its first twelve months, has concluded that Bill Clinton can fairly be called "the most philo-Semitic president in U.S. history." "His closest friends and most trusted aides were Jewish, his administration was crammed with Jewish appointees, both his nominees to the Supreme Court were Jewish—even his most famous girlfriend was Jewish. And Jews liked Clinton as much as he liked them. They appreciated his intellectuality and his social tolerance, his liberated wife, and his moderate liberalism. Jewish donors contributed generously to Clinton's election campaigns; after he left office, some of those former donors helped him to grow very rich very rapidly."[16] The election results of 1992, 1996, and 2000 can fairly be said to reflect the loyalty of Jewish voters to the Democratic Party under Clinton's leadership.

George Bush, by contrast, was not an attractive candidate for Jews—perhaps even less attractive than his father. In fact, Frum suggests, "It would be almost impossible to invent a candidate less likely to appeal to Jewish voters than George W. Bush. His personality seemed to fuse together in one body the three personality types most calculated to frighten and annoy Jews: the redneck, the Bible-thumper, and the upper-class frat boy. His social conservatism worried Jews, his apparent anti-intellectualism offended them, and above all, they resented his 'born on third base' background . . . So Bush entered office with fewer Jewish friends and supporters than any president since perhaps Dwight D. Eisenhower. There were no Jews in his cabinet and few on his staff."[17] Frum neglects to note that there were many Jews holding positions at secondary levels, in position to have great effect on policy toward Israel (notably, Undersecretary of Defense Paul Wolfowitz) and that these were markedly more friendly to Israel than the general run of Jews who had been at senior positions in the Clinton government.

It is clear, as I write in early 2004, that George W. Bush has been the best friend that Israel has ever had in the presidency of the United States. Commentators who find a contradiction here have not grasped the important fact that American politicians today are loyal to Israel today not primarily because Jewish supporters expect it of them but because they believe in Israel and identify with its cause. Despite what Muslims around the world claim; despite what the mainstream European politicians claim; and despite even what many American Jews imagine—it is not because of Jewish influence that presidents respond to Israel's need; often as not, it is in spite of it. That so many American Jews should ever have doubted Bush's commitment to Israel reflects upon their failure to understand and respect the broadly non-Jewish foundation of American Zionism today. Frum observes, "It was precisely the most religious members of the Bush administration who tended to be the friendliest to Jews as individuals and most sympathetic toward the State if Israel as a Jewish state."[18] Of particular note in this company is the Attorney General, John Ashcroft, who has been active over the years in Christian Zionist organizations. In July 2003, Tevi Troy, who had been policy director for Ashcroft when he was a Republican senator from Missouri, was appointed President Bush's liaison to the Jewish community.[19] This appointment suggests that, in its approach to the Jewish community, the Bush administration intends to stress the importance of good relations with Christian Zionists.

David Frum, who describes himself as "a not especially observant Jew,"[20] speaks of "the intense, devout secularism of the American Jewish community," which "baffled Bush" and which stands in the way of recognition of the authentic dedication to Israel of conservative Christians. He describes a cool reception at the Convention of the American Jewish Committee in May 2001, where Bush proclaimed: "I am a Christian. But I believe with the Psalmist that the Lord God of Israel neither slumbers nor sleeps" "The American Jewish community," Frum observes, is so terrified of non-Jewish religiosity that *any* reference to God by a non-Jew, no matter how friendly its intent, unnerved them. They do not trust people who talk too much about the 'Lord God.' And do not like it any better when such people remind them that the Lord God in question is their Lord

God, too."[21] It is difficult for American Jews to grasp that "those who believed most strongly in the Bible naturally felt the strongest affinity to the people of the Bible." This, according to Frum, is "a catastrophic political error."[22]

It is ironic that George Bush, who got only about 19 percent of the Jewish vote in 2000, has proven to be the most reliable champion of the Jewish state of recent times. But even more ironic than this is another generalization about the politics of culture that comes out of this election. Bush did extremely well among only one recognizable ethnic or cultural bloc, and that was Muslims—who, of course, now smite him hip and thigh for being under the thumb of the Jews! Bush had campaigned hard to win Muslim and Arab-American voters. Indeed, considerable embarrassment occurred later when attention was drawn to the fact that Bush had won endorsement of Muslim "charitable" organizations discovered, after 9/11, to be fronts for terrorist organizations and that he had sought the endorsement of Arab-American academics (including Sami al-Arian, a Professor of Computer Engineering at South Florida University, who later was charged with raising money for a front belonging to Palestinian Islamic Jihad).[23] Furthermore, it is just possible (but no more than that) that Muslim votes tipped the balance of the whole election of 2000.[24] The Tampa Bay Islamic Center claimed that its exit polls showed that 50,000 Muslims came to the polling places in Florida in November 2000, and that these voted 88 percent for Bush, 8 percent for Green Party candidate Ralph Nader (an Arab-American), and 4 percent for Al Gore. The reason for the Muslims' preference cannot be doubted: It was because Gore had chosen a Jew for a running mate. There is enormous racial, cultural, and economic diversity among those included under the heading "Muslim voters," but as one consultant on Muslim voters said to David Frum, "They all hate your people [the Jews]."[25]

PEACEMAKING

In the early months of the Bush presidency, the professionals in the State Department were, as always, keen to start up the peace process again. President Bush, however, was much less keen: He was determined to learn from the bitter experience of Bill Clinton, who, we recall, received the Oslo process as a gift from the heavens, and who thereafter worked without stint to bring about the definitive end of the conflict—only to see the Second Intifada start up. George W. Bush was not alone in believing that Clinton may have provoked this war by his hot pursuit of peace. To the extent that he did look in on the issue in these early months, Bush appeared to be following the guidelines of the Clinton policy—with the conspicuous difference that he was not prepared to consider Arafat on a basis of parity with the elected prime minister of Israel. In the early months of the Bush presidency, the Sharon government was frequently scolded by the U.S government for intemperate responses to escalating Palestinian violence, but it was noted that only rarely did the words of condemnation come directly out of the mouth of the president himself. Bush met frequently with Prime Minister Sharon (with whom he had established a warm relationship long before entering the presidency) but never once did he meet with Arafat.[26] Commentators speculated (correctly) that Bush despised Arafat. There was nothing that Bush could find to celebrate or even to identify with in a man whose life from his youth had been sleeplessly dedicated to violence. It puzzled him that his predecessor as president and now so many of his contemporaries among the European leaders seemed to trust this figure and even to romanticize his life. It was not enslavement to Jewish pressure that caused this preference for Sharon, for at this stage polls were showing very high levels of support within the American Jewish community for negotiations between Israel and Arafat and for an independent Palestinian state.[27]

The attack upon the United States by the internationally funded terrorist organization al-Qaeda put every ongoing U.S. foreign policy issue in a new light, as President Bush declared the beginning of a war "against terrorism and those who harbor terrorists." Not the least to be affected by the post-9/11 review was the matter of Israel. Still, in the weeks immediately following 9/11, when all attention was on Afghanistan and its neighbors, it was not immediately clear *how* policy toward Israel would change. In the babble that went up immediately from spokesmen for the administration, Israelis and friends of Israel noted one disturbing theme: that there must be an effort to reassure Muslims worldwide that the United States had not lost sight of *their* legitimate concerns. Specifically, they wanted to assure them that there would be no letting up on the effort at even-handedness in the matter of Israel and the Palestinians. Early indications were that the Americans were *increasing* pressure upon Israel for concessions to the other side. On September 26, 2001, Prime Minister Sharon responded publicly to the American call for a cease-fire with the Palestinians, and followed up this gesture by sending Foreign Minister Peres to meet with Arafat in Gaza to discuss resumption of the security arrangements agreed to some months earlier (the Mitchell Plan and the Tenet Plan). In October 2001, President Bush took the step that his critics said was most needed to reassure the Arab side of his goodwill—namely, a declaration of his personal support for a Palestinian state.

But, in the long run, 9/11 assisted Israel's cause. In simplest terms, it deepened the sense that most Americans had always had of a common cause with Israel. Hitherto, most Americans had imagined themselves exempt from the kind of conflict in which Israel seemed always to be embroiled, and to that extent could feel that they were condescending to assist the vulnerable Jewish people. Now the scales had departed from most eyes. The United States and Israel faced the same enemy. Americans would soon be dealing with that enemy on a daily basis unless they now took the very sort of actions that Israel had always taken against *its* internal enemy abetted by *its* external enemy—now disclosed as *America's* external enemy—worldwide radical Islam. The president said to congressional leaders on September 12: "They hate Christianity. They hate Judaism. They hate everything that is not them."[28] In days to follow President Bush and other administration spokesmen spoke frequently of the need to "defend civilization" and about fundamental distinctions between good and evil. Zealots of the peace process found such talk distressing, as the use of such absolutizing vocabulary undermines the quest for parity which is the heart of conflict resolution.

Bush's declaration that he favored the eventual creation of a Palestinian state had a clarifying effect, but it added nothing real to the situation, as most Israeli politicians, including by now Prime Minister Sharon himself, had made the same declaration at one time or another. It concentrated the mind. The real question had always been whether there was a Palestinian leader who could persuade the Palestinians to prove that they qualified for such statehood by settling down to a peaceful daily life long enough for the several unfinished peace agreements to be fulfilled.

Beginning in late 2001, a wave of suicide bombings brought daily life in Israel under a constant dark cloud of violent death. The government of Ariel Sharon revealed that certain of the now-deceased perpetrators were members of Arafat's own al-Aqsa Martyrs Brigade and their names had been on the list that the CIA had conveyed to the Palestinian Authority on Israel's behalf, together with specific information about this forthcoming action. There was nothing left, Sharon now declared, but to "destroy the authority of Arafat."[29] At first the Bush administration cautioned the Israelis to give Arafat more time and more room to quell the terrorists. And so Sharon held back while Arafat proclaimed at a rally in Ramallah (December 8, 2001), "We will sacrifice ourselves for our holy places. . . . We are willing to give seventy of our martyrs for every one of their martyrs in this campaign . . . We are all martyrs in paradise."[30] But the last nail in the coffin of Arafat's ambition to be recognized as a partner for peace by George W. Bush was the interception in the Red Sea on the night of January 2–3, 2002, by the Israeli Special forces of the merchant ship *Katrine*, manned by PA naval personnel under the direction of a lieutenant-colonel in the PA navy. The cargo—500 tons of major weapons, such as Katyusha rockets and anti-tank missiles—had originated in Iran and was meant to be floated ashore off Gaza. Arafat at first denied any knowledge of such an operation, but when the Israelis displayed the documents and the persons linking him directly to the operation, all hope was gone for any contact between Bush and Arafat.

On April 4, 2002, Bush said, "The chairman of the Palestinian Authority has not consistently opposed or confronted terrorism. At Oslo and elsewhere, Chairman Arafat renounced terror as an instrument of his cause, and he agreed to control it. He's not done so."[31] Bush had, by now, lost all patience with European politicians who wanted to keep up the fiction of Arafat as a fellow-statesman dedicated to peace. David Frum speaks of an occasion in the UN building when Arafat tried to work his way onto the path of the president so as to require a friendly acknowledgement and had to be physically blocked by the Secret Service.[32]

An indicator of the new tone in administration policy in the Middle East was the appointment (December 2002) of Elliot Abrams as senior director for Near East and South Asian Affairs at the National Security Council.[33] Abrams was notorious among Democrats as the good soldier who had stonewalled Congress rather than disclose what he knew of Iran-Contra while serving as assistant secretary of state for Inter-American Affairs to George Shultz; he was later forced to plead guilty to misleading Congress and was pardoned by President George Bush in December, 1992. Since then, Abrams had remained active in the neocon world, where he was known as an opponent of the Oslo Accords. In his book, *Faith or Fear: How Jews Can Survive in a Christian America* (1997), he brings to the attention of American Jews the work of Christian Zionists and protests the vilification of the "Christian Right," which had become endemic among leaders of national Jewish organizations.[34] These associations marked him as a bridge between an increasingly important part of the Jewish community and conservative Christians who were so important within the Republican Party and within the administration. The nomination of Daniel Pipes to the board of the U.S. Institute of Peace, an advisory body, further reflected the administration's approval of these same perspectives.[35]

GEORGE W. BUSH AND "CHRISTIAN OPINION" ON WORLD AFFAIRS

The moment President George Bush declared himself at war with the terrorists who were responsible for the 9/11 attacks a public relations war was inaugurated against him by the World Council of Churches, the National Council of Churches, USA, the National Council of Catholic Bishops—indeed, virtually all the organized religious institutions. In its press release, dated September 11, 2001, the NCC began *not* with judgment on the atrocities committed at the World Trade Center and at the Pentagon but with that body's "concern . . . to avert the danger of retaliatory actions against innocent people in the aftermath of Tuesday's attacks on the World Trade Center and the Pentagon." The example of "the false rush to judgment after the bombing of the Federal Building in Oklahoma City . . . when many Muslims in U.S. communities suffered threats, harassment and incidents of violence" was brought to mind, lest the president apply the "veneer of respectability to slaughter carried out for personal vengeance or political purpose."[36] About a week later, WCC General Secretary Konrad Raiser sent a "Pastoral letter to all Churches in the U.S.A." to plead that instead of a military response there ought to be "a form of justice that would name the evil and identify those responsible and bring them to trial in appropriate courts of law."[37]

It is regularly asserted in WCC declarations and publications that the government of the United States is contemptuous of "Christian opinion," which the WCC finds virtually equivalent to "world opinion" or "the conscience of mankind" as expressed at the UN. In an official publication of the WCC, Samuel Kobia of Kenya (then executive director of the Cluster on Justice, Peace, and Creation Team, today the general secretary of the WCC, succeeding Raiser) warned, "We should be concerned with the language of war from the White House because it exhibits the mentality of religious dualist fundamentalism strikingly similar to the language of the Taliban. . . . The dualistic mentality that only sees 'good and evil,' 'right and wrong,' and refuses to accept the moral ambiguity of human existence suggests that the only way to respond to violence is through violence. . . . It may well be that September 11th could have been avoided if America had declared war against terrorism after the East Africa bombings of 1998. But those who died then, by the hundreds were not Americans, but Africans whose lives matter little to the rich and powerful in the USA."[38] Racist slanders of this kind against the American government and people are routine in WCC publications, as is the habit of identifying George W. Bush as a "fundamentalist" or "literalist" Christian—one who shares with "fundamentalist Jews" and "fundamentalist Muslims" the apocalyptic mindset that prevents one from seeing humankind as one body.

Throughout the Bush years the WCC kept up its denunciations of Israel for her tyrannical suppression of the Palestinians, while sedulously neglecting mention of terrorist atrocities. Its line (identical to that offered by Jimmy Carter) was that "Israel's repeated defiance of international law, its continuing occupation and the impunity it has so long enjoyed are the fundamental causes of the present violence and threaten peace and security of both peoples."[39] Just a few days before the al-Qaeda attack upon the United States, WCC representatives attending the UN Conference on Racism, Racial Discrimination, Xenophobia, and Related Intolerance at Durban, South Africa, led in demanding an official denunciation of Israel for "systematic perpetration of racist crimes including war crimes, acts of genocide and ethnic cleansing."

In September 2002, President Bush began his campaign to persuade the UN Security Council to put an end to what the administration claimed was a decade and more of Saddam Hussein's defiance of the commitments that attended his surrender at the end of the Gulf War. Eventually, the Bush administration would lose patience with the UN and would proceed on its own to put together a Coalition of the Willing, which undertook the invasion of Iraq, which began in March 2003 and ended six weeks later. Throughout the campaign to recruit worldwide support, the Bush administration met considerable resistance from public opinion abroad. Among the NATO allies that refused to endorse the action were France, Germany, and Canada. Predictably, the WCC and the mainline churches steadfastly opposed the war, as did the Pope. This time, the religious leaders made a public issue of President Bush's refusal to give them time in his office to express their opposition in person. One hundred and twenty Methodist leaders, including seven bishops, took out a magazine ad entitled, "A Prophetic Epistle from United Methodists Calling Upon Our Brother George W. Bush to Repent," denouncing a range of policy actions of the president, some domestic and some foreign, which are "incongruent with Jesus' teaching."[40]

Does it follow that George Bush was acting in defiance of "Christian opinion," or of "the almost universal conviction of religious leaders" against the war (as claimed by Jimmy Carter in the *New York Times*, March 9, 2003)? The reality is that few Christian laypersons are aware of the positions taken on public issues by the ecumenical or denominational bodies that claim to represent their consciences. A more reliable indicator of the opinion of the laity is found in public opinion polls. In early 2003, these showed that not only did Christian laity of all denominations *not* support the antiwar proclamations made by their alleged spokesmen, but they *supported the war* by a greater percentage than did the general population.[41] On this, as on most key issues, George W. Bush was attuned to what polls have always shown to be the concerns of most self-described Christians, taking the positions that commentators persistently and obtusely speak of as "the agenda of the Christian Right."[42] On his first day in office, Bush signed an Executive Order banning all U.S. funding for all international programs advocating abortion (reversing an Executive Order left behind by Bill Clinton). Following through on a campaign theme, Bush gave recognition to faith-based organizations involved in humanitarian work (such as shelters, soup kitchens, drug-and-alcohol recovery) by means of an Executive Order of December 2002, which directed all federal agencies to provide equal treatment to such groups—thus reversing long-standing discrimination against programs identified with religious purposes in (among others) the Department of Housing and Urban Development, Health and Human Services, and Federal Emergency Relief Administration.[43] He has declared his support for an amendment to the Constitution ratifying that marriage is a union between a man and a woman.[44]

As the leaders of the major church organizations have denounced Bush for ignoring "religious opinion," so the major Jewish organizations have accused him of ignoring "Jewish opinion." The elitist bias is evident in both cases. Early in 2003, Jewish commentators noted a major effort of the Bush administration to broaden its Jewish support by, in effect, doing an end-run around the major Jewish organizations.[45] Just as Bush has gone around the Christian denominational leadership in order to appeal directly to Christian laity, so, recognizing the unlikelihood of winning the hearts and minds of the major Jewish organizations, Bush has appealed directly to American Jewish laity.

A LAST LOOK AT THE JIMMY CARTER ALTERNATIVE

As we have noted, George W. Bush's advocacy of military action in order to get at the sources of international terrorism put him at odds with the institutions that provide journalists and secular commentators with what they imagine is wholesale religious opinion. It also put him at odds with former President Jimmy Carter, who had been enjoying a striking increase in his public approval rating during the 1990s. No serious commentator attributed this to nostalgia, given that the years of Carter's presidency were still fixed in most minds as a time of economic troubles at home and weakness abroad. Rather, Carter won back the admiration of Americans by his *current* devotion to public service at home (including his work for Habitat for Humanity) and abroad (where, through his Carter Center, he contributed mightily to the reduction of many diseases rampant among the poorest populations in the world and shepherded several nations through the difficult work of achieving true democracy by assisting in the supervision of their elections.)

The one undoubted foreign policy accomplishment of Carter's presidency, the Camp David agreement between Israel and Egypt, gained increasing luster by comparison with the modest and problematical advances toward Middle East peace that the succeeding three presidents could show. As we have already noted, Jimmy Carter never gave up trying to persuade (and, through channels not open to public scrutiny, to coerce) his successors to abandon what he perceived as their pro-Israel policies. In an op-ed item published in *USA Today*, July 1, 2002, Carter pointed again to his accomplishments at Camp David and to his more recent role in supervising the elections held in the Palestinian Authority in 1996, and effectively proposed himself and his Carter Center as the "new mediator" who could bring "a just and lasting peace to the Arab-Israeli conflict."[46] This received little notice. But then, in October 2002,

Jimmy Carter was again on the front pages of the newspapers, and under circumstances that seemed to open up the possibility that he might again move public support away from the incumbent president's policy in the Middle East.

On October 11, 2002, word came that he was to receive the Nobel Prize for Peace. No informed commentator had expected this—and neither had Jimmy Carter. Carter's name had been before the Nobel Prize Committee ten times since 1978, when the committee awarded its prize to Menachem Begin and Anwar Sadat, the other two architects of the (first) Camp David Accords. Prompted by the debate about U.S. foreign policies that was building in the summer of 2002 around the Bush administration's plans for possible invasion of Iraq, the Nobel Prize Committee decided to take another look at the Jimmy Carter file. "In a situation currently marked by threats of the use of power," said the committee, "Carter has stood by the principles that conflicts must as far as possible be resolved through mediation and international cooperation based on international law, respect for human rights, and economic development."[47] Gunnar Berge, the head of the committee of five that made the choice, broke the organization's rules by boasting publicly about the political intention behind this selection: "With the position Carter has taken on this, it can and must also be seen as criticism of the line the current U.S. administration has taken on Iraq . . . It's a kick in the leg to all that follow the same line as the United States."[48]

Interviewed on *Larry King Live*, Carter again threw out the hint of his availability as a mediator of the Arab-Israeli conflict: "Although I hunger for a chance to help, I feel constrained to stay out of it because of proprieties about it. I don't see any hope for progress in the altercation between Israelis and Palestinians with this leadership. And the fight, apparently for control of the Likud Party is between Sharon and Netanyahu to outdo the other about how they can be most abusive toward the Palestinians and avoid any relation of a negotiating nature with Arafat."[49]

Jimmy Carter received his award and made his speech in Oslo—but there was no groundswell of interest in Carter's returning to public life in order to finish the unfinished business of Camp David. However, in December 2003, Carter was among the Nobel Prize winners and other dignitaries present at the signing ceremony in Geneva for the "Geneva Accord." This was an unofficial peace plan floated by certain out-of-office Israelis and Palestinians, which would (essentially) take all the parties back to the state of negotiations at the time at the end of the Camp David talks of July 2000. At Geneva, Carter denounced the Bush administration for its "bias toward Israel," and invited the world to imagine how different things might have been: "Had I been elected to a second term, with the prestige and authority and influence and reputation I had in the region, we could have moved to a final solution."[50]

THE COLLAPSE OF THE OSLO PROCESS

* * *

From the prophet even to the priest, everyone deals falsely. They have also healed the hurt of My people slightly [superficially], saying, "Peace, peace!" when there is no peace. (Jeremiah 6:13–14)

* * *

Yitzhak Rabin, in the second edition of his memoirs (1994), sets the Oslo process in the context of recent fast-paced political events that augured, he said, a new aeon of change, leading toward universal peace: "The world is turning upside-down before our eyes: the globes and atlases in your homes have become archeological findings . . . Ideologies that moved hundreds of millions vanished without a trace: ideas which brought about the death of millions died themselves overnight . . . We are undergoing the revolution of peace."[51] At about the same time (May 1994), Shimon Peres, foreign minister of Israel at the time of the Oslo negotiations and their principal champion on the Israeli side ever since, announced: "Today we have ended the Arab-Israeli conflict. Utopia is coming."[52]

This chapter on the policies of George W. Bush must be left incomplete. But as I write these words (in May 2004) it is clearer than ever that Utopia has not come and is not coming. Today only historians have any interest in talking about details of the Oslo Agreement. One by one, most of the advocates of the Oslo process have renounced their criminal utopianism. Between September 29, 1993 and October 1, 2003, 2,400 Arab Palestinians and 800 Israelis died by violence. Early in the year 2002, an ever-escalating series of assaults began upon civilian life in Israel, reaching a peak with the Passover Eve atrocity in Netanya (March 27–28, 2002.) This provoked Israel's Operation Shield, committed to destroying the entire infrastructure of terror throughout the PA. Arafat's own governmental compound in Ramallah was put under siege, and Arafat himself was confined to a few rooms in an undamaged wing. As the IDF took possession of the offices and facilities of the PA they came into possession of abundant documentation of Arafat's duplicity—proof of his close dealings with all the terrorist cells and with their sponsors throughout the Arab world. All this was shared with the government of the United States.

Thus was set the pattern, which is still in effect as I write (May 2004). There would be a suicide-bombing in Israel, followed by an IDF occupation of civilian areas within the PA and the closing of borders; this would usually effect a decline in terrorist actions, but never their elimination. Arafat would then make a statement deploring violence on all sides, which would then be held up by the UK and the EU as proof of Arafat's desire to establish a peaceful setting for further negotiations; Sharon would then agree to withdraw or curtail the occupying forces; then more suicide-bombers would slip through the borders in the midst of the thousands of workers, and the cycle would resume.

At a time when Israel was standing under almost universal condemnation for her use of force in her self-defense, the president of the United States stood virtually alone among world leaders in defending Sharon's Operation Shield. At the outset he said, "I fully understand Israel's need to defend herself; I respect that. It's a country that has seen a wave of suicide bombers coming into the hearts of their cities and killing innocent people. That country has a right to defend herself."[53]

Shortly into this process, the government of Israel declared its refusal to have further dealings with Yassir Arafat, and, as I write, continues to impose a virtual house arrest upon him by devastating everything in the vicinity of his offices in Ramallah and preventing him from taking to airplane or helicopter. Now there is a Road Map, which is virtually identical to the map that the first Bush administration unfurled in 1991 and which led at once into the morass of Madrid and ultimately to the Slough of Oslo. But this may be one of those cases where a little déjà vu can be a dangerous thing. American official attitudes toward Israel have changed dramatically since the days of G.H.W. Bush and James Baker. Expert State and Defense Department thinking is today more in line with popular thinking about the meaning of the struggle in the Middle East. The leaders of the Palestinian Authority, with great reluctance, responded to the situation created by Arafat's isolation by persuading him to appoint a prime minister, Abu Mazen, with whom both Prime Minister Sharon and President Bush met, but who proved incapable of putting an end to terrorism. In September 2003 Abu Mazen resigned, and another long-time Arafat associate, Ahmed Qurei (Abu Alaa) took his place. As of May 2004, the latter had accomplished no more than the former.

On April 14, 2004, President Bush met with Prime Minister Sharon in the White House and offered his whole-hearted support for Sharon's plan to work toward a total withdrawal of the Jewish settlements in Gaza and limited withdrawal of settlements in the West Bank. At a press conference, the two explained that this meant that Israel expected to retain after any final agreement with the Palestinians those settlements that were of longest-standing, most densely inhabited, and closest to Israel's original borders—this in light of the fact that "realities on the ground and in the region have changed greatly over the last several decades." With this, the government of the United States put behind forever its policy of considering all Jewish settlements outside the 1948 boundaries as obstacles to peace. A the same time, the two leaders agreed that an unqualified right of return of all Arab refugees was out of the question: Israel would welcome a small number with reasonable claims, while the others must expect the state of Palestine to take them in, or abandon their claims. This Israel-U.S. understanding, Yassir Arafat immediately announced, "means clearly the complete end of the peace process."[54]

Bush's performance throughout this critical time presents a considerable contrast to Ronald Reagan's in 1982, when Reagan removed the U.S. Marines from Lebanon in response to acts of terrorism against them, leaving Israel with no option but to withdraw from Lebanon. Adding to Israel's comfort was Bush's readiness to see Israel's campaign against the terrorists in the context of the worldwide escalation of hatred of Jews, sometimes disguised as "anti-Zionism," but still having all the hallmarks of the old "anti-Semitism." To a group of Jews invited to the White House for a dinner honoring the opening of an exhibit of materials of Anne Frank at the U.S. Holocaust Memorial Museum, Bush observed: "People who hate life and God, target the people of God."[55]

Retrospect and Conclusions

THE POLITICS OF AMERICAN ZIONISM

Not only casual observers but also serious students of the history of the U.S.-Israel connection seem to take for granted that the most important factor explaining the basic pro-Israeli disposition in American politics is the strength of the Jewish vote. This was never true, not even in the beginning of the story, and it is certainly not true today, when the entire Jewish population of the United States is less than 2 percent of the whole,[1] and when a considerable component of Jewish intellectuals has gone over to the anti-Zionist camp.

Here we need to glance at the role of Jews in recent American politics. The most important generalization under this head is simply that Jews participate disproportionately in politics, as they do in the cultural life, the arts, the academic life, and generally in the world where opinion and taste are made and disseminated. This circumstance is patient of explanation in normal historical terms: It is not a marvelous inexplicable phenomenon, nor is it a plot. Jews make up about 2 percent of the whole population of the United States, but because their interest in politics is well-developed Jews are careful to keep registered and active. About 80 percent are registered to vote at any time, whereas the national figure is about 50 percent. In New York State, for example, they are 9 percent of the population, but 18.3 percent of electorate; in California they are 3 percent of the population, 5.8 percent of the electorate; in Florida they are 4.7 percent of the population, 8.2 percent of the electorate.[2] The influence of Jews in politics is magnified by the fact that Jews participate, again in disproportionate numbers, in the financing and the direction of charities, cultural activities, and community activities of all kinds. Also, they are disproportionately active in public causes, including political campaigns. In some states, the actual number of Jewish voters is so small as to be utterly insignificant, yet again and again we find that senators and congressmen elected from such states have been among the most constant supporters of issues of close concern to Jews, and notably, of course, the cause of Israel. Jews contribute disproportionately to the financing of both major parties (and, for that matter, the minor ones), both at national levels and at local levels. Having good relations with Jews is normally assumed to be an asset in any political constituency.

A second generalization of equal importance to the first is that *Jews have stood aside, almost as a bloc, from the most important partisan trend of the last quarter-century.* Were it the case that the motive for all those Jews being in politics was to exercise raw power on behalf of Jews, then they have manifestly failed. The national election of 1980 marks the beginning of a period of decline of the Democratic Party and increase of the Republican Party. All this time, Jews and blacks have remained the only identifiable constituencies of voters that have resisted this trend. Jews provide somewhere between one-fourth and one-half of all Democratic campaign funds. If economic self-interest were the motive, then it must be said the Jews do not understand their basic interest: As Milton Himmelfarb has put it, Jews earn like Episcopalians and vote like Puerto Ricans.[3]

Reviewing the presidential elections of our period we find that the Republican share of Jewish vote was 10 percent when Dewey ran in 1948 and reached its highest point at 40 percent when Ronald Reagan ran in 1980.[4] In the most recent presidential election, it sank again (to 19 percent for George W. Bush in 2000).

With reference to our interests in this book, it is of utmost importance to distinguish the Jewish vote from the pro-Israel vote. Jewish organizations rate the performance of politicians first and foremost with respect to a certain set of "social issues," about which the leaders of these organizations claim American Jews are generally of one mind. Among these are "abortion rights" (FOR), public funding for education (FOR), school prayer (AGAINST), and "gay and lesbian rights" (FOR). It is the affinity of most Jews with most other Democrats on these "social issues" that keeps Jews voting as Democrats. Support for Israel, while an issue of great importance to most Jews, is by no means at the top of this list. Nowadays, while most Democrats still take a firm interest in the issue of support for Israel, those politicians who put support for Israel nearest to the top of their own priorities are not Democrats but Republicans.

In short, the Republican Party has been becoming more Zionist with each passing year since about 1980, while the Democratic Party has become less so—without losing its command upon the Jewish vote.

CHRISTIAN ZIONISM AND PATRIOTIC CONSERVATISM

The Republican Party has become the Zionist party as one consequence of its becoming the home of conservative Christians. Still, this should be understood as part of a larger story. The Republican Party has become the Zionist party as one consequence of its becoming the home of patriotic conservatives, not all of whom identify themselves as Christians. One of the major reasons why so many Democrats deserted Jimmy Carter in 1980 was that he appeared weak in the face of several challenges to America's security and self-esteem. These patriotic Democrats joined with patriotic Republicans to form a continuing constituency within the Reagan coalition. Patriotic conservatism is by no means coextensive with economic conservatism or libertarian conservatism or family values conservatism, but it does overlap in part with all of them.

Patriotic Republicans support Israel because they recognize that the people who hate Israel, the only democracy other than Turkey ever to exist in the Middle East, are people who hate America. Patriotic conservatives listen to the criticism leveled at Israel by the EU and by the UN, and they hear the same rhetoric leveled against the United States every time it takes up its task on behalf of civilization. There is the same disparagement of "reliance upon military might," of "occupation," of "unilateralism" and "contempt for world opinion." Republicans support Israel so much more militantly than Democrats do *not* because they are Jewish, and not really because Israel is Jewish, and certainly not because they are under the thumb of Jews, but because they identify Israel's cause with that of the United States. It is, in short, an ideological issue.

As the war against global terrorism has unfolded, Christian Zionists have provided some ideological reenforcement to arguments that make complete sense to patriotic conservatives in terms of national security for the United States. Patriotic Americans have taken to heart the television images of gleeful Palestinians celebrating in the streets following September 11, 2001, and later on pledging their eternal fidelity to Saddam Hussein, burning U.S. flags and effigies of George Bush, while the official television network of the PA broadcasts sermons by Palestinian Imams calling out, "O Allah, destroy the Jews, and their supporters. O Allah, destroy the United States."[5] While the world beseeches Sharon to refrain from participating in yet another "cycle of violence," Palestinian terrorist organizations go on and on recruiting eager suicide-bombers in numbers vastly greater than they can ever actually use. Militant Islamic organizations dominate the student leadership in all the schools and colleges. Pursuant to the Oslo Accords, the government of Israel armed the "police forces" of the PA, and the governments of Israel and the United States together trained the PA's "security and intelligence" apparatus—only to see it all be delivered into the service of the Second Intifada. In light of this experience, the notion of deliberately establishing a sovereign state controlled by a regime that has thrived on terror appears—strictly from the point of worldwide security—obviously unwise. Observing this, Republicans reflect, with Secretary of Defense Donald Rumsfeld, "If you have a country [Israel] that's a sliver and you can see three sides of it from a high hotel building, you've got to be careful what you give away and to whom you give it."[6] It would be like deliberately creating another Syria. This thinking is now general in the Defense Department and with civilian Republicans.

For the insight articulated by Secretary Rumsfeld there is no need for Christian Zionism. Still, the history of the United States demonstrates that arguments that turn on definitions of national security tend to have a short shelf life. An unanticipated decline of one prominent actor in world affairs or the sudden unanticipated rise of another will set the pundits rethinking the nation's security priorities. The only thing that gives security arguments longevity is ideology.

THE PRESIDENTS AND THE CYRUS LEGACY

Truman's self-identification with Cyrus the Restorer of the Jews was a matter of ideology. It followed from a profound conviction that Israel belonged in the world, as surely as the United States of America belonged in the world. The American constitutional process had put him, Harry Truman, in the seat of the president of the United States in that moment when the Jews of the world came before the community of the world, the United Nations, in the desperate state that followed upon the near-success of Hitler's final solution and presented for redemption the pledge made by the Great Powers in 1917 and confirmed thereafter repeatedly by the Great Powers and by the League of Nations—their pledge to create a home for the Jews in the land that the British called Palestine. Moreover, in this matter Truman had reason to believe that popular opinion would sustain him, against all the expert advice. And so it did. It did so *not* because people could see a strategic argument for creating Israel (there was none—and even today it is hard to make one) but because the case for creating Israel seemed ideologically compelling.

The effort to escape the legacy of the Cyrus, the Restorer and Benefactor of Israel, began in the presidency of Dwight Eisenhower. According to Eisenhower, Truman's one-sided support of Israel, though prettified as a high-and-mighty moral obligation, was motivated in reality by nothing more than "domestic politics." To replace this fundamentally immoral, one-sided policy, Eisenhower proffered the blessings of "even-handedness." The siren of even-handedness continued to sound throughout the presidencies of Eisenhower's four successors (Kennedy, Johnson, Nixon, and Ford). Nixon and Kennedy were both distinctly uncomfortable in the face of philosophical or theological reflection on the purpose in history—and therefore vigorously avoided the company of anybody who had such thoughts on his mind. Their historical philosophies were of the most rudimentary sort, and, such as they were, put them on the agnostic-to-cynical side of philosophy. Gerald Ford, who was more of a reader and more of a thinker than he let on, seems nonetheless to have got along without much reflection on history and history's purposes. Because of his essentially Evangelical outlook, he had a pious respect for God's presence in history; but nothing he ever said publicly suggests that that he ever saw the present State of Israel as a fulfillment of anything other than a secular political process.

However, it was not until Jimmy Carter became president that a full-fledged ideological alternative was found to Truman's policy.

THE PEACE PROCESS AS CONFLICT RESOLUTION

It was Jimmy Carter who found the way of getting presidents out from under the obligation of continuing the Cyrus legacy. Carter's goal was to substitute negotiation for military force in the solution of all world conflicts. To achieve this, the American policies everywhere in the world would have to be redesigned so that the United States could present itself *everywhere* as "a trusted mediator, even-handed, consistent, unwavering, enthusiastic, a partner with both sides and not a judge of either."[7] The case of Israel, he believed, was the place to start—precisely because the baneful allure of ideology was greatest there.

Carter's claims on behalf of the method of negotiation draw heavily upon the vocabulary and spirit of the literature on conflict resolution that has come to dominate the teaching and learning of university departments of political science and international relations, where historical study has virtually withered away. This, in turn, draws on a broader literature, which has flourished much longer in schools of social work. Common to all this literature is the argument that all "disputes" are grounded in arguments about the past, about history, and that their relief comes only when the historical record is willfully severed from the present state-of-things. According to this thinking, it is not only possible and desirable but necessary to level all distinctions between the claims of parties to a private dispute or a family dispute or a dispute among nations, establishing parity by deliberately setting aside the different outcomes for the two parties of the history of conflict to date, thus equalizing the moral capital on the two sides. Thus, the key to "solving the Arab-Israeli dispute" is to

establish parity of self-esteem. This is achieved by sidestepping and rec-
ommending to oblivion the history that has produced the present *inequal-
ity* in self-esteem.

Although many people of goodwill are beguiled by the irenic vocabulary
that governs conflict resolution, others, having a deeper appreciation of historical realities and an appreciation for original sin, detect a trap. History is
not a board game, as the advocates of conflict resolution pretend. As David
Wurmser, once director of the Middle East Program of the American Enterprise Institute, wrote, "Process oriented peace efforts blur the moral distinctions among nations by replacing patriotism—defending national values—
with internationalist conflict resolution—seeking compromise and peace as
the highest values. The enemy is no longer the entity that threatens the
national community's values, but the elements within the country that
reject compromise on the basis of such values. A nation is thus intellectually disarmed."[8]

In the matter before us, one side (Israel) enjoys the asset of strong
national identity, which historians explain as the outcome of several thousand years of inward growth and outward struggle. The other contestant
(Palestine) notoriously lacks these assets. Indeed, its qualification to be
called a nation is fragile.[9] One party (Israel) enjoys its own nation-state,
healthy capitalist economy, progressive educational system, social services,
modern culture, advanced scientific and scholarly institutions, a lively free
press, and the support of a loyal and politically powerful *Diaspora*. The
other side has none of these assets. Champions of a "negotiated solution"
insist that fairness requires treating both parties *as though* they had the
same assets. To achieve parity, both sides are *stipulated* to be "nations" or
"peoples" having histories of identical length and both have "diasporas."
Not only on the Palestinian side (of course) but also among Israeli politicians who have deep investments in the historical inevitability of the
"peace process," this argument for equating the authorities of mythical and
historical recollections of the past is highly prized.

Beginning with Jimmy Carter and continuing until the presidency of
George W. Bush, the policy of American presidents has been to "stand
above" the specific historical and theological memories that have engen-
dered the "Arab-Israeli conflict." This does not mean that they have
eschewed theological language, however. "Well, I mean," Bill Clinton,
explained, "it's our Holy Land too!" While it can be defended entirely in
secular terms, advancing the peace process can also be buttressed by selec-
tive use of scriptural passages when the president stands before an audience of religious Jews or Christians. Presidents have learned that some of
the most potent scriptural excerpts for the purpose exist in the Old Testament right alongside the very passages that religious Jews and Christian
Zionists have always preferred as sources for their own preaching in favor

of restoration—notably, from Isaiah and the other prophets. The trick is to ignore the context and glean the comforting, noncontroversial phrases. For example, in the same book of the prophet Isaiah where Christian Zionists find their favorite proof texts—including, "It shall come to pass in that day that the LORD shall set His hand again the second time to recover the remnant of His people who are left . . . He will set up a banner for the nations, and will assemble the outcasts of Israel, and gather together the dispersed of Judah, from the four corners of the earth" (Isaiah 11:11–12)—the presidents' speechwriters find proof texts for God's blessing upon the peace process: "Come now, and let us reason together, says the LORD" (Isaiah 1:18); and, "They shall beat their swords into plowshares, and their spears into pruning hooks. Nation shall not lift up sword against nation. Neither shall they learn war anymore" (Isaiah 2:4). What is mandatory, however, is the avoidance of scriptural references that support the Cyrus legacy (such as Isaiah, 11, just quoted).

As the secularization of our culture advances, it becomes increasingly easy to discredit historical arguments about the Middle East by pointing out that they are sustained consistently and fervently only by religious people. It takes a certain toughness of intellect to defend *historical* arguments when at any moment one will be hooted off the platform by the charge of Fundamentalism. At the same time, the ideology of Zionism has been losing credibility among American Jews. During the 1980s and the 1990s, American Jewish loyalty to Israel was steadily reduced—something that virtually every commentator has noted. This development took place within a larger context of increasing unfriendliness toward Israel and increasing insensitivity to her viewpoint among intellectuals and the media elites. In general, people whose views dominate in the media seemed less persuaded in 2004 than they were in the 1940s that blessing Israel has blessed America.

The American politicians who gave so much energy and attention to the peace process in the Carter years, and their successors who have continued this work, have all imagined that they had behind their efforts on behalf of the peace process the agreement of the best-educated people. There is no doubt that they did. What they lacked was active support of popular opinion. The spirit of hostility toward Israel, which is so strong within the academic and media elite community, contrasts starkly with the powerful pro-Israel bias in the popular culture. Today, in fact, the most *stable* component in the pro-Israel camp is the broadly based *popular* belief that America is blessed by preferring the interests of Israel to all other considerations in the Middle East. For most people, the adventures of Israel in the present world stand out in an extraordinary way, their importance seeming to be out of all proportion to the small size of the nation and the parties involved and the irrelevance of the geographical setting (in light of contemporary geopolitical realities). Even where theological conviction has retreated, something of a supernatural glow still seems to attach to these events in most minds.

One fascinating statistic will make our point: "While almost two thirds of American Jews favored the creation of a Palestinian state by the summer of 2002, fewer than half of Americans in general did so."[10] If this means what it appears to mean, American Jews are less Zionist than general, average, undifferentiated Americans!

*   *   *   *   *

The events of 9/11/01 began a rediscovery of the virtues of the "realist" school of commentary on foreign affairs that marked the 1950s (the era of Hans Morgenthau and George Kennan). It is now possible to speak positively again of civilization—even in history departments. The president of the United States has gone further, reintroducing the vocabulary of *good* and *evil*, and has been mocked by all the late-night comics, but has generally been applauded by people who are asleep at that hour but awake by 7 a.m. Enough has already happened to make it clear that President George W. Bush has a commitment of an altogether different kind to Israel than that of the first President Bush or that of his successor Bill Clinton. President Bush has declared himself the champion of the war "against terrorism and those who harbor terrorists," and has stood firm on the matter of acknowledging that these same mortal enemies of our civilization are the enemies that sought to prevent the birth of Israel in 1948 and against which Israel has been fighting for her survival for over a half-century. In a speech to the nation, September 7, 2003, President Bush said,

> For a generation leading up to September 11th, 2001, terrorists and their radical allies attacked innocent people in the Middle East and beyond, without facing a sustained and serious response. The terrorists became convinced that free nations were decadent and weak. And they grew bolder, believing that history was on their side. Since America put out the fires of September 11th and mourned our dead and went to war, history has taken a different turn. We have carried the fight to the enemy. We are rolling back the terrorist threat to civilization, not on the fringes of its influence, but at the heart of its power.[11]

Then, in a public statement on October 7, 2003, commenting on Israel's assault by air upon the terrorist camp in Syria, he aligned the cause of the defense of Israel and that of the defense of the United States perfectly: "America would do anything to defend its citizens, and we should expect no less from Israel."[12]

President George W. Bush draws his understanding of the meaning of Israel's struggle from a worldview secured by a confident and explicit Christian faith, which has reopened the possibility for the kind of commitment to Israel that marked the presidency of Harry S. Truman, over half a century ago.

Notes

ABBREVIATIONS USED THROUGHOUT

BA—Blood of Abraham
CZA—Central Zionist Archives, Jerusalem
DDE—Dwight D. Eisenhower
DSB—Department of State Bulletin
FRUS—Foreign Relations of the United States
GRFL—Gerald R. Ford Presidential Library; Ann Arbor, Michigan
HSTL—Harry S. Truman Presidential Library; Independence, Missouri
JCL—Jimmy Carter Presidential Library; Atlanta, Georgia
   /CO—Country
   /FO—Foreign Affairs
   /OSS—Office of Staff Secretary
   /SO—Staff Office
   WHCF—White House Central File
JPost—Jerusalem Post
JTA—Jewish Telegraphic Agency (www.jta.org)
KF—Keeping Faith
PPP—Public Papers of the Presidents of the United States; Washington, D.C.:
   U.S. Government Printing Office. These are cited as *PPP* followed by
   the initials of the president, and the year.
For example, *PPPHST:1945* = *Public Papers of the Presidents of the United*
   States: Harry S. Truman, volume for 1945
TP—Talking Peace
ZAL—Zionist Archives and Library, New York

INTRODUCTION

1. I use the New King James version for biblical quotations throughout the book.

2. Moshe Davis, "Reflections on Harry S. Truman and the State of Israel," in Allen Weinstein and Moshe Ma'oz, eds., *Truman and the American Commitment to Israel* (Jerusalem: Magnes Press/Hebrew University, 1981), 83–84.

3. 2 Chronicles 36:22ff; Ezra 1:1–8, Isaiah 44:28, 45:1.

4. Eliahu Elath, quoted by Moshe Davis in Weinstein and Ma'oz, *Truman and the American Commitment to Israel,* 84.

CHAPTER 1

1. David McCullough, *Truman* (New York: Simon & Schuster, 1992), 345–347.

2. McCullough, *Truman,* 324–332.

3. Merle Miller, *Plain Speaking: An Oral Biography of Harry S. Truman* (New York: Berkeley, 1974), 389–391.

4. Robert H. Ferrell, ed., *The Autobiography of Harry S. Truman* (Boulder: Colorado Associated University Press, 1980), 33–34.

5. HSTL/File: "Post-Presidential Invitations," General Baptist misc. folder #32.

6. Robert H. Ferrell, ed., *Off the Record: The Private Papers of Harry S. Truman* (New York: Harper & Row, 1980), 188 (item dated August 15, 1950).

7. Merlin Gustafson, "Harry Truman as a Man of Faith, "*Christian Century,* January 17, 1973.

8. From an autobiographical manuscript, dated May 14, 1934, in Ferrell, *Autobiography of Harry S. Truman,* 136–137.

9. McCullough, *Truman,* 598–599.

10. Abba Eban, *An Autobiography* (New York: Random House, 1977), 93–94 (citing Isaiah 11:12).

11. Quoted by Chaim Raphael, *Chaim Weizmann: The Revelation of the Letters* [Pamphlet] (London: Anglo-Israel Association, 1974), 17.

12. Barnet Litvinoff, ed., *Letters and Papers of Chaim Weizmann.* 15 vols. (London: Oxford University Press, 1956–1990), 2: nos. 169, 199, 12: nos. 61, 63.

13. Norman Rose, *Chaim Weizmann* (New York: Viking, 1986), 267.

14. Litvinoff, *Letters and Papers,* 22: no. 97; Chaim Weizmann, *Trial and Error: The Autobiography of Chaim Weizmann* (London: East and West Library, 1950), 458–459.

15. Litvinoff, *Letters and Papers,* 33: no. 131.

16. Sumner Welles, *We Need Not Fail* (Boston: Houghton, Mifflin, 1948), 63.

17. Harry S. Truman, *Memoirs,* vol. 2 (Garden City, NY: Doubleday, 1956), 158–159.

18. Paul C. Merkley, *The Politics of Christian Zionism, 1891–1948* (London: Frank Cass, 1998), 183 (citing HSTL/Eddie Jacobson Papers).

19. Donald Bruce Johnson, ed., *National Party Platforms* (Urbana, IL: University of Illinois Press, 1978), 403–413.

20. Eban, *Autobiography,* 88–89.

21. Golda Meir, *My Life* (New York: Putnam's, 1975), 245–254. (Golda Meir was the first Israeli Ambassador to Moscow.)

22. David Bercuson, *Canada and the Birth of Israel* (Toronto: University of Toronto Press, 1985), 181, 234–240.)

23. *FRUS:1948*, vol. 5, part 2, Department of State, Office of the Historian, Washington, D.C., 742–754.

24. *PPPHST:1948* (March 25, 1948), 190–193.

25. This story is told at greater length in my book, *The Politics of Christian Zionism*, 186–190.

26. HST, quoted in Miller, *Plain Speaking*, 233–247.

27. George F. Kennan, quoted in McCullough, *Truman*, 533.

28. *FRUS:1948*, vol. 5, part 2, Department of State, Office of the Historian, Washington, D.C., 972–993; McCullough, *Truman*, 614–617; Clark Clifford, with Richard Holbrooke, *Counsel to the President: A Memoir* (New York: Random House, 1991), 3–25; Forrest C. Pogue, *George C. Marshall: Statesman, 1945–1969* (New York: Penguin, 1987), 371–373.

29. Clifford, *Counsel*, 13–15.

30. McCullough, *Truman*, 633.

31. McCullough, *Truman*, 710.

32. *FRUS:1948*, vol. 5, part 2, Department of State, Office of the Historian, Washington, D.C., 1131–1132.

33. Benny Morris, *Righteous Victims: A History of the Zionist-Arab Conflict* (New York: Knopf, 1999), 218–219.

34. *FRUS:1948*, vol. 5, part 2, Department of State, Office of the Historian, Washington, D.C., 1415–1416.

35. *FRUS:1948*, vol. 5, part 2, 1430–1438.

36. Johnson, *National Party Platforms*, 432.

37. Frank Adler, *Roots in a Moving Stream* (Kansas City: Congregation of B'nai Yehudah, 1972), 217–219 (copy in HSTL/Jacobson papers); *FRUS:1948*, vol. 5, part 1, Department of State, Office of the Historian, Washington, D.C., 1430–1438.

38. *PPPHST:1948* (October 28, 1948), 913.

39. *FRUS:1949*, vol. 6, Department of State, Office of the Historian, Washington, D.C., 1072–1074.

40. Howard M. Sachar, *A History of Israel: From the Rise of Zionism to Our Time* (New York: Knopf, 1979), 335.

41. Eban, *Autobiography*, 156.

CHAPTER 2

1. Will Herberg, *Protestant, Catholic, Jew* (Garden City, NY: Doubleday/Anchor, 1960), 190.

2. This situation was only partly improved in May 2002, when Israel was "temporarily" admitted to a regional bloc called "West European and Others," and became eligible to participate, with unique restrictions, in some of the commissions. She was still excluded from the European caucuses in Geneva and from

the UN centers in Vienna and Nairobi. One important practical effect of these restrictions is that she can never be a member of the UN Human Rights Commission, from which comes the steady flow of declarations denouncing her (Embassy of Israel in Canada, May 23, 2002, via info@OTTAWA.mfa.gov.il).

3. Johnson, *National Party Platforms*, 497–499.

4. Mark G. Toulousse, *The Transformation of John Foster Dulles: From Prophet of Realism to Priest of Nationalism* (Macon, GA: Mercer U.P., 1985), 3–6.

5. Toulousse, *Transformation*, 4, 7, 124.

6. Isaac Alteras, *Eisenhower and Israel* (Gainesville: University of Florida Press, 1993), 56.

7. Alteras, *Eisenhower and Israel*, 99–100.

8. Milton S. Eisenhower, *The President Is Calling* (Garden City, NY: Doubleday, 1974), 87.

9. Dwight D. Eisenhower, *Ike's Letters to a Friend, 1941–1959*, edited by Robert Griffith (Lawrence: University of Kansas Press, 1984), 6.

10. See Heather and Gary Botting, Chapter 4: "The Cyclical Movement of History and Prophecy," in *The Orwellian World of Jehovah's Witnesses* (Toronto: University of Toronto Press, 1984), 60–75.

11. Merle Miller, *Ike the Soldier: As They Knew Him* (New York: Putnam's, 1980), 77–80.

12. Dwight D. Eisenhower, *The White House Years*, vol. 1, *Mandate To Change* (Garden City, NY: Doubleday, 1963), 100–101.

13. Miller, *Ike the Soldier*, 296–298.

14. Arieh J. Kochavi, *Post-Holocaust Politics: Britain, the United States, and Jewish Refugees, 1945–1948* (Chapel Hill: University of North Carolina Press, 2001), 91–95.

15. David Schoenbaum, *The United States and the State of Israel* (New York: Oxford University Press, 1993), 44–45, citing records of the Joint Chiefs of Staff.

16. Howard M. Sachar, *A History of the Jews in America* (New York: Knopf, 1992), 724.

17. Robert Ferrell, ed., *The Eisenhower Diaries* (New York: Norton, 1981), 318 (entry for March 8, 1956).

18. Eisenhower, *Ike's Letters to a Friend*, 175.

19. Sachar, *History of the Jews in America*, 724; Alteras, *Eisenhower and Israel*, 75–76, citing Dulles Papers.

20. Alteras, *Eisenhower and Israel*, 77.

21. Alteras, *Eisenhower and Israel*, 35.

22. Joseph Kraft, "Those Arabists in the State Department," *New York Times Magazine*, November 7, 1971.

23. Donald Neff, *Warriors at Suez: Eisenhower Takes America into the Middle East* (New York: Linden, 1981), 44, citing no. SS5-1: "Israel's Fundamental Problems."

24. Alteras, *Eisenhower and Israel*, 86.

25. Alteras, *Eisenhower and Israel*, 30–31.

26. Eisenhower, *The White House Years*, vol. 1, 155–156; *FRUS:1952–1954*, vol. 9, part 1, Department of State, Office of the Historian, Washington, D.C., 1–167.

27. *FRUS: 1952–1954*, vol. 9, part 1. Department of State, Office of the Historian, Washington, D.C., 3–25. The passage quoted is on page 7.

28. *FRUS: 1952–1954*, vol. 9, part 1, Department of State, Office of the Historian, Washington, D.C., 36–40. The passage quoted is on page 39.

29. Alteras, *Eisenhower and Israel*, 71, citing Israel State Archives, May 29, 1953.

30. Alteras, *Eisenhower and Israel*, 75–76, citing Dulles Papers.

31. *DSB* 28, number 729, June 15, 1953, 831–835.

32. Alteras, *Eisenhower and Israel*, 136–137.

33. *FRUS:1955–1957*, vol. 14, Department of State, Office of the Historian, Washington, D.C., 507–508.

34. *FRUS: 1955–1957*, vol. 14, Department of State, Office of the Historian, Washington, D.C., 504–505.

35. Alteras, *Eisenhower and Israel*, 143, citing *New York Times*, October 5, 1955.

36. Alteras, *Eisenhower and Israel*, 159.

37. Alteras, *Eisenhower and Israel*, 174–175.

38. *FRUS:1955–1957*, vol. 15, 857–859, and vol. 16, Department of State, Office of the Historian, Washington, D.C., 23–24; Alteras, *Eisenhower and Israel*, 177–178.

39. *FRUS:1955–1957*, vol. 15, Department of State, Office of the Historian, Washington, D.C., 347–908.

40. *FRUS:1955–1957*, vol. 15, Department of State, Office of the Historian, Washington, D.C., 859–874.

41. Stephen Ambrose, *Eisenhower*, vol. 2, *The President* (New York: Simon & Schuster, 1984), 329–330.

42. Portions quoted in Anthony Eden, *The Memoirs of Sir Anthony Eden*, vol. 2, *Full Circle*, and portions quoted in Neff, *Warriors*, 270.

43. *FRUS:1955–1957*, vol. 16, Department of State, Office of the Historian, Washington, D.C., 9–11.

44. Eden, *Memoirs*, vol. 2, 427.

45. *FRUS:1955–1957*, vol. 16, Department of State, Office of the Historian, Washington, D.C., 62–68.

46. Eden, *Memoirs*, vol. 2, 437.

47. *FRUS:1955–1957*, vol. 16, Department of State, Office of the Historian, Washington, D.C., 435–437.

48. Henry Kissinger, *Diplomacy* (New York: Simon & Schuster, 1994), 531.

49. Shimon Peres, *Battling for Peace: Memoirs* (London: Weidenfeld & Nicolson, 1995), 139–142.

50. Neff, *Warriors*, 205–206, citing interview with Eden's private secretary, *New York Times*, July 27, 1979.

51. Moshe Dayan, *Story of My Life: An Autobiography* (New York: Morrow, 1976), 226.

52. Dayan, *Story*, 221.

53. Dayan, *Story*, 348.

54. *FRUS: 1955–1957*, vol. 16, Department of State, Office of the Historian, Washington, D.C., 808–810 (October 28), and 821–825 (October 29, 1956); Eban, *Autobiography*, pp. 210–221; *New York Times*, October 31, 1956.

55. Ambrose, *Eisenhower*, vol. 2, 352–353, citing DDE to John Eisenhower.

56. Ferrell, *Eisenhower Diaries*, 331–332 (entry for October 15).

57. Eden, *Memoirs*, vol. 2, 525–526.

58. *PPPDDE:1956*, October 31, 1060–1062.

59. *FRUS: 1955–1957*, vol. 16, Department of State, Office of the Historian, Washington, D.C., 902–916; Ambrose, *Eisenhower*, 363–364.

60. Alteras, *Eisenhower and Israel*, 238–240; Cole C. Kingseed, *Eisenhowaer and the Suez Crisis of 1956* (Baton Rouge: Louisiana State University Press, 1995), 121–124.

61. Eden, *Memoirs*, vol. 2, 458–459.

62. Mark Tessler, *A History of the Israeli-Palestinian Conflict*, 803.

63. Alteras, *Eisenhower and Israel*, 290–291, citing interview with Eban, 1990.

64. Johnson, *National Party Platforms*, 557.

65. Johnson, *National Party Platforms*, 525–527.

66. Stuart Gerry Brown, *Conscience in Politics: Adlai Stevenson in the 1950s* (Syracuse, NY: Syracuse University Press, 1961), 151.

67. Brown, *Conscience*, 157.

68. Brown, *Conscience*, 158–161.

69. John Bartlow Martin, *Adlai Stevenson and the World* (Garden City, NY: Anchor, 1978), 239–240.

70. Brown, *Conscience*, 169–170.

71. Stevenson's response to President Eisenhower's national television address of October 31, 1956, quoted in Brown, *Conscience*, 171.

72. Eisenhower actually did somewhat better with the Jewish vote in 1956, gaining 40 percent to Stevenson's 60 percent, whereas in 1952 he had received only 36 percent to Stevenson's 64 percent. These figures should be compared with the national vote of 55 percent to 44 percent for Eisenhower in 1952, and 57 percent to 42 percent in 1956 (J. J. Goldberg, *Jewish Power: Inside the American Jewish Establishment* [New York: Addison Wesley, 1996], 34).

73. Martin, *Adlai Stevenson*, 393 and 392.

74. *PPPDDE:1957*, February 20, 147–156.

75. Sachar, *History of the Jews in America*, 728–729; Neff, *Warriors*, 433.

76. Steven L. Spiegel, *The Other Arab-Israeli Conflict: Making America's Middle East Policy, from Truman to Reagan* (Chicago: University of Chicago Press, 1985), 51, 436.

77. *New York Times*, February 18, 1957; Irwin Unger and Debi Unger, *LBJ: A Life* (New York: Wiley, 1999), 204–205.

78. *PPPDDE:1957*, January 5, 6–16.

79. This was done by a formal vote in the Knesset, June 3, 1957. (Alteras, *Eisenhower and Israel*, 305–306).

80. Miller, *Ike the Soldier*, 297.

81. Alteras, *Eisenhower and Israel*, 302–303.

82. Stephen Ambrose, *Eisenhower*, vol. 1, *The Soldier* (New York: Simon & Schuster), 420.

83. Johnson, *National Party Platforms*, 579 (Democratic), 605 (Republican).

84. Richard Reeves, *President Kennedy: Profile of Power* (New York: Simon & Schuster, 1993), 143.

85. Arthur M. Schlesinger Jr., *A Thousand Days* (Boston: Houghton, Mifflin, 1965), 566–567.

86. Dean Rusk, *As I Saw It* (New York: Norton, 1990), 382–383; Herbert S. Parmet, *JFK* (New York: Penguin, 1983), 226–235.

87. Parmet, *JFK*, 226, citing Joseph E. Johnson oral history interview at JFKL.

88. Parmet, *JFK*, 234.

89. Sachar, *History of the Jews in America*, 730–731; Warren Bass, *Support Any Friend* (New York: Oxford University Press, 2003), 55–56.

90. Richard G. Hutcheson, *God in the White House: How Religion Has Changed the Modern Presidency* (New York: Macmillan, 1988), 52.

91. Thomas Reeves, *A Question of Character* (New York: Macmillan, 1991), 161–162.

92. Schlesinger, *Thousand Days*, 106–109.

93. Theodore Sorensen, *Kennedy* (New York: Harper, 1965), 19.

94. Nigel Hamilton, *JFK: Reckless Youth* (New York: Random House, 1992), 358.

95. Reeves, *President Kennedy*, 155.

96. Joseph Califano Jr., *The Triumph and Tragedy of Lyndon Johnson* (New York: Simon & Schuster, 1991), 49n., 298, 302.

97. Califano, *Triumph and Tragedy*, 334–335.

98. Unger and Unger, *LBJ*, 83.

99. Unger and Unger, *LBJ*, 203–205.

100. William B. Quandt, *Peace Process: American Diplomacy and the Arab-Israeli Conflict Since 1967* (Berkeley: University of California Press, 1993), 38–37, 60, 507–508.

101. Rusk, *As I Saw It*, 389–390.

102. Rusk, *As I Saw It*, 389–390.

103. Rusk, *As I Saw It*, 383. Italics added.

104. Rusk, *As I Saw It*, 381.

105. Lyndon Johnson, *The Vantage Point: Perspectives of the Presidency* (New York: Holt, Rinehart, 1971), 291; Quandt, *Peace Process*, 29.

106. *PPPLBJ: 1967*, May 23, 561–563.

107. Johnson, *Vantage*, 3.

108. Abba Eban, *Personal Witness* (New York: Putnam's, 1992), 386–391.

109. Rusk, *As I Saw It*, 385–386.

110. Rusk, *As I Saw It*, 386–387.

111. Johnson, *Vantage*, 287–304; cf. Merle Miller, *Lyndon Johnson: An Oral Biography* (New York: Putnam's, 1980), 477–482.

112. Anatoly Dobrynin, *In Confidence: Moscow's Ambassador to America's Six Cold War Presidents* (New York: Times/Random House, 1995), 160–161.

113. Richard M. Nixon, *RN: The Memoirs of Richard Nixon* (New York: Grosset & Dunlap, 1978), 118.

114. William Safire, *Before the Fall: An Insider's Report on the Pre-Watergate White House* (Garden City, NY: Doubleday, 1975), 567.

115. Nixon, *RN*, 283.

116. Richard Reeves, *President Nixon: Alone in the White House* (New York: Simon & Schuster, 2001), 42, 332, 343, 370; cf. H. R. Haldeman, *The Haldeman Diaries* (New York: Putnam's, 1994), 95, 292.

117. Goldberg, *Jewish Power*, 34.

118. Richard M. Nixon, *In the Arena* (New York: Simon & Schuster, 1990), 88–93.

119. Quoted in Albert J. Menendez, *Religion and the U.S. Presidency: A Bibliography* (New York: Garland, 1986), 83–84.

120. Hutcheson, *God in the White House*, 82.

121. Quoted in Richard M. Nixon, *Leaders* (New York: Touchstone, 1990), 280.

122. Walter Isaacson, *Kissinger: A Biography* (New York: Simon & Schuster, 1992), 599.

123. Reeves, *President Nixon,* 241.

124. Nixon, *RN,* 478–479.

125. Stephen Ambrose, *Nixon,* vol. 2, *The Triumph of a Politician, 1962–1972* (New York: Simon & Schuster, 1989), 188–189.

126. Haldeman, *The Haldeman Diaries,* 132, with addition of portions deleted in the published edition but restored in Reeves, *President Nixon,* 170.

127. Nixon, *RN,* 481.

128. Tad Szulc, *The Illusion of Peace* (New York: Viking, 1978), 89–92, 197–199, 206–212.

129. Nixon, *RN,* 481–482.

130. Szulc, *Illusion of Peace,* 433.

131. Ambrose, *Nixon,* vol. 2, 626–627.

132. Johnson, *National Party Platforms,* 815.

133. Goldberg, *Jewish Power,* 34. For perspective, one should note that in 1968 the popular vote had been Nixon 43.4 percent, Humphrey 42.7 percent ; and in 1972, Nixon 60.7 percent, McGovern 37.5 percent.

134. Alexander Haig, Jr., *Inner Circles* (New York: Warner Books, 1992), 241–253; Martin Gilbert, *Israel: A History* (New York: Turner, 1998), 417; "King Hussein Sought Israeli Help in '70," *New York Times,* January 2, 2001.

135. Stephen Ambrose, *Nixon,* vol. 3, *Ruin and Recovery* (New York: Simon & Schuster, 1991), 167.

136. Gilbert, *Israel,* 452.

137. Henry Kissinger, *Years of Upheaval* (Boston: Little, Brown, 1982), 459–460.

138. Anwar el-Sadat, *In Search of Identity: An Autobiography* (New York: Harper & Row, 1977), 232–241, 325–327.

139. Janet Wallach and John Wallach, *Arafat: In the Eyes of the Beholder* (Rocklin, CA: Prima Publishing, 1992), 356.

140. Gilbert, *Israel,* 444–449.

141. Quandt, *Peace Process,* 156–157, 544, and note 29.

142. Isaacson, *Kissinger,* 22.

143. Marvin Kalb and Bernard Kalb, *Kissinger* (Boston: Little, Brown, 1974), 35–36.

144. Isaacson, *Kissinger,* 30.

145. Isaacson, *Kissinger,* 60.

146. *Jewish News,* May 21, 1976,Clipping in GRFL/HK (Henry Kissinger files), Box B1.

147. "Ford Vows Israel Security," *Jewish Exponent,* May 21, 1976. GRFL/HK/ Box B1: Rabbi Hertzberg.

148. Reeves, *President Nixon,* 42.

149. Ambrose, *Nixon,* vol. 3, 235.

150. Kissinger, *Years of Upheaval,* 467–468.

151. Ambrose, *Nixon,* vol. 3, 240.

152. Dobrynin, *In Confidence,* 293.

153. Ambrose, *Nixon,* vol. 3, 251; Quandt, *Peace Process,* 171.

154. Sadat, *In Search,* 239 (Appendix: Telegram from President Sadat to President Hafez al-Assad of Syria, October 20, 1973).

155. Morris, *Righteous Victims*, 427

156. Dobrynin, *In Confidence*, 294–295.

157. Dobrynin, *In Confidence*, 297.

158. *PPPRN:1973*, October 26, 896–906.

159. Dobrynin, *In Confidence*, 299–300.

160. Sadat, *In Search*, 270.

161. *PPPRN:1974*, June 10–June 19, 482–541.

162. Nixon, *RN*, 1007–1008.

163. Nixon, *RN*, 1013–1015.

164. Nixon, *RN*, 1013.

165. Kissinger, *Years of Upheaval*, 1126.

166. Nixon, *RN*, 1010–1013.

167. Nixon, *RN*, 1015–1017.

168. Nixon, *Leaders*, 287–288.

169. Goldberg, *Jewish Power*, 14–15, 203.

170. *PPPGRF:1974*, September 8, 101–103.

171. Hutcheson, *God in the White House*, 94.

172. I.F. Kenen, "President Gerald R. Ford," *Near East Report*, XIII, no. 33, August 1976. GRFL/ President Ford Committee Records [PFCR]/ Box F35.

173. See Herbert Stein, "Looking Over Ford's Record," *Wall Street Journal*, July 21, 1976. GRFL/ PFCR/Box F35.

174. Quoted by David Horowitz, in "U.S. Elections Worry the UN," *B'nai Brith Messenger*, July, 1976. GRFL/PFCR/Box H32.

175. Ibid.

176. GRFL/ Reichley /Box 4 ("Israel").

177. Hutcheson, *God in the White House*, 92.

178. Gerald Ford, *A Time to Heal: The Autobiography of Gerald R. Ford* (New York: Harper & Row, 1979), 10.

179. Attachment to memorandum, "Q & A Religious Questions," Dave Gergen to Bill Rhatican, September 23, 1976. GRFL/David R. Gergen's files 74–77, Box 8 ("Religion").

180. Ford, *Time to Heal*, 416–417.

181. GRFL/ PFCR/Boxes H32 and H45.

182. *PPPGRF:1976*, May 13, 1565–1569.

183. *Jewish Week*, May 20–26, 1976. GRFL/Reichley/Box 4.

184. *Jewish* News, May 21, 1976. Clipping in GRFL, HK/ Box B1.

185. *PPPGRF: 1976*, May 13, 1565–1569.

186. *PPPGRF: 1976*, October 12, 2489–2492.

CHAPTER 3

1. *PPPJC:1980*, April 23, 766–767.

2. David Kucharsky, *The Man from Plains: The Mind and Spirit of Jimmy Carter* (New York: Harper & Row, 1976), 30.

3. Jerald ter Horst, "Carter has religion—and votes," March 31, 1976. GRFL/ PFCR/Box H45 ("Carter Clippings: Politics and Religion").

4. Kucharsky, *Man from Plains*, 67.

5. "Carter and the God Issue," *Newsweek*, April 5, 1976.

6. *Playboy*, vol. 23:11 (November, 1976), 63f.

7. Martin Schram, *Running for President* (New York: Stein & Day, 1977), 304.

8. *Atlanta Constitution*, October 12, 1976, and other excerpts from Southern papers, clipping in GRFL/PFCR/Box 32.

9. Popular vote: 40,828,929 >39,148,940; electoral college vote: 297 > 240. Two percent of the popular vote went to several independents, including Eugene McCarthy.

10. *Time*, June 21, 1976.

11. Quoted in Schram, *Running*, 183–84.

12. May 6, 1976. Photocopy in GRF/A/Reichley/Box4:"Israel."

13. GRFL/PFCR/Box H45.

14. Quoted in *Sentinel*, May 6, 1976 (GRFL/Reichley/Box 4).

15. *Baltimore Sun*, September 8, 1976 (GRFL/PFCR/Box H32).

16. Goldberg, *Jewish Power*, 33–34.

17. Zbigniew Brzezinski, *Power and Principle: Memoirs of the National Security Adviser, 1977–1981* (London: Weidenfeld & Nicolson, 1983), 88.

18. Vance, *Hard Choices: Critical Years in America's Foreign Policy* (New York: Simon & Schuster, 1983), 164.

19. *PPPJCC:1977*, March 7–8, 329–336.

20. Jimmy Carter, *Keeping Faith* [*KF*] (New York: Bantam, 1982), 279–280.

21. Brzezinski, *Power and Principle*, 90.

22. Yitzhak Rabin, *The Rabin Memoirs* (London: Weidenfeld & Nicolson, 1979), 228.

23. Rabin, *Rabin Memoirs*, 228.

24. Carter, *KF*, 278; Goldberg, *Jewish Power*, 179–180; *New York Times*, June 23, 1977.

25. Brzezinski, *Power and Principle*, 97–98.

26. *PPPJC:1977*, April 4, 561–570.

27. Carter, *KF*, 282.

28. Sadat, *In Search*, 297–312.

29. Notably, Jimmy Carter, *Talking Peace* [*TP*] (New York: Dutton Children's Books, 1993), 9–18.

30. Carter, *KF*, 270–272.

31. David Hirst and Irene Beeson, *Sadat* (London: Faber & Faber, 1981), 7.

32. Nixon, *Leaders*, 297.

33. *PPPJC:1977*, December 25, 2173–2174.

34. Richard Hofstadter, *The American Political Tradition and the Men Who Made It* (New York: Vintage Books, 1954), 348.

35. Tessler, *History of the Arab-Israeli-Palestinian Conflict*, 507–508.

36. *PPPJC:1977*, April 25–26, 710–711, 720–723. Carter's preparations for his meeting with Hussein can be studied in JCL/SO/OSS/Handwritingfile/20.

37. Carter, *KF*, 285.

38. *PPPJC:1977*, April 22, 704 & May 9, 1977, 841–847; JCL/SO/OSS/Handwriting file/20.

39. Carter, *KF*, 285–286.

40. Jimmy Carter, *The Blood of Abraham* [*BA*] (Boston: Houghton, Mifflin, 1985), 67–73.

41. *PPPJCC:1977*, May 24–25, 1006–1012.

42. Carter, *BA*, 182–183 (italics added).

43. See, *Inter alia*, Dore Gold, *Hatred's Kingdom* (Washington: Regnery, 2003), 41–56.

44. For example, during the Ford-Carter debates (*PPPGRF:1976*, October 6, 2418–2421).

45. *PPPJCC:1977*, March 16, 1977, 382–402.

46. Amos Perlmutter, "The Courtship of Iraq," *New Republic*, May 3, 1980; Bruce W. Jentleson, *With Friends Like These* (New York: Norton, 1994), 33–37.

47. Carter, *KF*, 286.

48. *PPPJC:1977*, March 16, 382–404.

49. Edward Tivna, *The Lobby: Jewish Political Power and American Foreign Policy* (New York: Simon & Schuster, 1987), 102.

50. See Congressman Lee Hamilton to Jimmy Carter, May 23, 1977, and reply, Carter to Hamilton, July 5 1977 JCL/WHCF/CO-74-33. Originally "SECRET," Declassified 8/10/90.

51. Gertrude Hirschler and Lester B. Eckman, *Menachem Begin: From Freedom Fighter to Statesman* (New York: Shengold, 1979), 273.

52. *New York Times*, May 19, 1977; *Time*, June 6, 1977.

53. Carter, *KF*, 284.

54. Hirschler and Eckman, *Begin*, 15, 295.

55. Frank Gervasi, *Life and Times of Menachem Begin: Rebel to Stateman* (New York: Putnam's, 1979), 26.

56. *Time*, July 4, 1977.

57. *PPPJC:1977*, July 19–20, 1977, 1281–1284.

58. Sasson Sofer, *Begin* (New York: Basil Blackwell, 1988), 151, citing the Israeli newspaper, *Yediot Aharonot*, May 24, 1977.

59. "An in-depth study of the voting public of Israel, July, 1977" (JCL/Chief of Staff Hamilton Jordan)/Box 45 with attached Harris memo (SO/OCC/Handwritingfile/20); Memorandum, "Voting History of the American Jews," Hamilton Jordan to Jimmy Carter, July 1977.

60. "An in-depth study of the voting public of Israel, July, 1977" (JCL/Chief of Staff Hamilton Jordan)/Box 45 with attached Harris memo (SO/OCC/Handwritingfile/20); Memorandum, "Voting History of the American Jews," Hamilton Jordan to Jimmy Carter, July 1977.

61. *New York Times*, May 19, 1977 (italics added).

62. *Time*, May 30, 1977, 27.

63. Carter, *KF*, 288.

64. *PPPJC:1977*, July 19–20, 1281–1284, 1287–1292, 1295–1296; Carter, *KF*, 290–291.

65. Carter, *KF*, 291.

66. Madeleine Albright, during ZB Exit Interview (February 20, 1981), JCL, Oral History collection.

67. Ned Temko, *To Win Or To Die: A Personal Portrait of Menachem Begin* (New York: Morrow, 1987), 206–208; Moshe Dayan, *Breakthrough: A Personal Account of the Egypt-Israel Peace Negotiations* (New York: Knopf, 1981), 26–54; Robert Slater, *Warrior Statesman* (New York: St. Martin's, 1991), 394–398.

68. Carter, *KF*, 293–295; Brzezinski, *Power and Principle*, 107–110; Dayan, *Breakthrough,* 55–72; Slater, *Warrior Statesman,* 399–402.

69. Slater, *Warrior Statesman,* 399–400.

70. Text appears as Appendix #, in Carter, *BA*, 214–215.

71. JCL/Chief of Staff/ Box 45.

72. Carter, *KF*, 294.

73. Jimmy Carter Diary, October 4, 1977, as quoted in Carter, *KF*, 294.

74. Hirst and Beeson, *Sadat*, 273–274.

75. Raphael Israeli, *Man of Defiance: A Political Biography of Anwar Sadat* (London: Wiedenfeld and Nicolson, 1985), 228; Hirst and Beeson, *Sadat*, 255.

76. Israeli, *Man of Defiance*, 228; Hirst and Beeson, *Sadat*, 255.

77. Wallach and Wallach, *Arafat*, 364.

78. Hirschler and Eckman, *Begin*, 306.

79. Brzezinski, *Power and Principle*, 111–112.

80. Carter, *KF*, 296–297.

81. Sadat, *In Search,* 308–309.

82. Hirst and Beeson, *Sadat*, 262–263.

83. Carter, *KF*, 296–297.

84. Israeli, *Man of Defiance*, 232.

85. Text of speech appears as Appendix V in Sadat, *In Search,* 330–343. I quote from this text which varies slightly from the text in *New York Times*, November 20, 1977.

86. Ezer Weizman, *The Battle for Peace* (New York: Bantam Books, 1981), 33.

87. Gervasi, *Life and Times,* 69–70; Temko, *To Win Or To Die,* 213.

88. *PPPJC:1977*, November 20, 2042–2044.

89. Brzezinski, *Power and Principle*, 111.

90. Carter, *KF*, 297–299.

91. *PPPJC:1977*, November 30, 2053–2062.

92. *PPPJC:1978*, January 6, 1978, 46.

93. Dayan, *Breakthrough*, 99–100.

94. Dayan, *Breakthrough*, 99–100; *New York Times*, December 16, 1977.

95. *PPPJC:1977*, December 16–17, 2127–2128, 2133–2134, 2152–2153.

96. Weizman, *Battle for Peace,* 120.

97. Dayan, *Breakthrough*, 103.

98. Dayan, *Breakthrough,* 103–105.

99. *New York Times*, January 18 and 19, 1978.

100. Hirschler and Eckman, *Begin*, 319.

101. Diary entry, January 1, 178, quoted in Carter, *KF*, 300.

102. Carter, *KF*, 300–301.

103. *PPPJC:1978,* January 6, 62.

104. JCL/WHCF/CO-74-33 & 34.

105. Carter, *KF*, 313; *PPPJC:1978,* May 1, 1978, 812–14; JCL/WHCF/CO-74-34; *New York Times*, May 2, 1978.

106. JCL/WHCF/CO-74-34.

107. Carter, *KF*, 313.

108. JCL/Chief of Staff/Box 45.

109. Carter, *TP,* 9, 12.

110. Carter, *KF*, 316; *PPPJC:1978*, August 8, 1393.

111. Hirschler and Eckman, *Begin*, 331–332.

112. Carter, *KF*, 316–318; JCL/Chief of Staff/45 (September, 1978); JCL/SO/OSS/handwritingfile/Box 101.

113. Gaddis Smith, *Morality, Reason, and Power: American Diplomacy in the Carter Years* (New York: Hill and Wang, 1986), 165.

114. Carter, *KF*, 321.

115. Carter, *TP*, 12.

116. Carter, *KF*, 322.

117. Carter, *KF*, 327.

118. *PPPJC:1978*, September 6, 1501.

119. Carter, *KF*, 331; Weizman, *Battle for Peace*, 345.

120. Hirschler and Eckman, *Begin*, 332–33.

121. Carter, *KF*, 342.

122. Carter, *KF*, 328–338.

123. Carter, *TP*, 13.

124. Carter, *KF*, 342–346.

125. Temko, *To Win Or To Die*, 226.

126. Carter, *KF*, 350–356.

127. Hirschler and Eckman, *Begin*, 335.

128. Carter, *BA*, 43.

129. Carter, *KF*, 355–356.

130. Carter, *KF*, 351–370; Weizman, *Battle for Peace*, 348–369; Dayan, *Breakthrough*, 157, 171–172.

131. Brzezinski, *Power and Principle*, 262.

132. Brzezinski, *Power and Principle*, 263.

133. Weizman, *Battle for Peace*, 370; Anita Miller, Jordan Miller, and Sigalit Zetouni, *Sharon: Israel's Warrior-Politician* (Chicago: Academie Chicago/Olive, 2002), 142–144.

134. Carter, *KF*, 391–394.

135. Carter, *KF*, 394–401.

136. The texts of the completed documents can be found in *PPPJC:1978*, September 17 and September 18, 1523–1528.

137. Carter, *KF*, 398–399.

138. Carter, *TP*, 17.

139. *PPPJC:1978*, September 17, 1520–1523.

140. *PPPJC: 1978*, September 18, 1533–1537.

141. JCL/WHCF/FO-45 & 46.

142. Dan Raviv and Yossi Melman, *Friends In Deed* (New York: Hyperion, 1994), 183.

143. Memorandum: Edward Saunders to Jimmy Carter, September 18, 1978 (setting up meeting with Jewish leaders for September 19 (JCL/SO/OSS/Handwriting file/101.)

144. Quoted in Carter, *KF*, 405.

145. Dayan, *Breakthrough*, 191–198.

146. Dayan, *Breakthrough*, 199–251.

147. *PPPJC:1978*, December 7, 2174.

148. Carter, *KF*, 405–410; cf., memo, "Settlements in West Bank and Samaria," JCL/SO/OSS/Handwritingfile/102.

149. Spiegel, *Other Arab-Israeli Conflict*, 368; *New York Times*, December 20,1978.

150. *New York Times*, December 19, 1978.

151. JCL/WHCF/CO-74-35.

152. *PPPJC:1979*, March 2–5, 374–405.

153. Jimmy Carter Diary, March 8, 1979, quoted by Carter, *KF*, 418.

154. Brzezinski, *Power and Principle*, 284.

155. Carter, *KF*, 425.

156. Carter, *KF*, 427–428; *PPPJC:1979*, March 26, 287–288.

157. Dayan, *Breakthrough*, 200–203; Spiegel, *Other Arab-Israeli Conflict*, 365–366.

158. Carter, *KF*, 404–406.

159. JCL/WHCF/FO-45; Carter, *KF*, 408.

160. Spiegel, *Other Arab-Israeli Conflict*, 366–367; Dayan, *Breakthrough*, 235–236.

161. Carter, *KF*, 410.

162. Carter, *KF*, 406–407.

163. Spiegel, *Other Arab-Israeli Conflict*, 373 & note 195 (483).

164. *PPPJC:1979*, March 22, 453–455.

165. Jimmy Carter to Chairman Clarence Long, Foreign Operations Subcommittee, House Committee on Appropriations, October 12, 1978 (JCL/WHCF/F0-45.)

166. *PPPJC:1979*, August 8, 1418; Carter, *KF*, 427–428.

167. Brzezinski, *Power and Principle*, 283.

168. *Time*, October 2, 1978, 8.

169. *PPPJC:1978*, September 23, 1612.

170. *New York Times*, August 1, 1979.

171. *New York Times*, August 12, 1979.

172. Spiegel, *Other Arab-Israeli Conflict*, 375; Carter, *KF*, 491.

173. Brzezinski, *Power and Principle*, 105.

174. Wallach and Wallach, *Arafat*, 417–420.

175. Spiegel, *Other Arab-Israeli Conflict*, 375, referring to private interviews; *New York Times*, August 20, 1979.

176. Carter, *KF*, 491.

177. Carter, *KF*, 492–494; *New York Times*, March 5, 1980.

178. Spiegel, *Other Arab-Israeli Conflict*, 378; cf. Brzezinski, *Power and Principle*, 442.

179. Brzezinski, *Power and Principle*, 438–440.

180. *PPPJC:1980*, July 17, 1363–1367.

181. *PPPJC:1980*, October 29, 2528–2533.

182. Goldberg, *Jewish Power*, 34.

183. David Kimche, *The Last Option* (London: Weidenfeld & Nicolson, 1991), 115.

184. Carter, *BA*, 23.

185. Carter, *KF*, 274 (italics added).

186. Carter, *BA*, 113 (italics added).

187. "In that day there will be a highway from Egypt to Assyria, and the Assyrian will come into Egypt and the Egyptian into Assyria, and the Egyptians will serve with the Assyrians. In that day Israel will be one of three with Egypt and Assyria, even a blessing in the midst of the land whom the LORD of hosts

shall bless, saying 'Blessed is Egypt My people, and Assyria the work of My hands, and Israel My inheritance.'"

188. *PPPJC:1978*, February 18, 364–383.

189. Carter, *BA*, 9.

190. *PPPJC: 1978*, February 2, 263–265.

191. Carter, *BA*, 5–6.

192. Carter, *BA*, 5. (Italics added).

193. As quoted in Ramon Bennett, *Philistine* (Jerusalem: Arm of Salvation, 1995), 137.

194. Carter, *BA*, 7–8.

195. Carter, *BA*, 10.

196. Carter, *BA*, 10.

197. The reserve Army of Israel consisted of 200,000 men, slightly less than the Syrian Army (300,000) and one-quarter the size of the Egyptian Army (850,000) (Gilbert, *Israel*, 436).

198. Sadat, *In Search*, 266.

199. Morris, *Righteous Victims*, 404–413; Gilbert, *Israel*, 448.

200. Brzezinski, *Power and Principle*, 93. The fuller version of this same fantasy can be read in Sadat, *In Search*, 266–270.

201. Carter, *BA*, 15–16.

202. Carter, *BA*, 33; cf., Carter, *KF*, 423.

203. *PPPJC/1979*, March 9, 411–412.

204. Carter, *BA*, 5.

205. Carter, *BA*, 29–30.

206. Carter, *BA*, 8.

207. Carter, *BA*, 9.

208. Douglas Brinkley, *Unfinished Presidency: Jimmy Carter's Journey beyond the White House* (New York: Viking, 1998), 234–235.

209. Brinkley, *Unfinished Presidency*, 317.

210. Brinkley, *Unfinished Presidency*, 116.

211. Said K. Aburish, *Arafat* (London: Bloomsbury, 1998), 244.

212. Brinkley, *Unfinished Presidency*, pp. 328–329.

CHAPTER 4

1. Paul C. Merkley, Chapter Seven: "Christian Zionism and Christian Anti-Zionism," *Christian Attitudes towards the State of Israel* (Montreal and London: McGill-Queen's, 2001), 161–194.

2. Files of *Jerusalem Post*, December 1980 and January 1981, and Tivna, *Lobby*, 116.

3. Ronald Reagan, *An American Life: The Autobiography* (New York: Simon & Schuster, 1990), 32.

4. Garry Wills, *Reagan's America* (Garden City, NY: Doubleday, 1987), 36–42; Paul Kengor, *God and Ronald Reagan* (New York: HarperCollins, 2004), 17 and 345 (note no. 3).

5. Dinesh D'Souza, *Ronald Reagan* (New York: Simon & Schuster/Free Press, 1997), 213; Kengor, *God and Ronald Reagan*, 161–164.

6. This is well-documented throughout Kengor, *God and Ronald Regan*.

7. Reagan, *American Life*, 56.

8. D'Souza, *Ronald Reagan*, 213.

9. Diary, May 19 and August 8, 1982, as related in Reagan, *American Life*, 319–321.

10. Reagan, *American Life*, 316–317.

11. Lou Cannon, *President Reagan: The Role of a Lifetime* (New York: Simon & Schuster, 1991), 583–588, 728–732.

12. *PPPRR:1983*, March 8, 359–364.

13. Reagan, *American Life*, 570.

14. Reagan, *American Life*, 263.

15. Bob Slosser, *Reagan Inside Out* (Waco, TX: Word Books, 1984), 13–19; cf., Cannon, *President Reagan*, 288.

16. Wills, *Reagan's America*, 197–198.

17. Wills, *Reagan's America*, 383–385.

18. Alexander M. Haig, Jr., *Caveat: Realism, Reagan, and Foreign Policy* (New York: Macmillan, 1984), 168–169.

19. Reagan, *American Life*, 410–416.

20. *PPPRR:1981*, June 16 (President's News Conference), 520.

21. Reagan, *American Life*, 413.

22. Haig, *Caveat*, 184.

23. Dan Raviv and Yossi Melman, *Friends In Deed* (New York: Hyperion, 1994), 354.

24. William Martin, *A Prophet with Honor: The Billy Graham Story* (New York: Morrow, 1991), 474.

25. Haig, *Caveat*, 173–174.

26. *PPPRR:1981*, September 9–10, 766–775; Reagan, *American Life*, 414–416; Haig, *Caveat*, 188.

27. Spiegel, *Other Arab-Israeli Conflict*, 410.

28. Spiegel, *Other Arab-Israeli Conflict*, 409.

29. Spiegel, *Other Arab-Israeli Conflict*, 409.

30. Robert C. McFarland, *Special Trust* (New York: Cadell & Davis, 1994), 185–188.

31. Haig, *Caveat*, 171.

32. Haig, *Caveat*, 188–189; Spiegel, *Other Arab-Israeli Conflict*, 413–414; Quandt, *Peace Process*, 340.

33. Reagan, *American Life*, 422.

34. Quandt, *Peace Process*, 342–343.

35. George P. Shultz, *Turmoil and Triumph: My Years as Secretary of State* (New York: Scribner's, 1993), 44.

36. Reagan, *American Life*, 423–424.

37. *PPPRR:1982*, June 21, 799.

38. Shultz, *Turmoil*, 58.

39. *PPPRR:1982*, August 1, 996–997 and August 4, 1016.

40. Reagan, *American Life*, 427.

41. McFarland, *Special Trust*, 208.

42. Reagan diary, August 12, 1982, recalled in Reagan, *American Life*, 428.

43. McFarland, *Special Trust*, 209.

44. Shultz, *Turmoil*, 45–46, 75–78, 103.

45. Shultz, *Turmoil*, 77.

46. Shultz, *Turmoil*, 82–83.

47. Shultz, *Turmoil*, 99.

48. Shultz, *Turmoil*, 103.

49. Reagan, *American Life*, 438; Shultz, *Turmoil*, 107–110.

50. Shultz, *Turmoil*, 113–114; Miller, Miller, and Zetouni, *Sharon*, 167–174.

51. Reagan, *American Life*, 407–408, 441.

52. Shultz, *Turmoil*, 88–89

53. *PPPRR:1982*, September 1, 1093–1097.

54. Shultz, *Turmoil*, 98.

55. Shultz, *Turmoil*, 112.

56. McFarland, *Special Trust*, 206.

57. McFarland, *Special Trust*, 207.

58. Shultz, *Turmoil*, 215–216.

59. Shultz, *Turmoil*, 221–222.

60. *PPPRR:1983*, September 27, 1367–1368, September 29, 1389, October 12, 1444–1445; Shultz, *Turmoil*, 223–229.

61. *PPPRR:1983*, April 18, 550–551, April 20, 563–564, April 23, 576–579.

62. *PPPRR:1983*, October 23, 1498–1499, October 24, 1500–1504.

63. Shultz, *Turmoil*, 228–229.

64. Shultz, *Turmoil*, 231.

65. *PPPRR:1984*, February 2, 162.

66. *PPPRR:1983*, December 10, 1679–1685.

67. *PPPRR:1984*, February 3, 162.

68. *PPPRR:1984*, February 7, 185–186. See also, *PPPRR:1984*, "Presidential News Conference," 245–252.

69. Shultz, *Turmoil*, –230–231.

70. Reagan, *American Life*, 461–462, 465.

71. Cannon, *President Reagan*, 288–292. Among the sources cited by Cannon are "People for the American Way Study Warns of Impact of Armageddon Theology on U.S. Policy," *Business Wire*, April 1, 1985; Kenneth L. Woodward, "Arguing Armageddon," *Newsweek*, November 5, 1984; Daniel Schorr, "Reagan Recants His Path from Armageddon to Detente," *Los Angeles Times*, January 3, 1988.

72. *PPPRR:1984*, October 21, 1601–1608.

73. Cannon, *President Reagan*, 757

74. Shultz, *Turmoil*, 433–462; Peres, *Battling*, 297–312; Dan Kurzman, *Soldier of Peace* (New York: HarperCollins, 1998), 402–403.

75. Shultz, *Turmoil*, 939; Moshe Arens, *Broken Covenant American Foreign Policy and the Crisis Between the U.S. and Israel* (New York: Simon & Schuster, 1995), 22–23. Peres puts a different interpretation on this episode (Peres, *Battling*, 310–312).

76. Shultz, *Turmoil*, 941–948.

77. Morris, *Righteous Victims*, 605; Shultz, *Turmoil*, 457.

78. Shultz, *Turmoil*, 439.

79. Shultz, *Turmoil*, 432.

80. Shultz, *Turmoil*, 1016–1050.

81. Shultz, *Turmoil*, 1017.

82. Shultz, *Turmoil*, 1024–1025.

83. Shultz, *Turmoil*, 1038–1039.

84. *PPPRR:1988*, December 14 and 15, 1627–1628.

85. Quandt, *Peace Process*, 372–375.

86. Shultz, *Turmoil*, 1045.

87. Arens, *Broken Covenant*, 137.

88. Goldberg, *Jewish Power*, 213–214.

89. Goldberg, *Jewish Power*, 214–215.

90. George Bush and Victor Gold, *Looking Forward* (New York: Doubleday, 1987), 27.

91. Bush and Gold, *Looking Forward*, 69.

92. *PPPGB:1991*, January 28, pp. 70–73.

93. Martin, *Prophet with Honor*, 265, 368, 593.

94. George Will, *Suddenly* (New York: Macmillan/Free Press, 1990), 49–51.

95. James A. Baker, III, *The Politics of Diplomacy* (New York: Putnam's, 1995), 116.

96. Quandt, *Peace Process*, 340–342.

97. Baker, *Politics of Diplomacy*, 118.

98. Quandt, *Peace Process*, 385–391.

99. Quoted in Quandt, *Peace Process*, 389.

100. Kurzman, *Soldier of Peace*, 414–422; Arens, *Broken Covenant*, 74–78, 85–124.

101. Kurzman, *Soldier of Peace*, 415.

102. Baker, *Politics of Diplomacy*, 115–132. The words quoted are on 131.

103. Shultz, *Turmoil*, 239–241.

104. James Mann, *Rise of the Vulcans* (New York: Viking, 2004), 125–126; Shultz, *Turmoil*, 235–245.

105. Aburish, *Arafat*, 224–229.

106. Baker, *Politics of Diplomacy*, 1–16. The words quoted are on page 16.

107. Colin Powell, *American Journey* (New York: 1995), 474.

108. Brinkley, *Unfinished Presidency*, 333–342.

109. Brinkley, *Unfinished Presidency*, 330–332.

110. Brinkley, *Unfinished Presidency*, 246–247, cf., 240–241.

111. Brinkley, *Unfinished Presidency*, 224–226, 243–244.

112. Brinkley, *Unfinished Presidency*, 339.

113. Brinkley, *Unfinished Presidency*, 337.

114. Brinkley, *Unfinished Presidency*, 340.

115. *PPPGB:1991*, February 27, 187–188.

116. Powell, *American Journey*, 511–512; Arens, *Broken Covenant*, 173–202.

117. *PPPGB:1991*, March 6, 218–222.

118. The full text appears as Appendix N in Quandt, *Peace Process*, 502–503.

119. Michael R. Beschloss and Strobe Talbott, *At the Highest Levels* (New York: Boston: Little, Brown, 1993), 447.

120. Baker, *Politics of Diplomacy*, 541–555.

121. *PPPGB:1991*, September 12 (President's News Conference), 1139–1144.

122. Kurzman, *Soldier of Peace*, 441–442.

123. Jack W. Germond and Jules Witcover, *Mad as Hell* (New York: Warner, 1993), 135–136.

124. *PPPGB:1992*, August 13, 1348–1352.

125. *PPPWJC:1993*, August 30, 1403–1405 (italics added).

126. Gustav Niebuhr, "Books on Faith Are a Comfort, President Says," *New York Times*, October 4, 1994; cf., Kenneth L. Woodward, "Soulful Matters," *Newsweek*, October 31, 1994; Philip Yancey, "The Riddle of Bill Clinton's Faith," *Christianity Today*, April 25, 1994; Priscilla Painton, "Clinton's Spiritual Journey," *Time*, April 5, 1993.

127. Bob Woodward, *The Choice* (New York: Simon & Schuster, 1996), 55–57.

128. Sidney Blumenthal, *The Clinton Wars* (New York: Farrar, Straus & Giroux, 2003), 86.

129. Gustav Niebuhr, "Clinton Says Psalms Bring Him Relief," *New York Times*, February 3, 1994.

130. Elizabeth Drew, *On the Edge* (New York: Simon & Schuster, 1994), 296–297.

131. *PPPWJC:1993*, September 9, 1457–1458.

132. *PPPWJC:1993*, March 15, 303–308.

133. Kurzman, *Soldier of Peace*, 448–449.

134. Kurzman, *Soldier of Peace*, 443–444, 475.

135. Hanan Ashrawi, *This Side of Peace* (New York: Simon & Schuster, 1995), 220–221, 250–264.

136. Kurzman, *Soldier of Peace*, 455–456.

137. Drew, *On the Edge*, 42–48.

138. Michael Mandelbaum, "Foreign Policy as Social Work," *Foreign Affairs* January/February, 1996.

139. Ashrawi, *This Side of Peace*, 260–261.

140. Ashrawi, *This Side of Peace*, 253.

141. Ashrawi, *This Side of Peace*, 262–272.

142. Kurzman, *Soldier of Peace*, 459–460.

143. Drew, *On the Edge*, 297.

144. *PPPWJC:1993*, September 10 and 11, 1463–1466, 1475–1477; *Facts on File*, vol. 53, no. 2755, 677–686; *New York Times*, September 14, 1993.

145. *PPPWJC:1993*, October 21, 1794.

146. *New York Times*, February 12, 1993, *JPost*, June 4, 1992, and *PPPWJC:1998*, December 14, 2172.

147. Maureen Dowd, *New York Times*, September 14, 1993.

148. *PPPWJC:1994*, October 26, 1877–1878; Bennett, *Philistine*, 259–260, citing, "Disney World comes to the desert for a day," in *JPost*, October 28, 1994. Clinton offers the same misquotation again, *PPPWJC:1998*, December 13, 2172.

149. *PPPWJC:1993*, September 13, 1477–1482; Drew, *On the Edge*, 296

150. *PPPWJC:1993*, September 13, 1477–1480.

151. Yossef Bodansky, *The High Price of Peace* (New York: Random House/ Forum, 2002), 98.

152. Bodansky, *High Price*, 480.

153. Bodansky, *High Price*, 109.

154. Bodansky, *High Price*, 137–138; Alan Dershowitz, *The Case for Israel* (Hoboken, NJ: Wiley, 2003), 72.

155. Kurzman, *Soldier of Peace*, 476.

156. Kurzman, *Soldier of Peace*, 478–479; *PPPWJC:1995*, September 28, 1507–1513.

157. *PPPWJC:1994*, July 25, 1307–1315.

158. *PPPWJC:1994*, October 26, 1877–1879.

159. Kurzman, *Soldier of Peace*, 474; Gilbert, *Israel*, 576.

160. Kurzman, *Soldier of Peace*, 486.

161. Blumenthal, *Clinton Wars*, 487.

162. Dick Morris, *Behind the Oval Office* (Los Angeles: Renaissance Books, 1999), 256–258.

163. *PPPWJC:1996*, March 14, 444–451.

164. *PPPWJC:1996*, April 28–30, 653–670.

165. *PPPWJC:1996*, July 9, 1087–1095.

166. *PPPWJC:1996*, September 29–October 1, 1725–1742.

167. Thomas W. Lippman, *Madeleine Albright and the New American Diplomacy* (Boulder, CO.: Westview Press, 2000), 186–190.

168. Lippman, 91–94; Ann Blackman, *Seasons of Her Life* (New York: Scribner's, 1998), 272–293.

169. Bodansky, *High Price*, 169, 185–186.

170. *PPPWJC:1998*, January 8, 19.

171. Timothy Weber, "How Evangelicals Became Israel's Best Friend," *Christianity Today*, October 5, 1998, 38–49; Laurie Goldstein, "Falwell to Mobilize Support for Israel, " *New York Times*, January 21, 1998.

172. Blumenthal, *Clinton Wars*, 321–348

173. *PPPWJC:1998*, January 20–January 22, 80–108.

174. Weber, "How Evangelicals Became Israel's Best Friend," 38–49.

175. *PPPWJC:1998*, September 28, 1698–1699.

176. Blumenthal, *Clinton Wars*, 487, 777. For Clinton's version, see *PPPWJC:1998*, October 31, 1942–1943.

177. *PPPWJC:1998*, October 23, 1836–1842.

178. *PPPWJC:1998*,October 23, 1851–1854.

179. *PPPWJC:1998*, December 14, 2175–2179.

180. Khaled Abu Toameh, "Kaddoumi: PLO Charter Was Never Changed," *JPost*, April 22, 2004.

181. *PPPWJC:1998*, December 13, 2161–2172; cf., *PPPWJC:1998*, October 31, 1941.

182. *PPPWJC:1998*, December 15, 2180–2181.

183. *PPPWJC:1998*, December 13, 2164.

184. Bodansky, *High Price*, 212.

185. Bodansky, *High Price*, 221

186. Bodansky, *High Price*, 221, 223; Miller, Miller, and Zetouni, *Sharon*, 256–261.

187. Bodanksy, *High Price*, 313.

188. *PPPWJC:1994*, January 16, 81–91

189. *PPPWJC:1994*, October 27, 1881–1888.

190. Bodansky, *High Price*, 249.

191. Bodansky, *High Price*, 224–225, 242–264, 291–294; Blumenthal, *Clinton Wars*, 777.

192. Bodansky, *High Price*, 233–234; Excerpts from the texts of dozens of such sermons are to be found in Steven Stalinsky, "Palestinian Authority Sermons 2000–2003," *MEMRI* [Middle East Research Institute] Special Report no. 24, December 26, 2003.

193. Bodansky, *High Price*, 318–319.

194. Bodansky, *High Price*, 319–320

195. Bodansky, *High Price*, 321.

196. Bodansky, *High Price*, 332.

197. Dershowitz, *Case for Israel*, 111–112; Bodansky, *High Price*, 348–356.

198. Miller, Miller, and Zetouni, *Sharon*, 300–307.

199. Bodansky, *High Price*, 356.

200. Bodansky, *High Price*, 339–340, 357.

201. Later, it was disclosed that Prince Bandar bin Sultan, the Saudi Arabian ambassador to the United States, had been recruited to help Clinton move Arafat toward acceptance of these terms. Bandar recalls himself saying to Arafat, "If you take this deal, we will all throw our weight behind you. . . . If we lose this opportunity, it is going to be a crime." To the interviewer, Bandar said, "I still have not recovered, to be honest with you, inside, from the magnitude of the missed opportunity in January [2001]. . . . Sixteen hundred Palestinians dead so far. [March 2003.] And seven hundred Israelis dead. In my judgment, not one life of these Israelis and Palestinians dead is justified." (Elsa Walsh, "The Prince," *New Yorker*, March 24, 2003.)

202. Blumenthal, *Clinton Wars*, 780.

CHAPTER 5

1. David Frum, *The Right Man: The Surprise Presidency of George W. Bush* (New York: Random House, 2003), 3–4.

2. David Aikman, *A Man of Faith: The Spiritual Journey of George W. Bush* (Nashville: Nelson, 2004), 2–3.

3. Mansfield, Stephen, *The Faith of George W. Bush* (Lake Mary, Florida: Charisma House, 2003), 73.

4. Aikman, *Man of Faith*, 149. Prince Bandar bin Sultan, the Saudi Arabian Ambassador to the United States, describes the puzzlement that came over Prince Abdullah, the de facto ruler of Saudi Arabia, when the president offered grace before beginning a luncheon during the Princes' visit to the president's Texas ranch. (Elsa Walsh, "The Prince," *New Yorker*, March 24, 2003.)

5. Elizabeth Mitchell, *W.: Revenge of the Bush Dynasty* (New York: Hyperion, 2000), 198–205; Mansfield, *The Faith*, 59–69.

6. Frum, *Right Man*, 29–30.

7. Bob Woodward, *Bush at War* (New York: Simon & Schuster, 2002), 131.

8. Woodward, *Bush at War*, 45.

9. Mitchell, *W.*, 331.

10. Mansfield, *The Faith*, 152–153; Aikman, *Man of Faith*, 148–156; Benedict Brogan, "Campbell bans Blair from talking about his religion," www.telegraph.co.uk/news, May 5, 2003; William Shawcroft, *Allies* (London: Atlantic Books, 2003), 39–47; Peter Stothard, *Thirty Days* (New York: HarperCollins, 2003), 13, 40, 208–209, 232–233.

11. Frum, *Right Man*, 16.

12. An informal church service in which key members of his senior staff participated while aboard Air Force One, on a Sunday morning, is described in Kenneth T. Walsh, "A Sunday Service in the Air," *U.S. News & World Report*, May 19, 2003.

13. Sheryl H. Blunt, "The Unflappable Condi Rice," *Christianity Today*, September, 2003.

14. Frum, *Right Man*, 1, 24–25.

15. Powell, *American Journey*, 17, 158–160, 265–266.

16. Frum, *Right Man*, 246–247.

17. Frum, *Right Man*, 246–247.

18. Frum, *Right Man*, 249.

19. www.jta.org, July 2, 2003; Tevi Troy, "My Boss, the Fanatic," *New Republic*, January 29, 2001; Peter Beinart, "Bad Faith," *New Republic Online*, March 18, 2002.

20. Frum, *Right Man*, 17.

21. Frum, *Right Man*, 249–253.

22. Frum, *Right Man*, 249.

23. Frum, *Right Man*, 164–166; E. Lichtblau and J. Miller, "Threats and Responses: Indictment ties ULS Professor to Terror Group," *New York Times*, February 21 and 22, 2003; Frank Gaffney, Jr., "A Troubling Influence," *FrontPageMagazine.com*, December 9, 2003.

24. Grover Norquist, "The Natural Conservatives: Muslims Deliver for GOP," *American Spectator*, June, 2001.

25. Frum, *Right Man*, 160–164.

26. Aikman, *Man of Faith*, 121–124.

27. Frum, *Right Man*, 253.

28. Woodward, *Bush at War*, 45.

29. Bodansky, *High Price*, 515.

30. Bodansky, *High Price*, 516.

31. Frum, *Right Man*, 259.

32. Frum, *Right Man*, 256.

33. "Abrams back in capital fray at center of Mideast Battle," *New York Times*, December 7, 2002; Connie Bruck, "Back Roads," *New Yorker*, December 15, 2003.

34. Elliot Abrams, Chapter Four: "Evangelicals," *Faith or Fear* (New York: Free Press, 1997); Merkley, *Christian Attitudes*, 211–213, 219–220.

35. Matthew Berger, "Facing opposition in the Senate, Bush expected to push Pipes nomination," *JTA*, August 18, 2003.

36. NCCUSA, Press Release, September 11, 2001 (www.nccusa.org).

37. WCC general secretary, Rev. Dr. Konrad Raiser, "Pastoral letter to member churches in the USA," September 20, 2001.

38. Excerpt from, "Being Church in Africa Today," in *Echoes: Justice, Peace, and Creation News* (Journal of WCC), Geneva, #20, 2001.

39. WCC Press Releases July 1997, October 4, 1997, November 1997; March 1998; September, 21, 2001. The most recent WCC statements on "Israel/Palestine," together with history of the role that WCC has played in NGO actions and statements, can be found at www.wcc-coe.org/.

40. *WorldNetDaily*, June 6, 2003 (www.worldnetdaily.com); Elisabeth Bumiller, "Religious Leaders Ask If Antiwar Call is Heard," *New York Times*, March 10, 2003; *First Things*, May 2003, 80–81.

41. Gallup polls found that Americans who attend church regularly supported the war against Saddam by nearly 2:1, whereas those who never attend church or who say that religion is not important to them were evenly split, and overall public support was 56 percent (Mark Tooley, "Praise the Lord and George W. Bush," *Seattle Post-Intelligencer*, March 21, 2003).

42. Polls indicated that in the election of 2000, Bush won over Gore 57 percent to 40 percent among those who attend church regularly. Gore won 61 percent to 32 percent among those who say they "never attend church." Among white Protestants, Bush won 63 percent to 34 percent, and among white Catholics, 52 percent to 45 percent (Paul Kengor, "God & W. at 1600 Penn.," *National Review,* March 5, 2003, www.nationalreview.com).

43. Kengor, "God & W. at 1600 Penn."

44. Excerpts from "Interview with President Bush," www.abcnews.com, December 16, 2003.

45. Matthew E. Berger, "As Bush seeks Jewish voters, traditional groups feel ignored," *JTA,* June 23, 2003; Matthew Berger, "The president discusses his faith at New Year meeting with rabbis," *JTA*, October 5, 2003; Matthew E. Berger, "On Israel and Domestic Issues, Orthodox come out for Republicans," *JTA*, October 29, 2003; Paul M. Weyrich, "The Jewish-Christian Alliance," www.cnsnews.com, February 19, 2004; Ron Kampeas, "Survey: Jews Stay Democrats," www.jewish-times.com, January 16, 2004.

46. Carter Center Web site (www.cartercenter.org), July 19, 2002. Carter's claim to have a balanced view on this issue is easily disproved by examination of the several articles and op-ed pieces on the subject that he has written recently: *inter alia*: "America Can Persuade Israel to Make a Just Peace," *New York Times*, April 21, 2002, and "For Israel, Land or Peace," *Washington Post*, November 26, 2000; "The Choice For Israelis," *Washington Post*, September 23, 2003.

47. "Text: Announcement of 2002 Nobel Peace Prize," *New York Times*, October 11, 2002.

48. Jeffrey Gettleman, "Nobel Peace Prize Awarded to Carter with Criticism of Bush," *New York Times*, October 11, 2002; "Carter Wins Nobel Peace Prize," www.cnn.com/Worldnews, October 11, 2002.

49. www.cnn.com/TRANSCRIPTS, November 15, 2002/0111/15.

50. Elaine Sciolino, "Self-Appointed Israeli and Palestinian Negotiators Offer a Plan for Middle East Peace," *New York Times*, December 2, 2003. See also, "Jimmy Carter takes president to task," *Houston Chronicle*, April 9, 2004 (www.Houston-Chronicle.com).

51. Quoted in Gilbert, *Israel*, p. 566.

52. *Jerusalem Post*, 4 June, 1994.

53. Press conference, Crawford TX, March 3, 2002, as quoted in Frum, *Right Man*, 258.

54. "Transcript of Remarks by Bush and Sharon on Israel," and Brian Knowlton, "Bush Also Appears to Back Sharon on 'Right of Return' Issue," both *New York Times*, April 14, 2004.

55. *JTA*, June 12, 2003.

RETROSPECT AND CONCLUSIONS

1. According to the National Jewish Population Survey of 1990–1991, Jews were 5.5 million (around 2 percent) of the population. According to the same survey conducted for 2000–2001, the absolute number of American Jews had dropped to 5.2 million, and the total population of United States had grown in the same decade from 250 million (rounded figure) to 260 million. The percentage of Jews has thus dropped to *well below* 2 percent. See *JTA News*, September 9, 2003, and cf. Abrams, *Faith or Fear*, 1–2.

2. Goldberg, *Jewish Power*, 29–35.

3. Goldberg, *Jewish Power*, xxi.

4. Goldberg, *Jewish Power*, 33–35.

5. *JPost*, June 18, 2003.

6. Frum, *Right Man*, 262.

7. Carter, *BA*, 201–205.

8. David Wurmser, *Wall Street Journal Europe*, March 14, 1997, as quoted in *American Enterprise Institute Latin American Outlook*, April, 1997.

9. See, Rashid Khalidi, *Palestinian Identity* (New York: Columbia, University Press, 1997).

10. Frum, *Right Man*, 260.

11. *New York Times*, September 8, 2003.

12. *New York Times*, October 7, 2003.

Selected Bibliography

The Selected Bibliography includes only books frequently cited and a selection of the most valuable of other books consulted.

Abrams, Elliott. *Faith or Fear.* New York: Free Press, 1997.

Aburish, Said K. *Arafat: From Defender to Dictator.* London: Bloomsbury, 1998.

Aikman, David. *A Man of Faith: The Spiritual Journey of George W. Bush*, Nashville: Nelson, 2004.

Alteras, Isaac. *Eisenhower and Israel.* Gainesville: University of Florida Press, 1993.

Ambrose, Stephen. *Eisenhower.* Vol. 1, *The Soldier.* New York: Simon & Schuster, 1983.

Ambrose, Stephen. *Eisenhower.* Vol. 2, *The President.* New York: Simon & Schuster, 1984.

Ambrose, Stephen. *Nixon.* Vol. 1, *The Education of a Politician, 1913–1962.* New York: Simon & Schuster, 1987.

Ambrose, Stephen. *Nixon.* Vol. 2, *The Triumph of a Politician, 1962–1972.* New York: Simon & Schuster, 1989.

Ambrose, Stephen. *Nixon.* Vol. 3, *Ruin and Recovery.* New York: Simon & Schuster, 1991.

Arens, Moshe. *Broken Covenant: American Foreign Policy and the Crisis Between the U.S. and Israel.* New York: Simon & Schuster, 1995.

Ashrawi, Hanan. *This Side of Peace.* New York: Simon & Schuster, 1995.

Baker, James A, III. *The Politics of Diplomacy.* New York: Putnam's, 1995.

Blitzer, Wolf. *Between Washington and Jerusalem: A Reporter's Notebook.* New York: Oxford University Press, 1985.

Blumenthal, Sidney. *The Clinton Wars.* New York: Farrar, Straus & Giroux, 2003.

Bodansky, Yossef. *The High Price of Peace.* New York: Random House/Forum, 2002.

Brinkley, Douglas. *The Unfinished Presidency: Jimmy Carter's Journey beyond the White House*. New York: Viking, 1998.

Brzezinski, Zbigniew. *Power and Principle: Memoirs of the National Security Adviser, 1977–1981*. London: Wiedenfeld & Nicolson, 1983.

Cannon, Lou. *President Reagan: The Role of a Lifetime*. New York: Simon & Schuster, 1991.

Carter, Jimmy. *Why Not the Best?* Nashville: Broadman Press, 1975.

Carter, Jimmy. *A Government as Good as Its People*. New York: Simon & Schuster, 1977.

Carter, Jimmy. *Keeping Faith: Memoirs of a President*. New York: Bantam, 1982.

Carter, Jimmy, and R. Kirby Godsey. *Negotiations: The Alternative to Hostility*. Macon, GA: Mercer University Press, 1984.

Carter, Jimmy. *The Blood of Abraham*. Boston: Houghton, Mifflin, 1985.

Carter, Jimmy. *Talking Peace: A Vision for the Next Generation*. New York: Dutton Children's Books, 1993.

Clifford, Clark, with Richard Holbrooke. *Counsel to the President: A Memoir*. New York: Random House, 1991.

Dayan, Moshe. *Story of My Life: An Autobiography*. New York: Morrow, 1976.

Dayan, Moshe. *Breakthrough: A Personal Account of the Egypt-Israel Peace Negotiations*. New York: Knopf, 1981.

Dobrynin, Anatoly. *In Confidence: Moscow's Ambassador to America's Six Cold War Presidents*. New York: Times/Random House, 1995.

D'Souza, Dinesh. *Ronald Reagan*. New York: Simon & Schuster/Free Press, 1997.

Eban, Abba. *An Autobiography*. New York: Random House, 1977.

Eban, Abba. *Personal Witness*. New York: Putnam's, 1992.

Eden, Anthony. *The Memoirs of Sir Anthony Eden*. Vol. 2, *Full Circle.* London: Cassell, 1960.

Eisenhower, Dwight D. *The White House Years*. Vol. 1, *Mandate to Change*; Vol. 2, *Waging Peace*. Garden City, NY: Doubleday, 1963, 1965.

Eisenhower, Dwight D. *Ike's Letters to A Friend, 1941–1959*, ed. Robert Griffith. Lawrence: University of Kansas Press, 1984.

Eisenhower, Milton S. *The President Is Calling*. Garden City, NY: Doubleday, 1974.

Ferrell, Robert H., ed. *The Autobiography of Harry S. Truman*. Boulder: Colorado Associated University Press, 1980.

Ferrell, Robert H., ed. *Off the Record: The Private Papers of Harry S. Truman*. New York: Harper & Row, 1980.

Ferrell, Robert H., ed. *The Eisenhower Diaries*. New York: Horton, 1981.

Ford, Gerald R. *A Time to Heal: The Autobiography of Gerald R. Ford*. New York: Harper & Row, 1979.

Frum, David. *The Right Man: The Surprise Presidency of George W. Bush*. New York: Random House, 2003.

Gervasi, Frank. *Life and Times of Menachem Begin: Rebel to Statesman*. New York: Putnam's, 1979.

Gilbert, Martin. *Israel: A History*. New York: Turner, 1998.

Goldberg, J. J. *Jewish Power: Inside The American Jewish Establishment*. New York: Addison-Wesley, 1996.

Haig, Alexander M., Jr. *Caveat: Realism, Reagan, and Foreign Policy*. New York: Macmillan, 1984.

Haldeman, H. R. *The Haldeman Diaries*. New York: Putnam's, 1994.

Hirschler, Gertrude, and Lester B. Eckman. *Menachem Begin: From Freedom Fighter to Statesman*. New York: Shengold, 1979.

Hirst, David, and Irene Beeson. *Sadat*. London: Faber & Faber, 1981.

Hutcheson, Richard G., Jr. *God in the White House: How Religion Has Changed the Modern Presidency*. New York: Macmillan, 1988.

Isaacson, Walter. *Kissinger: A Biography*. New York: Simon & Schuster, 1992.

Israeli, Raphael. *Man of Defiance: A Political Biography of Anwar Sadat*. London: Wiedenfeld & Nicolson, 1985.

Johnson, Lyndon B. *The Vantage Point: Perspectives of the Presidency*. New York: Holt, Rinehart, Winston, 1971.

Johnson, Donald Bruce, ed. *National Party Platforms*. Urbana, IL: University of Illinois Press, 1978.

Kengor, Paul. *God and Ronald Reagan*. New York: HarperCollins, 2004.

Khalidi, Rashid. *Palestinian Identity*. New York: Columbia, University Press, 1997.

Kingseed, Cole C. *Eisenhower and the Suez Crisis of 1956*. Baton Rouge: Louisiana State University Press, 1995.

Kissinger, Henry. *White House Years*. Boston: Little, Brown, 1979.

Kissinger, Henry. *Years of Upheaval*. Boston: Little, Brown, 1982.

Kissinger, Henry. *Diplomacy*. New York: Simon & Schuster, 1994.

Kissinger, Henry. *Years of Renewal*. New York: Simon & Schuster, 1999.

Kucharsky, David. *The Man from Plains: The Mind and Spirit of Jimmy Carter*. New York: Harper & Row, 1976.

Kurzman, Dan. *Soldier of Peace: The Life of Yitzhak Rabin*. New York: HarperCollins, 1998.

Mansfield, Stephen. *The Faith of George W. Bush*. Lake Mary, FL: Charisma House. 2003.

Manuel, Frank E. *The Realities of American-Palestine Relations*. Washington, D.C.: Public Affairs Press, 1949.

Martin, John Bartlow. *Adlai Stevenson and the World*. Garden City, NY: Anchor, 1978.

Martin, William. *A Prophet with Honor: The Billy Graham Story*. New York: Morrow, 1991.

McCullough, David. *Truman*. New York: Simon & Schuster, 1992.

McFarland, Robert C. *Special Trust*. New York: Cadell & Davis, 1994.

Meir, Golda. *My Life*. New York: Putnam's, 1975.

Menendez, Albert J. *Religion and the U.S. Presidency: A Bibliography*. New York: Garland, 1986.

Merkley, Paul C. *The Politics of Christian Zionism, 1891–1948*. London: Frank Cass, 1998.

Merkley, Paul C. *Christian Attitudes towards the State of Israel*. Montreal & London: McGill-Queen's, 2001.

Miller, Anita, Jordan Miller, and Sigalit Zetouni. *Sharon: Israel's Warrior-Politician*. Chicago: Academie Chicago/Olive, 2002.

Miller, Merle. *Plain Speaking: An Oral Biography of Harry S. Truman*. New York: Berkeley, 1974.

Miller, Merle. *Ike The Soldier: As They Knew Him*. New York: Putnam's, 1980.

Miller, Merle. *Lyndon Johnson: An Oral Biography*. New York: Putnam's, 1987.

Mitchell, Elizabeth. *W.: Revenge of the Bush Dynasty*. New York: Hyperion, 2000.

Morris, Benny. *Righteous Victims: A History of the Zionist-Arab Conflict, 1881–1999*. New York: Knopf, 1999.

Neff, Donald. *Warriors at Suez: Eisenhower Takes America into the Middle East*. New York: Linden, 1981.

Nielsen, Niels. *The Religion of President Carter*. Nashville: Nelson, 1977.

Nixon, Richard M. *RN: The Memoirs of Richard Nixon*. New York: Grosset & Dunlap, 1978.

Nixon, Richard M. *In The Arena*. New York: Simon & Schuster, 1990.

Nixon, Richard M. *Leaders*. New York: Touchstone, 1990.

Norton, Howard, and Bob Slosser. *The Miracle of Jimmy Carter*. Plainfield: Logos, 1976.

Nutting, Anthony. *No End of a Lesson: The Story of Suez*. New York: Potter, 1967.

O'Brien, Conor Cruise. *The Siege*. New York: Simon and Schuster, 1986.

Peres, Shimon. *The New Middle East*. New York: Henry Holt, 1993.

Peres, Shimon. *Battling for Peace: Memoirs*. London: Weidenfeld & Nicolson, 1995.

Perlmutter, Amos. *Life and Times of Menachem Begin*. New York: Doubleday, 1987.

Perret, Geoffrey. *Eisenhower*. New York: Random House, 1999.

Pippert, Wessley G. *The Spiritual Journey of Jimmy Carter: In His Own Words*. New York: Macmillan, 1979.

Pogue, Forrest C. *George C. Marshall: Statesman, 1945–1969*. New York: Penguin, 1987.

Powell, Colin. *American Journey*. New York: 1995.

Powell, Jody. *The Other Side of the Story*. New York: Morrow, 1984.

Quandt, William. *Decade of Decisions: American Policy toward the Arab-Israeli Conflict, 1967–1978*. Berkeley: University of California Press, 1977.

Quandt, William. *Camp David: Peacemaking and Politics*. Washington, D.C.: Brookings Institution, 1986.

Quandt, William. *Peace Process: American Diplomacy and the Arab-Israeli Conflict Since 1967*. Berkeley: University of California Press, 1993.

Rabin, Yitzhak. *The Rabin Memoirs*. London: Weidenfeld & Nicolson, 1979.

Reagan, Ronald. *Where's the Rest of Me?* New York: Best Books, 1965.

Reagan, Ronald. *An American Life: The Autobiography*. New York: Simon & Schuster, 1990.

Reeves, Richard. *President Kennedy: Profile of Power*. New York: Simon & Schuster, 1993.

Reeves, Richard. *President Nixon: Alone in the White House*. New York: Simon & Schuster, 2001.

Rose, Norman. *Chaim Weizmann*. New York: Viking, 1986.

Rusk, Dean. *As I Saw It*. New York: Norton, 1990.

Sachar, Abram Leon. *A History of the Jews*. New York: Knopf, 1975.

Sachar, Howard M. *A History of Israel: From the Rise of Zionism to Our Time*. New York: Knopf, 1979.

Sachar, Howard M. *A History of the Jews in America*. New York: Knopf, 1992.

Sadat, Anwar el-. *In Search of Identity: An Autobiography*. New York: Harper & Row, 1978.

Safire, William. *Before the Fall: An Insider's Report on the Pre-Watergate White House* Garden City, NY: Doubleday, 1975.

Sammon, Bill. *Fighting Back: The War on Terrorism—From Inside the Bush White House*. Washington, 2003.

Schoenbaum, David. *The United States and the State of Israel*. New York: Oxford University Press, 1993.

Shultz, George P. *Turmoil and Triumph: My Years as Secretary of State*. New York: Scribner's, 1993.

Slater, Robert. *Warrior Statesman*. New York: St. Martin's, 1991.

Slosser, Bob. *Reagan Inside Out*. Waco, TX: Word Books, 1984.

Smith, Gaddis. *Morality, Reason, and Power: American Diplomacy in the Carter Years* New York: Hill and Wang, 1986.

Spiegel, Steven L. *The Other Arab-Israeli Conflict: Making America's Middle East Policy, from Truman to Reagan*. Chicago: University of Chicago Press, 1985.

Temko, Ned. *To Win Or To Die: A Personal Portrait of Menachem Begin*. New York: Morrow, 1987.

Tessler, Mark. *A History of the Israeli-Palestinian Conflict*. Bloomington: Indiana University Press, 1994.

Tivna, Edward. *The Lobby: Jewish Political Power and American Foreign Policy*. New York: Simon & Schuster, 1987.

Toulousse, Mark G. *The Transformation of John Foster Dulles: From Prophet of Realism to Priest of Nationalism*. Macon, GA: Mercer University Press, 1985.

Truman, Harry S. *Memoirs*. 2 vols. Garden City, NY: Doubleday, 1955 & 1956.

Tschirgi, Dan. *The Politics of Indecision: Origins and Implications of American Involvement with the Palestine Problem*. New York: Praeger, 1983.

Unger, Irwin and Debi. *LBJ: A Life*. New York: Wiley, 1999.

Vance, Cyrus. *Hard Choices: Critical Years in America's Foreign Policy*. New York: Simon & Schuster, 1983.

Wallach, Janet and John. *Arafat: In the Eyes of the Beholder*. Rocklin, CA: Prima Publishing, 1992.

Weinstein, Allen, and Moshe Ma'oz, eds. *Truman and the American Commitment to Israel*. Jerusalem: Magnes Press/Hebrew University, 1981.

Weizman, Ezer. *The Battle for Peace*. New York: Bantam, 1981.

Weizmann, Chaim. *Trial and Error: The Autobiography of Chaim Weizmann*. London: East & West Library, 1950.

Wills, Garry. *Reagan's America*. New York: Doubleday, 1987.

Wilson, Evan M. *Decision on Palestine: How the United States Came to Recognize Israel* Stanford: Hoover Institute Press, 1979.

Woodward, Bob. *The Agenda: Inside the Clinton White House*. New York: Simon & Schuster, 1994.

Woodward, Bob. *The Choice*. New York: Simon & Schuster, 1996.

Woodward, Bob. *Bush at War*. New York: Simon & Schuster, 2002.

Index

About the Author

Paul Charles Merkley is a Professor Emeritus in History at Carleton University, Ottawa. He is the author of five books including *The Politics of Christian Zionism, 1891–1948* and *Christian Attitudes towards the State of Israel.* He has been a Visiting Professor in Comparative Religion and American Studies at Hebrew University in Jerusalem.